American Literary Scholarship

1965

American Literary Scholarship

An Annual / 1965

Edited by James Woodress

Essays by Walter Harding, Richard Harter Fogle, Willard Thorp, Edward F. Grier, John C. Gerber, B. R. McElderry, Jr., Robert A. Wiggins, Frederick J. Hoffman, Richard Beale Davis, Louis J. Budd, J. Albert Robbins, C. Hugh Holman, William T. Stafford, Ann Stanford, Oliver Evans, Malcolm Goldstein, John T. Flanagan, Harry Finestone.

Indexed by Joseph M. Flora

Duke University Press, Durham, North Carolina, 1967

© 1967, Duke University Press. Library of Congress Catalogue Card number 65-19450. Printed in the United States of America by Heritage Printers, Inc., Charlotte, N. C.

Foreword

The present volume of *American Literary Scholarship* is the third annual issue in this series. The project which began rather tentatively during the academic year 1964–1965 seems well established, and the book has taken its place among the standard reference works in the field of American literature. Ten of the present contributors have been with the venture since the beginning, and to them in particular go the thanks of the profession. But at the same time students of American literature are nearly as much in debt to the other fourteen scholars who have contributed one or two essays to this series.

Only a few changes have been made in the plan of this volume over the preceding ones. We have added a chapter on folklore, and the miscellaneous chapter returns after a one-year's absence to cover both 1964 and 1965. The other chapters remain about the same, though users of this work may detect a trend among the contributors to be more evaluative and selective in their coverage and less all-inclusive than they were at first. The authors of the various essays, however, have been allowed to review the scholarship in their areas as they saw fit.

Once again the form of the bibliographical notation used follows closely the style adopted by the MLA bibliography. In general the articles reviewed give the author of the article, the title, the journal, the volume, and the pages. It may be assumed that in every case, unless otherwise stated, the year is 1965. When articles are cited from journals that page each number separately, the number of the issue is included. The periodicals in which the articles appear are represented by abbreviations or acronyms, and a key to the periodicals may be found in the front matter. Books cited are listed with author, title, place of publication, and publisher. The dates, as with journal citations, are 1965 unless otherwise noted.

As the third volume of this series goes to press, I should like to acknowledge my debts to Professor Joseph Flora for supplying the index, the Advisory Council of the American Literature Section and its secretary-treasurer Paul Carter for continued support of the project, Ashbel Brice and the Duke University Press for expertly solving editorial and production problems, and most of all Roberta Woodress for ministrations of all sorts during the planning and execution of this enterprise.

James Woodress

University of California at Davis

Table of Contents

Key to Abbreviations

ABC	American Book Collector	CLS	Comparative Literature Studies
AH	American Heritage		
AI	American Imago	Comment	Comment (New Zealand)
AJHQ	American Jewish Historical Quarterly	CRAS	Centennial Review of Arts and Science
AL	American Literature	Crit	Critique: Studies in Modern Fiction
ALS	American Literary Scholarship: An Annual		
		CritQ	Critical Quarterly
The American Novel	Wallace Stegner, ed., The American Novel from James Fenimore Cooper to William Faulkner (New York, Basic Books)	CUF	Columbia University Forum
		CWH	Civil War History
		DA	Dissertation Abstracts
		DR	Dalhousie Review
American Poetry	J. R. Brown, I. Ehrenpreis, and B. Harris, eds., American Poetry (London, Edward Arnold)	DramS	Drama Survey
		EA	Etudes Anglaises
		EIC	Essays in Criticism
		EIT	English in Texas
		EJ	English Journal
AN&Q	American Notes and Queries	ELH	Journal of English Literary History
AQ	American Quarterly	ELN	English Language Notes
ArQ	Arizona Quarterly	ES	English Studies
A&S	Arts and Sciences	E&S	Essays and Studies
ASch	American Scholar	ESA	English Studies in Africa (Johannesburg)
BA	Books Abroad		
BAASB	British Association for American Studies Bulletin	ESQ	Emerson Society Quarterly
		ETJ	Educational Theater Journal
BB	Bulletin of Bibliography	EUQ	Emory University Quarterly
BBr	Books at Brown		
BNYPL	Bulletin of the New York Public Library	EWR	East-West Review (Doshisha Univ., Kyoto)
BSTCF	Ball State Teachers College Forum	Expl	Explicator
		ForumH	Forum (Houston)
BuR	Bucknell Review	FN	Fitzgerald Newsletter
CCC	College Composition and Communication	FR	French Review
		FuS	Furman Studies
CE	College English	GaHQ	Georgia Historical Quarterly
CEA	CEA Critic		
CEJ	California English Journal	GaR	Georgia Review
ChiR	Chicago Review	HC	Hollins Critic
CHSB	Cincinnati Historical Society Bulletin	Hist. & Lit.	Heinz Bluhm, ed., Essays in History and Literature Presented by Fellows of the Newberry Library to Stanley Pargellis (Chicago)
CJF	Chicago Jewish Forum		
CL	Comparative Literature		
CLAJ	College Language Association Journal		
CLQ	Colby Library Quarterly		

HLQ	Huntington Library Quarterly
IEY	Iowa English Yearbook
JA	Jahrbuch für Amerikastudien
JAF	Journal of American Folklore
JEGP	Journal of English and Germanic Philology
JFI	Journal of the Folklore Institute
JGE	Journal of General Education
JHI	Journal of the History of Ideas
JJQ	James Joyce Quarterly
JL	Journal of Linguistics
KFR	Kentucky Folklore Record
KM	Kansas Magazine
KN	Kwartalnik Neofilologiczny (Warsaw)
KR	Kenyon Review
LCrit	Literary Criterion (Univ. of Mysore)
LM	London Magazine
L&P	Literature and Psychology
MASJ	Midcontinent American Studies Journal
McNR	McNeese Review
MD	Modern Drama
MEB	Missouri English Bulletin
MFS	Modern Fiction Studies
MHR	Missouri Historical Review
MinnR	Minnesota Review
MissQ	Mississippi Quarterly
MLQ	Modern Language Quarterly
ModA	Modern Age
MP	Modern Philology
MQ	Midwest Quarterly
MQR	Michigan Quarterly Review
MR	Massachusetts Review
MRR	Mad River Review
MSS	Manuscripts
MTJ	Mark Twain Journal
NCF	Nineteenth-Century Fiction
NCHR	North Carolina Historical Review
NEQ	New England Quarterly
NMQ	New Mexico Quarterly
N&Q	Notes and Queries
NRF	Nouvelle Revue Française
NS	Neueren Sprachen
NVT	Nieuw Vlaams Tijdschrift
NYFQ	New York Folklore Quarterly
OPL	Osservatore Politico Letterario

OW	Orient/West
PAAS	Proceedings of the American Antiquarian Society
PAPS	Proceedings of the American Philosophical Society
Paunch	Paunch (Buffalo, N. Y.)
PBSA	Papers of the Bibliographical Society of America
PELL	Papers on English Language and Literature
Person	Personalist
PMHB	Pennsylvania Magazine of History and Biography
PMLA	Publications of the Modern Language Association
PNJHS	Proceedings of the New Jersey Historical Society
PrS	Prairie Schooner
PsyR	Psychoanalytic Review
PUA	Proceedings of the Utah Academy of Arts and Sciences
PULC	Princeton University Library Chronicle
QH	Quaker History
QJS	Quarterly Journal of Speech
RES	Review of English Studies
RLC	Revue de Littérature Comparée
RLit	Russkaja Literatura (Leningrad)
RLMC	Rivista di Letterature Moderne e Comparate (Florence)
RS	Research Studies
RUS	Rice University Studies
SA	Studi Americani
SAQ	South Atlantic Quarterly
SatR	Saturday Review
SB	Studies in Bibliography
SCB	South Central Bulletin
SDR	South Dakota Review
SEEJ	Slavic and East European Journal
Serif	The Serif (Kent, Ohio)
SFQ	Southern Folklore Quarterly
SF&R	Scholars' Facsimiles & Reprints
ShawR	Shaw Review
SIR	Studies in Romanticism
SM	Sammlung Metzler
SNL	Satire Newsletter
SoR	Southern Review
SR	Sewanee Review
SS	Scandinavian Studies
SSF	Studies in Short Fiction

SUS	*Susquehanna University Studies*
SWR	*Southwest Review*
TamR	*Tamarack Review*
TCL	*Twentieth Century Literature*
TDR	*Tulane Drama Review*
TFSB	*Tennessee Folklore Society Bulletin*
Thoth	*Thoth* (Dept. of Eng., Syracuse Univ.)
THQ	*Tennessee Historical Quarterly*
TM	*Temps Modernes*
Topic	*Topic* (Wash. and Jeff. College)
TQ	*Texas Quarterly*
TSB	*Thoreau Society Bulletin*
TSE	*Tulane Studies in English*
TSL	*Tennessee Studies in Literature*
TSLL	*Texas Studies in Literature and Language*
TUSAS	Twayne United States Authors Series
UKCR	*University of Kansas City Review*
UMPAW	University of Minnesota Pamphlets on American Writers (Minneapolis, Univ. of Minnesota Press)
UMPEAL	University of Miami Publications in English and American Literature (Coral Gables, Univ. of Miami Press)
UNCSCL	University of North Carolina Studies in Comparative Literature
UR	*University Review*
VQR	*Virginia Quarterly Review*
WF	*Western Folklore*
WHR	*Western Humanities Review*
WMQ	*William and Mary Quarterly*
WR	*Wiseman Review* (London)
WSCL	*Wisconsin Studies in Contemporary Literature*
WWR	*Walt Whitman Review*
XUS	*Xavier University Studies*
YR	*Yale Review*
YULG	*Yale University Library Gazette*

Part I

1. Emerson, Thoreau, and Transcendentalism

Walter Harding

i. Emerson

a. **Editions.** Important studies continue to be made in textual editing. Merton M. Sealts, in *Journals and Miscellaneous Notebooks of Ralph Waldo Emerson*, Vol. V, *1835–1838* (Cambridge, Mass., Harvard Univ. Press), continues the meticulous editing of the earlier volumes of this series, covering the years of *Nature*, "The American Scholar," the Divinity School Address, Emerson's settling in Concord, and the establishment of his friendship with Thoreau, Alcott, and Margaret Fuller. It is by far the richest volume of the series yet to appear. With each new volume we realize more strongly that this is one of the major editorial accomplishments of our time. The only other significant editorial work of the year is Carl Ferdinand Strauch's "Critical and Variorum Edition of the Poems of Ralph Waldo Emerson" (*DA*, XXVI, 2226) which confines itself to forty-six of Emerson's most important poems.

b. **Biography.** Remarkably little was done on Emerson biography. Ralph H. Orth, in "Emerson Lectures in Vermont" (*Vt. Hist.*, XXXIII, 395–399), gives a brief account of Emerson's visits to the Green Mountain State and reprints in full a contemporary newspaper account of his December 9, 1858, lecture in Burlington. And Kenneth Walter Cameron has produced another of his miscellaneous catchalls in *Emerson's Workshop* (Hartford, Conn., Transcendental Books), which includes such items as "Emerson's Reading in Periodicals through 1836," "Miscellaneous Broadsides and Documents Concerning Emerson, Thoreau, and Concord," "Thematic Key or Index to Emerson's Manuscripts," and "College Papers of George Moore, Friend of Emerson."

c. **Criticism.** Greatest interest seems to have centered in critical analysis of Emerson's ideas. Therman B. O'Daniel, in "Emerson as a Literary Critic" (*CLAJ*, VIII, 157–189), makes the broadest examination to date of Emerson's literary criticism, pointing out that although Emerson had "a penchant for saying disparaging things about the critic's function," he left behind a large body of critical comment. The "three essential principles" upon which he based his literary criticism were "Nature, Beauty, and Morality." And, in applying these principles, while he occasionally made some mistakes in judgment, time has shown that he made a surprising number of correct appraisals. Mr. O'Daniel concludes his study with summaries of Emerson's comments on authors as varied as Shakespeare, Wordsworth, Montaigne, Alcott, and Abraham Lincoln. René Wellek, in *The Age of Transition*, the third volume of his *History of Modern Criticism* (New Haven, Yale Univ. Press), also examines Emerson's critical theories and concludes that despite oft-spoken charges of inconsistency, Emerson is instead guilty of "monotony, repetitiveness, and inflexibility," and that he is "almost frightening in the purity of his doctrine." (Wellek also gives brief glances at the critical theories of Thoreau, Jones Very, and Margaret Fuller.) The book, as one might expect, is beautifully written, amazingly comprehensive—at least so far as Emerson is concerned, and touched with a wit that makes for delightful reading. In another essay on "Emerson and German Philosophy" in *Confrontations* (Princeton, Princeton Univ. Press), Wellek suggests that Emerson read the German philosophers more for a confirmation of his own opinions than in a search for new ideas, and thus he accepted none of their philosophies in their entirety.

Christopher Collins, in "The Uses of Observation: a Study of Correspondential Vision in the Writings of Emerson, Thoreau, and Whitman" (*DA*, XXVI, 352), has studied the development and use of the "relationship perceived to exist between external phenomena and internal realities" in the works of Emerson and Thoreau, and concluded that Emerson saw the whole world as "a vast symbol of the inner world of the Divine Self," while Thoreau consistently declared that the outer world corresponds to the inner world, giving man in nature the opportunity to explore his own undiscovered self. Mary Worden Edrich, in "Emerson's Apostasy" (*DA*, XXV, 7242–7243), suggests that the concept of Emerson as a religious radical has been long overstressed, that his Divinity School Address is unrepresentative, and that the furor over it was caused more by his "lack of appropriateness of rhetoric and diplomacy" than by its theological heresy. Harold L. Berger, however, in "Emerson and Carlyle: the Dissenting Believers" (*ESQ*, No. 38, pp. 87–90), asserts that Emerson, like Carlyle, "rejected Christian orthodoxy [though they] remained unimpeachable theists." Adapa Ramakrishna Rao has examined "Emerson's Attitude toward Humanitarian Reform" (*DA*, XXV, 1964, 2519) and concluded that "the emphasis clearly falls on self-regeneration, as opposed to horizontal reform measures." John G. Cawelti, in "Self-Improvement and Self-Culture: Ralph Waldo Emerson" in his study of *The Apostles of the Self-Made Man* (Chicago, Univ. of Chicago Press), suggests that "Emerson made an impressive synthesis of the diverse ideals of self-improvement, success, and self-culture which had developed in the early nineteenth century, shaping them into a pattern with his own transcendental philosophy" but that many of his followers then debased his ideas into "ritualistic self-deception."

In making a general analysis of Emerson's style, Sidney P. Moss, in "Analogy: the Heart of Emerson's Style" (*ESQ*, No. 39, pp. 21–24), asserts that analogy was for Emerson "an essential device for discovering identity in variety, for linking the solid with the ethereal, and for expressing ulterior meanings through the medium of the physical world." Confining himself to a specific example, Robert S. Matteson, in "Emerson and the Aeolian Harp" (*SCB*, XXIII, 1963, 4–9), points out that surprisingly the aeolian harp was a favorite image of the tone-deaf Emerson who likened the artist's necessity of waiting for the inspired moment to the harp's need for an appropriate breeze. Donald Ross, Jr., has given us a detailed analysis of "Emerson's 'Brahma'" (*ESQ*, No. 39, pp. 42–43), his most difficult and controversial poem.

d. **Influence.** Indications of Emerson's influence have been found in widely scattered places. In the most rewarding study, Hyatt H. Waggoner's "Emily Dickinson: the Transcendent Self" (*Criticism*, VII, 297–334), it is demonstrated that Emerson was a major resource for the poet "despite her awareness of the criticisms that might be made of his doctrines, criticisms in fact a good many of her poems *had* made." A close analysis of a number of her poems indicates just how vital that influence was. Agostino Lombardo, a contemporary

Italian critic, in "Lombardo on Emerson and American Art" (*ESQ*, No. 39, pp. 28–34 [trans. by J. Chesley Mathews from *La Ricerca del Vero*, Rome, 1961]), suggests that Emerson's greatest accomplishment was his inspiration of Thoreau, Hawthorne, Whitman, and Melville. On the other hand, Alfred S. Reid, in "Emerson and Bushnell as Forerunners of Jamesian Pragmatism" (*FuS*, XIII, 18–30), asserts that Emerson's influence on William James has generally been overstated and that Horace Bushnell was actually a far greater influence. Turning abroad, Eugene F. Timpe, in examining the books and periodicals concerning *American Literature in Germany 1861–1872* (UNCSCL, XXXV, 62–70), found amazingly little interest expressed in either Thoreau or Emerson, while Martin Christadler, in studying "Ralph Waldo Emerson in Modern Germany" (*ESQ*, No. 38, pp. 112–130), came to the conclusion that because the Nazis perverted Emerson's philosophy to their own use in the thirties, the Germans of the fifties have been wary of his philosophy. Adrian H. Jaffe, in "Emerson and Sartre: Two Parallel Theories of Responsibility" (*CLS*, I, 1964, 113–117), finds parallel ideas but no indications of any direct influence in the ideas of the two philosophers. And David Finnegan, in "The Man Himself: Emerson's Prose Style" (*ESQ*, No. 39, pp. 13–15), thinks "Emerson's idealism no longer . . . relevant in a scientific age," but does find his freshness of style still appealing.

ii. Thoreau

a. **Editions.** There have been no important additions to the Thoreau canon. *Over Thoreau's Desk: New Correspondence 1838–1861* (Hartford, Conn., Transcendental Books), edited by Kenneth Walter Cameron, is devoted for the most part to correspondence of the Thoreau family pencil business and such peripheral matters as the court suit in which Thoreau's aunts were involved rather than documents pertaining directly to Thoreau himself. And Paul O. Williams has brought to light a forgotten first printing of a few paragraphs of Thoreau's *Cape Cod* in "Thoreau in the *Boatswain's Whistle*" (*ESQ*, No. 38, p. 133).

b. **Biography.** Of my own *Days of Henry Thoreau* (New York, Knopf) I can say only that it is the first full-length biography of Thoreau to appear in a quarter of a century and that it is an attempt, based on a great deal of newly discovered documentary evidence, to portray "Thoreau the man."[1] In *Thoreau and His Harvard Classmates* (Hartford, Conn., Transcendental Books) Kenneth Walter Cameron reprints in facsimile the rare *Memorials of the Class of 1837 of Harvard University* and appends several other previously published documents on Thoreau's life at Harvard. Edwin Moser, in a brief note, "Thoreau's Theme Grades" (*TSB*, No. 91, pp. 1–2), corrects a long-standing misinterpretation of penciled comments on the manuscripts of some of Thoreau's college themes. Roland Robbins, in "House Hunting for Henry D. Thoreau" (*TSB*, No. 92, pp. 1–2) reiterates the story of his 1945 excavations at Walden Pond. Virginia S. Eifert, in "The Botanist, Thoreau" in her *Tall Trees and Far Horizons* (New York, Dodd, Mead) gives a very readable account of Thoreau's botanical interests as displayed on his 1857 trip to the Maine woods, although she has apparently completely overlooked the many details Thoreau recorded in his *Journal*.

c. **Criticism.** Thoreau studies seem to have concentrated on his sources. The most important is John Aldrich Christie's *Thoreau as World Traveler* (New York, Columbia Univ. Press), which examines his voluminous reading in travel literature and demonstrates how he used it constantly as a source for metaphors to raise his own writing from the parochial to the universal. Christie's masterly study not only gives us a good deal of insight into Thoreau's techniques of writing, but also, and almost incidentally, a comprehensive survey of the popular travel literature of the mid-nineteenth century. John Lawrence Magnus, Jr., in "Thoreau's Poetic Cosmos and Its Relation to Tradition: a Study of His Reading and His Writings, 1837–1854" (*DA*, XXVI, 2219), like Christie, reaches the conclusion that Thoreau "developed the comforting ability to invoke [from his reading] precisely the appropriate tradition to justify his own opinion—whatever it might be." Carl F. Hovde, studying the "Literary Materials in Thoreau's *A Week*" (*PMLA*, LXXX, 76–83) in particular, demonstrates that Thoreau, in studding his first book with quotations, drew chiefly upon English and American poetry, Oriental literature, and local histories and travel books, and concludes, like

---

1. Joel Porte in the *Christian Science Monitor* (Feb. 10, 1966) reports that the book is "singularly free of special pleading" and provides "a meticulously accurate chronicle" of Thoreau's life—Ed.

Magnus, that Thoreau often wrenched these quotations out of context to make them fit his own conclusions. William Bysshe Stein, in two articles, "Thoreau's First Book: A Spoor of Yoga" (*ESQ*, No. 41, pp. 4–25) and "Thoreau's *Walden* and the *Bhagavad Gita*" (*Topic*, No. 6, 1963, pp. 38–55) devotes himself to studies of the Oriental influence on Thoreau, though I fear he tends somewhat to overstate his case. Kenneth Walter Cameron, in two source studies, "Thoreau's Two Books of Pindar" (*ESQ*, No. 38, pp. 96–112) and "Henry Thoreau and the *Entomology* of Kirby and Spence" (*ESQ*, No. 38, pp. 138–142) confines himself primarily to reproducing pages in facsimile from books in Thoreau's personal library.

There have been several particularized studies of *Walden*. The most significant is Joseph J. Moldenhauer's "Rhetoric of *Walden*" (*TSB*, No. 91, p. 3), a critical study of Thoreau's major stylistic techniques in his masterpiece and their relation to its artistic structure and to Transcendental theories, strategies, and goals of expression. Gerry Brenner confines his study to one chapter of the book, in "Thoreau's 'Brute Neighbors': Four Levels of Nature" (*ESQ*, No. 39, pp. 37–40), and suggests, not completely convincingly, that "by tracing Thoreau's sequential observations of animals in this chapter, one can observe the animal cosmos in its comparative levels of natural, unnatural, preternatural, and supernatural behaviour." In an even more particularized discussion of a portion of that chapter, Francis D. Ross, in "Rhetorical Procedure in Thoreau's 'Battle of the Ants'" (*COO*, XVI, 14–10), attempts to indicate the meaning that underlies Thoreau's handling of point of view. J. Golden Taylor, in "Thoreau's Sour Grapes" (*PUA*, XLII, 38–49), discusses the genesis and evolution of the sour grapes metaphor in the first chapter of *Walden* and demonstrates how Thoreau gradually developed the symbol.

Understandably, fewer articles have been devoted to Thoreau's lesser works. Although most readers have considered Thoreau's first book a loosely structured volume, J. J. Boies, discussing "Circular Imagery in Thoreau's *Week*" (*CE*, XXVI, 350–355), argues that its "controlling metaphor is the circle" and, approached from this viewpoint, the book has an unexpected artistic unity. Arthur Lewis Ford, Jr., makes the first extended "Critical Study of the Poetry of Henry Thoreau" (*DA*, XXV, 1964, 2980) and suggests that while it is not great poetry, it is worthy of more serious study than it has yet received, particularly as a precursor of Whitman's experimental poetry. Carl Bode, in "Thoreau's Young Ideas" in his *Half-World of American Culture* (Carbondale, Southern Illinois Univ. Press), points out that Thoreau's poetry also proves that he had developed in his youth many of the ideas and attitudes that we usually associate with his maturity. (This volume also reprints several earlier essays on Thoreau by Professor Bode.) Lauriat Lane, Jr., in "Thoreau at Work: Four Versions of 'A Walk to Wachusett'" (*BNYPL*, LXIX, 3–16), makes an extended examination of four different versions (two manuscript and two printed) of Thoreau's early essay and demonstrates how the revisions made the writing more vivid, more real, and more universal. Lee A. Pederson's catalogue of "Americanisms in Thoreau's *Journal*" (*AL*, XXXVII, 167–184) lists eighty-one items that antedate the earliest corresponding citations in the *NED*, *DAE*, and *DA*, and 160 other items which are without reference in these dictionaries. It is a pioneer work which should open whole new fields for lexicographical study (see also **Folklore**, p. 256).

A more generalized study is Nina Baym's "Thoreau's View of Science" (*JHI*, XXVI, 221–234) which suggests that Thoreau gradually turned more and more against science and scientists when he became aware of the fact that his Transcendentalist philosophy and science were incompatible. (Such a conclusion, however, ignores the fact that Thoreau's interest in science was greatest in the last years of his life and that his one important contribution to scientific theory, "The Succession of Forest Trees," was written only a little more than a year before he died.) There are two studies of Thoreau's reaction to the West. C. A. Tillinghast, in "The West of Thoreau's Imagination: the Development of a Symbol" (*Thoth*, VI, 42–50), suggests that although Thoreau quickly became disillusioned with the materialism of the Western pioneer, he often used the idealized West as a symbol of youth, hope, and imagination. Edwin Fussell, in two essays, "Henry David Thoreau" and "Thoreau's Unwritten Epic," both in his *Frontier: American Literature and the American West* (Princeton, Princeton Univ. Press), makes a much more intensive study but unfortunately couches his findings in obtuse prose. He also seems to be unaware of Thoreau's sense of humor and thus often misses his point. Lawrence Bowling, in "Thoreau's Social Criticism as Poetry" (*YR*, LV, 255–264), avers that "Thoreau was not a social reformer, in the modern sense of the term; . . . [that] most of his so-called social criticism may be best appreciated, not when viewed as objective observations of social conditions . . . but when read as poetry." Theodore M. Brown, in "Thoreau's Prophetic Architectural Program" (*NEQ*, XXXVIII, 3–20), finds that Thoreau has scattered through his writings a plea for a new architecture "based upon minimum physical means and maximum human values" that anticipates the theories of such modern architects as Frank Lloyd Wright. Joel Porte, in "Thoreau on Love: a Lexicon of Hate" (*UR*, XXXI, 1964, 111–116, 191–194), asserts that Thoreau, in recognizing "the immitigable necessity of love and hate as concomitants of each other in a love relationship" also anticipated the theories of many modern psychologists.

There have been two symposiums devoted to Thoreau. In *The Thoreau Centennial* (Albany, State Univ. of N. Y.), I have edited the papers gathered by Lewis Leary for the 1962 centennial. Most rewarding perhaps are Carl Hovde on "Conception of Character in *A Week*," Joseph Moldenhauer on "*Walden*: the Strategy of Paradox," and J. Lyndon Shanley's provocative analysis of Thoreau's frame of mind in his last years. There are also essays by Raymond Adams, Reginald Cook, Walter Harding, Donald Harrington, Howard Mumford Jones, and Braj Kumar Nehru. The wide variety in subject matter and approach gives "ample indication of Thoreau's multifaceted appeal today." *Paunch* (No. 24) is in large part devoted to studies of Thoreau from the rather unconventional approach of the editors of that magazine. Included are essays by Robert D. Callahan, Arthur Efron, Wade C. Thompson, and Kingsley Widmer that seem to be concerned chiefly with Thoreau's sexuality, phallic symbolism in his works, and allied topics. They will undoubtedly provoke some of Thoreau's more ardent and uncritical followers to violence, but if read with a healthy skepticism and a sense of humor (something the authors themselves at times lack), they prove quite stimulating.

d. **Influence.** Eugene F. Timpe has surveyed briefly the influence of "Thoreau in Germany" (*TSB*, No. 93, pp. 1–3) from the mid-nineteenth century to the present day. Robert S. Fogarty, in "A Utopian Literary Canon" (*NEQ*, XXXVIII, 386–391), reports on forgotten commentaries which show a surprising sympathy for Thoreau's works in the *Circular* of the Oneida Community.

iii. Transcendentalism and the Minor Transcendentalists

a. **Editions.** N. Scott Momaday's edition of *The Complete Poems of Frederick Goddard Tuckerman* (New York, Oxford Univ. Press) gives us for the first time a good standard edition of one of our best sonneteers. The texts of all his poems are given with variants clearly indicated. Most important, we at last have a dependable version of his most important poem, "The Cricket." Momaday's introduction is competently done and his various appendixes will be of aid to scholars. Yvor Winters' foreword, as one might expect, is bound to stir up some violent reactions. Mordecai Marcus, in "The Text of Tuckerman's Poems" (*MR*, VII, 1966, 403–406), corrects some of Mr. Momaday's comments on the text of "The Cricket."

John Michael Moran, Jr., has edited the "Collected Poems of Franklin Benjamin Sanborn of Transcendental Concord" (*ESQ*, No. 90, pp. 1–131). Sanborn's poems are far from great literature, but Moran has performed a real service for the student in gathering the widely scattered poems into one collection. C. Carroll Hollis, in "A New England Outpost, as Revealed in Some Unpublished Letters of Emerson, Parker, and Alcott to Ainsworth Spofford" (*NEQ*, XXXVIII, 65–85), gives the texts of many letters to a Transcendentalist enthusiast in Cincinnati, Ohio, who later became Librarian of Congress. Donald H. Williams presents a brief letter to Fannie Hardy Eckstorm in "T. W. Higginson on Thoreau and Maine" (*CLQ*, Ser. VII, pp. 29–32). Kenneth Walter Cameron prints a minor Greek translation by Jones Very in "Jones Very's Harvard Greek Exhibition and Daniel Webster" (*ESQ*, No. 38, pp. 133–135).

b. **Biography.** The most important book in this field is unquestionably Charles H. Foster's *Beyond Concord: Selected Writings of David Atwood Wasson* (Bloomington, Indiana Univ. Press) which includes the first extended biographical study of Wasson, one of the almost forgotten minor Transcendentalists, an ample selection from his works, and a comprehensive bibliography of his writings (by Robert C. Albrecht). This is exactly the type of volume we need for the other minor figures of the movement.

Ruth M. Baylor, in *Elizabeth Palmer Peabody: Kindergarten Pioneer* (Philadelphia, Univ. of Pa. Press), has concentrated perhaps more on the kindergarten movement than on Miss Peabody. Although Mrs. Baylor is obviously devoted to her cause and has done a good deal of research, she imbeds her findings in almost inscrutable educationese. John B. Wilson, in "Grimm's Law and the Brahmins" (*NEQ*, XXXVIII, 234–238), describes Miss Peabody's interest in the philological theories of Dr. Charles Kraitsir and points out briefly their influence on a number of the Transcendentalists.

Lawrence Charles Porter, in "New England Transcendentalism: a Self-Portrait" (*DA*, XXVI, 372), documents the image the Transcendentalists had of themselves from their letters, journals, and essays. René Welleck, in "The Minor Transcendentalists and German Philosophy" in his *Confrontations* (Princeton, Princeton Univ. Press), points out that the Transcendentalists did more direct reading in German philosophy than has been supposed, but that its influence was so diffuse that it cannot readily be pinpointed. John B. Wilson, in "Darwin and the Transcendentalists" (*JHI*, XXVI, 286–290), shows that many of the Transcendentalists not only actively supported Darwin's evolutionary theories, but as a matter of fact anticipated them. Robert C. Albrecht, in "The Theological Response of the Transcendentalists to the Civil War" (*NEQ*, XXXVIII, 21–34), suggests that most of the Transcendentalists, under the emotional stress of the Civil War, "reverted to the religious concepts they had apparently rejected years before." Although Perry Miller's uncompleted *Life of the Mind in America from the Revolution to the Civil War* (New York, Harcourt, Brace and World) does not deal with Transcendentalism directly, it is vitally important reading for anyone who wishes to understand the mind of the period. It deservedly won a Pulitzer Prize.

c. Criticism.   Tony Tanner's "The Transcendentalists," in his *The Reign of Wonder: Naivety and Reality in American Literature* (Cambridge, Cambridge Univ. Press), makes one of the most stimulating surveys in recent years of the contributions of the Transcendentalists. He concentrates on their "interest in the naive eye with its unselective wonder, [their] interest in the vernacular with its immediacy and concrete directness, and [their] effort to slough off the Past and concentrate exclusively on the present moment." He thinks Emerson's greatest contribution is that he made his fellow man "wonder at the usual," and Thoreau's that he made an "intimate undemanding acquaintance" with the physical world. As an interesting sidelight, he points out that "it is really with the Transcendentalist writers that the first-person singular achieved its preeminence as a literary strategy." John B. Williams, in "The Impact of Transcendentalism on the Novels of Herman Melville" (*DA*, XXVI, 1052–1053), suggests that Melville in his most creative years was much closer to the Transcendentalists than has usually been assumed. Arnold Smithline, in "*Eureka*: Poe as Transcendentalist" (*ESQ*, No. 39, pp. 25–28), suggests that Poe in *Eureka* was much closer to the Transcendentalist position than his snide remarks elsewhere about the movement would indicate. Fred E. H. Schroeder, "Andrew Wyeth and the Transcendental Tradition" (*AQ*, XVII, 559–567), argues that the Transcendentalists' use of attachment and detachment are "keys to understanding both the purpose and technique of Andrew Wyeth's art."

An interesting series of articles on the problems of teaching the American Transcendentalists in Roman Catholic colleges are a feature of *ESQ* (No. 39), including Francis S. Duggan on "Doctrine and the Writers of the American Renaissance" (pp. 45–51), Francis E. Kearns on "Emerson and the American Catholic Scholar" (pp. 63–68), John J. McAleer's thoroughly delightful "Transcendentalism and the Improper Bostonian" (pp. 73–78), and Joseph X. Brennan's "The American Catholic and American Literature" (pp. 85–93). Their general conclusion is that while Roman Catholics once viewed the Transcendentalists with suspicion, "many clerical/religious graduate students now find that literature much more intelligible and compatible and meaningful than that of more recent origin." And the irony of the situation is that "as time goes on the literature of the American Renaissance [may] find one of its securest niches and many of its most dedicated devotees in the Catholic educational pantheon." Also included in the symposium are Reginald Cook on "Ancient Rites at Walden" (pp. 52–56) and J. Russell Reaver on "Mythology in Emerson's Poems" (pp. 56–63), dealing respectively with Thoreau's and Emerson's use of myth; John B. Pickard's "The Religion of 'Higher Laws'" (pp. 68–72), analyzing a chapter from *Walden*; and Gay Wilson Allen's "James's *Varieties of Religious Experience* as Introduction to American Transcendentalism" (pp. 81–85), suggesting a new teaching approach for the period.

Americo D. Lapati, in *Orestes A. Brownson* (TUSAS), offers a "primer" summarizing Brownson's religious, socioeconomic, and political views and his literary criticism, thus providing a cross-index to his thought. Unfortunately the writing is rather uninspired and at times opinionated. It nevertheless should serve as a useful tool for those who wish to have a quick summary of the opinions of that weathercock of American thought who confuted himself almost annually.

As I emerge from this survey of the year's writings on Emerson, Thoreau, and the Transcendentalists, I find myself repleted with the plethora of scholarly trivia that the "publish or perish" philosophy— or the inability of editors to say "No!"—has inundated us with. An astonishing number of writings published by our scholarly journals and our university presses state the obvious, restate what has already been well said, or mumble so obscurely that one cannot be sure what was intended. And yet, paradoxically, there is so much of value that cries out to be done in the field. When are we going to see a good solid biography of Christopher P. Cranch? What about a scholarly edition of the works of Jones Very, one of our most sadly neglected poets? What about a study of Charles DeB. Mills's orientalism? What about a good study of the influence of Transcendentalism on educational theory and practice? Perhaps we need a serious redirection of scholarly energies.

New York State University College at Geneseo

2. Hawthorne

Richard Harter Fogle

i. Dissertations

Among the dissertations on Hawthorne in 1965 are one textual study, two examinations of Hawthorne's use of the emblem, a reappraisal of his appearance-and-reality theme, a study of his concept of nature, a re-estimate of his indebtedness to John Bunyan, a historical and critical assessment of his theory of the prose romance, and an analysis of "moralistic techniques" in his tales and sketches. J. Donald Crowley, in "Nathaniel Hawthorne's 'Twice-Told Tales': A Textual Study Based on an Analysis of the Tales in the Three Major Collections" (*DA*, XXV, 7242), concludes that the Riverside Edition text of 1883 is radically corrupt; that Hawthorne himself made relatively few revisions in the *Tales*, either in manuscript or in print; that revisions in the 1837 and 1842 editions were Hawthorne's and not bowdlerizations emanating from Mrs. Hawthorne; that Hawthorne's revisions were primarily omissions of certain passages from the original periodical and annual publications; and that the selections for 1837 and 1842, emphasizing Hawthorne's most recently published work rather than the earlier tales from New England history, are illustrative of Hawthorne's efforts to become a genuinely popular writer. Crowley's textual study is doubtless a direct or an indirect product of the labors now in progress at Ohio State upon the Centenary Edition.

It is interesting to find two full-scale treatments of the emblem in Hawthorne attempted in the same year. Some time ago in the notable introduction to his selections from Hawthorne's short studies Newton Arvin proposed the "emblem" as a more precise term than either "allegory" or "symbol" to describe Hawthorne's characteristic mode. Arvin's enterprise was worthy; in particular it would have been a good idea to rescue our author from the pejorative connotations with which academic critics had surrounded "allegory." F. O. Matthiessen's superb *American Renaissance* had one unfortunate

result, for example; it associated Hawthorne with the mode of allegory, and Melville with the preferable mode of symbol, and the
distinction was too categorical to be wholly just to Hawthorne.
Matthiessen's distinction was forcefully repeated in Charles Feidel-
son's work, and others have followed it. Arvin's effort to find a new
and better term was therefore appropriate and timely, but until now
it has gained no adherents. One suspects that Arvin's word, "em-
blematist," has struck most Hawthorne scholars as too unattractive
for use.

Donald Gene Darnell, "Hawthorne's Emblematic Method" (*DA*,
XXV, 5903), maintains that Hawthorne's crucial scenes are composed
in accordance with the concept of the emblem and its formal divisions into motto, picture, and explanatory poem. "Thus," he says,
"the scene in Hawthorne becomes the unit for analysis." Darnell attributes the appearance of the emblem in Hawthorne almost wholly
to the influence of Spenser and Bunyan. John Owen Rees, Jr., "Hawthorne and the Emblem" (*DA*, XXVI, 357), traces much of Hawthorne's literary technique back to emblem writers ranging from as
early as the sixteenth century to as late as the nineteenth. Emblem is
to be found in many popular picture books, and in the *New England
Primer*. Spenser and Bunyan show the influence of emblem; in particular Hawthorne knew Bunyan's *Divine Emblems* and his *Choice
Emblems*, which according to Rees had an impact on The Artist of
the Beautiful." Correspondingly, "The Great Stone Face" may have
been influenced by Holmes and Barber's nineteenth-century *The Religious Allegories*.

Menno M. Friesen re-examines the appearance-and-reality theme
in "The Mask in Hawthorne's Fiction" (*DA*, XXV, 5276). Hawthorne
finds men predominantly evil, and correspondingly disposed to conceal their true natures. They are therefore prone to psychological
concealment (concealment of their evil from themselves); social
concealment (of their evil from others); and moral-religious concealment (inhumanity toward others with moral codes and religious
creeds as pretexts). Hawthorne's intent is to dramatize man's evil
and his attempts to conceal it, and he preaches that man must remove
his mask and change the human heart itself. David Bert Kesterson,
in "Nature in the Life and Works of Nathaniel Hawthorne" (*DA*,
XXVI, 1023), deals with an oft-discussed but unexhausted topic. He
concludes that for Hawthorne wild nature is necessary for occasional

inspiration, but cultivated nature is what man needs more fundamentally as a link between himself and the natural world. Hawthorne's major symbolic treatments of nature are always related to the themes of isolation and withdrawal. Nature is basically amoral, man a moral being; therefore nature can be only an occasional resource, not a permanent asylum.

In "Nathaniel Hawthorne and John Bunyan" (*DA*, XXV, 1964, 2964–2965), Merlene Ann Ogden also reconsiders a familiar subject, which however has seldom or never been given full-scale consideration. She finds that, although there are only nine direct references to Bunyan in Hawthorne outside "The Celestial Railroad," and three of these are in *Our Old Home*, Bunyan's influence is nevertheless strong, and his method of religious allegory and the dream-vision have a strong attraction for Hawthorne. Bunyan's pilgrimage theme, the quest for release from the burden of sin, doubt, and despair, are Hawthorne's basic patterns, and the effect of the comparison is to place him firmly in the tradition of religious allegory.

John Caldwell Stubbs, in "The Theory of the Prose Romance: A Study in the Background of Hawthorne's Literary Theory" (*DA*, XXV, 4709), sees Hawthorne as the culmination of the romance tradition. His most notable precursors in theory are Dunlap in his *History of Fiction* (1814), and Scott and Bulwer Lytton in various essays and prefaces. These were examined and popularized by the periodical reviewers. In the development of the theory of the romance in America verisimilitude was the leading criterion for the first twenty years of the nineteenth century, but the success of Cooper brought about freer critical discussion. In the period 1820–1840 critics emphasized the importance of using native American materials in the prose romance, which was so flourishing that between 1840 and 1850 no less than 112 works were published in the United States that were specifically described as romances. Hawthorne knew the romance tradition thoroughly, and his theory of fiction is an elaboration of previous critical dicta.

In "Hawthorne as Truth-Teller: An Analysis of Moralistic Techniques in the Tales and Sketches" (*DA*, XXVI, 2734–2735), J. A. Zaitchik treats Hawthorne "as a writer who accepted the literary value of both psychological and moralistic exploration, a writer for whom the question, 'How should a man act?' was no less important than the question 'How does a man act?' "

ii. Articles

In contrast to Mr. Zaitchik, Sister M. Evelyn Joseph holds that the suggestive quality of Hawthorne's art renders it impervious to moralistic interpretation. His fiction is psychological, not moral, though not without moral standards. Hawthorne believes, however, that merely human values are inadequate for accurate judgment ("Substance as Suggestion: Ambiguity in Hawthorne," *Renascence*, XVII, 216–220). The argument is important in the light of recent emphasis upon the exclusively psychological and humanistic aspects of Hawthorne's fiction, though obviously Sister Evelyn's stance is not humanistic. Zaitchik's balance between the psychological and moral seems preferable, but in this particular instance the two positions are not as far apart as the abstract statement of them makes them sound.

The recent work of Frederick C. Crews is the most prominent instance of the psychological humanism just mentioned. Mr. Crews's insistence upon his own objectivity, coupled with his insistence that Hawthorne must participate in his own world view, is an interesting phenomenon. In his "The Ruined Wall: Unconscious Motivation in *The Scarlet Letter*" (*NEQ*, XXXVIII, 312–330), he takes as his text Hawthorne's comment on the state of Arthur Dimmesdale in Chapter XVIII, "A Flood of Sunshine":

> And be the stern and sad truth spoken, that the breach which guilt has once made into the human soul is never, in this mortal state, repaired. It may be watched and guarded; so that the enemy shall not force his way again into the citadel, and might even, in his subsequent assaults, select some other avenue, in preference to that where he had formerly succeeded. But there is still the ruined wall, and near it, the stealthy tread of the foe that would win over again his unforgotten triumph.

Crews finds the passage difficult enough to examine with considerable care, remarking that "To resolve this confusion we must first of all guess what Hawthorne intended to say." Perhaps, however, it might be sufficient to attend carefully to what he did say, without finding it necessary to translate his utterance into terms that would better satisfy his critic. The crux is the word "guilt," which for Crews has neither meaning nor reality; "guilt-feelings" would be much more intelligible. His acute and well-written essay confines Hawthorne's scope to psychological exploration.

In another extensive study of *The Scarlet Letter* William H. Nolte rejects what Crews terms "Christian neo-orthodoxy" in favor of his own version of Romanticism ("Hawthorne's Dimmesdale: A Small Man Gone Wrong," *NEQ*, XXXVIII, 168–186). (Nothing derogatory is intended by the phrase "his own"; only a reservation concerning the ultimate definition.) Nolte substantially agrees with the conclusions of F. I. Carpenter's well-known "Scarlet A Minus," particularly with reference to Hester Prynne. Hawthorne, he believes, is Romantic in his sympathy with Hester, and treats Puritanism with "bitterness and hatred" in *The Scarlet Letter*. Considering his wrongs, Chillingworth is not so black as the critics have supposed. On the other hand, little can be said for Dimmesdale, who believes that he is almost certainly damned, and confesses at the end only in a last desperate try for salvation. Hawthorne treats him with contempt.

Nolte makes thus an interesting protest against the recent tendency to give Dimmesdale more stature than Hester in the novel. One may agree that to choose sides thus is undue partisanship; but one would have to continue that any partisanship is harmful in such a case. To deflate Dimmesdale is to deflate *The Scarlet Letter* as well. The critic underrates Hawthorne's emphasis upon Dimmesdale's agony and the real difficulty of the self-confession and revelation upon which the book hinges.

In the first number of the now happily revived *Southern Review*, Austin Warren maintains an interpretation of Hawthorne which he effectively presented as long ago as 1934 in the American Writers Series *Representative Selections*. "*The Scarlet Letter*: A Literary Exercise in Moral Theology" (*SoR*, I, 22–45) is a wise essay which despite its title does not place moral and theological above literary considerations. In several respects his conclusions resemble Nolte's. Hester's outlook is fundamentally naturalistic; she is less penitent than stoic, and Warren cannot accept the penitence with which Hawthorne tries to invest her at the end. Like Nolte, Warren has reservations about the artistry of *The Scarlet Letter's* concluding chapters, although he sees the issues involved more complexly. As one would anticipate, Warren is far more sympathetic with the minister than is Nolte, since he is far more sympathetic with the problems of his beliefs and his nature.

Among 1965 articles on Hawthorne's tales, Sidney P. Moss tackles perhaps the most difficult of them all in "A Reading of 'Rappaccini's

Daughter'" (*SSF*, II, 145–156). Noting that critics have invariably found it difficult to pin the story down to a single theme, Moss suggests that attempts to capture it in statement might well be frankly abandoned. "Perhaps the best way to formulate the theme, then, is by a series of related propositions which have the virtue of reflecting the complexity of the entire allegory." It remains a question, however, whether the method conveys an adequate sense of the story's artistic unity, or, if one likes, its lack of it. L. Hugh Moore, Jr., considers the case of Owen Warland a little too briefly and rigidly in "Hawthorne's Ideal Artist as Presumptuous Intellectual" (*SSF*, II, 278–283). "The Artist of the Beautiful" is Hawthorne's most affirmative tale, and its appraisers have been too frequently misled by its irony and humor into reductive readings of it as a satire. It is certainly true, as Moore says, that Warland is imperfect, but he understands and comes to terms with his limitations.

In "The Biblical Context of 'Ethan Brand'" (*AL*, XXXVII, 115–134), Ely Stock examines the possibilities of enriching the story's associations with great thoroughness. He finds Brand's resemblances to Cain, especially the Cain of Byron's drama, the most significant of the parallels he discusses. Mary Rohrberger approaches Hawthorne's tales from the direction of modern theory in "Hawthorne's Literary Theory and the Nature of his Short Stories" (*SSF*, III, 23–30), emphasizing organic unity of technique and structure with meaning. "Artistically," she says, "his purpose is to signify truth, rather than to profess it."

iii. Books

Henry G. Fairbanks, in *The Lasting Loneliness of Nathaniel Hawthorne: A Study of the Sources of Alienation in Modern Man* (Albany, N. Y., Magi Books), is just in finding Hawthorne catholic though never Catholic. His volume is well-researched and essentially well-balanced. One cannot avoid a slight and doubtless unworthy irritation at the discovery that the cause of Hawthorne's loneliness was his failure to find a religion; the conclusion in this instance is predictable and a little professional. Also, Mr. Fairbanks has nothing to say to the student of Hawthorne's fiction as such.

> Of this predicament [alienation] and this search [for reunion] the classic American embodiment is Nathaniel Hawthorne. It is his

reflection of the common malaise of his countrymen and their restlessness which makes him a significant, representative author. Without this, he might be remembered for one romance and a handful of short stories; for time has dealt unkindly with his allegorical mode, and his inventive faculty was always as thin as his moralizing has become increasingly tedious.

Nevertheless, the book is honest, and profitable in its use of the notebooks and the letters.

My *Hawthorne's Fiction: The Light and the Dark,* revised from the first (Univ. of Okla. Press) edition of 1952, is almost unaltered in the existing text, but contains new interpretations of "The Birthmark" and "My Kinsman, Major Molineux," while it omits the annotated bibliography of Hawthorne criticism with which the previous edition concluded. *Hawthorne's Fiction* differs from the two most comparable works, Hyatt H. Waggoner's *Hawthorne* and Roy R. Male's *Hawthorne's Tragic Vision,* in its greater emphasis upon "traditional" English Romanticism, although it is in substantial agreement with Waggoner and Male. It differs also from Millicent Bell's *Hawthorne's View of the Artist,* which likewise emphasizes Romanticism, in its friendlier (or less critical) attitude toward the Romantic inclinations it discovers. Few alterations have been made in the 1952 text, despite its undoubted susceptibility of improvement, because I have seen little occasion to change the opinions then expressed.

Terence Martin's *Nathaniel Hawthorne* (TUSAS) is a mature, responsible, and well-rounded study. The format and purposes of the Twayne United States Authors Series are primarily calculated to produce useful basic handbooks, but Martin goes beyond the necessities of the type. He gives a reasoned estimate of Hawthorne's "Life and Career" and his chief literary theories and tendencies, with detailed analyses of six representative tales and the four major novels. His notes are brief but helpful, and his more extensive selected bibliography is balanced and central. His small volume (not so small, as a matter of fact, when one notices the closeness of the print) is a very respectable contribution to Hawthorne scholarship.

iv. New Editions

Two important editions of *The House of the Seven Gables* are to be noticed here, with what in the larger view may be disproportionate attention. Since the editing of American classics is much in the air

these days, the amount of space given them here is topically and tem-
porarily appropriate. There is considerable difference between the
two editions. Hyatt H. Waggoner's Riverside Edition (1964) is an
individual enterprise that represents the taste and judgment of a
single scholar; the Ohio State Centenary Edition (1965) is the product of many hands and pooled resources, plus the Hinman machine.
The difference referred to, however, is much less evident in the text
of *The House of the Seven Gables* than in the tone and emphasis of
the editorial comment which in each case supplements it.

Waggoner supplies an excellent critical and interpretative introduction to the novel, which continues the reflections of his chapter in
Hawthorne: A Critical Study in terms more fully adapted to the general reader. Thus, for example, he remarks the "spirals" theory of history underlying Hawthorne's treatment of the past, but more briefly
than in his earlier work. He strongly asserts the "redemptive" aspects
of the book as a central conviction of Hawthorne: "The purgation
effected by suffering endured and accepted, and the redemptive
power of love, have at last made possible a real movement beyond
the compulsions of the past." Waggoner defends Hawthorne's characters against Henry James's charge that they are mere ideas: they
are created out of his experience, and universalized by his imagination. Judge Pyncheon, least real among them, is a failure of sympathy
rather than of verisimilitude. Waggoner notes the modern relevance
of his powerful materialism: "If Hawthorne were writing the book
today, he would have to make him a suburban Republican active in
the Chamber of Commerce, opposed to fair housing laws because
they endanger the rights of property, a member of a country club that
excludes almost everyone, willing chairman when his turn comes of
the United Fund or Community Chest Drive. . . . " He concludes
that *The House of the Seven Gables* should be judged in terms of the
American tradition of "romance"; then "it becomes ever more apparent that he wrote in the main stream of the greatest American fiction."
It is radically democratic, and not social but supra-mundane.

Waggoner describes his editorial procedures with great care in
his "Note on the Text." Finding some three thousand variations between the manuscript and the first edition, he felt obliged to produce
a "critical" text rather than follow either exclusively. His statement of his textual accomplishment is modest, discriminating, and
critically important. "There is a sense," he avows, "in which it would

be perfectly true to say that not one of the thousands of changes the printers made in Hawthorne's manuscript—from hyphens to words—make any important critical difference, when 'critical' is understood as having to do with interpretation and evaluation of the novel." Hawthorne's own interest in his text was critical, not bibliographical nor minute. He was interested in his words, not in punctuation, capitalization, nor even very vitally in spelling. Consequently the state of his manuscript was such as to force many changes upon his printers to make it fit for publication. Yet the changes are insignificant to criticism, and Waggoner claims only two significant discoveries from his examination of the manuscript—significant, that is, to interpretation. One is that about three chapters from the end it improves—the handwriting is clearer, the punctuation is more consistent, and mental lapses, frequent earlier, now tend to disappear. Waggoner speculates that at this point "a significant clarification of his own work occurred in Hawthorne's own mind," and that the improved text may be new composition rather than copy. The second discovery concerns Hepzibah. Originally called "the Old Maid' almost throughout, she becomes in revision of the manuscript "our poor Hepzibah," "our forlorn shop-keeper." These and other less uncomplimentary appellations show that Hawthorne's conception of her has clearly grown more sympathetic as he has progressed.

Waggoner's decision on punctuation, which involves the greatest number of variants, remains to be discussed. He concludes that "there is only one really desirable choice, and that is to reproduce Hawthorne's punctuation so far as the manuscript makes that possible, making the changes that are necessary but doing so conservatively." Hawthorne's punctuation was old-fashioned even for his own time, his practice rhetorical and emotional rather than grammatical and logical. But his editor believes it genuinely expressive. "His hesitant, tentative, circling style, that could even be called irresolute if we wanted to apply a word that necessarily carries some derogatory connotations, appears, when we read it in his own punctuation, even more clearly what we have always known it to be."

This edition is an extremely satisfying production, in which the editor has done his full duty by his text, explained his rationale and procedure with great lucidity and literary balance, and has been able to apply first-class critical intelligence, an intimate knowledge of Hawthorne as a whole, and long commitment to him as a scholar and a teacher. The moderation with which Waggoner views his editorial prerogatives and achievements is not the least of the many virtues of this text. Hawthorne's fiction is still the primary target toward which the reader's aim is directed.

Waggoner's work rates one footnote in the more recent Centenary *House of the Seven Gables* (Columbus, Ohio State Univ. Press). Its textual editor, Professor Fredson Bowers, concludes his introduction with the statement that "the text of *The House of the Seven Gables* is established here for the first time in the relative purity of its manuscript form." To this the annotation is added,

> When this Introduction was in proof, a paperback Riverside Edition of *The House of the Seven Gables* (Boston, 1964) appeared, edited by Hyatt H. Waggoner, and based on a manuscript–first edition collation. The above statement, therefore, is no longer true. However, the Riverside text will be found to differ considerably from the Centenary text in its transcript of the manuscript and its estimate of the amount of authorial proof-correction. (p. lx)

Since a reasonable period intervened between the appearance of the Riverside edition and the publication of the Centenary volume, Professor Bowers' ignorance of the existence of a competing text seems unnecessary. And although his remarks are neutral, they are nevertheless in effect insulting in their refusal to take Waggoner into account, whether favorably or unfavorably. Waggoner's work is the first edition from the manuscript since the original first edition, and considered specifically as a student of Hawthorne he is of higher stature and more deeply committed than any of the scholars involved in the Ohio State project. Even if the Centenary textual introduction was already in proof, it would appear that at the least a considerably fuller note would have been practicable. This treatment of a scholar of high repute suggests, I trust incorrectly, that the Ohio State editors have assumed sole authority over the texts of Hawthorne.

The two texts are very similar. Bowers' different opinion is no doubt correct as to the sheer number of variants of all kinds, but significant variations are negligible. I have made a representative sampling, admittedly without the aid of the Hinman machine (although I am at the moment about ten feet away from one), which includes the preface, the first three long paragraphs of Chapter I, the first seven paragraphs of Chapter X, the first thirteen paragraphs of Chapter XV (some of them dialogue and consequently brief), and the entire concluding Chapter XXI. In this material there are nine variants, none of them verbal and none of them of consequence.

In the Preface Waggoner prints a semicolon and em dash (;—, p. 4) to the Centenary em dash (—, p. 2). On the same page he omits a comma before a parenthesis, which the Centenary includes. The two versions of the first three paragraphs of Chapter I are identical. On page 128 (Chapter X), Waggoner reads "New-England" to the Centenary's "New England" (p. 146): a difference more or less canceled out by his "East Wind" (Chapter XV, p. 192) to Centenary's "East-Wind." In the earlier case Waggoner's choice is the more explicable, since his "New-England" is grammatically an adjective. His "colonel" (p. 193) is Centenary's "Colonel," and on page 194 he prints a comma after a parenthesis [),], while Centenary reverses the order [,)] on page 225. In the final chapter one encounters Waggoner's "Now it . . ." (p. 268); Centenary's reading is "Now, it . . ." (p. 311). And Waggoner's "thither," (p. 270) is Centenary's "thither;" (p. 314).

The passages I have examined show no important discrepancies and no discernible differences of tendency, unless it be a very slight preponderance of literalness in the Centenary's adoption of the styling [,)], an impossible usage today. There are no doubt slight divergences here and there: Waggoner accepts the printer's emendation of Hawthorne's "barn-door fowl" to "barn-yard fowl," while Centenary comments that the OED sanctions "barn-door" in references as late as Sir Walter Scott. Waggoner reasons that "barn-door" is simply a mental slip of Hawthorne's among quite a number of others in the manuscript and in his proof-reading. In this instance the problem of idiom is too difficult to permit of any certainty, but posterity has sided with the printer and Waggoner. "Barn-door fowl" would immediately strike a twentieth-century reader as a false note.

What the comparison predominantly demonstrates is overwhelming agreement on the adoption of Hawthorne's very heavy pointing, except where, as Waggoner remarks, it is manifestly inadvertent and unintelligible (e.g., "likewise, although, an unintelligible, one, as such clues . . ."). There is substantial agreement, too, on the import of this kind of pointing. In a passage cited earlier in part, Waggoner notes that

> Hawthorne's very heavy use of marks of separation, though illogical when compared to modern grammatical punctuation, is, in the end, in its cumulative effect, expressive, even though he himself had probably never given the matter any thought. His hesitant, tentative, circling style, that could even be called irresolute if we wanted to apply a word that necessarily carries some derogatory connotations, appears, when we read it in his own punctuation, even more clearly what we have always known it to be. (p. xxxii)

In the Centenary volume Professor William Charvat writes, as quoted by Bowers,

> It comes to me now, for the first time, that Hawthorne's style is essentially parenthetical, and that this characteristic reflects the basically essayistic, generalizing, and speculative quality of his fiction. His parentheses give him the latitude and flexibility that this quality requires. He modulates the degree of isolation of a unit by selecting (usually) just the right pair of separators: parentheses, or dashes, or commas. I don't think he did this selecting consciously. (pp. xlvii–xlviii n.)

These conclusions, in both instances reached primarily through contact with Hawthorne's manuscript, are very close together.

These two texts of *The House of the Seven Gables* are both admirable in themselves. The Riverside Edition is greatly preferable in critical acumen and general humanity. Despite the enormous competence and industry behind the Centenary volume (here one may as well read volumes), its pleasures are intended for highly specialized bibliographers, and steadfast literary historians of a type that are now rather to be respected than heeded. When this definitive edition of Hawthorne was announced I was prepared, with what now seems undue innocence, to welcome it wholeheartedly. It quickly appeared, however, that its concern with Hawthorne as an important and a unique American writer was small; he was merely a corpus of important texts upon which scholars could exercise their virtuosity. Mr. Bowers has used his undoubted talents largely in praise of his own vocation of bibliography, and Mr. Charvat has employed his great knowledge of literary history and of bookmaking chiefly in reassuring us that Hawthorne is now safely accounted for as a normal nineteenth-century American with a turn for literature, and may consequently be filed and forgotten. Charvat concludes his introduction to *The House of the Seven Gables* by asking, "Was he [Hawthorne] foreseeing the developing taste for realism which was to dominate the next era in fiction, when Twain and Howells tended to ignore or disguise the marble and emphasize the mud of common and humble life? In this work and in the next one, *The Blithedale Romance*, Hawthorne was at least on the edge of what was to become the main stream of American fiction." As literary history in terms of trends and movements this is a sensible and uncontroversial statement; it is plausible, too, as regards Hawthorne—witness the Custom-House Essay. In a critical context, the notion of *The House* and *Blithedale* as forerunners of Howells is—startling.

With major editions of Irving, Howells, Melville, and Twain in preparation, well supported and manned with many scholars, the issues of purpose and emphasis are of great moment. To avert possible misunderstanding, the matter of textual thoroughness is not in question here. Obviously the more accurate the text the better—though with careless fellows like Hawthorne, Melville, Shelley, and Shakespeare what constitutes accuracy is not a problem that can be decided in advance, by predetermined rules. One may hope, however, not for less expert editing but for a less exclusive emphasis upon editing alone. Literary studies have always given adequate prestige and emolument to editorial labors; there is no present need at all for a campaign for greater recognition of their value.

University of North Carolina at Chapel Hill

3. Melville

Willard Thorp

1965 was an atypical year in Melville studies. No editions were published; very little was written about the early novels; and only one full-length book appeared. In the course of the next few years, however, a collected edition of Melville's works will be issued. It is now under way at Northwestern University and the Newberry Library. Harrison Hayford, the general editor, has written an account of the progress of the edition to date, which will be found at the end of this chapter. The one book of the year, Paul Brodtkorb, Jr.'s *Ishmael's White World*, is summarized below, in the section on *Moby-Dick*.

i. Redburn

H. Bruce Franklin's "Redburn's Wicked End" (*NCF*, XX, 190–194) advances the startling idea that though Redburn has seen plenty of evil and wrong in the course of his initiation, in the end he commits a great wrong himself. He deserts Harry Bolton, now alone and homeless in a strange land. The reader will hear in the dialogue in which Redburn commits Harry to Goodwell "the echoes of all Melville's time-servers as they confront their victims." Mr. Franklin has not asked himself the inevitable question: why should Melville wish to alter, in this abrupt fashion, a characterization he has so carefully built up? Heinz Kosok believes that *Redburn* has received too little attention as a work of art. His "'A sadder and a wiser boy:' Herman Melvilles *Redburn* als *Novel of Initiation*" (*JA*, X, 126–152) is an admirable attempt to do justice to the novel. He deals first with the "I" of the story. The first-person narrator is conscious of how he is telling his tale. He has experienced subsequent rovings and has looked on far more perilous scenes, yet the older "I" has not lost the younger Redburn's feeling for the worth of man. (We learn a surprising amount along the way, about the "I" who is now grown up.) Herr Kosok, next, has interesting things to say about the compactness and the symmetrical structure of the novel. The initiation theme is first clearly announced in Chapter VI: "He is Initiated in the Business of Cleaning out the Pig-pen." This theme is carried through a series of disillusionments on the voyage, with more to come in Liverpool. Melville uses the "prosy old guide-book" passages to place side by side the four time-planes of the novel: the father's *Wanderjahre*, the childhood, youth, and maturity of Redburn. By this time Redburn's initiation is complete. He has confronted both death and evil. In discussing next the isolation theme, Herr Kosok shrewdly observes that Redburn seems all the more isolated because the officers and sailors he encounters are so little differentiated. The article concludes with a careful analysis of the characterizations of Harry and Carlo. Together they add up to the young Redburn in the mingling of innocence and experience. "Carlo nimmt die extreme Gegenpostion zu dem unausgeglichenen Harry ein; während er nie unreif gewesen zu sein scheint, wird Harry nie erwachsen werden. Zwischen beiden steht Wellingborough, dessen Ausgangspunkt dem Harrys gleicht, der sich aber nach vielen Konflikten der Ebene Carlos annähert."

ii. *Moby-Dick*

Leon Howard's chapter, "Herman Melville, *Moby Dick*," in *The American Novel* (pp. 25–34), is necessarily synoptic but contrives to make some good points, the most original of which is this: the distinctive power of *Moby-Dick* is derived from the author's good fortune in being able to incorporate within himself and dramatize in a novel the major intellectual conflict of a century. "Melville felt the conflict deeply, but he had to invent his own symbols in order to give it meaning." Nathalia Wright resolves the question in her title, "Moby Dick: Jonah's or Job's Whale?" (*AL*, XXXVII, 190–195), in favor of Job. "The quotation in 'Extracts' and Father Mapple's sermon aside, the story of Jonah and the whale is referred to only three times, each time facetiously." On the other hand Ishmael's references to the sea monster in Job are of serious import, and "all convey the awesome tone of the original description." The best point made in Beongcheon Yu's "Ishmael's Equal Eye: The Source of Balance in *Moby-Dick*" (*ELH*, XXXII, 110–125) takes us beyond the

novel. "This anguished Melville of 1856, incapable of either belief
or unbelief, is no longer the same Melville who created Ishmael, but
rather the Melville who has somehow lost Ishmael's 'equal eye.'" In
"A Note on Quakerism and *Moby Dick*: Hawthorne's 'The Gentle
Boy' as a Possible Source" (*QH*, LIV, 94–102), Gerhard Friedrich
first shows how Melville assigns to the Quakers in his novel a carefully conceived scale of essential values and imperfections. He then
suggests that Melville may have taken hints for his theme from the
agonized questions of the nature of God by the mother in "The
Gentle Boy": "What has God done to me? Hath He cast me down
never to rise again? Hath He crushed my very heart in His hand?"

It would take some time to count the articles and sections of
books which describe the Ishmaelean consciousness and assess Melville's remarkable technical feat in making Ishmael the "center of
consciousness" of the novel. Paul Brodtkorb, Jr. has now done the
job thoroughly in *Ishmael's White World: A Phenomenological Reading of* Moby Dick (New Haven and London, Yale Univ. Press). It
is a dense book, because the arguments come thick and fast. I shall
have to content myself with noting here a few passages in which
Mr. Brodtkorb pauses to summarize his intentions. What he has
attempted is "a descriptive analysis of the Ishmaelean consciousness;
a consciousness which we, as readers cannot escape. It constitutes
for us all we can know of Ishmael and his world." At all times
Ishmael "*is* whatever character he reports, even when he reports
what logically he could not know; for he is the writer, entering into
the souls of others. . . . And, similarly, when he disappears from
the action, he quite simply *is* the action; why should he not be?"

Mr. Brodtkorb ordered his study as follows. Chapter I is concerned with establishing a governing principle of Ishmael's pre-
reflective vision. Chapters II through V "make use of the following
major categories, which overlap and parallel rather than strictly
exclude each other: Ishmael's existence as an intentional consciousness may be divided into his apprehension of (1) his world, exclud-
ing other people; (2) his body, and his consciousness of the bodies
of others; (3) other people, including himself as character; (4)
time." Chapter VI formally "defines the complex emotion or sequence
of emotions in which Ishmael (his book, his world, his total history)
is founded."

A passage in the last page of the book is a good summary of the author's overall intention.

Ishmael's book is founded in his own boredom, dread, and despair. These moods are the unity of his consciousness, and of his book. They are the correlatives of his book's "objects," and as moods they are neither frivolous nor fleeting. Certain romantic philosophies would hold that they are nothing less than ontological: they are not something we have, but something we are. Whether or not that is true, *Moby Dick* tries to persuade us to become these moods in order to discover their meanings within ourselves; it does so by submerging the initially amusing character Ishmael into the ambiguous voice of the narrator, whose feelings in relation to his strange world provide analogues for ours.

The book has some faults. Passages from the novel are occasionally interpreted as if we were dealing with a philosophical treatise. There is rather too much reliance on Kierkegaard's categories in settling points at issue. Occasionally Mr. Brodtkorb spins out an idea until the thread breaks, as when he comments on the fact that we are never told Ishmael's real name. But this is, I believe, an important book. It should not be undertaken in an idle hour.

iii. Pierre

I did not comment in *ALS, 1964* on Valentina Poggi's *"Pierre:* Il 'Kraken' di Melville" (*SA*, X, 1964, 71–100). It is one of the best of recent articles by a foreign scholar. Basing her arguments on Chapter LIX ("Squid") of *Moby-Dick*, the author sees Pierre as confronted by ambiguities in his relations with others as frightful and baffling as the terror which the apparition of the faceless and frontless squid aroused in the members of the crew of the *Pequod*. Melville's remark about krakens in a letter to Hawthorne (November 17?, 1851) was not made casually. He was already thinking of a formless, chance-like apparition of life (*Pierre*) which would be related to *Moby-Dick* as the kraken is to the leviathan. In *Moby-Dick* there are hints of possible answers to the questions posed. Melville does not permit Pierre to resolve any of the "ambiguities." Almost from the beginning his life has "no perceptible face or front." It is an apparition and there is no way by which he can grapple with it. In speculating why Melville so completely thwarts his hero, the author comes to this conclusion: "Personalmente, credo che in quest'opera si debba riconoscere un'espressione spesso incontrollata di agnoscia esistenziale." In any event, "il Melville di *Pierre* fa l'effeto di un uomo che si è visto costretto a negare nell'uomo ogni capacità di sanità e grandezza morale, e non riesce a rassegnarsi a questo pensiero."

In "*Pierre* and *Manfred*: Melville's Study of the Byronic Hero" (*PELL*, I, 230–240) Joseph J. Mogan, Jr., states categorically that "Manfred is clearly Pierre's progenitor." But the resemblances which he finds between the two works are too general to justify such a statement. In "Pierre and Robin: Melville's Debt to Hawthorne" (*ESQ*, No. 38, pp. 90–92) John L. Kimmey argues for a definite Hawthornean influence on *Pierre*. In "My Kinsman, Major Molineux" a young, Adamic youth comes to the city, at night, in search of a relative who will, he hopes, help him. He is treated badly in a series of encounters: "the essence of each face-to-face encounter is eager anticipation followed by disillusionment, renunciation, and finally bewilderment." Again, as in Mr. Mogan's argument for the influence of *Manfred* on *Pierre*, the resemblances between the two works do not seem to me particular enough to posit any definite "borrowing."

iv. The Confidence-Man

The debate continues and the two contestants who are in the lists this year are strong-minded and determined. In "Appearance and Reality in Melville's *The Confidence-Man*" (*ELH*, XXXI, 1964, 418–442) Philip Drew disagrees with three points that are often made in studies of the novel: (1) the confidence-man is a trickster; (2) those who trust him are fools, while those who distrust him are wise; (3) the novel's message is that innocence, faith, and trust are doomed. The dissenting Mr. Drew argues that "even the most dubious of the confidence-man's transactions are susceptible of an innocent explanation." Every incident narrated is innocent in itself to a trusting eye, but filled with dubious circumstance to the reader who is himself without confidence. If we decide, in reading the novel, that only a rogue or a simpleton asks for charity, this decision is our own, not Melville's. "It is in ourselves that we must then locate the failure of confidence which is the subject of the book." Enter Lawrence Grauman, Jr., as, literally, the Devil's advocate. In "Suggestions on the Future of *The Confidence-Man*" (*PELL*, I, 241–249) he argues that from the second chapter on the confidence-man appears in seven different guises, "each of them, on the allegorical level, an avatar of the Devil." Here is news indeed. No Melvillean has ever ventured this far out. Still, Mr. Grauman will not agree that Melville despaired because "Christ, for some inscrutable reason, has been displaced as God's agent by the Devil." Man is not villain but victim, and "Melville's grief is that of compassion."

v. Tales

In "Melville's *L'Homme Révolté*" (*ES*, XLVI, 390–402) John V. Hagopian concludes that Melville must be recognized as America's first existentialist writer. Basing his study on "Bartleby," "Benito Cereno," and *Billy Budd*, he finds four similarities in theme and technique in the three tales. They all involve (1) a realistic, historically oriented human situation; (2) presentation from the point of view of a naïve or uncertain observer who gradually gains insight into the horror of that situation; (3) an "official view" which in some way justifies the forces of authority and power; and (4) a revolt against those forces which is both necessary and futile. Judith Slater's "The Domestic Adventurer in Melville's Tales" (*AL*, XXXVII, 267–279) argues that "the Ishmael theme" is carried over into six of the tales, "Cock-a-Doodle-Doo!," "The Lightning-Rod Man," "I and My Chimney," "Jimmy Rose," "The Apple-Tree Table," and "The Piazza." In these tales we are shown, as it were, "the future of Ishmael," and this is the question which is posed in each of them: "how can such an individual without sacrificing his complexity of vision adjust himself, as he must, to 'home'?" The "domestic adventurers" of these tales possess to some degree "a doubleness of vision which is foreshadowed in Ishmael's development." The article is, I think, over-ingenious.

One of the best papers of the year is Herbert M. Smith's "Melville's Master in Chancery and his Recalcitrant Clerk" (*AQ*, XVII, 734–741). Much follows from the fact that the narrator in "Bartleby" has recently enlarged his "snug business" in becoming Master in Chancery. The main concern of Chancery law (a survival in America of the authority of the sovereign) is with "principles of ideality instead of precedent, principles of absolute instead of relative justice." Melville's new Master soon has on his hands an unexpected

"case" in equity. He had hired Bartleby as a consequence of the
increase in his volume of work. Now he is challenged in his legal
thinking by "the exactly apposite problem of Bartleby." The story
takes on new meaning when one recognizes the reasons why Melville placed his narrator in the new office. Even the key word of the
story, "prefer," relates to the Master's obligations. "Only in equity
pleading is the preference of the plaintiff for one kind of restitution
over another a consideration." Norman Springer's "Bartleby and the
Terror of Limitation" (*PMLA*, LXXX, 410–418) supplements Mr.
Smith's article. Mr. Springer concentrates on the Master's flawed
and limited perception of the situation. "It is one of Melville's successes that he forces us to see and feel this yawning incomprehensibility the narrator faces, an incomprehensibility great in its effect
because it is so carefully surrounded by all the concrete paraphernalia of the comprehensible."

It has become fashionable of late to view Captain Delano as a
dolt. E. F. Carlisle's "Captain Amasa Delano: Melville's American
Fool" (*Criticism*, VII, 349–362) carries this notion as far as it can
go. " 'Benito Cereno,' then, reveals an awareness, frequently dramatized in American fiction, of the failure of optimism—of the inadequacy of the Great American Boob." Delano suffers from three major
misconceptions. His optimism causes him to misread life. Though
he professes to be "republican" in his dealings, he easily accepts
Negro slavery and oppression. He seems excessively concerned with
himself. His attention to superficial details and to himself "helps to
cloud his vision and mislead him." Seymour L. Gross's "Mungo Park
and Ledyard in Melville's *Benito Cereno*" (*ELN*, III, 122–123)
makes a small but interesting point. When Melville revised the story
for inclusion in *Piazza Tales*, he substituted Ledyard for Mungo
Park in the passage in which Captain Delano sentimentalizes about
the slumbering Negresses. Why this change? Probably because Melville read an article in *Putnam's* in the issue in which the first instal-
ment of "Benito Cereno" appeared. In this article, "About Niggers,"
Ledyard is referred to as remarking on the friendliness of the African
women he encountered. In "The Narrator of 'Norfolk Isle and the
Chola Widow'" (*SSF*, III, 52–62) Howard D. Pearce attempts to
answer the question he raises: Is the narrator of this tale Melville
or is he creating a fictive "I" to tell the tale? The conclusion is not

very firm. "It would be difficult not to see Melville standing behind, not residing in, this narrator, fully aware of the incompleteness of the narrator's view of the events and aware as well of his attempt to color the events to suit his own sensibility."

vi. Poems

William B. Dillingham's " 'Neither Believer Nor Infidel': Themes of Melville's Poetry" (*Person*, XLVI, 501–516) finds that the four predominant themes in the poetry deal with innate depravity, the endless human search, man's eternal loneliness, and the folly of dogma. "An examination of his poetry reveals the older Melville unmellowed by time, unsatisfied in his probings, and, as ever, impatient with final answers." In "Hawthorne, Melville, and the *Monitor*" (*AL*, XXXVII, 33–40), Leo B. Levy argues that in writing his four poems about the famous warship, Melville borrowed ideas from Hawthorne's 1862 *Atlantic* essay, "Chiefly About War Matters." The parallels are striking, to be sure, but suggest that the two men were thinking along the same lines—about the increasing mechanization of American life and the implications of the kind of warfare which the *Monitor*'s engagement introduced. Melville would say, in "A Utilitarian View of the Monitor's Fight":

> War yet shall be, but warriors
> Are now but operatives;

Hawthorne's meditations were more elegiac. "Then went down all the navies of Europe, and our own. Old Ironsides, and all, and Trafalgar and a thousand other fights became a memory never to be acted over again." Elémire Zolla's "La struttura e le fonti di *Clarel*" (*SA*, X, 1964, 101–134) promises more than the article delivers. By "structure" the author means only "la struttura ideologica," and the section on this subject discusses chiefly Melville's recurrent stress on the destruction of religious faith by modern science. Only three "fonti"—Disraeli's *Tancred*, the symbolism of dust in *The Marble Faun*, and Chateaubriand's *Itinéraire de Paris à Jerusalem*—are considered. Strangely, the author makes no use, no mention even, of Walter Bezanson's edition of *Clarel*, though two Melville studies published subsequently are cited.

vii. Billy Budd

John W. Rathbun's "Billy Budd and the Limits of Perception" (NCF,
XX, 19–34) provides a good, middle-of-the-road reading of the story.
The author is most persuasive in his remarks on its total impact. He
observes, rightly, that "the final chapters constitute an ironic epilogue,
in which in a series of tonally contrasting events we see the impact of
Billy's death on the state, Captain Vere, and the seamen." Sister Mary
Ellen's "Parallels in Contrast: A Study of Melville's Imagery in
Moby-Dick and Billy Budd" (SSF, II, 284–290) makes ingenious use
of the images in the two fictions in order to discover Melville's
changed view of the heroic man. Here is the core of the argument:
Melville made a "three-way division of the images characterizing
Ahab" in writing Billy Budd. "The hyperbolic images of god, hero,
king, Adam, magnet, and light apply to Billy Budd. The foreboding
images of eyes, brow, darkness, fire, and snake apply to Claggart. The
distinguishing images of captain, aristocrat, intellectual, and efficient
leader apply to Captain Vere." Robert Shulman's "Montaigne and
the Techniques and Tragedy of Melville's Billy Budd" (CL, XVI,
1964, 322–330) is a definitive treatment of the subject and corrects
misconceptions in some earlier studies. Enlisting Montaigne on Vere's
side was "a useful strategy for winning initial approval for a character
who will later strain that acceptance." Actually Vere is made to re-
spond to only a limited range of the Essays. From the differences between Montaigne and his disciple Vere ironic overtones emerge. For
example, Vere asks the court whether "private conscience should not
yield to that imperial one formulated in the code under which alone
we officially proceed." Montaigne's answer would have been em-
phatically in the negative. "Montaigne's own celebration of the values
of compassion, freedom, personal loyalty, private integrity, and individual conscience serve to remind us of what Vere has disregarded."
John S. Reist, Jr.'s "Surd Evil and Suffering Love" (Universitas, II,
1964, 81–90) is a well-argued theological consideration of Billy
Budd.

I hope that Edward H. Rosenberry's "The Problem of Billy Budd"
(PMLA, LXXX, 489–498) will be widely read. It is a thorough, well-
reasoned attempt to bring order out of the conflicting assessments of
Billy Budd. As the author remarks, if some kind of consensus cannot
be reached, we are in for a continuing combat over the tale of the

kind which has plagued "The Turn of the Screw." Mr. Rosenberry's chief quarrel is with the ironists, though he understands why, in this age when we have been "thrown off balance by a barrage of ironic works" (as Wayne Booth has said), the irony-hunters have been having their say. There is plenty of irony in *Billy Budd*, but it is not satiric irony. It is the Aristotelian kind (reversal of fortune, "irony of fate"). Among the deluded readings of the story which Mr. Rosenberry attacks are these: "the refusal to honor the author's proffered coin of meaning"; reading the novel in the light of Melville's attack on naval discipline in *White-Jacket*; the confusion of dramatic facts with the personal views of author or reader; an equally powerful preconception of the characters of *Billy Budd*. In advancing his own views, Mr. Rosenberry is chiefly bent on building up the case for Vere. In a world "in which mutiny is a serviceable metaphor for the moral and theological condition of man, an imposed order is the only kind that is possible, and the articles under which Captain Vere takes his authority are not radically different from those under which Moses took his." *Billy Budd* was conceived as the kind of story in which "accommodations" are not available.

viii. Miscellaneous

New biographical information about Melville seldom turns up these days, but Hershel Parker has edited an important document which gives us more light on his early career. This is the 1846 London Journal of Gansevoort Melville, now in the Gansevoort-Lansing Collection of the New York Public Library. Mr. Parker published "Gansevoort Melville's 1846 London Journal" in three instalments in *BNYPL* (LXIX, 633–654; LXX, 36–49 and 113–131). It has been issued as a separate publication. The diary will be of use to Melville scholars because it tells in detail of Gansevoort's arrangements for the publication of *Typee* and provides some information about the relations between the two brothers. It is also a valuable document for diplomatic historians. Mr. Parker has written an excellent introduction containing information about Gansevoort's oratorical services to the Democratic party and his relations with his superior in London, Minister Louis McLane, a "peace man," who disliked Gansevoort because he thought him a warmonger. As Mr. Parker says, the Journal is "the best evidence in Gansevoort's defence." Mr. Parker's "New Cross-

Lights on Melville in the 1870's" (*ESQ*, No. 39, pp. 24–25) comments
on an article which appeared in *Harper's* for January, 1873–"The
Sailors' Snug Harbor." This piece presents a pen portrait of Thomas
Melville but makes no mention of Herman. Mrs. Frances Thomas
Osborne's "Herman Melville through a Child's Eyes" (*BNYPL*,
LXIX, 655–660) is a delightful account of visits to Grandpa and
Grandma Melville in the house on Twenty-sixth Street. The visits
began when this granddaughter was five; Melville died three years
later. The piece is longer than the similar one Eleanor Melville Met-
calf wrote for Weaver's biography.

Three general studies of Melville's literary career are decidedly
worth attention. The chapter on "The Demonic, Herman Melville" in
Loren Baritz' *City on a Hill: A History of Ideas and Myths in America*
(New York, John Wiley, 1964, pp. 271–331) is of particular interest
because it is the work of an intellectual historian. Mr. Baritz' purpose
was to discuss the thought of a group of men who "developed the
most complex and interesting view of America, men whose definitions
of the nation were subtle enough to include both success and failure."
He traces Melville's intellectual journey that began "in the buoyant
temper of Young America and ended in a private world of unmiti-
gated and unmediated torment." The climax of Melville's disillusionment is to be seen in *Clarel*.

> Winthrop had sermonized about the assignment of the new world
> as the home of the Saints, recreated men; Edwards had taught of
> the sunrise in the west, with all that implied; Adams had written
> of the wisdom of the past as merely preparatory for the grand
> climax of America; Taylor [of Caroline] had argued that his land
> could recapture Eden; and Emerson had sung and sung his hymns
> to the present.

Finally, Melville, in *Clarel*, transformed the idea of America as a city
on a hill into a "satire of the heaven."

> Columbus ended earth's romance:
> No New World to mankind remains!

The second general study is Philip Drew's "The Two-Headed Symbol" (*Listener*, LXXIV, 300–301), originally a B.B.C. Third Pro-
gramme talk. Mr. Drew asks why it is that we do not experience in
finishing a Melville narrative that "feeling of finality most poignantly
experienced when the hero shoots the villain at the end of a Western
film." The reason is that Melville locates his story "at a point where

the general morality is not simply vague but in fact continues to support simultaneously two incompatible doctrines." The later novels and stories are not "attempts at allegory which fail because of an insufficiently precise system of correspondences, but exact embodiments of intrinsically ambiguous situations, pivoting on ethical anomalies." Melville repeatedly maneuvers us into a position where "the whole weight of the book bears down on our own equivocal systems of assessment." Robert Beum's "Melville's Course" (*DR*, XLV, 17–33) attempts to account for the fluctuations between success and failure in Melville's writing. His conclusion is speculative but provocative. "In general, Melville's control of theme and structure and language improves as he . . . achieves—if only for the purposes of his art —a vision which, however tragic, is not bitter or nihilistic. . . . Conversely style and form begin to deteriorate . . . whenever Melville begins to lose faith in the existence of discoverable truths, or in life as something at least partly and potentially dignified and admirable. He could not make Pyrrhonism eloquent."

In 1964 members of the Faculty of Philosophy of the University of Tübingen published a *Festschrift* for Shakespeare—*Shakespeare: Seine Welt—Unsere Welt* (Max Niemeyer). To this volume Hans-Joachim Lang contributed "Melville und Shakespeare" (pp. 134–161). Herr Lang makes no attempt to search for verbal influences, believing that there has been enough digging of this kind. He is looking for larger influences. In at least two instances he makes original observations. Studying the interpretations of Shakespeare offered by the leading popularizer of the day, H. N. Hudson, he noted that Hudson presented Shakespeare as a nationalist, a model of common sense, and a political conservative. When Melville discovered Shakespeare for himself, he dissented strongly from these interpretations. Herr Lang argues that Shakespeare—particularly his dark characters —made possible the conception and "Sprachgestaltung" of *Moby-Dick*. In discussing *Pierre*, he recalls Emerson's remark that the speculative genius of his century was "a sort of living Hamlet." Small wonder that Melville should drive his probings at the very axis of reality through a Hamlet figure.

Two articles deal with the influence of Melville on other writers. We know, from a letter to the Dutch novelist Maartens, that Barrie greatly admired Melville, but David Park Williams, in "Hook and Ahab: Barrie's Strange Satire on Melville" (*PMLA*, LXXX, 483–488), demonstrates that Barrie made extensive use of passages from Melville in writing *Peter and Wendy* and *Peter Pan*. The transformations he effected, which are ingenious and delightful, Mr. Williams summarizes as follows.

> So Barrie's dark, inscrutable captain is pursued by the hungry, ticking crocodile—time running out on Hook. So Melville's dark, inscrutable captain pursues the White Whale—eternity eluding Ahab. The whale's pearly tomb-like jaw becomes Peter Pan's pearly baby teeth; the Typee girls become scaly mermaids; and the gold watch of a whale's inner life becomes a clock striking six within the crocodile. The mutilated Roundhead Ahab becomes the mutilated Cavalier Hook—and through Barrie's dark, inscrutable imagination filters the rhetoric and fury of his admired Melville.

Manuel García Blanco has discovered that Unamuno was an enthusiastic reader of Melville ("Unamuno y el novelista norteamericano Melville," *Insula*, XIX, 1964, 216–217, 5). The Spanish novelist owned *Moby-Dick, Omoo*, and *Typee*. He made extensive notes in the Everyman *Moby-Dick*, which he bought in Paris in 1925. In Unamuno's *Cancionero, Diario Poética* there are two poems (Nos. 787 and 1,121) based on Melvillean themes. Sr. Blanco remarks that the marginalia and underscorings in the three novels would be worth study, but he has left it to someone else to do the job.

Scholars in search of reviews of Melville's books have overlooked a journal which reviewed him consistently and favorably. In *"The Spirit of the Times Reviews Melville"* (*JEGP*, LXIV, 57–64), John T. Flanagan notes that *The Spirit* reviewed or devoted at least a few lines to nearly all of Melville's works of fiction, the exceptions being *The Piazza Tales* and *Israel Potter*. The review of *Moby-Dick* is long and laudatory. Most remarkable is the assessment of *Pierre*. "Every work written by this author possesses more than common interest, and abounds in strange and wild imaginings, but this book outstrips all his former productions, and is quite equal to 'Moby Dick, or the Whale.'"

Two articles make corrections in the record. In spite of the fact that Melville explicitly wrote that he is "not talking of Mr. Emerson now" in the passage about "men who *dive*" (letter of March 3, 1849, to Evert Duyckinck), biographers have persisted in believing that he *did* have Emerson in mind. In "A Note on Melville's 'Men who *Dive*'"

(*BNYPL*, LXIX, 661–664) Heyward Ehrlich makes use of a letter from Evert to his brother George (March 4, 1839) which would seem to settle the matter. Evert explains that "Duycking" in the family coat of arms "means *diving*—that is to say seeking the hidden pearls of truth." Melville, who must have known this bit of family lore, is punning on the family name in the passage in question. Duyckinck, not Emerson, is the man who dives. As a student of Hawthorne, Hubert H. Hoeltje is annoyed because "Hawthorne and his Mosses" has had an unwarranted influence in Hawthorne criticism. In "Hawthorne, Melville, and 'Blackness' " (*AL*, XXXVII, 41–51), he points out that the famous essay does not present the contents and style of the book on which it is based. Melville read into it his own "blackness." Though both Hawthorne and his wife appreciated Melville's praise, neither of them ever wrote anything in approval of the interpretation. Indeed, Sophia confided to her mother that the anonymous reviewer (Melville) "does not know how this heart and this intellect are enshrined."

It begins to look as if Melville will have the kind of posthumous fame as a dramatist that has come to Henry James. In both instances, of course, the adapters have done the work and deserve much of the credit. The Coxe-Chapman *Billy Budd Foretopman* was a *succès d'estime* on Broadway in 1951 and has been produced scores of times since then. A musical setting of "Bartleby" opened in New York in a double bill with Edward Albee's *The American Dream* on January 21, 1961, but closed after sixteen performances. The libretto was prepared by Albee and James Hinton, Jr. Robert Lowell's adaptation of "Benito Cereno," which received enthusiastic notices at the time of its premiere in November, 1964, now forms the third part of his trilogy *The Old Glory* (New York, Farrar, Straus, and Giroux). Benjamin Britten's *Billy Budd* (London, 1952; revised version, 1961) is considered by many critics to be the best of his operas. Jean-Paul Renvoisé has made a study of the genesis and musical structure of this work ("Billy Budd: opéra de Benjamin Britten," *EA*, XVIII, 367–382). Of special interest to Melville scholars will be M. Renvoisé's account of the way the librettists, Eric Crozier and E. M. Forster, went about solving their problems in adapting the tale. Incidentally, Britten was moved to compose the opera after he read the brief account of *Billy Budd* in Forster's *Aspects of the Novel*.

ix. Dissertations

Four dissertations completed in 1965 have been recorded in *DA*.
Edgar Afton Dryden's "Herman Melville's Narrators and the Art of
Fiction: A Study in Point of View" (*DA*, XXVI, 3298–3299) maintains that because of his deep concern with the problems of the
writer of fiction Melville's narrators through *Moby-Dick* are "portraits of the artist at work." *Pierre* marks the beginning of the period
in which Melville "seriously questions the ability of the artist to discover truth in a world of lies." *The Confidence-Man* dramatizes "the
artist's surrender to the world of lies." In "Benito Cereno" and *Billy
Budd*, Melville used a new narrative method. Their narrators,
through their ability to be at one and the same time "involved in and
detached from experience, are able to create a fiction which is also
the vehicle of truth." Victor Myers Hoar, Jr.'s "The Confidence Man
in American Literature" (*DA*, XXVI, 2753–2754) is a general survey
of the subject, from the early Southern humorists through Faulkner.
John Edward Semmens' "Point of View in the Early and Later Fiction of Herman Melville" (*DA*, XXVI, 1028) contends that beginning with "Bartleby" Melville's handling of point of view is characterized by authorial disengagement. By standing apart as he did, he
was able "to give attention to structural demands that his subjective
involvement in the early fiction had prevented." John Brindley Williams, in "The Impact of Transcendentalism on the Novels of Herman
Melville" (*DA*, XXVI, 1052–1053), concludes that even though Melville criticized the Transcendental religious faith in a benevolent
nature, his writings show an interest in Emersonian self-reliance and
in "the portrayal of symbolic correspondences between nature and
the mind." Melville was in agreement with Transcendental ethics in
many respects.

We now have abstracts of three dissertations written in 1964.
Malcolm Orrin Magaw's "Melville and the Christian Myth: The
Imagery of Ambiguity" (*DA*, XXV, 4126) proposes the thesis that
"Melville's art, in effect, does not explore the Christian myth; it
explores the enigmas that have preoccupied human beings since the
beginning of history." The ambiguity of his allusive Christian imag-
ery "underscores the dualism and relativism of his metaphysics."
James Lawrence Guetti, Jr., "The Failure of the Imagination: A

Study of Melville, Conrad, and Faulkner" (*DA*, XXV, 4145–4146), furnishes a close reading of *Moby-Dick*, "Heart of Darkness," and *Absalom, Absalom!* He discovers in these works the "dramatization of a character's or a narrator's failure to compose or structure his imaginative experience." Though this technique has connotations of failure for the central characters and even the narrators of these and other novels by these authors, "at the same time it is the most suggestive and powerful of the techniques of prose fiction." Raj Kumar Gupta's "Form and Style in Herman Melville's *Pierre*" (*DA*, XXVI, 1631–1632) is a chapter-by-chapter study of the epic and dramatic conventions, symbolism, and imagery of the novel. Mr. Gupta concludes that *Pierre* is not a failure, "but a successful literary performance and one of Melville's greatest artistic achievements."

Two dissertations written more than a decade ago have now been abstracted: Edward Fiess, "Byron and Byronism in the Mind and Art of Herman Melville" (*DA*, XXV, 4145); and George Raymond Creeger, "Color Symbolism in the Works of Herman Melville" (*DA*, XXV, 6620).

Martin L. Pope's "The Wandering Quest: A Study of Herman Melville" (Columbia, 1965) has not yet been entered in *DA*.

x. The Collected Melville

The Northwestern University Press and the Newberry Library of Chicago have announced their joint publication of the collected writings of Herman Melville, under the editorship of Harrison Hayford, Hershel Parker, and George Thomas Tanselle.

Originating through the Center for Editions of American Authors of the Modern Language Association, this edition will include Melville's fiction, poetry, and miscellaneous uncollected writings. It is planned that the edition will number fifteen volumes, to be published over the next four years. Its purpose will be to establish the original texts of Melville's writings based on intensive literary research.

Each of the previously published works will consist of three sections: (1) the work itself as Melville finally intended it, free from editorial and printing corruptions; (2) textual variants; and (3) a historical afterword by a contributing scholar. In addition, there will be (1) a descriptive bibliography by Mr. Tanselle and (2) an annotated bibliography of writings about Melville and his works, by the editors. *Typee* and *Omoo* will be published during the spring of 1967.

All texts are being prepared by the central editorial board named above. Serving as contributing scholars will be Walter Bezanson, Merlin Bowen, Richard Fogle, Elizabeth Foster, William Gilman, Howard Horsford, Leon Howard, William Hutchinson, Leland Phelps, Gordon Roper, Roma Rosen, Merton Sealts, Jr., Morris Star, Willard Thorp, and Nathalia Wright.

Each volume in the series may be purchased either individually or, beginning spring 1967, on a subscription basis.

Princeton University

4. Whitman

Edward F. Grier

i. Editions, Texts, and Textual Studies

Again, in 1965, the most important work on Whitman has been editorial, for *Leaves of Grass: Comprehensive Reader's Edition,* edited by Harold W. Blodgett and Sculley Bradley (New York, New York Univ. Press), marks a distinct advance over any text of *Leaves* we have had in accuracy and fullness. As our insight into the genesis of the canon of *Leaves* has grown, the problem of selecting the text to be edited has become more complex, but although recent volumes of selections have tended to follow, with some critical justification, a chronological order, and the 1855 and 1866 texts have been reprinted, the present editors have conservatively and wisely chosen the classic solution: they reprint the last authorized version. Their text was therefore printed "from a photographic facsimile . . . corrected for mechanical defects" of the green cloth, hardbound issue of the 1891–1892 edition. The editors chose this issue for they discovered that the paperbound "deathbed" issue, designed as gifts for Whitman's friends, "does not contain the verbal changes and mechanical variants which first appeared in Whitman's revised *Leaves of Grass* in 1888 and 1889" (pp. l-li). Although the editors can offer no explanation for this anomaly, they reprint the variants in footnotes. They have further respected the 1892 text by following the spill-overs of that edition as far as possible, thus avoiding any possible confusion about line-endings and stanzas. The lines are also numbered.

I have not compared the text of this edition with that of the 1892 edition, but I have noticed a few misprints. In the poems, page 57, line 633, "worrry" should be "worry." In the editorial material, page lii, line 18, one finds "accidnetally"; on page 50, note to lines 464–476, "*PMA*" should be "*PMLA*"; and on page 413, note to line 49, "53" should be "63."

As everyone knows, the *Collected Writings* has been planned on a most ample scale, and the *Comprehensive Reader's Edition* does not disappoint us. In addition to the full text, the volume also contains all of Whitman's prefaces as they first appeared. (Floyd Stovall, in his *Collected Prose Writings, 1892,* has printed them as they appeared in *Complete Prose Works.*) Thus we have the 1856 letter to Emerson now easily available, as it should have been long ago, for as a statement of Whitman's intentions it is secondary only to the 1855 Preface. But there are more riches. Since Whitman through the years omitted poems and passages of poems, the editors have included the forty-five omitted poems and a selection of twenty-eight omitted passages which they feel have a substantial interest and identity of their own. The omitted passages are reprinted in the text of the last edition in which they appeared. One wishes, however, that the editors had more closely cross-referenced the omitted passages to the poems from which they were dropped; even if one knows that two passages omitted from "The Sleepers" are to be found elsewhere in the volume, it would be handy for a number of reasons to be told in the introductory note to that poem that they appear on pages 626–628. The editors have also included forty-three of the sixty-five known uncollected poems, twenty-two of which are from manuscript. Some of these are complete; others, such as "The Two Vaults," are unfinished. Others seem to this reader to be fragments, not without a certain completeness, but essentially the sort of passages which could be fitted into any one of a number of Whitman's more loosely constructed chants and therefore perhaps more properly to be included among the uncollected manuscript fragments of which the editors print sixty. But this is a quibble. Talk about "comprehensive"! It is almost with a feeling of satiation that one finds a gallery of the best-known Whitman portraits in black and white and, as frontispiece, a color plate of the little-known Alexander portrait (a handsome painting, even though Whitman did not like it).

The notes are as generously planned as the presentation of texts. The bibliographical and textual notes are excellent. The editors have briefly summarized the textual history of each poem, often with reference to secondary literature. In the notes to individual lines and passages, they have often cited variant readings either from the editions prior to 1892 or from manuscript sources. Their citations of secondary material are not, however, always given with an eye to the use of a reader. For example, on page 50, in a note to lines 464–476 of "Song of Myself" (Sec. 22) they comment on Whitman's use of the Hegelian dialectic and cite the studies of Boatwright and Parsons. On page 261, note on line 4 of "On the Beach at Night Alone," they again refer to Hegel, and give a cross-reference to the note on page 50. So far, so good. But on page 274, in the note on "Roaming in Thought," they cite six studies of Whitman's Hegelianism, including Boatwright and Parsons, but give no cross-reference. In other words, the inexperienced reader, or even the experienced one, has a good chance of missing the most useful note, that on page 274. The note on studies of the structure of "Song of Myself" omits several important articles, although the editors may have a rather strict definition of "structure." Several reviewers have commented adversely on the notes which either interpret passages or explain words, and I concur in their judgments. The interpretive notes might well have been omitted entirely, for they get in the way. The explanatory notes often explain the obvious or familiar, but leave the obscure or difficult unexplained. For example, in their notes to "Salut au Monde!" the editors very properly annotate the place-names. But if Teheran and the Oder River are to be identified, why not Derne and Mogador?

This last objection is perhaps captious, for the defects are as nothing in the light of the magnificent manner in which Messrs. Blodgett and Bradley have carried out their arduous task. We are all indebted to them.[1]

Two paperback editions, both eminently useful for the classroom and private reading have appeared. One is an anonymously edited volume which announces itself on cover and title page to be *Leaves of Grass* (Garden City, N. Y., Doubleday Dolphin Books, n.d.), but which, on examination, proves to be a reprint of *Leaves of Grass*, 1855. An editorial note says that "The text is a faithful copy of the original [not, of course, in typography or design], and has not been

---

1. If, at this point, a general remark "for the good of the profession" may be permitted, this reviewer hopes, now that textually accurate editions of American writers are beginning to appear, that scholars (and critics) will cease the dubious and lazy practice of citing any old paperback edition at hand.

edited or abridged in any way." Despite the dark doubts aroused by the misleading title and the anonymity of the note, this statement is correct, allowing for the presence of five minor and obvious misprints (pp. 12, 23, 25, 54, 141) and a gratuitous paragraph break on page 27. (I am indebted to Miss Janice Bulleigh, who made the preliminary collation.) The third paragraph of the Preface is considerably separated from what precedes, but inspection of the original shows a separation at the same place approximately 1/32 inch wider than the others. Was this a mistake at the Rome Brothers' printshop or was it an indication by Whitman that the first two paragraphs are preliminary matter? Despite such very refined editing, however, this reprint omits the horizontal double rules that Whitman placed before each of the last six poems in lieu of the common title of "Leaves of Grass" and thus separates the poems only by a space. But, *mirabile dictu*, the marks of suspension are all correct. By an excess of zeal, even the original misspellings are retained. Such an analysis has been, perhaps, overelaborate for a cheap reprint, but this reprint is in fact inexpensive and it is reliable (even though the misspellings might have been corrected). Since Cowley's edition of 1959 requires extensive correction, this text can be considered reliable. *Whitman's "Song of Myself"—Origin, Growth, Meaning* (New York, Dodd, Mead, 1964) edited by James E. Miller, Jr., is a textbook which will be very useful in advanced courses. The 1855 and 1892 texts are given on facing pages and the apparatus is enriched by early versions from the Triggs variorum and Holloway's *Uncollected Poetry and Prose*. The text of the 1855 edition is essentially sound. The marks of suspension are correct with the exception of line 1146 (Sec. 44), where Whitman used six instead of the four dots he used elsewhere. There are also irregularities in the correction of spelling errors. "Furs" (l. 770, Sec. 32) remains, and "tressels" (l. 1064, Sec. 42) becomes "tressles." "Ouvre" (l. 665, Sec. 31) is corrected. "Nation" (l. 330, Sec. 16) is misprinted "nations." The 1855 Preface is not included but there are essays on the structure of "Song of Myself" by Strauch, Jarrell, Chase, Pearce, Cowley, and the editor. The usual "case book" questions and topics for students are also there.

There have been further studies which bear on Whitman's text. In "A New Whitman Letter" (*WWR*, XI, 102–103), George Montiero prints a letter of October 20, 1866, to Theodore F. Dwight, which quotes the price of the 1867 edition. William White, in "Whitman's *Leaves of Grass*: Notes on the Pocketbook (1889) Edition" (*SB*, XVIII, 280–281), explains the reasons for the existence of two states of the binding, one with flap and tuck, the other in common book style. The latter was suggested by Dr. Bucke, and twenty were so bound. At least 104, and possibly 280, were bound with flap and tuck. Mr. White, in "A 'Strange Coincidence' in Walt Whitman" (*WWR*, XI, 100–102), points out certain remarkable coincidences, including identical textual errors, between *Walt Whitman's New York*, edited by Henry W. Christman (New York, 1963) and "Brooklyniana," published by Emory Holloway in *Uncollected Poetry and Prose of Walt Whitman*, II, 222–321 (New York, 1921). In "Whitman Bibliography in Russia" (*WWR*, XI, 77–79), DeWolfe Miller reports on a new bibliography. *WWR* continues to carry an annotated bibliography of Whitman publications and to publish bits of Whitmaniana in each issue.

ii. General Studies, Including Biography

M. [O.] Mendelson, *Zhizn' i tvorchestvo Uitmena* [Life and Works of Whitman] (Moscow, Nauka) is one of two theses on Whitman mentioned by Miller (above). Mr. Mendelson, who is on the faculty of the Gorky Institute of World Literature and a member of the Soviet Academy of Sciences, has apparently published an earlier book on Whitman (1954). Although the bibliography of the present work lists much of the standard or recent "bourgeois" scholarship through 1962, there are some omissions as well as faulty entries. He mentions Bucke in his text, but does not cite him in the bibliography; he has apparently not seen *The Presence of Walt Whitman* (see below). Periodical criticism is cited only from the various collections which have appeared in the last few years. There are excusable weaknesses due to lack of firsthand knowledge of background, although there must be better authorities on American journalism in the 1840's than Charles Dickens. In his interpretations, Mendelson seems to follow the usual Soviet line that Whitman is the poet of the people. Thus the contradiction between "I" and "en masse" looms large for him, and he discusses it interestingly. He lays, however, too much emphasis on Whitman's involvement in the slavery question, which he considers to be fundamental in his development. He brushes aside psychological or mystical interpretations with contempt, and he seems to be uninterested in the genetic development of the text.[2]

Gay Wilson Allen, in "A Note on Comparing Whitman and Nietzsche" (*WWR*, XI, 74–75), comments on C. N. Stavrou's *Whitman and Nietzsche* (see *ALS, 1964*, p. 46). He admits the existence of striking parallels between Whitman and Nietzsche in many respects, but finds the two writers completely incompatible in the matters of sympathy, love, death, immortality, and the superman. James F. T. Tanner, in "The Superman in *Leaves of Grass*" (*WWR*, XI, 85–100), mentions neither Stavrou nor Allen, but finds as does Allen that the similarities spring from the fact that both read Emerson. He also perceives differences, but does not pursue them. Whitman's Superman, proclaimed in Section 46 of "Song of Myself," is the result of an evolutionary process implicit in the progress of the cosmos. He will be athletic, arrogant, affectionate, invincible, scholarly (it would perhaps be more correct to say "genius"), but chiefly, he will be divine, and it is the function of the poet, as "the true son of God," to produce the new man. Incidentally, "Superman" is so shopworn and so abused a term that one hopes a substitute can be found for it.

Recent criticism has had much to say about America as the Garden, about Adam, pastoral, innocence, childhood, the vernacular, and so on. Tony Tanner, in *The Reign of Wonder: Naivety and Reality in American Literature* (Cambridge, Cambridge Univ. Press), takes up the general theme, but with an awareness that innocence and wonder were not American inventions, as some American critics have seemed to think, but are part of the Romantic point of view. Tanner's concerns are literary, rather than cultural, and he sees the stylistic swing from minute particulars and sweeping generalizations as a literary manifestation of the Romantic distaste for analysis which was heightened by American conditions. His chapter on Whitman is perhaps not so fresh as might be, since Whitman has been a major topic in discussions of this particular thematic cluster, but Tanner

2. Since I cannot read Russian, I hope that by the time these notes appear Mendelson's book will have been properly reviewed in the journals. I wish to thank my colleague, Professor Sam F. Anderson, who patiently scanned the book for me and translated several sections viva voce. Of course he is not responsible for my statements.

has interesting things to say about Whitman's style, the catalogues and the structure of "Song of Myself."

Whitman also receives only a chapter in Edwin Fussell's *Frontier: American Literature and the American West* (Princeton, Princeton Univ. Press). Fussell attempts, with considerable success, to untangle the various meanings of "west," "frontier," and related terms and advances the theory that "the first American republic," the life principle of which was the Western dream, collapsed about 1860—not 1890. This is not the place for an extended critique of Fussell's Frontier Theory, but one may remark in passing that it is far more sophisticated than Turner's and far less the victim of the "Heart of America" myth, of which the Turner thesis is a document rather than an analysis. In short, Fussell's version of the theory is far more useful to the literary student, and, one suspects, the historian, than is Turner's. Whitman, of course, appeared at the moment of collapse, and Fussell examines, first, his involvement with the Frontier and, second, his successes and failures in the imaginative transformation of it. His literary thesis is that Whitman's decline after 1860 is to be accounted for by the failure of the Frontier as a vital cultural myth; that is, the imagined New World and the real disappeared together, and Whitman could no longer, despite his efforts, sustain his role as their prophet.

In some respects Mr. Fussell pushes his thesis too far, for it is difficult to interpret the doubts of "Calamus" and "Out of the Cradle" in his terms. Something, of course, can be done with "As I Ebb'd with the Ocean of Life." His connection of all sorts of traditional Romantic dualisms with the Frontier myth also is strained. One fruitful metaphorical extension of the Frontier, which is mentioned only briefly in one of the chapters on Melville, is not developed as fully as it might have been. This is Charles Olson's remark, in *Call Me Ishmael*, that in the 1840's and 1850's the sea was as truly Frontier as anything on land. Had Mr. Fussell followed up this brilliant hint, he would have been able to say some interesting things about Whitman's striking sea and space imagery, for example "Song of Myself," Section 52. He is excellent on Whitman's later years, and, in a way, almost rehabilitates them, if not as years of great poetry, then as years of occasional flashes of insight as to the function of literature in a post-frontier age. On the whole, though, the Whitman chapter is one of the weakest in the book. It seems almost tired. One has a feeling, nevertheless, that *Frontier* is the sort of book of which every reader will praise every chapter but that on his own specialty. This means of course that it is an immensely stimulating book.

John Paul Pritchard, in *Literary Wise Men of Gotham: Criticism in New York, 1815–1860* (Baton Rouge, Louisiana State Univ. Press, 1964), reveals the existence of a better-defined local body of theory than one had realized to exist, aside from the Young America group. Mr. Pritchard insists that "the student of Whitman will profit from detailed study of the periodical literature in his background," and indicates several points at which Whitman's theory and practice are related to the ideas he would have been reading about or that were his by birthright, notably his lack of regional bias. Aside, however, from a few figures like H. T. Tuckerman, W. A. Jones, Evert Duyckinck, the Young Americans around the *Democratic Review*, and a bird of passage like Poe, the New York literati seem to have been merely gentlemen in tail coats, lacking the vigor of the Boston-Concord group. One can almost think that Whitman was rebelling against this environment. Some of his most characteristic notions, his Transcendentalism, his arrogant nationalism, and his primitivism, run counter to New York thought. His New York background is important, but one must remember that like all geniuses he was almost sui generis and that his own tribute to Emerson touches the heart of the matter.

Bernard Duffey also reads Whitman in terms of his age in the second part of a two-part article (see *ALS, 1964*, p. 138), "Romantic Coherence and Romantic Incoherence in American Poetry" (*CRAS*, VII, 1963, 219–236; VIII, 1964, 453–464). He treats Whitman, at least in part, along with Melville, as an example of a shift from a coherence based on a deistic-evangelistic ethical spirituality to an incoherence based on the triumph of fact where "only personal temperament and private circumstance were available." William A. Little, in "Walt Whitman and the *Nibelungenlied*" (*PMLA*, LXXX, 562–570), surveys Whitman's interest in the Middle High German epic. He apparently does not realize that the sources of the three manuscripts he discusses were all identified by Floyd Stovall in 1954, since he nowhere cites Stovall's article. His dating is probably correct and as close as we will ever get.

Among other papers collected in R. W. B. Lewis' *Trials of the*

Word (New Haven, Yale Univ. Press) is "Walt Whitman: Always Going Out and Coming In," reprinted from *Major Writers of America*, I, edited by Perry Miller. Despite a surprising number of small biographical errors there are many happy insights and judgments. Mr. Lewis was also editor of *The Presence of Walt Whitman: Selected Papers from the English Institute* (New York, Columbia Univ. Press, 1962), which should be mentioned even at this late date. A number of the essays in it appropriately fall under the rubric of General Studies. James A. Wright, himself a poet, calls our attention to "The Delicacy of Walt Whitman." It is true that Whitman could be extremely delicate and that his delicacy has been useful to poets today just as his yawp has been, but Mr. Wright seems to make Whitman lead forward to genteel poetry. Samuel Hynes in "Whitman, Pound, and the Prose Tradition" throws light on Pound's uneasy relationship to Whitman and relates it to two major traditions in American poetry, that of a poetry of things and that of the magic of words. James E. Miller, Jr., in "Whitman and Thomas: The Yawp and the Gab," demonstrates an unexpected literary significance of Whitman to Thomas' poetry.

There have been a few studies of Whitman's relationships with his contemporaries. In "Charles Kent's 'Most Affectionate and Overflowing Tribute to Whitman's Great Gifts'" (*WWR*, XI, 3–19), William Leo Finkel reprints a London review of the 1868 Rossetti *Selections*, which pleased Whitman and Rossetti. Robert L. Peters, in "Edmund Gosse's Two Whitmans" (*WWR*, XI, 19–21), presents further evidence that in 1896 Gosse distorted his diary account of his 1885 visit to Whitman. Phyllis Grosskurth's *The Woeful Victorian: A Biography of John Addington Symonds* (New York, Holt, Rinehart and Winston), is informative about Symond's private life, but less informative about the Whitman-Symonds relationship than Harold W. Blodgett's *Walt Whitman in England*. Mrs. Grosskurth had access to private papers, but apparently did not find any Whitman letters. Florence B. Friedman, in "New Light on an Old Quarrel: Walt Whitman and William Douglas O'Connor" (*WWR*, XI, 27–52), confirms from papers newly available that the quarrel was over Sumner's policies, as Perry originally suggested. Apparently Whitman in those years was a hot-tempered and much more violent person than the picture handed down by his friends depicts, and it was he who initiated the break by shaking his finger in O'Connor's face and walking out of his house. The further "New Light" is that Mrs. O'Connor had been in love with Whitman since 1864 and that Whitman, who had known it at least since late 1870, had rejected her as deftly as he had Mrs. Gilchrist. Mrs. O'Connor's feelings were apparently made clear to her husband after Whitman had left the house, or at least in the course of the quarrel, for husband and wife separated until O'Connor's final illness.

The Nassau Review (Vol. I), devoted its entire spring issue to the record of a Whitman celebration held in May. Charles E. Feinberg wrote on Whitman's reputation ("Walt Whitman: Yesterday, Today and Tomorrow," pp. 1–18), George A. Brenner on "Whitman and You" (pp. 84–98), and J. L. Davenport on "Walt Whitman's Salute 'To You'" (pp. 81–83). John F. Kiley has a poem, "Whitman as Player" (p. 80), as does Art Sullivan—"Incident at Sunken Meadow" (pp. 99–100). The principal item is a dramatic narrative by Paul Shyre, "A Whitman Portrait" (pp. 19–79), which was acted at the celebration and has been announced for New York production in the 1966-1967 season.

iii. Studies of Individual Editions and Poems

The Presence of Walt Whitman (see above) also contains a very valuable group of papers on the 1860 edition and, in particular, on "Out of the Cradle Endlessly Rocking." Roy Harvey Pearce's "Whitman Justified: The Poet in 1860," which has appeared in substance as the introduction to his facsimile of the 1860 edition, makes sweeping claims for the superiority of the 1860 edition to all others and defines it as one of the great "archetypal autobiographies." One need not go all the way with Mr. Pearce to admire his analysis of the text of the edition. Three other contributors confine themselves to "Out of the Cradle": Stephen E. Whicher, "Whitman's Awakening to Death: Toward a Biographical Reading of 'Out of the Cradle Endlessly Rocking'"; Paul Fussell, Jr., "Whitman's Curious Warble: Reminiscence and Reconciliation"; Richard Chase, "'Out of the Cradle' as a Romance." Although the palm goes to Mr. Whicher's, all three of these essays are among the finest things we have had on the poem in many years. Christopher Collins, in "Whitman's Open Road and Where It Led" (*Nassau Review*, I, 101–110), points out that "Song of the Open Road" (1856) develops a "pattern of disen-

gagement, observation, and the ache for contact." Only as a result of
Whitman's emotional crisis of 1858 was his inner loneliness assuaged.
In "The Autoerotic Metaphor in Joyce, Sterne, Lawrence, Stevens
and Whitman" (*L&S*, XV, 92–106), Neil D. Isaacs finds in "Out of
the Cradle" the same motives of rocking, light, water, music, tumes-
cence, and detumescence that he finds in works by the other authors
named.

Arthur Golden, in "New Light on Leaves of Grass: Whitman's
Annotated Copy of the 1860 (Third) Edition" (*BNYPL*, LXIX, 283–
306), makes a real contribution to our knowledge of Whitman's
process of revision by rather thoroughly exploding the traditional
opinion that his revisions between 1860 and 1866 were motivated by
sexual prudence or a growing conventionality of literary taste. Mr.
Golden reports that the revisions in the famous "Blue Book," not all
of which were carried over to the 1867 edition, were dictated first
of all by a desire to reject any foreign influences on a nation then
struggling to maintain its unity. The hostility of France and England
toward the Union no doubt contributed to Whitman's nationalism.
As for the striking omissions from "Calamus," Mr. Golden points out
that regardless of the merits of some of the deleted poems, Whitman
was concealing nothing, but was probably motivated by a desire to
tighten up the group by eliminating repetitions. "Children of Adam"
underwent no major changes.

A number of individual poems have been discussed by critics.
In "Figures of Repetition in Whitman's 'Songs of Parting' " (*BNYPL*,
LXIX, 77–82), Vernon V. Chatman III finds that Whitman uses fif-
teen figures which do not involve meaning. It is to be regretted that
Mr. Chatman did not use a wider sampling of poems. Ronald Christ,
in "Walt Whitman: Image and Credo" (*AQ*, XVII, 92–103), finds that
"To a Locomotive in Winter" is a useful example of a number of
characteristics of Whitman's poetry and mind, including his attempt
to find a technological counterpart for his organic nature symbols."
William A. Friedman's "Whitman's 'The World Below the Brine' "
(*Expl*, XXIII, Item 39) analyzes the poem as an approximation of
the doctrine of the Great Chain of Being. James A. Kilby, in "Walt
Whitman's 'Trippers and Askers' " (*AN&Q*, IV, 37–39), goes to
rather tortuous extremes by interpreting the words ("Song of Myself," Sec. 4) as meaning "drivers employed by another and paid by
the trip" and "beggars" in preference to "skeptics or opponents" for

the one and "inquisitive people" for the other. Edward A. Martin, in "Whitman's 'A Boston Ballad (1854)'" (*WWR*, XI, 61–69), gives a thorough study of the historical occasion of the poem and the growth of the text and relates the tone to the American comic tradition. Francis E. Skipp has contributed two notes on "The Sleepers." The first, "Whitman's 'Lucifer': A Footnote to 'The Sleepers'" (*WWR*, XI, 52–53), comments on the fact that the original reading for "Lucifer" in an omitted passage, according to a manuscript in the University of Virginia library, was "Apollyon." In Revelation 9:4, 5, 11, Apollyon is the scorpion-locust of God's revenge on the wicked. One may speculate that Whitman assigned Apollyon's role to Lucifer because the latter was, for Whitman, a more sympathetic figure, even though he was not, traditionally, the scourge of God. In "Whitman and Shelley: A Possible Source for 'The Sleepers'" (*WWR*, XI, 69–74), Mr. Skipp finds suggestive parallels between the last twenty-two stanzas of "The Witch of Atlas" and Sections 1–2, 7–8 of Whitman's poem. If these are true sources, "The Sleepers" is something less than the spontaneous utterance it has always been taken for. Despite, however, the coupling of Whitman and Shelley by some of the former's admirers, there is little evidence that Whitman was interested in Shelley, and "The Witch of Atlas" is a most un-Whitmanesque poem.

University of Kansas

5. Mark Twain

John C. Gerber

In reading the Mark Twain scholarship for 1965 one gets the impression that many of the old veins are playing out. There are still the encomia for Huck, the fretting over the last chapters in *Huckleberry Finn*, the fascination with innocence and initiation, and other such perennial preoccupations. But the yield is steadily less. There is too much of what Northrop Frye disparagingly calls commentary, and too little analysis taking place within disciplined intellectual and aesthetic contexts. If a meaningful distinction can be made between criticism and scholarship, the scholars offer more of interest in 1965 than the critics. Some of the work reported here on the Clemens family and on *The Gilded Age*, for example, should have continuing value. Everything considered, though, the year was probably most notable for the publication of attractive and inexpensive editions. If this seems a rather testy evaluation of the Mark Twain scene, 1965, it is not meant to be. The fact that twenty inexpensive editions of major novels appeared in one year should be the most reassuring fact possible to Twain enthusiasts. Mark Twain is almost making a runaway of it as the most read major American author.

i. Texts and Editions

None of the new editions is the result of careful textual study, but almost all of them are attractively printed. As paperback Perennial Classics, Harper and Row reprinted *Life on the Mississippi*, *Tom Sawyer*, *The Prince and the Pauper*, *Huckleberry Finn*, *A Connecticut Yankee*, and Charles Neider's version of the *Autobiography*. Grosset and Dunlap added *The Prince and the Pauper*, *Tom Sawyer Abroad*, and *Tom Sawyer Detective* to their hardback Companion Library. Doubleday put out Junior Deluxe Editions of *Tom Sawyer* and *The Prince and the Pauper*. Whitman added *Tom Sawyer* and an abridged version of *Huckleberry Finn* to their Whitman Classics list.

Bantam, Blackie, and Watts all issued editions of *Huckleberry Finn*, Heritage *The Prince and the Pauper*, Dodd *The Prince and the Pauper and Other Stories*, Airmont *Life on the Mississippi*, and Dell *Tom Sawyer Abroad* and *Tom Sawyer Detective* in one volume. Norton reissued its annotated edition of *Huckleberry Finn*. Grosset and Dunlap, incidentally, names Samuel Clemens as author instead of Mark Twain, a decision not calculated to help its young readers.

Primarily for the adult market is Charles Neider's abridged version of *The Gilded Age*, which he calls *The Adventures of Colonel Sellers* (Garden City, N. Y., Doubleday). Fresh from having put together collections of Mark Twain's novels, essays, sketches and tales, and short stories, and from having rearranged the *Autobiography*, Neider now has found another way of making Mark Twain marketable. What he does is to stitch together with his own transitions those portions of *The Gilded Age* which he presumes to have been written by Twain. Doubleday advertises the result as being "in effect, a new work." For better or for worse, it *is* a new work.

In making his selections Neider has relied on what Mark Twain himself claimed as his in a letter to Mrs. Fairbanks, in another to Dr. John Brown, and in notations in a copy of the book he gave to his friend William Seaver. Neider says that he has "not been able to discover in the manuscript anything which challenges Clemens' ascription of authorship in the two letters and the Seaver copy." Clearly Neider has not studied the manuscript—or such parts of it as are extant—as closely as Bryant French and Hamlin Hill, mentioned later in this chapter. As French points out, mutual interpolations and rewritten passages, though minor in nature, were frequent, and caused a greater interweaving of the collaborators' work than would appear from the basic division reported by Twain. French adds that to a greater degree than would appear in this basic division, Twain's ideas and even philosophy were absorbed into much of what was written by Warner. In short, though what Neider has included can in a gross kind of way be called Mark Twain's, it is not pure Twain; nor has he cut out pure Warner.

Neider does nothing to restore the text to Twain's last intent. Indeed, the change from Beriah Sellers back to Eschol Sellers does just the opposite. What counts in restoring a text like this is to rid it of everything that does not carry the authority of the author's final wish. That Twain made the change to Beriah Sellers at the behest of a real Eschol Sellers is beside the point. Besides, since "Eschol" was Warner's idea, Neider should be happy to find a reason to excise it. What *can* be said for his book is that it, like his other volumes, makes something of Twain's easily available. Like the *Autobiography*, though, this new work is not real, one hundred proof Twain. It is Twain diluted by Neider.

A few letters have become available through publication. Several of these were written to A. B. Paine, and are now in the collection of Chester Davis at Perry, Missouri. They appear in the *Twainian* for July-August (pp. 1–4). Most of them are by Jervis Langdon, one of the three executors of the Clemens estate. Primarily they deal with the details of putting the estate in order. One notation indicates that the estate was worth $541,136.07. The September-October *Twainian* (pp. 1–3) carries letters from George A. Mahan of Hannibal to A. B. Paine about the gift of the Clemens house to the city of Hannibal and the selection of an artist by the Mark Twain Monument Commission. In "Once Again: Mark Twain and German" (*MTJ*, XII, iv, 16), John J. Weishert reprints a Mark Twain letter that originally appeared in the Louisville *Anzeiger* on May 1, 1919, although it was written twelve years before. In it Twain felicitates the *Anzeiger* in garbled English and German on its fiftieth anniversary.

The *Twainian*, incidentally, has begun the practice of reprinting newspaper reviews of Twain's lectures in full. Also, it has begun to reprint sections from *A Mark Twain Lexicon*, the reference work by Robert L. Ramsey and Frances Guthrie Emberson (Columbia, Univ. of Missouri, 1938) that is now completely available again in a Russell and Russell reprint, 1963.

ii. Biography

The most significant volume of biography to appear in 1965 is *Susy and Mark Twain* (New York, Harper and Row). Arranged and edited by Edith Colgate Salsbury, the book gives us a strikingly intimate view of the Clemens family from 1872 to 1896. It is set up as though it were a play with the names of the speakers in capital letters in the left-hand margin. Playing the role of narrator, Mrs. Salsbury provides the necessary transitions and explanations. She does this briefly and unobtrusively—and quite satisfactorily. The "speeches" of the others are statements made by them, principally in writing, culled from over eighty sources. As the title would suggest, the major characters are Susy and her father.

What emerges is the picture of a family whose devotion to one another was extraordinary. Although Mrs. Clemens was frequently called upon to make decisions, the tone and pace of the family were obviously set by Twain himself. To the others he communicated much of his capacity for affection, too much of his inner tension. Susy and Jean were nervous girls; Mrs. Clemens seldom had good health. It is worth noticing that Clara, who was the least close to her father and the least affected by him, was the healthiest and the most relaxed. Susy was the most affected. A sensitive and talented girl, she adored her father while disliking his public image as a humorist. Others have already put it better: she adored Sam Clemens, hated Mark Twain. She wrote about him, sponsored family activities that would please him, could not stay a single year at Bryn Mawr away from him. It is interesting to speculate how much of her moral priggishness was due to an attempt to please her father. Meningitis took her, but separated from her father and Clara, on whom she increasingly depended, she was run down when the disease struck. Twain may have had more prescience than we have believed when he berated himself for being the cause of her death.

Mrs. Salsbury's book makes it more evident than ever that his wife and daughters supplied psychic needs in Twain that were deep and compelling. In time, the family came to mean really too much to him. Separation brought pain, and death self-accusing agony. Although few of the excerpts that Mrs. Salsbury includes can be considered fresh discoveries, her book assembles them in a narrative form that has movement and ends up being quite moving. As a result, one can better understand Twain and, what is more, better understand what he is projecting into the young people in his fiction. The influence of Susy and her sisters on the character of Joan of Arc is obvious. Their influence on other works, though less obvious, must be equally certain.

The only complete biography to appear is by Monroe Stearns: *Mark Twain* (New York, Franklin Watts). Presumably written for young teenagers it packs into its 186 pages a surprising amount of factual material. The style is readable, and the narrative moves along at a lively clip. Yet in at least two important ways the work is disappointing. For one thing, Stearns has not kept up with the scholarship. He is still attributing the "Quintus Curtius Snodgrass Letters" to Twain, and he thinks the *Mysterious Stranger* as it stands is altogether Twain's work. Much too often, too, he presents his own partly baked psychoanalysis as fact: that Twain, for example, secretly wished that his brother Henry would die, that Twain had never been intimate with a woman before his marriage, that he felt subtly rejected by his wife. One suspects that Stearns is trying to jazz up the book for the teen-agers, or make it seem more profound to them. How profound the work *really* is can be gleaned from the Foreword where the author says that "Mark Twain is an important sociologist also because he was a humorist, not a satirist. . . . Had he been a satirist, he would have condemned his 'damned human race' for failing to be the gods they ought to be."

Ralph Gregory's *Mark Twain's First America* (Florida, Mo., Friends of Florida) provides a small compendium of facts about the early years of Florida. It indicates that John Marshall Clemens quickly became a busy and influential citizen, and that his move to Hannibal in 1839 was not necessarily because he lacked business acumen. "Two Comstock Journalists: Samuel L. Clemens and William L. Wright as Reporters and Authors" (*MHR*, LIX, 428–438) by Linda Boeser is a brief factual comparison of Twain, who was on the staff of the *Territorial Enterprise* for about two years and Dan De Quille, who was on it for thirty-one. Both men later capitalized on their Western experiences, Twain in *Roughing It* and De Quille in *The Big Bonanza*. Miss Boeser advances the interesting possibility that *Roughing It* sold the better of the two in part because Twain's bigger-than-life accounts coincided more closely with the image of the West in the dime novels of the time. Jon Swan's "Innocents at Home" (*AH*, XVI, Feb., 58–61, 97–101) provides a fascinating account of how Twain enthusiastically welcomed Gorki to New York in 1901 and subsequently dumped him when he discovered that Gorki was accompanied by a mistress. J. Harold Smith, in "Mark Twain's Basic Political Concepts: Man, Parties, Democracy" (*MHR*, LIX, 349–354) assembles some fairly well-known attitudes of Twain on political matters. The same issue of *MHR* reprints a slight piece from the Columbia *Statesman* for February 22, 1907, that describes Twain's white suit with its silk braid down the outside seams of the trousers and its white zig-zag embroidery around the edges of the coat. And Richard H. Powers in "To Mark Twain's Missionary Defenders" (*ForumH*, IV, 10–17) provides yet another summary of the Brooks-De Voto controversy. He comes out on the side of Brooks.

Not quite a matter of Twain biography but interesting anyway is an account by Dewey Ganzel that scrapes some of the tar and feathers off J. C. Hotten: "Samuel Clemens and John Camden Hotten" (*Library*, XX, 230–242). Ganzel finds Hotten not at all the unscrupulous pirate that Twain and, later, Paine, Merle Johnson, and others make him out to be. Author of over thirty-five books himself and actually a champion for international copyright, Hotten, Ganzel believes, was a discriminating reader and careful editor. Hotten once said that he had offered to pay Twain for "any work that he might do for him" but had never received a reply.

iii. Criticism

The year produced no major work of criticism, and only three or four short works that apply to Mark Twain's writings as a whole. Of these the most interesting is Sherwood Cummings' "*What Is Man?*: The Scientific Sources" (*Essays in Determinism in American Literature*, Kent, Ohio, Kent State Univ. Press, pp. 108–116). Cummings with good reason attacks those who contend that Twain's determinism emerged from his Calvinistic upbringing or from a guilt complex or from some other psychological phenomenon while blandly accepting Crane, Norris, Bierce, and Dreiser as conscious participants in a broad ideological and literary movement. Twain's determinism, Cummings contends, was just as much the result of *his* participation in the movements of his time. In "Mark Twain's Visual and Aural Descriptions" (*MTJ*, XII, iv, 1–9, 16), William C. Clark asserts that Twain is almost always more effective in handling sounds than sights. In the same issue of *MTJ* Donald Chaput suggests that although Mark Twain's literary debts to others were enormous, he could still argue with propriety for perpetual copyright, as he did in 1899 before the Copyright Committee of the British House of Lords. Chaput seems to think that Twain was unoriginal because many of his characters were based on real people. C. Merton Babcock in "Mark Twain and Mencken: A Literary Kinship" (*Menckeniana*, No. 14, pp. 4–5) reminds us that Mencken freely admitted his indebtedness to Twain.

Eugene J. McNamara completed a dissertation at Northwestern on "Mark Twain's Theory and Practice of Fiction," Benjamin Pfeiffer completed one at Nebraska on "Religious, Moral, and Social Ideas in the Works of Mark Twain," and Robert C. Regan completed one at California (Berkeley) on "The Unpromising Hero in the Writings of Mark Twain."

iv. Innocents Abroad

The popular notion that Twain from almost the outset of the *Quaker City* cruise relied heavily on Mrs. M. M. Fairbanks for literary advice is rather vigorously attacked by Dewey Ganzel in "Clemens, Mrs. Fairbanks, and *Innocents Abroad*" (*MP*, LXIII, 128–140). Ganzel concludes from the evidence that they were never close associates until Mark Twain discovered in Alexandria that nearly a third of the letters he had dispatched to the *Alta California* were lost. At that point he enlisted the help of Mrs. Fairbanks as a copyreader. Becoming more specific about the guidebooks Mark Twain used, Ganzel, in "Samuel Clemens, Guidebooks, and *Innocents Abroad*" (*Anglia*, LXXXIII, 78–88), singles out Josiah Leslie Porter's *A Handbook for Travellers in Syria and Palestine* (1858), *Galignani's New Paris Guide for 1867*, and William H. Neligan's *Rome: Its Churches, Its Charities, and Its Schools* (1858).

v. The Gilded Age

Undoubtedly we shall learn more about *The Gilded Age* and Twain's relation to it, but it seems unlikely that there will be need for another full-length study after Bryant Morey French's *Mark Twain and The Gilded Age* (Dallas, Southern Methodist Univ. Press). French is convinced that the themes of the book are precisely what Mark Twain and Warner say they are in the preface to the British edition: "all pervading speculativeness and the shameful corruption of the age." He believes that these themes are so compensating in their effect that they cut through the unresolved problems of design, structure, and refinement. The volume, then, he concludes, is not the hopeless hodgepodge it has been accused of being.

French takes up in turn the circumstances of composition, the sources of the people and happenings used in the book, the autobiographical elements, and the relation of the work to the historical *gestalt*. In addition, he provides a chapter on the play *Colonel Sellers* and some interesting appendixes. Despite the care that has obviously gone into *Mark Twain and The Gilded Age* it is not completely satisfying. Its arrangement, for example, forces the author into repetition, and the scholarly paraphernalia frequently becomes overpowering. Furthermore, one sometimes feels that French is too willing to overlook or to explain away manifest weaknesses. Nevertheless, one does come away from the work with a higher esteem for *The Gilded Age*. For once one perceives the extent of the book's basis in fact he begins to agree with French that much of what has been passed off as farce must now be viewed as comic satire. At the very least, French's volume equips us so handsomely with historical information that we can all reread *The Gilded Age* with greater insight.

In "Toward a Critical Text of *The Gilded Age*" (*PBSA*, LIX, 142–149), Hamlin Hill indicates the extraordinary complexity of establishing its text. Among other things the editor must take into account the fact that Twain and Warner both worked on the manuscript; that Twain then went to Europe and left Warner to revise the manuscript, galleys, and page proof of the American edition; and that Twain proofread the English edition. Apparently the American typesetters followed the manuscript scrupulously whereas the English typesetters frequently took it upon themselves to regularize the accidentals. Yet the English edition in the last nine chapters is probably closer to Twain's last intent than any portion of the American edition or any other portion of the English edition since it apparently was set from manuscript or galleys and not from the page proof carrying Warner's revisions. Even so, the American edition is the soundest for use as copy-text though there are four other sources of substantive variants. Anyone thinking of putting out an authoritative edition of a popular nineteenth-century American author should read Hill's careful analysis and ask himself if he is likely to live long enough.

Dated June 1, 1911, a letter reprinted in the *Twainian* (May-June, p. 1) from Joseph H. Twichell to A. B. Paine tells that so far as Twichell can recall Twain paid Warner nothing for relinquishing his right to share in the profits of *The Gilded Age* as a play: "There was some unpleasantness between them about it." A short critical piece by Joseph T. Gordon, "*The Gilded Age* and *Democracy*" (*ForumH*, IV, vi, 4–9), suggests parallels in these works of Twain and Adams, parallels in character, episode, and scope.

vi. Tom Sawyer

Vincent Stewart, in "Out of the Looking Glass: Illusion and Reality in *Tom Sawyer*" (*MEB*, XXII, 1–8), argues that *Tom Sawyer* dramatizes how Tom, failing to hold on to the world of his imagination, learns to accommodate himself to the world of reality. Donald A. Winkelman indicates briefly that Mark Twain uses folklore in Tom Sawyer to add local color and an air of realism, "Goodman Brown, Tom Sawyer, and Oral Tradition" (*KFQ*, X, 43–48). He reinforces the point in "Three American Authors as Semi-Folk Artists" (*JAF*, LXXVIII, 130–135). For those who enjoy a poker-faced spoof, one of the best is John Halverson's "Patristic Exegesis: A Medieval *Tom Sawyer*" (*CE*, XXVII, 50–55). Strongly indebted to the *Book of the Duchess*, suggests Halverson solemnly, *Tom Sawyer* is a condemnation of the folly and vice to which concupiscence leads.

vii. Huckleberry Finn

As always, *Huckleberry Finn* receives the bulk of the critical attention. And again the range in interpretation is great. On the one hand Huck is the voice of the Oversoul; on the other he is a nasty little materialist. The range in penetration is equally great.

Tony Tanner's subject leads him into idolatry, perhaps in spite of himself. His book, *The Reign of Wonder* (Cambridge, Cambridge Univ. Press), concerns itself with the use of the child's point of view in American fiction, the stance of wonder as he calls it. In arguing that this has been a way of confronting existence preferred by American writers, he devotes about a fourth of his book to Mark Twain and most of that fourth to *Huckleberry Finn*. Twain, Tanner suggests, found his *métier* in the talk of outlaws, who, as he continued to write, became younger and younger until in *Huckleberry Finn* he used a young boy to tell the entire story. With the boy he could abandon not only the high rhetoric of the establishment but could strike out at its falsity and its institutions. But though the point of view of boyish wonder was immensely rewarding to Twain in terms of language and strategy, Tanner believes it provided him with few hints about form. After *Huckleberry Finn* he was as uncertain about his style and strategy as he had been before. There is little that is fundamentally new in Tanner's account; his debt to Henry Nash Smith is especially obvious. But he writes well, and there are numerous small insights that are provocative.

Henry Nash Smith, himself, is represented by a chapter on *Huckleberry Finn* in *The American Novel* (pp. 61–72). Written for oral presentation over the Voice of America, the chapter discusses what Smith considers Huck's major characteristics to be, and suggests that they are the characteristics of Americans generally. The result is a shrewd assessment of Huck, but as a picture of the American type, it is, at the moment at least, too flattering to be convincing.

Four articles interpret parts of the novel. "Twain's *The Adventures of Huckleberry Finn,* Chapter I" (*Expl,* XXIII, Item 62), by Daniel R. Barnes, praises the special aptness in the Widow Douglas' attempt to teach Huck something about "Moses and the Bulrushers." Like Pharaoh's daughter, the widow has adopted a foundling; like Moses, Huck is more or less to deliver a member of an oppressed race from bondage. That Huck should "take no stock" in the story adds an ironical dimension. "Huck's First Moral Crisis" (*MissQ,* VIII, 69–73), by Sidney J. Krause, argues that Huck's first moral crisis occurs in Chapter XVI where Huck saves Jim from capture by hinting there is smallpox on the raft. Ray B. Browne, "Huck's Final Triumph" (*BSTCF,* VI, 3–12), once again brings up the ending. Browne feels it is indispensable for the working out of the real purpose of the book, Huck's search for personal liberation. Without the ending, we would not realize how Huck has grown away from Pap and Jim and Tom, and now can be "true to himself because there is no reason to be false to himself in order to be true to society." "'No Money for to Buy the Outfit': *Huckleberry Finn* Again" (*MFS,* X, 341–348), by William R. Manierre, takes out after Huck in a fashion designed to upset most of those who like to recall Huck's major crisis as a triumph of a sound heart over a deformed conscience. Manierre does not think it much of a triumph. To be sure, Huck has to struggle before he can decide to go to hell rather than surrender Jim, but there is little in the book to indicate that this moral triumph should be taken very seriously. Almost invariably thereafter, Huck accepts the values of Tom and the slaveholding and materialistic Establishment.

Five articles call attention to parallels between *Huckleberry Finn* and other literary works. In "Twain and Scott: Experience Versus Adventures" (*MP,* LXII, 227–236), Sidney J. Krause finds significant differences between Mark Twain and Scott in the use of adventures. Whereas Scott simply fabricates adventure for its own sake, Krause believes that Twain inserts romantic adventure into the stream of experience in order to highlight the difference between the "trash" of romance and the "facts" of experience. J. M. Ridland, "Huck, Pip, and Plot" (*NCF*, XX, 286–290), finds that Huck's great struggle and ultimate decision to help Jim are remarkably like Pip's actions in *Great Expectations* when he helps and then is ashamed of helping the escaped convict Magwitch. Additionally the smashup of the raft suggests the collision on the Thames of the steamer and the rowboat containing Pip. Ridland believes that Twain, unlike Dickens, is unable to invest such incidents with plot significance.

Two articles have the same title: "Huck and Holden." The one by George de Schweinitz (*EIT*, I, 34–40) lists structural, thematic, and tonal resemblances between *Huckleberry Finn* and *Catcher in the Rye*. The other, by Deane M. Warner (*CEA*, XXVII, March 4a–4b), throws in Henry Fleming for good measure, and finds all three protagonists are innocents seeking initiation into the adult world. Huck finds hypocrisy, Fleming meaninglessness, and Holden these plus filth. With no consideration given to irony, Warner's treatment of Fleming is especially unsatisfactory. William Rossky, in "*The Reivers* and *Huckleberry Finn*: Faulkner and Twain" (*HLQ*, XXVIII, 373–387), discovers resemblances between Huck and Lucius, Jim and Boon and Ned. A more fundamental parallel lies in the development of the idea that initiation into adulthood brings a painful awareness of human deception and cruelty. Happily, the rebellion of the outcast innocent in these and other American novels leads to a higher wisdom. It is a provocative notion, and gives rise to speculation as to just how much wiser Huck really is by the end of the novel—as against how much wiser the reader is.

For what it is worth, William R. Linneman, in "*Punch* and *Huckleberry Finn*" (*ELN*, II, 293–294), reports that Roundabout, a columnist in *Punch* (January 4, 1896), finds the novel more Homeric than any other book in English.

viii. A Connecticut Yankee

In "The Uses of History in Mark Twain's *A Connecticut Yankee*" (*PMLA*, LXXX, 102–110), James D. Williams discusses the historical works that Mark Twain borrowed from in writing *Yankee*. Their authors include W. E. H. Lecky, Saint Simon, Taine, and Carlyle, of course, and also J. Hammond Trumbull, Henri Forneron, Andrew Carnegie, Edward Jarvis, and Charles Ball. Twain was no dedicated scholar, but his reading was surprisingly catholic. As Williams points out, he used what he read partly to be funny but more importantly to support his basic historical theory that the past by comparison with the present is odious. Whatever he may have claimed, therefore, Twain never really made a serious attempt at being factually accurate. Indeed, the longer he worked on the volume the more he sought out the cruel and the unjust in history to support his thesis and not to create an historically accurate picture. Also on the subject of source material, John DeWitt McKee's "Three Uses of the Arming Scene" (*MTJ*, XII, iv, 18–19, 21) observes that though Twain drew heavily from Malory's *Le Morte D'Arthur*, there is no arming scene in Malory so complete as the one in *Yankee*. McKee finds possible sources in *Sir Gawain and the Green Knight* and in Chaucer's *Sir Topas*.

ix. Short Selections

Details concerning the various editions of *1601* are given in Martha Anne Turner's "Mark Twain's '1601' through Fifty Editions" (*MTJ*, XII, iv, 10–15, 21). Miss Turner thinks the best of these is the one that was printed in Chicago for Franklin J. Meine in 1939 and reprinted in 1961. Miss Turner is willing to start the Brooks-De Voto scrap all over again by maintaining that *1601* discloses "the man himself beneath the external trappings of convention." Sidney J. Krause, in "Cooper's Literary Offences: Mark Twain in Wonderland" (*NEQ*, XXXVIII, 291–311), argues that as the champion of realism Twain nevertheless creates his own wonderland in attacking Cooper's romanticism. What Twain does is to turn Cooper's mildly ridiculous situations into sheer madness, combining understatement with exaggeration, sweetness with abuse. Indeed, Mark Twain's wonderland becomes so enchanting that few scholars have bothered to check its literal accuracy. A bit hard to follow, Krause's essay is nevertheless useful in reminding us that Mark Twain on the warpath could scalp a fact without compunction.

University of Iowa

6. Henry James

B. R. McElderry, Jr.

i. Bibliography, Texts, Manuscripts

Leon Edel published *The Henry James Reader* (New York, Scribner's), including ten short novels and tales, with brief introduction. Napier Wilt and John Lucas edited *Americans and Europe* (Boston, Houghton Mifflin), eight stories on the international theme. Leon Edel (*TLS*, June 17, p. 523) denied the rumor that a new cache of James letters has turned up; and he printed the correct text of a letter to Edmund Gosse, miscopied in Mrs. Phyllis Grosskurth's recent book on John Addington Symonds. In a later issue of *TLS* (August 19) Mrs. Grosskurth accepted the correction, and Lyall H. Powers commented on the presence of other errors in typescript copies of Gosse correspondence in the Brotherton Collection at Leeds. A previously unpublished letter from James to Stopford Brooke, edited by Fred L. Standley, appeared in the *Victorian Newsletter* (No. 27, Spring, p. 29).

Brian Birch, "Henry James: Some Bibliographical and Textual Matters" (*Library*, XX, 108–123), contends that attention to the famous reversed chapters in the first American edition of *The Ambassadors* has obscured the superiority at various points of that edition to the first English edition. Birch also gives some attention to revisions of *The Wings of the Dove* and *The Golden Bowl*. His evidence leads him to conclude reluctantly that the Edel-Laurence *Bibliography* is misleading and inadequate in its description of the text of both the New York Edition and the London edition of 1921–1923.

Hershel Parker, "An Error in the Text of *The American*" (*AL*, XXXVII, 316–318), draws attention to the end of Chapter XI in the first edition, in which three short speeches are mistakenly run together. Though the New York edition corrects the error, the early text is frequently reproduced in popular editions of the novel.

ii. Biography

The writer of this chapter published in the Twayne series a critical
biography of James, covering all the fiction and plays, with some
notice of the nonfictional work, and an emphasis of James's thoroughly professional career as writer. The book gives for the first time a
convenient and complete list of the 135 fictional pieces, with dates
of their original appearance. *NCF* (XX, 304–305) commented favorably on this volume; *MFS* (XI, 198–199) less favorably.[1]

Millicent Bell, *Henry James and Edith Wharton* (New York,
Braziller), draws upon unpublished letters of James, Edith Wharton,
and their friends to give for the first time a full account of their
association. Though Mrs. Wharton met James as early as 1887 or
1888, their close friendship was from 1903 until James's death in
1916, a period when the Whartons lived chiefly in Europe. The difficulties of their marriage, which led to Mrs. Wharton's divorce in
1913, were well known to James, and are a major reason why letters
of this period have remained unpublished. Though James was deeply
sympathetic, there is no suggestion of a love affair between him and
Mrs. Wharton. She was, however, in love with Walter Berry, their
mutual friend. This relationship, and friendships with Paul Bourget,
Howard Sturgis, and many others are clarified and appreciatively
evoked. On the literary side, to which Mrs. Bell devotes the second
part of her book, James's undoubted influence on Mrs. Wharton is
much more complex than is usually thought. Mrs. Wharton did not
enjoy the later fiction of James, the very work he was doing when
their friendship began. Though they agreed on general principles,
Mrs. Wharton's later fiction shows a conscious effort to depart from
James's practice.

Though more critical than biographical, two articles explore
further James's relation to Edith Wharton. Abigail Ann Hamblen
emphasizes "The Jamesian Note in Edith Wharton's *The Children*"
(*UR*, XXXI, 209–211); and Vittoria Sanna, in "I rommanzi di Edith
Wharton e la narrativa jamesiana" (*SA*, X, 1964, 229–291), reviews
her work as an extension of James, sometimes achieving a greater
vitality, as in *The Age of Innocence* as compared with *The Golden
Bowl*.

1. Oscar Cargill in *AL*, XXXVII, 516, writes that the book is "admirable for
coverage in brief space of the man and his work"—Ed.

George Monteiro's *Henry James and John Hay: The Record of a Friendship* (Providence, Brown Univ. Press) brings together and supplements material previously published in a series of short articles. Though useful, the volume does not substantially change the impression that Hay's friendship was agreeable but incidental to James.

iii. Criticism: General

Elmer Borklund's "Recent Approaches to James" (*JGE*, XVI, 327–340) is a cogent article-review of several recent works on James. In reading Edel's biography, Borklund finds it "embarrassing to learn so much about a man who cared so much for freedom and privacy." Borklund detects a logical dilemma in Wayne C. Booth's reservations about James; easily convicts Maxwell Geismar of serious misinterpretation of the facts in James's stories; points up the value of Cargill's study of the novels; and emphasizes the obfuscatory style of Laurence Holland's recent book. James, according to Borklund, eludes both his friends and his foes. He should be studied in the light of Wallace Stevens, with due attention to pleasure, abstraction, and change.

Though not critical in the strict sense, Robert L. Gale's *Plots and Characters in the Fiction of Henry James* (Hamden, Conn., Archon Books) provides a valuable help to future interpreters of James. It includes objective plot summaries, alphabetically arranged by title, and a dictionary of the more than fifteen hundred named characters in the stories. Oscar Cargill provides an appreciative foreword, with amusing illustrations of the difficulties of keeping in mind all the details of James's vast house of fiction.

Naomi Lebowitz, in *The Imagination of Loving: Henry James's Legacy to the Novel* (Detroit, Wayne State Univ. Press), emphasizes the depth of character relationship in Jamesian fiction and James's skill in portraying it. It is the absence of such relationships in French fiction, she thinks, that led him to distrust the naturalistic movement. Turning to *The Sacred Fount*, Miss Lebowitz suggests that the narrator is "an elated novelist thoroughly enjoying the game of sharing composition with his more conscious characters." In her chapter on *The Golden Bowl*, which appeared as "Magic and Metamorphosis in *The Golden Bowl*" (*SR*, LXXIII, 58–73), Miss Lebowitz supports Dorothea Krook in ranking this novel as James's greatest achievement. A final chapter relates James to later novelists, especially to

Saul Bellow. The book has many fresh insights and unhackneyed quotations; it suffers from over-allusiveness and from frequent disregard of chronological sequence in discussing James's fiction. Similar in emphasis, but more succinct, is Irene Samuel's "Henry James on the Imagination and the Will to Power" (*BNYPL*, LXIX, 117–130). Examining *The Princess Casamassima*, *The Tragic Muse*, *The Spoils of Poynton*, *The Ambassadors*, and *The Wings of the Dove*, Miss Samuel shows interesting variations in James's representation of imaginative characters. Though the unimaginative, wilful characters often appear to succeed, "their obtuseness is their triumph and their doom."

Michael Millgate's *American Social Fiction: James to Cozzens* (Edinburgh, Oliver and Boyd; New York, Barnes and Noble) points out that James never "solved the contradiction between his need to write about the business man and his inability to do so." The uncompleted novel *The Ivory Tower*, Millgate thinks, shows no advance from the treatment of Christopher Newman in *The American* and Adam Verver in *The Golden Bowl*.

The theme of American innocence in James is treated by three writers. Tony Tanner, *The Reign of Wonder: Naivety and Reality in American Literature* (Cambridge, Cambridge Univ. Press), traces through the Transcendentalists and later American writers the influence of the doctrine that wonder is a better method of achieving truth than analysis. Nearly the last third of the book is devoted to James: "He took the untutored eye . . . and subjected it to a dynamic, unprogrammed education." This idea is developed principally through examination of *The Sacred Fount*, *What Maisie Knew*, and *The Awkward Age*. Part of the discussion of *The Sacred Fount* appeared in 1963 (*E&S*, XVI, 37–55). Cleanth Brooks, "The American 'Innocence': in James, Fitzgerald, and Faulkner" (*Shenandoah*, XVI, i, 1964, 21–37), compares Christopher Newman with Fitzgerald's Gatsby and Faulkner's Sutpen; despite obvious differences, Brooks thinks that all three characters are in some degree virginal and naïve. Kermit Vanderbilt, in "James, Fitzgerald, and the American Self-Image" (*MR*, VI, 289–304), sees some touches of evil in Newman, and thinks that James's revisions deepened that emphasis. Fitzgerald, Vanderbilt believes, had not yet read *The American* when he wrote *The Great Gatsby*.

John A. Clair, in *The Ironic Dimension in the Fiction of Henry*

James (Pittsburgh, Pa., Duquesne Univ. Press) makes radically new applications of James's announced principle of "operative irony" (*The Art of the Novel*, p. 222). In the early story "The Four Meetings" and the late story "The Jolly Corner" Clair finds Caroline Spencer and Alice Staverton to be liars duping the men involved. From these stories, Clair proceeds to "The Turn of the Screw," *The Spoils of Poynton*, and *The Golden Bowl*, in which close reading raises doubts about characters often regarded as "good" or well-intentioned. Mr. Clair may be too eager to find irony, but he will force objectors to read James with very sharp attention.

In *Trials of the Word* (New Haven, Yale Univ. Press), R. W. B. Lewis reprints two previously published essays and adds a third. "Hawthorne and James: The Matter of the Heart," which earlier appeared in *The Hawthorne Centenary Essays* (See *ALS, 1964*, pp. 18–19), sees James in *The Bostonians* casting "a Hawthornian eye on a non-Hawthornian world." "*The Wings of the Dove*," previously published in *MFS*, 1957, emphasizes that the novel goes below the surface of manners to psyches. The new essay, "The Sense of Fair Play," traces the moral basis of drama in *The Spoils of Poynton*.

In "The Question of Freedom in Henry James's Fiction" (*CE*, XXVI, 372–376, 381), Quentin G. Kraft concedes that freedom in James often seems passive and is usually limited; nevertheless, he concludes, the freedom is real. Jonah Raskin, in "Henry James and the French Revolution" (*AQ*, XVII, 724–733), shows that James was more concerned with social problems than is usually thought. His allusions to the French Revolution are frequent throughout his career. Though he was essentially conservative by temperament, James saw some parallel between Victorian society and the *ancien régime*, and had some revolutionary sympathy, as is illustrated in *The Princess Casamassima*. That such sympathy was not excessive is indirectly shown by Linda W. Wagner in "The Dominance of Heredity in the Characterizations of Henry James" (*SDR*, II, 69–77).

Nathalia Wright's *American Novelists in Italy, the Discoverers: Allston to James* (Philadelphia, Univ. of Pa. Press) traces James's long and deep interest in Italy in its historical context. James sympathized with the new Italy as well as the old, and despite all the complexities of Italian life, he saw, especially in Italy's architecture, a sense of proportion that was symbolic of moral values. Miss Wright suggests that as James wrote *The American Scene* Italy was an im-

portant background for his judgments. In his fiction it is striking how
frequently Italy is the scene of self-realization. The associated theme
of James's interest in art, and its influence on his impressionistic
description, is treated by Giorgio Melchiori in "Il 'Déjeuner sur
l'herbe' di Henry James" (SA, X, 1964, 201–228).

James's fictional technique receives attention in four articles and
two important republications. Walter O'Grady, "On Plot in Modern
Fiction: Hardy, James, and Conrad" (MFS, XI, 107–115), rejects E.
M. Forster's well-known definition of plot by pointing out that the
cause of external events must have an internal effect on character.
In this respect O'Grady finds James's fiction well balanced: the flow
of his fiction is constantly inward. J. A. Ward, in "James's Idea of
Structure" (PMLA, LXXX, 419–426), finds James developing from a
neoclassicist appreciation of form to an organicist view in which opposites are reconciled. His ultimate concept of form is that it exists
to reveal an unknown or unknowable factor in character. In another
article, "Picture and Action: The Problem of Narration in James's
Fiction" (RUS, LI, 109–123), Ward defines James's problem as the
subordination of action to picture. Transience and epiphanies were
of little interest to him. He sought rather a developing awareness of
character; hence his frequent use of such inconsequential outer
events as meetings, where internal action could lead to a development
of ideas. In "Locksley Hall Revisited: Tennyson and Henry James"
(REL, VI, iv, 9–25), Giorgio Melchiori relates several half-concealed
echoes of Tennyson to the later method of literary allusion in Pound
and Eliot. This article also appears, in Italian, in Arte e Storia: Studi
in onore di Leonello Vincenti (Torino, Giappichelli). Cornelia
Pulsifer Kelley's The Early Development of Henry James (Urbana,
Univ. of Illinois Press, 1930; reissued with an introduction by Lyon
Richardson) stands out as a solid and still valuable achievement.
The work is very slightly revised, and a selective bibliography of
James studies from 1930 to 1965 has been added. Pelham Edgar's
Henry James, Man and Author, first published in 1927, has also been
reissued (New York, Russell and Russell, 1964).

Three discursive works on James's period allude only incidentally to James, but they offer useful background for the interpretation
of his works: Ray Ginger, An Age of Excess: The United States from
1877 to 1914 (New York, Macmillan); Helen Howe, The Gentle
Americans, 1864–1960: Biography of a Breed (New York, Harper

and Row); and Louise Hall Tharp, *Mrs. Jack* (Boston, Little, Brown). The last of these, a biography of Mrs. Isabella Stewart Gardner, includes a few letters from James.

Thirteen dissertations treat general themes in James. Frances Bownell Burstein, "The Picture of New England Puritanism in the Fiction of Henry James" (*DA*, XXV, 1964, 2977–2978), finds that James's fictional treatment of Puritanism is "historically accurate and perceptive"; James himself, she thinks, was religious in the sense of denying materialism and affirming spiritual reality. Jan Kadetsky Solomon, "The Puritan, the Gentleman, and the Artist: A Study of the Conflict Between Ethics and Aesthetics in the Novels of Henry James" (*DA*, XXV, 7278–7279), thinks that James gave increasing weight to aesthetic considerations in the later novels. She contrasts "the stern and selfless morality of Isabel Archer" with the more subtle Maggie Verver in *The Golden Bowl*, who is an ethical character able to operate in the aesthetic world—a view of Maggie Verver that has been challenged by Joseph J. Firebaugh (*EIC*, 1954, pp. 400 ff.). Maude Cardwell Ross, "Moral Values of the American Woman as Presented in Three Major American Authors" (*DA*, XXV, 5262–5263), considers Maggie Verver in relation to Hester Prynne and Eula Varner but reaches no unexpected conclusions. Ruth Taylor Todasco, "The Humanism of Henry James: A Study of the Relation Between Theme and Imagery in the Later Novels" (*DA*, XXV, 1964, 3559), finds that the "free spirits" of James's fiction illustrate William James's concept of "the full life." Aesthetic and moral considerations in James are also touched upon in James Seymour Westbrook, Jr.'s "Sensibility and Society: A Study of Themes" (*DA*, XXV, 1964, 3560). Edward Duncan Aswell, "The Art of Aggression: The Short Fiction of Henry James, 1888–1898" (*DA*, XXV, 4141), reaches the doubtful conclusion that "the act of imagination appropriately becomes a celebration of the claim of the personal will to absolute sovereignty, its right to distort and imprison the substance of life around it, and finally to renounce itself." Martha Banta, "The Two Worlds of Henry James: A Study in the Fiction of the Supernatural" (*DA*, XXVI, 1035–1036), is the background for her previously reported study, "Henry James and 'The Others'" (*NEQ*, XXXVII, 1964, 171–184).

Arnold H. Chadderdon, "Comic Method in Henry James's Fiction" (*DA*, XXVI, 2205), studies James's skill in assimilating alien elements and creating a free play of mind that frequently suggests Molière. Charles K. Fish, "Henry James and the Craft of Fiction: The Years of Exploration, 1864–1871" (*DA*, XXV, 1964, 3568), analyzes sixteen early stories and the novel *Watch and Ward*. James showed from the beginning an eagerness to experiment with point of view and with the contrasting materials of American and European life. Two short notes by Fish are mentioned below in the section on James's short stories. Gerald Bryan Hoag, "Henry James and Formalist Criticism of the Novel in English in the Twentieth Century" (*DA*, XXVI, 2753), believes that James's concept of organic form derives from Coleridge, and has been a guiding force on critics from Joseph Warren Beach to Wayne C. Booth and Mark Schorer. Sidney Howard White, "Henry James's *The American Scene*" (*DA*, XXVI, 1030–1031), points out the essential validity of James's views of American society in the early 1900's and relates James's artistic problem in formulating his impressions to the discussion of such matters in the Prefaces, written almost concurrently. Alan Holder, "Three Voyagers in Search of Europe: A Study of Henry James, Ezra Pound, and T. S. Eliot" (*DA*, XXVI, 1646–1647), finds these three American writers a natural triad; all saw the present as inferior to the past. James in particular was unhappy with American literature, society's lack of form, the American preoccupation with business, and the general neglect of discipline. Holder's article, "T. S. Eliot on Henry James," previously reported (*PMLA*, LXXIX, 1904, 490–497), is closely related to his dissertation. Rainer Ortwin Schulte, "Henry James and Marcel Proust: A Study in Sensibility" (*DA*, XXVI, 3352), finds common elements in these writers: a growing sense of disillusion and a style notable for the rhythmical use of parentheses, repetition, and concrete metaphors.

iv. Criticism: Individual Novels

Four writers restudy *The Portrait of a Lady*. Joseph H. Friend, "The Structure of *The Portrait of a Lady*" (*NCF*, XX, 85–95), considers it as a quest novel. He points out James's frequent use of irony as one means of avoiding the sentimental clichés associated with the pattern. Tony Tanner, "The Fearful Self: Henry James's *The Portrait of a Lady*" (*CritQ*, VII, 205–219), concludes that Isabel is defined by her fears. She, like Osmond, is an egotist, but as a result of her mistakes she attains a truer vision of herself. John Rodenbeck, "The Bolted Door in James's *Portrait of a Lady*" (*MFS*, X, 330–340), shows the peculiar force of a recurrent image in the novel. Richard Poirier's "Henry James, *The Portrait of a Lady*," in *The American Novel* (pp. 47–60), critically examines Isabel's romantic concept of freedom. An element of her weakness is her failure to see that Osmond's transcendental aversion to society is actually a corrupt self-love.

James B. Colvert, in "Views of Southern Character in Some Northern Novels" (*MissQ*, XVIII, 59–68), suggests that Basil Ransom in *The Bostonians* is modeled on James's boyhood acquaintance Eugene Norcom, mentioned in *A Small Boy and Others*. The sexuality of Ransom is "an intuitive anticipation of the image of the Southerner in contemporary literature" as in the novels of Wolfe and Faulkner.

In "Self and Secularization in *The Princess Casamassima*" (*MFS*, XI, 116–128), D. G. Haliburton explores the problem of society and self in Hyacinth, who has a positive commitment to revolution, but takes his own life rather than obey the command to commit a murder which has no meaning for him. Emily K. Izak, "The Composition of *The Spoils of Poynton*" (*TSLL*, VI, 460–471), shows that some inconsistencies in the novel result from James's change of plan after he published the opening chapters: to the original mother-son conflict, James added the theme of the son's love for Fleda Vetch. N. Krishna Rao, "The Idea of Refinement in Henry James's *The Awkward Age*" (*LCrit*, VI, 56–60), sees the pose of refinement as a cloak for corruption; in this and in the helplessness of Nanda, the novel anticipates *The Wings of the Dove*. Not until *The Golden Bowl*, however, does James "transform moral turpitude to moral responsibility."

In "What Maisie Knows: A Study of Childhood and Adolescence" (*AL*, XXXVI, 485–513), John C. McCloskey critically reviews previous discussion of the novel and develops his own interpretation. He rejects, for example, Cargill's suggestion that Maisie intuitively sees herself as Mrs. Beale's rival for the affection of Sir Claude. Maisie, in McCloskey's view, is at the end of the story her father's daughter, with little emotion and little moral sense. She has grown hard and selfish, with "an ego that will satisfy itself at the cost of what it regards as everything."

Jean Frantz Blackall's *Jamesian Ambiguity and* The Sacred Fount (Ithaca, Cornell Univ. Press) extends the argument of her previously published article (*PMLA*, LXXVIII, 1963, 384–393). She sees James's novel as a combination of high comedy and the sinister. An interesting addition to the material for interpreting this difficult novel is her chapter on Ludwig II of Bavaria, the admirer of Wagner whose psychological peculiarities were notorious when *The Sacred Fount* was written. Giorgio Melchiori, in "Cups of Gold for the Sacred Fount: Aspects of James's Symbolism" (*CritQ*, VII, 301–316), surveys possible influences on the increasing symbolism of his later stories: the French symbolists, d'Annunzio, the Grail story, the publication in 1893 of an important edition of Blake, containing "The Mental Traveller." This poem may lie back of a notebook entry of February 16, 1894, and thus link *The Sacred Fount* to Blake. Walter Isle, in "The Romantic and the Real: Henry James's *The Sacred Fount*" (*RUS*, LI, 29–47), sees the narrator as "a romantic confronting the materials of reality." It is the confusions of the narrator that mask the success of the author in his mastery of a form that points to the later work of Proust, Joyce, and Virginia Woolf.

Robert N. Hudspeth, "The Definition of Innocence: James's *The Ambassadors*" (*TSLL*, VI, 354–360), develops ideas related to those in the two articles mentioned above on James and Fitzgerald. Strether, initially an innocent, attains an understanding of how evil can occur within his own culture. Mrs. Pocock remains brutally obstinate, and refuses to see. U. C. Knoepflmacher, " 'O Rare for Strether'; *Antony and Cleopatra* and *The Ambassadors*" (*NCF*, XIX, 333–344), sees in the Shakespearean allusion in Book III a key to Strether: James portrays him as deceived by his romantic imagination. Knoepflmacher's extension of the irony in this scene to an interpretation of the whole novel, though highly ingenious, will seem to most readers unwarranted. J. Davis, in "Intention and Achievement in Narrative Technique: Henry James's *The Ambassadors*" (*KN*, XII, 245–253), points out that James enters the story by comments on characters, by explaining motives, and by moderating dramatic scenes, much as George Eliot and Meredith had done. The standard judgments of Lubbock and Beach that James gains all his effects by emphasizing the point of view of Strether should be modified. Henry L. Terrie, Jr., in "The Image of Chester in *The Ambassadors*" (*ES*, XLVI, 46–50), shows a number of interesting parallels of scene in the novel and James's essay on Chester written for the *Nation* in 1872 (reprinted in *Transatlantic Sketches*, 1875). Elliot L. Gilbert, in "Kipling and James: A Note on Travel" (*Kipling Journal*, XXXI, No. 152, 7–9) suggests that Kipling's "An Error in the Fourth Dimension" (*The Day's Work*, 1898) is "a miniature version of the real choice involved in *The Ambassadors*," that is, Strether's choice to return to America.

Quentin G. Kraft, in "Life Against Death in Venice" (*Criticism*, VII, 217–223), notes that though the actual death of Milly is not narrated in *The Wings of the Dove*, it functions much as May Bartram's does in "The Beast in the Jungle." Like Marcher in the story, Milton Densher gains a sharper vision: he now sees Milly as the "princess of life" in the face of death.

v. Criticism: Short Stories

Once more "The Turn of the Screw" received major attention. The chief publication was *An Anatomy of The Turn of the Screw* (Austin, Univ. of Texas Press), by Thomas M. Cranfill and Robert L. Clark, Jr. Cranfill surveys the controversy over interpretation by dividing commentators into apparitionists and non-apparitionists, and on this basis he analyzes crucial points in the story in twenty short chapters. He concludes that the children are the victims of the governess' harassment, stimulated by her hallucinations. This interpretation, he contends, is not only justified by the clues in the story, but it constitutes a richer reading experience than the apparitionist interpretation. A chapter of this work, "James's Revisions of 'The Turn of the Screw,'" was separately published (*NCF*, XIX, 394–398). The appended bibliography of nearly three hundred references, largely the work of Mr. Clark, is ingeniously keyed with symbols indicating points emphasized by each critic.

Stanley Trachtenberg, "The Return of the Screw" (*MFS*, XI, 180–182), picking up Louis D. Rubin, Jr.'s suggestion that Miles is to be identified with Douglas (*MFS*, IX, 314–328) argues that Miles was corrupt, and that as Douglas he has hidden the truth for many years. The article ignores the difficulties in accepting such a theory. Robert M. Slabey, "The Turn of the Screw: Grammar and Optics" (*CLAJ*, IX, 68–72), cites three ambiguities in the use of pronouns, and draws attention to the unusually acute vision attributed to the governess; he concludes that the ghosts are "true as fiction," but does not indicate whether he intends this phrase to apply to the governess's narrative or to James's story as a whole. Hildegard Domaniecki, "Complementary Terms in The Turn of the Screw: The Straight Turning" (*JA*, X, 206–214), hardly succeeds in making a satisfactory case for regarding the terms "straight" and "turn" as consistently symbolic in the story. Marcel Schneider, "Henry James et Benjamin Britten" (*NRF*, XIII, 713–716), praises the opera based on James's story for its restraint. A. W. Thomson, in "The Turn of the Screw: Some Points on the Hallucination Theory" (*REL*, VI, iv, 26–36), replies to Dorothea Krook (*The Ordeal of Consciousness in Henry James*, 1962) that Edmund Wilson's theory that the governess suffers from hallucinations (which Miss Krook rejects) does not rule out her own emphasis of the innocence and corruption of the children. Some of the ambiguities in the story, Thomson thinks, may result from a change of intention as James wrote the story.

Six other stories, ranging from "The Story of a Masterpiece" (1868) to "The Bench of Desolation" (1909) received attention. Charles Fish, whose dissertation is noted above, shows in "Indirection, Irony, and the Two Endings of James's 'The Story of a Masterpiece'" (*MP*, LXII, 241–243), that James originally ended the story with the dramatic slashing of the portrait. At the insistence of the editor of *The Galaxy*, James added a comment, but he successfully resisted the temptation to sentimentalize. James's letter to the editor parallels his critical objections to George Eliot's authorial comment at the end of *The Mill on the Floss*. In another article, "Description in Henry James's 'A Light Man'" (*ELN*, II, 211–215), Fish demonstrates James's early skill in making external description serve his narrative purpose. Samuel I. Bellman, "Henry James's 'The Madonna of the Future' and Two Modern Parallels" (*CEJ*, I, 47–53), finds parallels between James's story and works by Bernard Malamud and Robert Towers; as described, the parallels seem less notable than the differences. J. A. Ward, "Structural Irony in 'Madame de Mauves'" (*SSF*, II, 170–182), traces the complex technique of this fine early story. John H. Randall, "The Genteel Reader and Daisy Miller" (*AQ*, XVII, 568–581), provides an amusing and useful review of contemporary comment. The first readers of the story tended to see the story in conventional patterns, reduced by Randall to such titles as "Only a Woman, or Daisy Revealed." They did not see the story as a criticism of gentility itself. In such criticism the story anticipates both Edith Wharton and Fitzgerald. Ora Segal, "'The Liar': A Lesson in Devotion" (*RES*, XVI, 272–281), protests the usual interpretation of Lyon or Mrs. Capadose as the villain of the piece. Using a parallel from "The Tree of Knowledge" (1900—twelve years later than "The Liar"), Segal argues that the leading character in each story shrinks from essential knowledge; rather than villainy, there is a failure in imaginative perception. In another article, "The Weak Wings of Pride: An Interpretation of James's 'The Bench of Desolation'" (*NCF*, XX, 145–154), Segal concludes that though Herbert Dodd's acceptance of Kate Cookham at the end seems to be a renunciation of his past, the reconciliation strikes a sad rather than a bitter note. A notable feature of the story is James's capacity to create a steady sympathy for Herbert Dodd, unmarred by condescension. Earl Rovit, "The Ghosts in James's 'The Jolly Corner'" (*TSL*, X, 65–72), finds allegorical emphasis in the dreams of Alice Staverton, and hence support for Quentin Anderson's allegorical interpretation of the later novels.

University of Southern California

7. Faulkner

Robert A. Wiggins

In 1965 interest in Faulkner remained high at about the level of the two previous years. The *PMLA* bibliography lists a total of eighty-six items, fourteen more than the year before. There are eleven dissertations entirely on Faulkner and four more that include him as a major part of the study. On the list are ten items published abroad (other than in England), two of them books. The *PMLA* list does not adequately cover foreign publications, and, therefore, is probably not a reliable indication of foreign interest in Faulkner.

i. Bibliography

AL, *PMLA*, and *MFS* contain current checklists. A monograph by Gordon Price-Stephens, "The British Reception of William Faulkner: 1929–1962" (*MissQ*, XVIII, 119–200), chronicles the ups and downs of Faulkner's literary reputation in England, reaching the not surprising conclusion that Faulkner came gradually to be respected as an original and gifted writer. The survey draws upon daily and weekly papers, but also reflects judgments made elsewhere in books, scholarly journals, and general articles. The reason for including this item under bibliography is that there is a generous, useful appendix of selected reviews of each of Faulkner's works appearing in British publications. This is a welcome supplement to similar studies by Lowrey (1956), Emerson (1962), and Woodworth (1959) on Faulkner's American and French reputations.

ii. Texts

James B. Meriwether, in *Essays, Speeches, and Public Letters of William Faulkner* (New York, Random House), has authoritatively edited from original typescripts and correspondence, when available, all of Faulkner's mature articles, speeches, book reviews, introductions to books, and letters intended for publication. Omitted are apprentice writings and the University of Mississippi pieces previously compiled by Carvel Collins (1962). The few essays in the slim volume (over half the book is made up of letters-to-the-editor items) show Faulkner skilfully using relatively spare prose in such magazines as the *Atlantic, Harper's, Holiday,* and *Sports Illustrated.*

Random House has reprinted facsimile editions (not noted in *PMLA*) of the first editions of *The Marble Faun* and *A Green Bough, Pylon,* and *The Unvanquished.* Others are promised in the laudable effort to keep all of Faulkner in print.

iii. Biography

The long-awaited Faulkner biography has yet to come, though some biographical materials have been made available. Joseph Blotner is at work on a biography, and the first fruits of his researches are offered in *William Faulkner's Library—A Catalogue* (Charlottesville, Univ. Press of Va.). In his introduction Blotner properly reminds us to be cautious in drawing conclusions from the list of some 1200 volumes of the personal library Faulkner left in 1962. James A. Webb and A. Wigfall Green, in *William Faulkner of Oxford* (Baton Rouge, Louisiana State Univ. Press), have edited a number of reminiscences by various Oxford citizens who knew Faulkner. All but three of these were edited from tape recordings. A translation of an article by Maurice Edgar Coindreau that first appeared in *Preuves,* "The Faulkner I Knew" (*Shenandoah,* XVI, ii, 27–35), offers memories of Faulkner by his French translator. Coindreau concludes that Faulkner increasingly lived in Yoknapatawpha rather than in this world. In "The Ways That Faulkner Walked: A Pilgrimage" (*ArQ,* XXI, 133–145), H. Edward Richardson takes a stroll through Oxford and interviews Phil Stone and Mack Reed. The biographical harvest remains slight.

iv. Criticism

The 1965 bibliography continues to be dominated by criticism, but there seems to be an increase in studies involving Faulkner's sense of, and use of, history. E. O. Hawkins, Jr., locates a source for an anecdote in *Requiem for a Nun* (*MissQ,* XVIII, 248–251). Elmo Howell rummages around in various anthropological works in "William

Faulkner and the Chickasaw Funeral" (*AL*, XXXVI, 523–525) to find
that Faulkner is often inaccurate in confusing Choctaw and Chickasaw customs. "Artistically his Indian stories are valid, in spite of the
curious hodgepodge of fantasy and unassimilated lore." This sounds
like a historian's judgment rather than a literary critic's. The aesthetic
requirements of the story demand that Sam Fathers be buried above
ground, and Faulkner was too good an artist to let facts get in the
way of truth. Mr. Howell similarly looks at fact versus fiction in "William Faulkner and the Andrews Raid in Georgia, 1862" (*GaHQ*,
XLIX, 187–192) and "In Ole Mississippi: Faulkner's Reminiscence"
(*KM*, pp. 77–81).

History seems more relevant to Faulkner's achievement in other
studies. M. E. Bradford, for example, in "Faulkner and the Jeffersonian Dream: Nationalism in 'Two Soldiers' and 'Shall Not Perish'"
(*MissQ*, XVIII, 94–100), shows the Griers as yeomen characters, an
example of Faulkner re-examining his heritage and finding a part of
it in the "Jeffersonian dream of the freeholder's Republic of independent men who will 'keep alive [the] sacred fire [of liberty].'"
Sutpen, of course, is a natural for this kind of study. His life mirrors
the history and the heritage of the South, moral as well as social and
political, according to Melvin Backman in "Sutpen and the South: A
Study of *Absalom, Absalom!*" (*PMLA*, LXXX, 596–604). One might
quibble with his contention that *Absalom, Absalom!* is Faulkner's
most historical novel, but one cannot deny that he has done a
thorough job of relating the character of Sutpen to the history of the
frontier South and finding reflected both the pride and the shame of
the South. Donald M. Kartiganer is less convincing in "Faulkner's
Absalom, Absalom!: The Discovery of Values" (*AL*, XXXVII, 291–
306). He argues that Faulkner sees Thomas Sutpen as embracing the
values of Jefferson as a representative pre-Civil War Southern plantation owner—not at odds with the values of the community, but na-
kedly and in a somewhat brutal form reflecting the same values. The
thesis seems curiously at odds with one of the themes he develops in
his dissertation ("The Individual and the Community: Values in the
Novels of William Faulkner," *DA*, XXV, 4701–4702): that the values
in the best Faulkner of his mid-period are antisocial, centering upon
the individual versus the community. The error is in implicitly viewing Faulkner as a social critic rather than novelist.

Robert Penn Warren as a Southerner himself is entirely convincing in "Faulkner: The South and the Negro" (*SoR*, I, 501–529), when he asserts that Faulkner views the past as an ambiguous mixture of values worth cherishing and the source of dynamic evil. Faulkner shows the romantic pull of the past, but also realizes that submission to the romance of the past is a form of death. This ambiguity is reflected in Faulkner's treatment of the Negro, who is both nigger and human being. The fullest treatment of the Negro, however, is in Charles H. Nilon's *Faulkner and the Negro* (New York, Citadel), which is not listed in the *PMLA* bibliography. He finds slavery and the attempt to possess the land to be two seminal evils that mold Negro character in Faulkner's world. The Negro is examined in detail in eight novels and seventeen short stories. While focusing on the tragic aspect he neglects Faulkner's comic use of the Negro. On the same subject Walter F. Taylor, Jr., ("The Roles of the Negro in William Faulkner's Fiction," *DA*, XXV, 2990) finds the portrayal of the full-blooded Negro Faulkner's least successful characterization, but concludes "few writers have portrayed the reactions of whites to Negroes with more subtlety, or explored more elaborately the total meaning of the Negro for white society." According to Glenn O. Carey ("William Faulkner as a Critic of Society," *ArQ*, XXI, 101–108), Faulkner sometimes slights areas needing criticism, but he consistently speaks out for the rights of man, and he is foremost an artist, not a propagandist.

The religious readers of Faulkner have been busy. It is futile, of course, to try to fit him into anything approaching an orthodox Christian framework, but many continue to be fascinated by his use of Christian imagery. In "The Structural Function of the Christ Figure in the Fiction of William Faulkner" (*DA*, XXV, 5941–5942), Warren G. Rubel sees Faulkner as an optimist offering to men a promise of hope. "The Christ figure became for him a significant token of this promise for man." Francis L. Kunkel, in "Christ Symbolism in Faulkner: Prevalence of the Human" (*Renascence*, XVII, 148–156), not surprisingly finds the most plentiful such symbolism in Joe Christmas and the Corporal. Charles Clerc, in "Faulkner's *The Sound and the Fury*" (*Expl*, XXIV, Item 29), sees associations between Quentin and St. Francis as illuminating the allusive complexity of the sister-water-death imagery in the Quentin section. The thesis of John W. Hunt's *William Faulkner: Art in Theological Tension* (Syracuse, Syracuse Univ. Press) provides the apparatus for some insightful reading of the novels. One must have reservations about the tension theory, for theology does not equate with metaphysics. Fortunately the enlightening readings proceed from a sensitive critical intelligence rather than necessarily from application of the theory. A Faulkner concordance would undoubtedly be useful to many investigators, but George K. Smart's *Religious Elements in Faulkner's Early Novels: A Selective Concordance* (UMPEAL, No. 8) is not it. The work includes only *Soldier's Pay*, *Mosquitoes*, and *Sartoris*, and only by stretching the imagination can such terms as *chaotic* be regarded as religious, particularly when in the Faulkner context there is no discoverable religious significance. The image hunters need to be equipped with more than this popgun.

In the area of imagery Louise Dauner has made an interesting identification ("Quentin and the Walking Shadow: The Dilemma of Nature and Culture," *ArQ*, XXI, 159–171). In the Quentin section she finds shadow imagery evoking the opposing self, the dark half of the psyche. J. N. Pratt, in "Faulkner's *The Sound and the Fury*" (*Expl*, XXIII, Item 37), relates the sparrow on the ledge to Caddy and death, both objects of Quentin's unnatural love; and John K. Simon, in "The Scene and the Imagery of Metamorphosis in *As I Lay Dying*" (*Criticism*, VII, 1–22), comments upon apocalyptic imagery.

The largest number of studies deals with matters of style and meaning related to theme. In "Faulkner's Rhetoric" (*DA*, XXV, 5017), Corey Gail Wall finds Faulkner to be a conscious artist working in the tradition of the impressionistic novel, as also does S. L. Weingart in "The Form and Meaning of the Impressionist Novel" (*DA*, XXVI, 1656). W. M. Brylowski, on the other hand, places Faulkner in the Transcendental tradition, since "the essence of Faulkner's intuition is in that realm of mythic thought which is prior to logical reason" ("Man's Enduring Chronicles: A Study of Myth in the Novels of William Faulkner," *DA*, XXV, 6617–6618). In William Sherman Chisholm's "Sentence Patterns in *The Sound and the Fury*" (*DA*, XXV, 7254–7255), linguistics and the computer combine elaborately to confirm that there are some relationships between grammatical and rhetorical styles. Robert D. Harwick, in "Humor in the Novels of William Faulkner" (*DA*, XXVI, 1646), contends that humor provides the unifying element in four novels. Victor Strandberg identifies what he calls the "principle of inversion" operating in Faulkner's technical equipment in "Faulkner's Poor Parson and the Technique of Inversion (or William Faulkner: An Epitaph)" (*SR*, LXXIII, 181–190). His principle involves a form of reversal of expectation, using, for example, the least likely character as a divine instrument. His analysis of the sermon in the Negro church by Parson Shegog is intended to illustrate the technique, but apart from one's reservations about the "principle," the reading is illuminating in revealing the power of the scene and its use to summarize the theme of the book. In "Faulkner's Poetic Prose: Style and Meaning in 'The Bear'" (*CE*, XXVII, 243–247), Richard Lehan discusses symbolism in *The Bear* that points toward the story's meaning. But the meaning is essentially numinous, since it is couched in metaphor (hence is poetic); it is "a meaning that stems from complex verbal associations and double meaning, meaning that at best is crudely expressed once it is paraphrased."

The structural argument about *Go Down, Moses* is raised again by Marvin Klotz in "Procrustean Revision in Faulkner's *Go Down, Moses*" (*AL*, XXXVII, 1–16). He argues that its appearance as a novel was in the service of book publishing economics in which novels sell better than collections of short stories. He holds that the revisions damaged the earlier versions as individual stories. Mr. Klotz argues his point too hard, for he does not sufficiently allow for Faulkner's characteristically episodic structure in all his novels. John M. Muste is probably closer to the mark when he argues, in "The Failure of Love in *Go Down, Moses*" (*MFS*, X, 366–378), that the work is unified by common motifs of the McCaslin family, a hunt, and concern for white-Negro relationships, but most of all by the theme of the white man's failure to love. Glauco Cambon, in "Faulkner's 'The Old People': The Numen-Engendering Style" (*SoR*, I, 94–107), sees the wilderness as a godhead with Sam Fathers as its priest. Sam ritually adopts Ike and confirms him as a novice. The "sense of Nature's sacredness as a progressively disappearing value to be re-attained through special rituals pervades the style of 'The Old People.'"

The 1965 bibliography includes a number of studies of characters. By and large these studies resist the temptation to regard Faulkner's characters as real people, but some of them seem to err just as seriously in wanting to make the characters function too much as symbols. Jessie Coffee corrects the apparent error of identifying the Nancy mentioned in *The Sound and the Fury* who fell in a ditch and was shot by Roskus with Nancy the prostitute in "That Evening Sun." In "Faulkner's *The Sound and the Fury*" (*Expl*, XXIV, Item 21) she argues persuasively that the Nancy picked clean by the vultures was a large animal—probably a cow. Cleanth Brooks, in "The American 'Innocence': In James, Fitzgerald, and Faulkner" (*Shenandoah*, XVI, iii, 21–37), compares Sutpen with Newman and Gatsby to define innocence in the American experience. In "The Second Mrs. Bundren: Another look at the Ending of *As I Lay Dying*" (*AL*, XXXVII, 65–69), David F. Sadler sees the introduction of the woman by Anse the day after Addie's burial as pointing up the loss of the values Addie represented. The woman with the gramophone signifies the family's embracing new materialistic values. The explanation for Abner Snopes's burning barns lies in his implacable will, according to Charles Mitchell in "The Wounded Will of Faulkner's Barn Burner" (*MFS*, XI, 185–189). James F. Farnham, in "Faulkner's Unsung Hero: Gavin Stevens" (*ArQ*, XXI, 115–132), sees Stevens painfully developing through the Snopes trilogy toward a realistic sense of acceptance in his conflict with Snopesism and in his unrequited love for Eula Varner Snopes. There is something to be said for seeing Stevens as the embodiment of Faulkner's tragic yet hopeful view of man, but I think there is danger in equating this with Faulkner's own realistic approach to existence. The same error and conclusion are found in George Leroy Friend's "Levels of Maturity: The Theme of Striving in the Novels of William Faulkner" (*DA*, XXV, 6622–6623). He studies a number of characters to determine their level of maturity in relation to the theme of striving and concludes that Faulkner is no naturalist-determinist, since he is on the side of free will. He states that Faulkner "insists on a mature striving to accept whatever *is* as the reality that must be coped with and prevailed over." The error in such studies consists in the unstated assumption that Faulkner's own personal values and beliefs must be those illustrated by characters of whom he seems to approve. Based on Meyerhoff's *Time in Literature*, Agnes Schelling Pollock's "The Current of Time in the Novels of William Faulkner" (*DA*, XXV, 7276–7277) finds that Faulkner's characters were shaped by their concepts of time.

A psychological analysis is represented by William Richard Brown in "William Faulkner's Use of the Material of Abnormal

Psychology in Characterization" (*DA*, XXVI, 1036–1037). He contends that pseudo-normality (statistical norm) is represented by Flem Snopes, while Popeye and Christmas, in their absence of a sense of guilt, serve as scapegoats for a guilty society.

Faulkner's last book, *The Reivers*, comes in for its share of attention in four studies. J. M. Mellard, in "Faulkner's 'Golden Book': *The Reivers* as Romantic Comedy" (*BuR*, XIII, iii, 19–31), uses Northrop Frye's system to classify comic characters and finds that "characters, structure, and themes belong, first, to the mode of comedy generally and, second, to the form of romantic comedy specifically." In "*The Reivers* and *Huckleberry Finn*: Faulkner and Twain" (*HLQ*, XXVIII, 373–387), William Rossky concedes that numerous studies have commented upon the resemblances between Mark Twain and Faulkner, but he here explores parallels between the two books more thoroughly than has yet been done. In another article, "*The Reivers*: Faulkner's *Tempest*" (*MissQ*, XVIII, 82–93), Rossky claims that as *The Tempest* stands in relation to Shakespeare's major tragedies so does *The Reivers* stand in relation to Faulkner's major works of the twenties and thirties. It is comedy, but it must not be dismissed as *mere* comedy. It is Faulkner's final summing up and acceptance of the human condition. By coincidence Olga Vickery also uses comparison with *The Tempest* to begin her discussion of *The Reivers*. This is a revision of her previously published book, *The Novels of William Faulkner, A Critical Interpretation* (Baton Rouge, Louisiana State Univ. Press), in which she has added two chapters, one on *The Reivers* and a concluding one. She treats *The Reivers* as a comic epic in, for the most part, a satisfying way, though I must confess I feel she slights the comic in favor of the epic. In the concluding chapter she makes a convincing case in describing the episodic structural patterns in Faulkner's novels.

All things considered, 1965 was not a vintage Faulkner year. There was no single really outstanding new contribution. But it was a good representative Faulkner year with a considerable amount of solid work produced. Moreover there is the indication of not just sustained, but increased, interest and the promise that it will continue for some time.

University of California at Davis

8. Hemingway and Fitzgerald

Frederick J. Hoffman

The most noteworthy facts of criticism and scholarship in 1965[1] are these apparently contradictory ones: (1) there is still much interest in the gaudy details of personality, and this interest affects the kind and quality of publication; and (2) there is an increasing effort to formulate the meaning of the literature itself. These two matters are not unrelated; critics of Hemingway and Fitzgerald still see them as strongly inspiriting and personally dominating what they write, and discussions of them purely along formalistic lines are not frequent. There is less emphasis on the personality in the case of Fitzgerald than there is for Hemingway, but that is undoubtedly because Hemingway's death is still within fairly recent memory. Attempts to provide an interpretive comprehension of the entire work of both men have been on the increase, though they differ markedly, as between Hemingway and Fitzgerald.

i. Bibliographies and Texts

Two collections of Fitzgerald's writing were published in 1965; there were no new Hemingway publications, though one suspects strongly that unpublished manuscripts do abound. The Fitzgerald writings include John Kuehl's editing of *The Apprentice Fiction of F. Scott Fitzgerald, 1909–1917* (New Brunswick, N. J., Rutgers Univ. Press) and *Letters to His Daughter*, edited by Andrew Turnbull (New York, Scribner's). About the first of these I have already said as much as need be said, in *ALS*, 1964 (p. 82). The second is a misfortune. I suppose one may argue that the letters to "Scottie" from 1933 to 1940 are a unit by themselves and therefore belong together and

---

1. I occasionally refer to 1964 work, if there is an item I did not discuss in last year's *ALS*; also, since the time of writing this essay is July of 1966, any important items that have appeared in the first six months of that year may be evaluated. Not every bit of criticism and scholarship is specified in the essay; it is in that sense selective.

alone, in their splendid isolation. But the truth is that these letters are identical with those found on pages 3–102 of the 1963 volume of letters. The only thing new in this 1965 publication is an introduction by Fitzgerald's daughter, and even this was first published elsewhere (*Esquire*, LXIV, iv, 95–97). Considering how many documents of Fitzgerald remain to be published, this performance can only be called an expensive act of supererogation. Mrs. Lanahan's short piece is very lively, very candid, and most entertaining. She confesses that being the child of a "Famous Author" is a not altogether enviable position: "The pay is good, and there are fringe benefits, but the working conditions are too hazardous" (p. ix). In what follows, Mrs. Lanahan shows an undoubted love of her father, and describes quite instructively the circumstances of her daughterhood. The span of the letters is in itself worthy of reflection: in 1933, she was eleven years old and gone off to camp; the troubles in the family had just begun to harden. In the seven years that followed, the Fitzgerald fortunes steadily declined. The letters are in themselves masterpieces of composition, written in a genuine sense from profound moral and material difficulties, but transcending these as well as using them as "lessons." Mrs. Lanahan shrewdly takes measure of the reasons for their being written. They *were* directed to her, but they comprehended much in his life that was almost too painful for her to assimilate. She ends her little foreword with this word of admonition: "Listen carefully to my father, now. Because what he offers is good advice, and I'm sure if he hadn't been my own father that I loved and 'hated' simultaneously, I would have profited by it and be the best educated, most attractive, most successful, most faultless woman on earth today" (pp. xv–xvi).

Texts were in short supply in 1965. Concern about texts, at least in Fitzgerald's case, received its usual scrupulous attention, in Matthew J. Bruccoli's *Fitzgerald Newsletter*. The variety of items preserved in this sequence includes texts of letters, reviews of Fitzgerald books, checklists of minor items, discussions of the development of texts, and other interesting (as well as potentially valuable) details. Some sense of their flavor may be gained from this item, a letter of June, 1925, from Fitzgerald to Van Wyck Brooks (*FN*, No. 29), in which Fitzgerald has this to say about Henry James: "I think if [he] hadn't had at least one poignant emotional love affair with an American girl on American soil he might have lived there [all his life,] twice as long, tried twice as hard, had the picaresque past of Huck Finn & yet never struck roots." Of course the possibilities, for both Fitzgerald and Hemingway, are all but inexhaustible. Fitzgerald has the advantage of a patient scholar, whose appreciation of details is not governed by their immediate pertinence, but is rather sustained by the hope of future relevance. Bruccoli is slowly accumulating the kind of material that should eventually be extremely useful to the author of the definitive biographical and critical study of Fitzgerald.

ii. Memoirs and Biography

For better or worse, both Hemingway and Fitzgerald continue to interest the public often in terms of their personalities. Scribner's move in duplicating the publication of Fitzgerald's letters to his daughter is a case in point, despite the genuine intrinsic value of the writing therein. Hemingway has received the major share of attention along these lines, however. The months and years leading to his suicide are just now being explored, aside from a few scarehead books, based on quite unreliable evidence. The memoirs of his brother Leicester and his sister Marcelline have value but are limited in scope. Hemingway's health, his attitudes toward death, and the alternations of despair and optimism which characterized his actions are now all a matter of public concern, or at least of interest. His widow has failed in her effort to enjoin the publication of the first long study of these years, and it is likely that his life will in future biographies be studied without much discretion. The culprit in the case is A. E. Hotchner's *Papa Hemingway: A Personal Memoir* (New York, Random House, 1966), a book whose almost total frankness made it a solid best-seller; it is difficult, though necessary I suppose, to thank Hotchner for the act of digging up and accumulating this noxious pile. In the spring of 1948, Hotchner first met Hemingway in Cuba, to which he was sent by the *Cosmopolitan* magazine for the purpose of signing up Hemingway for a contribution. The association between the two continued fitfully, but most profitably for Hotchner, from that time until Hemingway's death in the summer of 1961. He had also had the job of translating some of Hemingway's work into television scripts, so that the relationship was not altogether without "literary" results. Hemingway appears to have accepted Hotchner's presence after a while, perhaps even at times to have required it, and the strangely updated Boswellian intercourse continued, the tape recorder at first slowing it down but later encouraging Hemingway to speak, perhaps to say more than he would in more normal circumstances.

In the time of Hemingway's worst illness (mental and physical), Hotchner's frankness began to take its toll. There is really no way of judging the reliability of his evidence, but his record will undoubtedly stand for a few years at least. It is ironic that Hemingway, who had in the early 1950's threatened to stop the presses because Philip Young had offered a very intelligent and basically right few paragraphs of psychological analysis (in his *Hemingway*, New York, Rinehart, 1952), here allows his eager recorder to report everything. *Papa Hemingway* is, despite its see-all attitude, most valuable for its short views of Hemingway with his friends, on his yacht, in his cups, with his cats, and with his wife. The memoir has wheels within wheels. Since Hemingway was writing *A Moveable Feast* part of the time that Hotchner knew him, he would go back in his mind to the 1920's, reflecting in the 1950's about the beginnings of his career as a writer. As the early years went by, in silent-movie form, Hemingway provided a commentary upon them, how serious and how sincere it will be easy to determine. For example, "The characters in *Sun Also Rises* were tragic, but the real hero was the earth and you get the sense of its triumph in abiding forever" (p. 50).

Of course the matters of paramount interest had to do with Hemingway's illness and death. The parallels with his father's suicide in 1928 were startling, and Hotchner gives the entire sequence of events an aura of gloomy inevitability. There was a definite turn toward the old Hemingway after the two airplane crashes in Africa in 1954; when Hotchner saw him afterward, in Venice, he was shocked by the change: "What was shocking to me now was how he had aged in the intervening five months. What there was of his hair (most of it had been burned off) had turned from brindle to white, as had his beard; and he appeared to have diminished somewhat—I don't mean physically diminished, but some of the aura of massiveness seemed to have gone out of him" (p. 83).

There is probably little point in going elaborately into the record, beyond pointing out that in publishing it Hotchner has opened a door Mary Walsh Hemingway had been determined to keep closed

but didn't succeed in locking. Two consequences of Hotchner's book
appear to me important: the first, and perhaps the unfortunate one,
is that interest in Hemingway will continue to concentrate upon his
rather bumptious, gesturing, external personality and how it grew;
the other, much more useful, is that the amount of insight his book
gives us into Hemingway's fears and uncertainties (in short, into
the somewhat less than public performer) may some day go into
a sensible and correct final estimate of him as personality and writer.
To this latter end, the weeks of agony and depression, of shock-
treatments in Rochester, Minnesota, of alternating hilarity and despair, will of course make an important contribution. His analyst, he
had once told Ava Gardner, was "Portable Corona number three . . .
I'll tell you, even though I am not a believer in Analysis, I spend a
hell of a lot of time killing animals and fish so I won't kill myself. . . .
When a man is in rebellion against death, as I am in rebellion against
death, he gets pleasure out of taking to himself one of the godlike
attributes, that of giving it" (p. 139).

iii. Criticism

There is a logical transition from Hotchner's memoir to at least some
types of Hemingway criticism. Philip Young's valuable 1952 study
of Hemingway, the beginning of mature Hemingway criticism, has
of course been widely distributed, often translated, and much
quoted. It has now been reissued as *Ernest Hemingway: A Reconsideration* (University Park, Pennsylvania State Univ. Press, 1966).
This edition is substantially like the 1952 book, with a chapter before
and one after, and the original volume in between, which "has been
revised extensively in minor ways" (p. iv). Some of the minor revisions have to do with alterations in tense made necessary by the
fact that in the interim Hemingway had died. Unfortunately, Young
has dropped page references, though he has added explanatory footnotes within the text itself. Occasionally a revision suggests a change
of mind about his subject matter, or at least a desire to refine what he
has said. The following change can serve as an example: in the 1952
edition (pp. 19–20) he says: "When one extracts from the book as we
have done the stories in which Nick appears one sees that actually
Hemingway has plotted out a story which covers perhaps as much as
twenty years in the life of Nick Adams, first leading actor in a co-

herent drama which he has been steadily writing ever since 1923."
This sentence becomes, in the 1966 edition (pp. 47–48): "When one
extracts from [*In Our Time*] as we have done the stories in which
Nick appears one sees that Hemingway has plotted a story which
covers perhaps as much as twenty years in the life of Nick Adams,
first leading actor in a coherent drama to which he dedicated nearly
four decades of his life." Though there is relatively little difference
between the two versions, the changes made become fairly substantial in the total economy of the new edition. The impression they
now give is that Young's study is no longer a "passing commentary,"
but is rather an achieved work of criticism.

Of course the most interesting new matter is contained in the
foreword and the afterword. The foreword, originally published in
the *Kenyon Review* under the title "Our Hemingway Man" (*KR*,
XXVI, 1964, 676–707), tells the strange story of Young's struggle with
Hemingway to get permission to quote him, a privilege he was
almost denied because of certain references he had made to Freud
and Fenichel concerning Hemingway's "repetition compulsions"
and the traumatic effect of the 1918 wound. "To tell a writer he
has a neurosis, Hemingway did write me, is as bad as telling him
he has cancer: you can put a writer permanently out of business
this way" (p. 3). In any case, the relationship between Young and
his subject is an absorbing example of what might happen when one
ventures to explore a man's work while he is living and breathing
and resenting and grieving. The account is almost, in one sense,
a comedy of misunderstandings, of misplaced and aberrant good intentions, of injured feelings and outraged taste. The truth is that
Young's treatment of this aspect of Hemingway's work was precise
and right; it was also put forth modestly enough. Hemingway's
behavior with respect to it was exorbitant, but it in one sense testi-
fied to the fact that he was becoming more and more sensitive about
his own psychological nature, for fear that it might be accurately
diagnosed.

As for the afterword, part of which also originally appeared in
the *Kenyon Review*, it begins with a straightforward and quiet summary of the close of Hemingway's career, remarking by the way upon
the strange coincidences of Hemingway's death and his father's. The
report on the last years is much superior to Hotchner's, because
Young sees them with some clarity and with no desire to gossip. The

question—which is half a critical and half a biographical question—is why could such a man, who "had so convincingly bespoken courage, endurance and indomitability commit suicide" (p. 263)? Young's answer is, simply, that there were two Hemingways, that the Hemingway who pulled the trigger was "not himself." He was "a very sick old man," and the "worst of all his illnesses was a severe depression of the spirit that provides the will to endure" (p. 264).

We now have a reconstituted book, once again in print, and with interesting and perhaps useful additions. As for Young's having modified downward his earlier enthusiasm for *The Old Man and the Sea*, this is all to the good, but he seems at the same time to want to substitute for it another book he may admire in its place. This is *A Moveable Feast*, for which, I fear, he has an undeserved admiration he will some day also have to retract. Of all the appraisals of that strange posthumous book, I much prefer Andrew Lytle's (*SR*, LXXIII, 339–343) and Tony Tanner's (*Encounter*, XXIII, 1964, 71–75). Tanner's judgment is admittedly rather harsh; and, since he is at the same time reviewing Turnbull's editing of the Fitzgerald Letters, Fitzgerald enjoys a kind of post-twenties triumph of esteem. One detects in *Feast*, says Tanner, "The over-assertiveness of a man troubled by anxiety and fear, a man whose tight tough confidence seems strained by wariness and suspicion, a man mythologising himself to avoid confronting himself" (p. 72). In a somewhat similar vein, Hemingway comes out second-best again, this time to Faulkner, in an obituary essay by Leslie Fiedler on "The Death of the Old Men" (*A&S*, Winter, 1963–1964, pp. 1–5). One of the last persons to see Hemingway alive, Fiedler sums up the end of the "Old Man" in this fashion: at the end "One quarry was left him only, the single beast worthy of him: himself" (p. 4).

The echoes are monotonously forbidding. What their ultimate influence will be upon criticism and biography, it is hard to say; but it is true that, like Fitzgerald shortly after his less spectacular death in December, 1940, Hemingway is being re-evaluated in terms of the character and circumstances of his life's conclusion. There are a number of essays on Hemingway's views of death and of growing old. Harvey Curtis Webster's ("Ernest Hemingway: The Pursuit of Death," *TQ*, VII, 1964, 149–159) is perhaps the least effective. There is really not much here, except for the clichés of past criticism. *In Our Time*, Webster says, contained eighteen dead men, one dead woman, and ten corpses of animals; but in *For Whom the Bell Tolls*, Hemingway "finally came to terms with death." Despite his limitations, "with great art and with great intensity, he nevertheless showed man, encompassed by death, confronting, meeting, accepting, and transcending it, as a man will, I presume, in more fortunate ages than our own" (p. 159). In "The Concept of Maturity in Hemingway's Short Stories" (*CLAJ*, VIII, 1964, 149–156), Bernard Knieger says very little more. The term *maturity* is susceptible to a too easy form of stoicism, in any case. Gabriel Motola's "Hemingway's Code: Literature and Life" (*MFS*, X, 319–329) takes off from the fact of Hemingway's suicide, saying that it requires a re-examination of his code; this is followed by a summing-up of the code, as Motola sees it. He comes to the fairly conventional halfway conclusion about Robert Jordan of *For Whom the Bell Tolls*, but has an interesting and rather new approach to Hemingway's own ending: he had depended much upon luck in his life, but toward the end was beginning to run out of luck. He was desperately ill, and unfortunately for him, "they" (meaning his killers, like the fascist cavalrymen of *For Whom the Bell Tolls*) would not come. He had therefore to take care of his own death. At least this *seems* to be Motola's conclusion; it is all much confused with Hemingway's "inability to understand the close proximity of his 'emotional' coward to his hero," which "results in his refusal to pass judgment, specifically on his father, thereby creating the root of his intellectual and emotional confusion" (p. 329). To explain a confusion is, I suppose, an improvement over holding it up to exclusive scorn; Hemingway now seems to be suffering from both kinds of mistake.

Given this kind of environment, it was probably inevitable that such a book as Robert W. Lewis, Jr.'s *Hemingway on Love* (Austin, Univ. of Texas Press)[2] should have come along. Originally a doctoral dissertation at the University of Illinois, this study assumes a number of approaches to the subject: the psychoanalytic (it is far

2. There were a number of more limited studies of Hemingway: Stanley Cooperman on *The Old Man and the Sea* (*CE*, XXVII, 215–220); William White's very good essay on the reportorial essays collected in *The Wild Years* ("Novelist as Reporter," *OW*, IX, 1964, 77–92); John S. Rouch on *The Sun Also Rises* (*MFS*, XI, 361–370); Sidney P. Moss on the same novel ("Character, Vision, and Theme in *The Sun Also Rises*," *IEY*, No. 9, 1964, pp. 64–67); Phillips G. and Rosemary R. Davies' investigation of the source of the short story "Fifty Grand" in the Mickey Walker-Jack Britton fight of 1922 (*AL*, XXXVII, 251–258); and assorted shorter notes in *Explicator* and other magazines.

more complicated and more pretentious in this respect than is
Young's approach), the "philosophy of adultery," allegedly based
upon Denis de Rougement's *Love in the Western World* (in other
words, the "Tristan-Iseult syndrome" of p. 7), the more or less free-
floating terms *eros* and *agape*. The effect of these and other approaches is stifling; Hemingway sinks, drowns, is lost from sight,
and one sees only the form of the author, attempting to administer
artificial resuscitation. Certainly a book of this length deserves to
make *some* contribution, but the terms get into each other's way, and
the results contrast forbiddingly with the bright intelligence of
Philip Young. It is not that Lewis is not bringing germane matters to
bear upon Hemingway's work; he does this surely. But he is so
preoccupied with defining and redefining that he all but ends with
the task of definition, which is not the best way, by any means, of
getting near to what Hemingway has been saying. Hotchner is at
one extreme (the extreme of gossip) of the spectrum; Lewis is to
be found at the other extreme, that of a bemused terminological
speculation.

It is, of course, necessary to rescue Hemingway from the assumption that all criticism of him is bound to turn into one or another of
the extremes. Philip Young's book is a testimony of that, and there
are a number of useful speculations about individual works. Perhaps
the most sophisticated short study is Daniel Fuchs's "Ernest Hemingway, Literary Critic" (*AL*, XXXVI, 431-151). While the title is
just a bit misleading, the essay is a sharp analysis of Hemingway as
a man of culture and perception, whose prejudices do not need
always to be handled in Lillian Ross's way, but can in fact be profitably examined. Hemingway's prose, says Fuchs, is "motivated by a
comic contempt of standard English in its aspect of respectability,
gentility, polite euphemism, though it never forgets it in its aspect
of biblical plainness and repetition" (p. 433). What follows is an
attempt to set Hemingway up as an antagonist of "literature" (the
term here used in the sense that Verlaine used it when he said, "*Et
tout le reste est littérature*"). It is an interesting and a sophisticated
kind of review and a worthy enterprise.[3]

3. I should mention here once again the book edited by Roger Asselineau,
The Literary Reputation of Hemingway in Europe (Paris, Lettres Modernes),
a most useful collection of essays, though uneven. The best essays are by Professors Welland, Asselineau, Papajewski, Skard, Åhnebrink, and Parker. Arturo
Berea's comments on *For Whom the Bell Tolls* are printed in an appendix.

When one approaches the year's work on Fitzgerald, the major ornament is Henry Dan Piper's *F. Scott Fitzgerald: A Critical Portrait* (New York, Holt, Rinehart and Winston).[4] It is an important book; the only real objection to it is the one made by Eric Solomon (*FN*, No. 30, pp. 1–2), that in view of its late arrival on the scene it simply echoes others on the subject and its subdivisions. It is, he says, "nevertheless valuable" (p. 1). I should say that is more than valuable, and that it stands its own ground. One other book-length study, Richard Lehan's *F. Scott Fitzgerald and the Craft of Fiction* (Carbondale, Southern Illinois Univ. Press, 1966)[5] is both more ambitious (in one or two respects at least) and less. Its scope cannot be compared to that of Piper's study, nor is it the result of as many years of scholarship. Yet Lehan has a number of interesting thematic speculations: on the influence on Fitzgerald of Oswald Spengler's *The Decline of the West* ("I read him the same summer I was writing *The Great Gatsby*," he wrote Max Perkins in June of 1940, "and I don't think I ever quite recovered from him," *Letters*, pp. 289–290); on various Romantic and *fin de siècle* influences; and on Fitzgerald's sense of time—more specifically, his sense of the importance and the evanescent quality of youth. In addition, Lehan offers some original research into Fitzgerald's relations with Ginevra King, and the effect of them upon several of his characterizations, most notably those of Daisy Buchanan and Jordan Baker (the latter apparently derived from Edith Cummings, a close friend of Miss King's).

The conclusion of Lehan's book is one of a number of interesting speculations that recent Fitzgerald critics have provided. Fitzgerald's concern with the moral implications of wealth is confused with his sense of the romantic spirit. Gatsby, for example, is both morally implicated (to a degree Fitzgerald could never clearly see) in the indictment of the moneyed world, and a bright Romantic, whose power is irrational and illusory. Fitzgerald never succeeded in defining precisely the dividing line that separates one kind of culpability from another, and was himself drawn into the vortex where

4. I have already made a number of remarks about Piper's book in *ALS, 1964* (pp. 83–84), and I have no reason to modify the high praise I gave the book then.

5. Since this book had not yet been published at the deadline for my review, I have read a copy of the page proofs, for which I thank both author and publishers. I have not seen Harry T. Moore's preface, which was not included in the proofs.

definitions are all but impossible. "His craft was a means of flight
for him—into a brighter and better world where he could relive his
hurts and where people would act as he could expect" (p. 179).

Just how much this conclusion depends upon a sense of Fitzgerald
the man, I should think would require a full reading of Lehan's
text to determine. Whatever the degree, it is testimony once more
to the all but inseparable relationship of personality and text in the
realities of Hemingway and Fitzgerald. It is possible to write criticism of either without attending to this relationship; it has been
done, and sometimes skilfully and well. The most effective of these
non-personal approaches is likely to associate Fitzgerald and James
in the tradition of manners or in terms of manners and literary form.
Kermit Vanderbilt's essay, "James, Fitzgerald, and the American
Self-Image" (MR, VI, 289–304), is more explicitly a study of the
relationship of The Great Gatsby to James's The American (which
is all the more remarkable since Fitzgerald had not read The American before Gatsby was published). The parallels are interesting
enough; they are, Vanderbilt is sure, what T. S. Eliot had in mind
when he wrote Fitzgerald, saying that "In fact it seems to me to be
the first step that American fiction has taken since Henry James."[6]
Vanderbilt has in mind what he calls "the isolated, aggressive, virginal
American spirit in search of fulfillment amid the complexities of an
advanced social order" (p. 290). He even suggests the contrasting
relationship of Christopher Newman and Gatsby to the green world
of Long Island. Newman had paid it a visit just after he had made a
fine moral decision, and had found the landscape gratifyingly rewarding; Gatsby, however, sees not much more than a green light at
the end of the Buchanan dock. James's Long Island has become "both
the closed suburbia of the Buchanans and the open wasteland of Dr.
T. J. Eckleburg and the morally bankrupt Wilsons" (p. 299).

Joseph N. Riddel's "F. Scott Fitzgerald, the Jamesian Inheritance,
and the Morality of Fiction" (MFS, XI, 331–350) is both a more
elaborate and a more subtle treatment of approximately the same
theme. The source of Riddel's perspective is in the preface to the
New York Edition of The Portrait of a Lady, more specifically this
sentence: "There is, I think, no more nutritive or suggestive truth
in this connexion [that is, of the morality of art] than that of the

6. In The Crack-Up, edited by Edmund Wilson (New York, New Directions,
1945), p. 310.

perfect dependence of the 'moral' sense of a work of art on the amount of felt life concerned in producing it."[7] Morality is closely related to consciousness, according to which "felt life" is measured. James suggests "no less than an equation of the moral conscience and the artist's imagination" (pp. 331–332). With these and other points in mind, Riddel examines Fitzgerald's fiction. The success of *The Great Gatsby* is largely the success "of method becoming conception" (p. 335), while the early fiction is flawed and therefore fails to communicate because Fitzgerald is involved in, is swallowed by, his creations. The points made in this essay cry out for expansion; nothing short of a monograph could "prove" by way of providing indicators of so subtle an issue.

The essay is nevertheless, like Fuchs's on Hemingway, a suggestion of how far criticism can go by way of renewing itself from the swirl of autobiographical influences, without either abstracting itself or becoming too embarrassingly ridden by terminological clichés. John N. Miller's dissertation, "Romanticism, Irony, and the Novels of F. Scott Fitzgerald" (*DA*, XXV, 4151–4152), has something of the same promise, in its analysis of Fitzgerald's growth in terms of the "polarity" of personal vision and external actuality. William Wasserstrom's "The Strange Case of F. Scott Fitzgerald and A. Hyd(Hid)ell" (*CUF*, VIII, 5–11) is a sad mixture of tendentious criticism and editorializing, in which the assassination of Kennedy and the atmosphere of *Tender Is the Night* are somehow strangely involved. G. C. Millard's "F. Scott Fitzgerald" (*ESA*, VIII, 5–30) errs on exactly the opposite side: it is all too coherent, too intelligible, and it pays for these virtues by using a term, "disenchantment," that too easily accounts for everything in Fitzgerald.

Other Fitzgerald criticism concerns itself with separate works: Sy Kahn's, with *This Side of Paradise* (*MQ*, VII, 1966, 177–194), and especially with Amory Blaine as the first of a sequence of "noble" Fitzgerald heroes, who are in defeat "more humane . . . than the people and forces that undo them" (p. 194); William H. Hildebrand's study of *The Great Gatsby* (*Serif*, II, 19–26) makes a stab at image criticism, with not much success (in the end, the value of the essay comes not from the images but from the way his powers of generalizing can rescue him from them). There are at least two criticisms of

7. *The Portrait of a Lady*, New York Edition (New York, Scribner's, 1908), III, ix-x.

"Babylon Revisited," one of the most discussed of Fitzgerald's stories: Roy R. Male's (*SSF*, II, 270–277), which situates the story in a group in which the protagonist returns after a prolonged absence (p. 27); and Thomas F. Staley's (*MFS*, X, 386–388), a not too successful attempt to use the story as an illustration of Fitzgerald's preoccupation with time. Finally, two studies of *Tender Is the Night* mark the extremes of modern criticism: James Ellis' (*UR*, XXXI, 43–49), which is moderately successful in its attempt to define Dick Diver's basic problems, but is scarcely original in so doing; and a fascinatingly different approach offered by Lee M. Whitehead, "*Tender Is the Night* and George Herbert Mead" (*L&P*, XV, 180–191), in which Mead's work, *Mind, Self and Society*, is used with great effectiveness. With respect to the latter, there is no question of direct influence; Whitehead simply applies his knowledge of Mead to a reading of the novel, with fascinating results.[8]

iv. Conclusion

Despite the sometimes admirable essays in formalist, thematic, or philosophical criticism, the major impact both Hemingway and Fitzgerald still have upon even sophisticated audiences is directly related to the ways in which they comported themselves in the world, the ways in which they lived and the manner of their dying. This is at least partly true because neither has yet had a definitive biography. Fitzgerald has been treated more fully in this respect than has Hemingway (of course, we await Carlos Baker's authorized treatment). Because the biographies are as yet not certain, memoirs tend to take their place; and such a book as Hotchner's has an immediate (though I rather imagine not a prolonged) success. It is also true that no writers have carried so much of the burden of being "culture heroes," so that everything associated with them, private or public, seems to have a magic or an eponymous significance. They

8. I should also like to mention these essays: Barry Edward Cross, "Success and Failure in *The Last Tycoon*" (*UR*, XXXI, 273–276); E. Fred Carlisle, "The Triple Vision of Nick Carraway" (*MFS*, XI, 351–360); and, for special reasons, Helen F. Blackshear's "Mama Sayre, Scott Fitzgerald's Mother-in-Law" (*GaR*, XIX, 465–470). This last is the slightest of memoirs, but it does communicate something of the quality of Zelda's formidable mother. As for Scott, Mama Sayre admitted he was handsome, but "he was not good for my daughter" (p. 467). There is some question as to whether Mama Sayre was "good" for Zelda.

are not charismatic creatures (Faulkner qualifies far more in that role), but they have not ceased being public property. Hemingway is, of course, the most affected by this circumstance. Some of the moral paradoxes and ambiguities discussed in this essay, as well as some of the rather simple-minded questions (as, how can a man who has celebrated courage all of his life commit suicide?) result from the unsettled character of Hemingway scholarship generally. The quality of any period of literature fluctuates often; new discoveries cause changes of view and demeanor; and speculation is rife when an artist yields so easily and so often to public image-making. Somewhere beyond the gossip, the clacking of tongues over deathbeds and other beds, lies the beginning of a hard core of critical accomplishment. This latter it is the task of responsible scholarship and criticism both to explain and to preserve.

University of Wisconsin at Milwaukee

Part II

9. Literature to 1800

Richard Beale Davis

The number of studies of our early literature increased markedly in 1965 over the preceding two years. The count of books and essays on individual authors and their writings remained about the same; but treatments of general and genre subjects and edited texts of single works and period anthologies appeared much more frequently. Scholars writing of the period seemed eager to make available obscure or previously unpublished texts and to analyze minds and movements in their broader historical contexts. Though some of these publications represent the middle and southern colonies or states, they are preponderantly concerned with New England. A survey of work during 1965 indicates the pressing need for more edited texts and studies of literature produced west and south of the Hudson, a literature we now know exists—thanks to a handful of spadeworkers in some instances here represented—and is more significant than scholars fascinated by the New England mind have ever taken the time or space to observe.

i. Bibliography, Libraries, and Publishing History

Adequate bibliography for the period continues to be a pressing necessity, but some useful and significant contributions were made in the area. D'Alte A. Welch continued "A Bibliography of American Children's Books Printed Prior to 1821" (*PAAS*, LXXIV, Pt. 2, 260–382). Charles E. Clark printed in "The Literature of the New England Earthquake of 1755" (*PBSA*, LIX, 295–305) a list of twenty-seven items he discussed critically in another essay noted below. Marcus McCorison and Wilmarth S. Lewis gave, with illuminating introductory essays, *The 1764 Catalogue of the Redwood Library Company of Newport, Rhode Island* (New Haven, Yale Univ. Press), a list of over fifteen hundred books and pamphlets, altogether representative of a New England gentleman's library of the period.

Quite different but equally interesting is the new enlarged edition of Pierce W. Gaines's *Political Works of Concealed Authorship in the United States 1789–1810 With Attributions* . . . (Hamden, Conn., Shoe String Press), highly valuable to all students of historical and political literature. Included are several poems, among them some assigned to Thomas Green Fessenden and St. George Tucker. Useful too is Thomas R. Adams' *American Independence: The Growth of an Idea. A Bibliographical Study of the American Political Pamphlets Printed Between 1764 and 1766 Dealing With the Dispute Between Great Britain and Her Colonies* (Providence, Brown Univ. Press). Containing 230 titles, it omits all writing on local disputes, all newspaper essays, all poetry, satire, and plays. Intended "for people concerned with the study of the origins of the American Revolution," this bibliography is weak primarily in its failure to include locations of pamphlets in the South and parts of the West and Southwest. From Georgia to California there are many extensive collections left uncited. Though the editor asserts that he has not intended completeness, he has ignored the possible usefulness of his bibliography to most scholars outside his own region and Philadelphia. The list begins with a Virginia pamphlet by Richard Bland, but very few items written outside New York, Pennsylvania, and New England are included.

Wendell D. and Jane N. Garrett, in *The Arts in Early American History: Needs and Opportunities for Study* (Chapel Hill, Univ. of N. C. Press), with an introductory essay by Walter Muir Whitehill, have on the whole compiled a very disappointing bibliography, though it is partially redeemed by Whitehill's fine essay. The list is fairly good on printing, even though it omits some valuable items on the *Virginia* and *South Carolina Gazettes*. It by no means includes, as it claims, "the basic writings in a variety of fields," especially not in painting, architecture, and music, scanty as they are.

The history of several early pamphlets and books, their reception and dissemination here and in Great Britain, have received attention. In "American Broadside Whipt" (*AN&Q*, III, 67–68), W. H. Blumenthal tells the rather amusing story of a "false and scurrilous letter" of 1755 attacking an officer's behavior at the Battle of Lake George. The broadside epistle was ordered to be given forty stripes and burnt. G. Thomas Tanselle, in "Early American Fiction in England:

The Case of *The Algerine Captive*" (*PBSA*, LIX, 367–384), traces the reception and format of Royall Tyler's novel when it appeared in the United Kingdom. He examines the charge that the English edition was stripped of American scenes and associations and altered in wording and deleted of paragraphs and chapters. He concludes that, although there were some changes, the book preserved its American character and was actually in some English editions improved in style. D. L. Jacobson shows in "Thomas Gordon's *Works of Tacitus* in Pre-Revolutionary America" (*BNYPL*, LXIX, 58–64) how this translation was *the* edition read and pondered by Whigs, who noted its emphasis on the right, or the duty, to resist tyranny or alter political institutions in keeping with changing times and needs. And in " 'The Court of Fancy' in England" (*PBSA*, LIX, 48–49), Robert D. Harlan indicates that the one hundred copies of Thomas Godfrey's poem shipped to England in 1763 by David Hall, Franklin's printer, were advertised but left no perceptible impression.

Edwin Wolf II in his usual interesting fashion analyzes "A Parcel of Books for the Province in 1700" (*PMHB*, LXXXIX, 428–446) from an invoice made out to Penn and docketed in the hand of James Logan. It is not a Quaker theological list but a varied collection of sermons, essays, philosophy, history, and memoirs. Stewart M. Robinson's "Notes on the Witherspoon Pamphlets" (*PULC*, XXVII, 53–57) controverts the prevalent idea that all of Witherspoon's library was burned, for six hundred pamphlets bound in sixty neat volumes are now housed at Princeton. They were clearly the sources for many of their owner's lectures and political ideas. Charles W. Mignon makes clear many obscurities or puzzles encountered by the scholar studying the Puritan poet in "Some Notes on the History of the Edward Taylor Manuscripts" (*YULG*, XXXIX, 168–173), for he gives many details of papers at Yale and of some elsewhere, and something of their provenance.

Percy G. Adams has solved one of the persistently puzzling bibliographical problems in travel literature in "The Case of Swaine Versus Drage: An Eighteenth Century Publishing Mystery Solved" (*Hist. & Lit.*, pp. 157–168). Certain accounts of voyages in search of the Northwest Passage have been attributed to Theodorus Drage by some, to Charles Swaine by others. Through a complex and masterly bit of detective work, assembled bio-bibliographical elements, comparative handwriting, and sound reasoning, Adams has shown that the sometime clerk of the ship *California* and the Carolina S.P.G. missionary were one and the same man, the author of two important accounts of 1748–1749 and 1760.

ii. Texts

The number and high quality of texts printed for the first time or reproduced from rare early editions in 1965 is quite encouraging. Two useful works by major New England writers appeared, but more remarkable were the dozen or so Southern authors represented, and the wide variety of the latter subjects and forms. There were also several anthologies devoted exclusively or primarily to writing before 1800.

Josephine K. Piercy's edition of *The Tenth Muse* (*1650*), *and, From the Manuscripts, Meditations Divine and Morall Together with Letters and Occasional Pieces by Anne Bradstreet* (Gainesville, Fla., SF&R) supplies a long-needed facsimile of the poet's first volume and reproduces the only known handwritten copy of certain additional poems and prose pieces. The brief introduction is inadequate, however, to an understanding of the reproduced manuscript portion. One must read Professor Piercy's study of Anne Bradstreet (noted below) and the Ellis edition's preface to understand the relationships among the poems here gathered. The editor fails to comment, as Ellis did, on the fact that part of the manuscript reproduced is not in the author's hand but in that of her son Simon.

Another scholar, Jeannine H. Rowlette, in "The Works of Anne Bradstreet" (*DA*, XXV, 4707–4708), indicates that she has prepared a reliable text of all the poetry, including some never before published, and has compared all available copies of the 1650 and 1678 editions, by machine when possible. She considers the second edition the authoritative one and intends to bring out a corrected "complete poems" based upon it.

Norman S. Grabo has edited for the first time from the original manuscript *Edward Taylor's Treatise Concerning the Lord's Supper* (East Lansing, Mich. State Univ. Press, 1965–1966). Reminding us that Taylor's poems are to be comprehended fully only through the prismatic light of his sermons rather than through the plain glass of the verse itself, Grabo demonstrates how this tract or series of eight sermons on the sacrament is actually, in its proliferation of the "wedden garment" as gospel righteousness, an extended discussion of the favorite imagery represented most obviously in his best-known poem "Huswifery," the prose itself being an elaborated cluster of metaphors, an able reply to Solomon Stoddard's advocacy of open communion, and another evidence of Taylor's orthodox Calvinism. Grabo's comparison of Edwards' and Taylor's doctrine, psychology, and rhetorical method indicates not only their essential harmony (if not identity of concepts of God and the covenant of grace) but also their contrast in temperament and tone: Edwards' dignity and serenity, Taylor's imagination and tenseness. To the reader familiar with the best Puritan sermons by other divines or with Taylor's *Christographia*, these sermons as literature will prove disappointing. Hortatory and repetitive, they are really outlines with the divisional doctrines stated and partially explicated. With the help of Grabo's introduction and the learned and pertinent commentary in his notes, one sees them most significantly as an exposition of "the function of metaphor" in the Puritan's—particularly Edward Taylor's—expression of his theology and as an exposition of their author's depth of theological learning and of his doctrinal sources.

Most welcome is the reprinting with adequate introduction of *The Diary of Edward Taylor* (Springfield, Mass., Connecticut Valley Historical Museum, 1964), which had appeared once before, in 1880. Far less significant to an understanding of Taylor than other things so far printed, it does present the record of his journey from England to Boston, his three years at Harvard, and his overland trip to Westfield to take up his pastorate.

Also useful is "John Cotton's Letter to Samuel Skelton," edited by David D. Hall (*WMQ*, XXII, 478–485), an important piece of evidence in the dispute over Congregationalism in 1630. It is also declared to be our "only source of information about the events at Salem in the summer of 1630," though it does not resolve certain problems of Cotton's consistency or of the relationship between the Plymouth and Salem churches.

The publication of texts of Southern writers may be considered chronologically. Thus one should begin with the magnificent first modern edition, in facsimile with elaborate introduction, of Richard Hakluyt's *The Principall Navigations Voiages and Discoveries of the English Nation . . . 1589* (Salem, Mass., Peabody Museum; Cambridge, Eng., Hakluyt Society, 2 vols.), edited by David B. Quinn and Raleigh A. Skelton with a new index by Alison Quinn. The introduction explains the character of the book, its inception and production, sources, and non-literary materials, and includes a provisional checklist of surviving copies. Writers who may be called American and Southern include Thomas Hariot and Ralph Lane of the Roanoke Island colony, who wrote *on* as well as *about* the soil of the New World. The black-letter text reproduction is not at all difficult to read, and the modern index renders easy the search for writers and events. Here is gathered what may be called the first English-language literature of the New World, and in the original format. Perhaps along with it should be noted Louis B. Wright's readable anthology of writings, many from this 1589 Hakluyt, *The Elizabethans' America: A Collection of Reports by Englishmen on the New World* (London, Edward Arnold; Cambridge, Mass., Harvard Univ. Press). Its forty-odd items, two or three by New Englanders, again include Lane and Hariot, and in addition, the later George Percy, John Smith, Christopher Newport, William Strachey, Alexander Whitaker, John Pory, Ralph Hamor, and John Rolfe, all of whom lived and some of whom died in Virginia. The same editor has made available in a new paperback series *A Voyage to Virginia in 1609: Two Narratives, Strachey's "True Reportory" and Jourdain's Discovery of the Bermudas* (Charlottesville, Univ. Press of Va., 1964), presenting the complete texts of two significant pamphlets well printed and edited.

Two years ago (see *ALS, 1963,* p. 101) Edmund and Dorothy Berkeley published their *John Clayton, Pioneer of American Botany,* a study of the eighteenth-century Virginia physician-naturalist who contributed so much to botanical science and literature. Now the Berkeleys as editors have brought out *The Reverend John Clayton, A Parson with a Scientific Mind: His Scientific Writings and Other Related Papers . . . with a Short Biographical Sketch* (Charlottesville, Univ. Press of Va.), presenting another and earlier Clayton (1657–1725) who was sometime rector of James City and later Dean of Kildare. His essays on the air and temperature of Virginia, a journey beyond the Appalachians in 1671, the aborigines, and other Virginia subjects appear along with papers written later in London or Ireland. This is a useful collection of a "curious" clergyman's

observations in natural history and experiments in other branches
of science, many of them appearing in print for the first time.
A new reprint series is devoting itself largely to the reproduction
of historical and literary materials concerning the original thirteen
colonies. Perhaps the most valuable so far is William Stith's 1747
History of the First Discovery and Settlement of Virginia (original
imprint Williamsburg; now Spartanburg, S. C., The Reprint Co.),
with the extremely helpful index originally issued by the Virginia
State Library in 1912. Almost as valuable is Charles Campbell's
History of the Ancient Colony and Dominion of Virginia (original
imprint Philadelphia; now Spartanburg, S. C., The Reprint Co.),
another study from original sources of this early colony. Other
southern, New England, and middle colonies are also to be represented in reprints of scarce early writing.

But perhaps the greatest step taken by scholars in the last decade
or two to reveal the Southern colonial mind was the publication of
Jack P. Greene's edition of *The Diary of Colonel Landon Carter of
Sabine Hall, 1752–1778* (Charlottesville, Univ. Press of Va., 2 vols.).
Carter's diary is at once more revelatory of a mind and of a way
of life than is William Byrd II's. Called by his editor "the most
prolific and most polished author of his generation in Virginia and
perhaps in any of the colonies south of Pennsylvania," Carter, in his
tracts-for-the-times (including four major pamphlets and nearly
fifty essays in American and British journals), usually published
anonymously, never achieved a literary or political reputation among
his contemporaries to compare with that of certain lesser men.
Like the younger Franklin and Jefferson, he was a scientific investi-
gator. He was elected to two learned societies in recognition of
his observations and experiments. In Greene's volumes we have
firsthand evidence of a colonial Southerner as complex psychologi-
cally as a Cotton Mather and at times as sensitive and morbid as any
New England Puritan. Never repetitious as Byrd's entries are in
content and style, Carter's diurnal jottings vary in length from a
score of pages to a few lines or nothing at all, and in content from
terse rehearsal of facts to long introspective broodings. Favorite
themes are the imperfection of all created things and virtue as the
best policy. The diarist also comments on the cuttings of the stone
capitals for his piazza; his rector's weakness in gambling; his chil-

dren's ingratitude and lack of integrity; his medicinal treatments for family, friends, and slaves; the great balls held on religious holidays and birthdays; and finally in his last years his own physical condition. Books, religion, a free school, agriculture, poetical epitaphs, all these and much else interested this Virginia aristocrat who lived as simply and as frugally as Byrd.

By reproducing and analyzing the variant texts, Edwin Wolf II has, in "The Authorship of the 1774 Address to the King Restudied" (*WMQ*, XXII, 189–224), done a great deal to determine precisely what part John Dickinson, Patrick Henry, and Richard Henry Lee had in composing this document of the Continental Congress. George F. Jones has edited and translated "Von Reck's Second Report for Georgia" (*WMQ*, XXII, 319–333), which gives more interesting details of the colony in its first stages, of men, towns, gardens, aborigines, fauna, and flora. And J. A. Leo Lemay's edition of *A Poem by John Markland of Virginia* (Williamsburg, Va., William Parks Club) makes available in modern reprint, with introduction and notes, another work by the author of "Typographia." The verses are a "Poetical Address" to Lord Baltimore on his visit to Williamsburg in 1733 by a man who was apparently a fairly well-known English poet before he settled in Virginia and became one of the literary circle at the colonial capital.

Representing the Revolutionary generation are the materials included in Robert L. Brunhouse's edition, *David Ramsay, 1749–1815: Selections from His Writings* (Philadelphia, American Philosophical Society). Born and educated in the middle colonies, Ramsay in 1774 moved to South Carolina and from that state published his long line of speeches, essays, and sketches from 1778 well into the nineteenth century. He wrote on soil, politics, the deaths of Washington and Rush, medicine, and most importantly he wrote a *History of South Carolina*. His letters begin from the Eastern Shore of Maryland and Virginia and continue in time and space into South Carolina. Among his host of correspondents famous in their day and ours were Benjamin Rush, Theodorick Bland, John Witherspoon, Samuel Stanhope Smith, Adams, Jefferson, and Jay.

From South Carolina too came *John Wesley's First Hymn-Book: A Collection of Psalms and Hymns. Charles-Town, Printed by Lewis Timothy, 1737* (Charleston, Dalcho Historical Society; London, Wesley Historical Society, 1964), a facsimile reproduction of the first

Anglican as well as first Methodist hymnal printed in America. The introduction by Frank Baker and George W. Williams gives the history of the book and points out its basic part in shaping the hymnody which was "the crowning glory of the Methodist movement." It also discusses Wesley in America as selector and reviser of hymns.

Two multi-volume editions of southern philosopher-statesmen were continued this year. Julian Boyd, editing *The Papers of Thomas Jefferson*, Vol. XVII, *July 1790 to November 1790* (Princeton, Princeton Univ. Press), has made this volume especially noteworthy for the damning evidence it offers, in documents and introductory essays, of Alexander Hamilton's nearly or actually treasonous intrigues with British officials. William T. Hutchinson and William M. E. Rachal, in editing *The Papers of James Madison*, Vol. IV, *1 January 1782–31 July 1782* (Chicago, Univ. of Chicago Press), have brought out a volume which contains mostly personal letters about public business.

Statesmen of the middle colonies or states are represented in the continuation of *The Papers of Benjamin Franklin*, Vol. VIII, *April 1, 1758 through December 31, 1759*, edited by Leonard W. Labaree *et al.* (New Haven, Yale Univ. Press) and *The Papers of Alexander Hamilton*, Vol. VIII, *February 1791–July 1791*, Harold C. Syrett *et al.* (New York, Columbia Univ. Press). The Franklin volume contains several quasi-literary essays as well as others on electricity, trade, and statecraft; the Hamilton volume has almost nothing of literary interest.

Students of the novel will welcome the reprint of Susanna Rowson's *Charlotte Temple, a Tale of Truth* (New York, Twayne), edited by Clara M. and Rudolf Kirk, a clear-type reproduction of the text of the most popular American novel during the first sixty years of our history. Scholars of the earlier periods will be even more interested in William K. Bottorff's "An Edition of *American Poems, Selected and Original*, 1793" (*DA*, XXV, 4696–4697), an abstract discussing critically the little-known first American poetic anthology, its contributors and contributions (the anthology itself is to appear in facsimile in 1966). Equally interesting is the outline of a modern compilation, Kenneth E. Silverman's "Colonial American Poetry: An Anthology" (*DA*, XXVI, 359–360), apparently a well-balanced representation by type, area, period, and individual author of verse from John Smith to Freneau and Brackenridge.

Four published anthologies are of some importance, especially two of them. *The American Frontier: A Social and Literary Record* (New York, Holt, Rinehart and Winston), edited by Merton C. Babcock, will be useful primarily as a handy source for certain early materials. More specialized and significant is *Pamphlets of the American Revolution 1750–1776* (Cambridge, Mass., Harvard Univ. Press, Belknap), edited by Bernard Bailyn, the first volume of four projected designed to include the most distinguished essays or arguments on political theory (some actually are sermons and verse) leading to the Revolution. The fourteen essays in this initial volume represent both sides of the question, each is self-explanatory, and each supports the editor's contention that "the controversy was an ideological-constitutional struggle." New England writers number ten, Pennsylvania two, Virginia and Maryland one each. One may wonder that Landon Carter is unrepresented, though his friend Richard Bland's essay is one of the most entertaining and literarily facile of those included.

Frederick Rudolph, in *Essays on Education in the Early Republic* (Cambridge, Mass., Harvard Univ. Press, Belknap), has brought together a volume which in organization much resembles Bailyn's. The essays here collected are of the last quarter of the eighteenth century and represent varied attitudes on such subjects as religion-and-education and female education. Some are specific, some general. Even the Calvinists among the authors are optimistic, representing the "fluid and plastic temper, the deep sense of a nation being formed, a people's character being shaped, the destiny of man everywhere being changed for the better." Benjamin Rush, Noah Webster, Simeon Doggett, Samuel Harrison Smith, and Samuel Knox are among the authors included. All the eight essays are genuinely democratic, agreeing with Jefferson that education must produce an aristocracy of virtue and talents.

From a literary point of view the two-volume anthology edited by Russel B. Nye and Norman S. Grabo, *American Thought and Writing* (Boston, Houghton Mifflin) is easily the most important of the year. Volume I, *The Colonial Period*, is strongly New England-oriented. The introduction includes a lucid explanation of the covenant-theology as a derivative of Calvinism, but its comparison-contrast of education in New England and the South is misleading, for it fails to mention—much less consider—plantation and free schools in the South. Maryland printing is overlooked, and the five kinds of verse included contain no Southern example for the entire colonial period. For all practical purposes *Puritans* seems to be synonymous with *colonial Americans*. There is no Dr. Alexander Hamilton, no Ebenezer Cooke, no Samuel Davies, no John Clayton (either of them), no Hugh Jones (any of them), and even no William Byrd. Volume II, *The Revolution and Early Republic*, covers a period in which Southerners could by no count be entirely escaped. Washington, Jefferson, Galloway, Harper, and Cartwright are here, but equally or more significant American thought is offered by the missing, e.g., Madison, George Mason, John Taylor, and William Wirt. The introductions to both volumes are well written and most discerning as far as they go, but point of view and mode of selection seem, particularly in Volume I, as conservative—or narrow and provincial—as they are in Barrett Wendell's literary history.

iii. Biography

Although there is considerable biographical information in several of the edited texts of diaries and journals noted above and in certain of the primarily critical studies noted below, only two books appeared which are essentially biographies. One of these represents the first generation of Virginia writers, the other a new interpretation of Franklin's life.

S. G. Culliford's *William Strachey 1572–1621* (Charlottesville, Univ. Press of Va.) is an assemblage of data on Strachey and his family and contains some analysis of his writings. Unfortunately it is a British dissertation of some fifteen years ago which the author has not brought up to date. More recent publications on John Smith and George Sandys, for example, supply information on the colony and even on such figures in Strachey's career as Sir Thomas Glover, information which might have improved the perspective and rounded out the picture. The text demonstrates no use of the few items of more recent date which have been added to the bibliography.

An already established reputable Franklin scholar, Alfred Owen Aldridge, in *Benjamin Franklin, Philosopher and Man* (Philadelphia, Lippincott), has attempted a study which mingles biography and criticism. The result is an intriguing if still enigmatic portrait of the subject as man and as philosopher. Aldridge declares Franklin's political philosophy remains the great intellectual puzzle of his life, in part the result of Franklin's reactionary social concepts and his practical benevolent ethics. The apparent paradoxes are resolved more satisfactorily in the book by Conner discussed below.

Aldridge has used many materials he himself uncovered and has taken full advantage of the edition of Franklin's *Papers* noted above. The author is very good on Franklin's French associations, on which he has published a book, and he handles multitudinous details with sympathy and a degree of objectivity as well as necessary selectivity. The declared emphasis is on the Philadelphia philosopher's complexity, but to many readers it will appear to be on the warmly human side of the subject, particularly his sex life, which receives most attention. In style the book leaves much to be desired. Chapters are short and sometimes appear truncated. Documentation (no annotation) consists of brief bibliographies by chapters which are not entirely satisfactory. The book does bear out the contention that Franklin fully deserved the inscription VIR under his portrait.

iv. Criticism and Literary and Cultural History

The Puritan, Quaker, and political mind in varied manifestations received a great deal of attention in 1965. Drama, fiction, musical literature, and verse were examined in books and essays. The writings of individuals from Anne Bradstreet to Woolman and Brown were the objects of analyses, brief and extensive.

Of the New Englanders, Bradstreet, Edwards, Taylor, and Cotton Mather were most frequently examined. Josephine K. Piercy, in addition to her edition of the poems noted above, published the first modern and extended study of the author in *Anne Bradstreet* (TUSAS). Professor Piercy aimed to analyze Bradstreet's poetry and prose for its revelation of the author's spiritual growth and her personal struggle with orthodoxy and also to trace her development as a writer. The result is a running commentary with quotations in which it is sometimes difficult to see evidence of spiritual growth, nor does there seem any more evidence of real struggle with orthodoxy than in an Edward Taylor. The writer rather naïvely assumes, in studying her subject's development in her art, that the departure from heroic couplets was an anticipation of the Romantic poets, when it seems in reality to show her kinship with the other baroque poets of her time and looks backward to Elizabethan freedom rather than forward. Bradstreet's love of nature may be paralleled in dozens of her contemporaries; one does not have to jump to Wordsworth to get a parallel. Perhaps some of the weakness in what the book attempts lies in the lack of sufficient biographical materials to frame a study of development. The author also seems little aware of the considerable body of similar religious poems based on the Bible in Sandys and his contemporaries.

The critical introduction and notes to Grabo's edition of *The Treatise Concerning the Lord's Supper* make it the most significant Taylor publication of the year, but there were others worth noting. Donald E. Stanford's *Edward Taylor* (UMPAW, No. 52), a brief study, emphasizes Taylor as the Calvinist poet whose prose and verse are extrapolations of his belief in the covenant of grace and prime examples of a Puritan working of an established tradition of which Baxter's *The Saints Everlasting Rest* is one example. Leo M. Kaiser and Stanford have together written on "The Latin Poems of 'Edward Taylor'" (*YULG*, XL, 75–81), proving by various means that these verses are actually the writing of Chauncy on the death of John Davenport. Donald Junkins, in "Edward Taylor's Revisions" (*AL*, XXXVII, 135–152), compares certain of Taylor's poems in the *Poetical Works* with drafts in his Manuscript Book, concluding that the final forms show meticulous craftsmanship in improving upon first jottings. Junkins finds 616 places in the "Preparatory Meditations" where Taylor revised—almost always for the better—substantives, meter, rhyme, and image. In sum, Taylor was an artist who had a procedure. Finally, Jean L. Thomas, "Drama and Doctrine in *God's Determinations*" (*AL*, XXXVI, 452–462), examines these poems of Taylor's and finds them nearer to the dramatic homiletic tradition going back to the Middle Ages than to either the morality play or the literary meditation. She examines *God's Determinations* in relation to a few of the sermons and devotional works which could have been known to Taylor and considers to what extent he may have used them to dramatic advantage.

Three essays are concerned with relatively minor phases of Cotton Mather's life and work. Phyllis Franklin, in "Mather's Desire for Membership in the Royal Society" (*AN&Q*, III, 70–71), takes up again the question previously raised by Manierre. Paola Jandolo, "Cotton Mather e la stregoneria" (*SA*, X, 9–56), discusses the Puritan priest's relation to witchcraft through a series of quotations from his writings with running commentary. The author feels that Calef's work was unjust to Mather by connecting him inseparably with a tragedy in which his part was but minor. William R. Manierre II, who has devoted a great deal of attention to this Puritan, in "A Description of 'Paterna': The Unpublished Autobiography of Cotton Mather" (*SB*, XVIII, 183–205), argues that the publication of this little-known work would serve no useful purpose, among other reasons because most of it is already in print or published paraphrase, as he demonstrates by a survey of its content.

J. A. Leo Lemay, in "Jonson and Milton: Two Influences on Oakes' *Elegie*" (*NEQ*, XXXVIII, 90–92), shows two places in *The Elegie upon the Death of the Reverend Mr. Thomas Shepard* (1677) unmistakably echoing Jonson's verse and another indebted to *Samson Agonistes*. Richard D. Birdsall in "Ezra Stiles and the New Divinity Men" (*AQ*, XVII, 248–258) sees the Yale president as moving gradually from the Old Light position toward the New and finally developing an Old Calvinist position supposedly as evangelical as the New Divinity but without its stern doctrine. John E. Van de Wetering, in "God, Science, and the Puritan Dilemma" (*NEQ*, XXXVIII, 491–507), employs Thomas Prince as an example of the Puritan endeavoring to buttress religion and morality with Newtonian science: "The result was too often bad science and a lost moral." Charles E. Clark (his bibliography of the literature of the Earthquake of 1755 has been noted above), in "Science, Reason, and an Angry God: The Literature of an Earthquake" (*NEQ*, XXXVIII, 340–362), examines the impact of that marvelous "Providence." Clark discusses some of the thirteen sermons and fifteen other works, some inveighings against a heedless people who had forsaken their Calvinistic God, others evidence of science struggling to be born, and almost all conscious examples of the uniqueness and special mission of America. On the whole, Clark sees few evidences in other writers of this literature of the unresolved science-religion conflict Van de Wetering saw in Prince's work. LeRoy Moore, Jr., in "Religious Liberty: Roger Williams and the Revolutionary Era" (*CH*, XXXIV, 57–76), looks back at the great iconoclast's thought and sees in it anticipations of Baptist elder John Leland, of Thomas Jefferson, and of James Madison.

The New England expatriate and Philadelphian Benjamin Franklin was the individual colonial most written about. Besides Aldridge's biography already noted, there were several essays on his career and writings, a study of his political theory and development, and one consideration of his "mind." Ralph L. Ketcham's *Benjamin Franklin* (New York, Washington Square Press, Great American Thinkers Series) finds "a marvelously harmonious and interesting human being who dealt constructively with an amazing range of problems during a long and fruitful life." Ketcham devotes chapters to his subject's early reading, his personal brand of deism, and his public philosophy as sage. Though clear and entertaining, this attempt at analyzing a great American thinker is astonishingly uncritical. There is a good summary composed in considerable part of quotations from Franklin, but there is none of the depth of analysis, no presentation of the paradoxical complexity, which other writers have seen in this mind. The book on Franklin's politics reviewed below is much superior on the political side of his mind, and Aldridge has insights Ketcham lacks. Ketcham has been too much impressed by Franklin's own word and has thus oversimplified or failed to face the apparent contradiction and paradox.

Paul W. Conner's *Poor Richard's Politicks: Benjamin Franklin and His New American Order* (New York, Oxford Univ. Press) is certainly the best book of the year on Franklin. Using an impressive number of primary and recent secondary sources, Conner suggests that Franklin possessed an integrated political theory of government inseparable from his views on economics and sociology. In successive chapters Conner probes the consistencies and apparent contradictions in Franklin's fifty-year development of a theory of harmonious order as the basis for a state. Objective, admitting weaknesses, balancing contemporary laudation with contemporary attack, this account is the best we have of the political theory of this Founding Father, as it sprang from eighteenth-century thought, events in Europe and America, Franklin's personal background and interests, and the classics. The book suggests more than it states. Its possible weakness lies in the occasional tendency to see in Franklin development from published political and social theory we have no evidence he ever read. It is on the whole a mature book from a young scholar.

The shorter pieces as usual reveal the many sides of Franklin's attractiveness. Richard Cary's "Benjamin Franklin, Printer-Plenipotentiary" (*CLQ*, Ser. VII, pp. 115–124) sketches pleasantly the avocational and professional interests of the envoy in England and France. L. W. Labaree, in "Benjamin Franklin's British Friendships"

(*PAPS*, CVIII, 423–428), discusses the associations with the naturalists, electrical scientists, and men of varied interest, almost all of
them great names in history. These personal relationships made
Franklin "this country's first great diplomatic representative." In
"Franklin's Suppressed 'Busy-Body'" (*AL*, XXXVII, 307–311), J. A.
Leo Lemay demonstrates how Bradford's suppression of the first
edition of the *American Weekly Mercury*, containing the addition to
the "Busy-Body No. 8," because the printer considered it too dan-
gerous to publish, has prevented our seeing that Franklin was very
early on the antiproprietary side. Julian Smith's "Coming of Age in
America: Young Ben Franklin and Robin Molineux" (*AQ*, XVII,
550–558) points out similarities of experience in the *Autobiography*
and Hawthorne's tale which appear to indicate that part of the inspiration for the latter came from the former.

Perhaps the finest study yet made of one of Franklin's sometime
fellow-citizens is Edwin H. Cady's *John Woolman* (New York,
Washington Square Press, Great American Writers Series), a little
book which surveys, and covers, a large mind. Cady sees Woolman
as "a genuine American saint" whose aesthetic and moral imagination
are as sorely needed today as they ever were. Acutely conscious of
the irony of Woolman's serenity in the presence of social enmity, the
author traces the Quaker's life and thinking in his writings, from
the early essays through the *Journal*. Each pamphlet or book is
weighed against or with the secular and religious mind of the time
and the social situations Woolman faced so directly, and each is
analyzed for structure, imagery, and spirit. The *Journal*, Cady points
out, was not kept but composed, partly in the tradition of Quaker
journals and partly as a work of art. Sympathy and depth of insight
mark the study from start to finish, and the last impressive chapter
demonstrates the relevance of Woolman's mind and spirit to the
American tradition from Jonathan Edwards to Martin Luther King.

A good summary of obvious and not-so-obvious aspects of Woolman's moral philosophy, including excellent examples and modern
parallels, is made by Phillips Moulton in "John Woolman: Exemplar
of Ethics" (*QH*, LIV, 81–93). Moulton like Cady feels that Woolman
has much to say to our day as he had to his, as an example of sensitivity and sympathy in a callous age.

Two essays concern Thomas Jefferson as writer and/or bibliophile.
George B. Watts's "Thomas Jefferson, the 'Encyclopédie' and the

'Encyclopédie methodique'" (*FR*, XXXVIII, 318–325) traces the Virginian's interest from 1780 in obtaining a set of the *Encyclopédie* and his later attempts to obtain the *Encyclopédie methodique*. Watts also shows how certain information supplied by Jefferson was twisted or distorted when it appeared in articles in these works and how his influence and ideas at least informed the authors of many other essays. William Raymond Smith, in "The Rhetoric of the Declaration of Independence" (*CE*, XXVI, 306–309), sees Jefferson's concept of order forming the basis for his great document and as responsible for the "quiet tone of measured deliberative statement of what exists." In other words, an understanding of Jefferson's assumptions about the nature of the universe is the best guide to an understanding of the sources of his rhetorical technique. Phrase and clause march by the logical necessity of their author's beliefs.

Several uncollected items are identified as the work of Jefferson's friend Freneau in Philip Marsh's "Freneau's Use of Addison's 'L'" (*PNJHS*, LXXXIII, 287–288). Marsh uses the initial to identify the authorship of numerous essays and poetic translations from 1790 to 1827. Another Jeffersonian is treated by Ira M. Thompson in *The Religious Beliefs of Thomas Paine* (New York: Vantage), a rather naïve and oversimplified treatment of Paine's concept of God and attitude toward Christian dogma.

Other political writers of the Revolution received brief attention. John W. Ellsworth's "John Adams: The American Revolution as Change of Heart" (*HLQ*, XXVIII, 293–300) sees Adams' shift from loyalty to independence as inspired not by polemical tracts such as those of James Otis, but actually by Adams' pondering of the tangible threats to liberty which the British actions in America represented. J. F. S. Smeall produces "The Evidence That Hugh Brackenridge Wrote 'The Cornwalliad'" (*PMLA*, LXXX, 542–548), giving textual, editorial, and biographical arguments to show that the friend of Freneau and Madison wrote the 720-line poem which appeared in the *United States Magazine* in 1779.

John Dickinson received somewhat more extensive treatment. In addition to Edwin Wolf II's essay noted above, there was the full-length study by David L. Jacobson, *John Dickinson and the Revolution in Pennsylvania, 1764–1776* (Berkeley, Univ. of Calif. Press), which surveys Dickinson's part in precipitating the American Revolution and analyzes his political system and methods through his writ-

ings (1774–1775). Jacobson concludes that Dickinson was not a
systematic thinker but a politician who spoke for the needs of his
time, his emphasis being upon the limits placed on government by
the people's necessities.

An interesting Anglo-American politico-literary connection is to
be seen in John R. Moore's "Defoe's 'Queries Upon the Foregoing
Act': A Defence of Civil Liberty in South Carolina" (*Hist. & Crit.*,
pp. 133–155). Defoe employed the accounts of the colony by Caro-
linians John Ash and Joseph Boone in his tract attempting to aid
the Dissenters against the Proprietary Government-High Church
party.

Late eighteenth-century writing which was primarily belletristic
received scattered brief attention, the largest part of it devoted to
Charles Brockden Brown. Kenneth Bernard, in "*Arthur Mervyn:
The Ordeal of Innocence*" (*TSLL*, VI, 441–459), sees this novel as
the author's "most complete portrait of the world around him, and as
such the closest of his books to the traditional English novel." Its
constant theme of "innocence and experience" ends in Mervyn's
acceptance of experience, in which he foreshadows the heroes'
decisions in Hawthorne, Melville, and James. Marisa Bulgheroni's
"Charles Brockden Brown tra il romanzo e la storia" (*SA*, X, 1964,
57–69) sees Brown as transforming the European conception of
romance in a tradition continued by Cooper and Hawthorne. Brown
appears as the originator of the realistic tale of the "truth of the
heart" balanced in the subtle position between the romance and the
novel continued by his greater successors including Melville, Twain,
and Crane. Paul Levine's "The American Novel Begins" (*ASch*,
XXXV, 134–148) also emphasizes the difference between the European and the American novel, seeing that difference essentially in
the nervous rhythm of the American variety. He surveys Brown's
work, especially *Edgar Huntly*, as the first fiction in which *movement*
becomes the subject of the novel. Harvey M. Craft, in "The Opposition of Mechanistic and Organic Thought in the Major Novels of
Charles Brockden Brown" (*DA*, XXV, 5926), again examines the
mental processes displayed, and Paul Witherington, in "Narrative
Technique in the Novels of Charles Brockden Brown" (*DA*, XXV,
2992), sees the fiction as a series of experiments with currently
fashionable forms only partially successful because of Brown's weakness in showing character in action or in moving his plot forward

by dialogue. Yet Witherington like others sees Brown as foreshadowing the techniques of the later American romancer. David B. Hirsch, "Charles Brockden Brown as a Novelist of Ideas" (*BBr*, XX, 165–184), points out in *Wieland* and *Ormond* Brown's attempts to project his own insights through character development, to depict men of ideas in action. Hirsch concludes that Brown's work is largely a failure because he could never successfully substitute any ideology for lost religious faith, or solve the quandary that action produces evil but that all men must act. And Jane T. Flanders has done a full-length parallel-source study in "Charles Brockden Brown and William Godwin: Parallels and Divergences" (*DA*, XXVI, 3334–3335).

Jack Bailey Moore's "Native Elements in American Magazine Short Fiction, 1741–1800" (*DA*, XXV, 5261) sees in the generally anonymous tales conscious attempts, as in the native drama mentioned below, to represent the uniquely American in the depiction of the Indian, the Negro slave, the Yankee, the Southerner, the middle class businessman, the Revolutionary War soldier, and less frequently the farmer, backwoodsman, and bluestocking. Amidst the conventional sentimentality are anticipations of later fictional fantasy and the comic as employed by Poe and Twain.

"Royall Tyler and the Question of Our Speech" (*NEQ*, XXXVIII, 454–474), by Roger B. Stein, suggests that "*The Contrast* is a sensitive register and indeed a dramatic statement of 'the question of our speech' [James's phrase] at a crucial juncture of American literary history." Tyler's play indicates the variety and quality of American speech, the patterns of metaphor, the speech as mask, a delight in wordplay. It marks the beginning of the search for "a supple national idiom" which yet continues. In "The Development of a Native Tradition in Early American Comedy" (*DA*, XXVI, 2752), Daniel F. Havens indicates how native dramatists from Tyler to Mowatt adapted British dramatic conventions to their own needs in a conscious attempt at literary independence. These adaptations appear especially in the clearly defined pattern of native characters, a tradition of earthy humor, and an insistent exploration of national and regional themes. Hugh F. Rankin's *The Theatre in Colonial America* (Chapel Hill, Univ. of N. C. Press) gives a good historical account, including first performances, amateur productions, the early repertory companies, plays, audiences, and prologues. He indicates that the Southern cities were overwhelmingly the most receptive to the theater. But there is little or nothing on theatrical criticism and little evaluation of the effect of the theater on culture generally. Newspaper sources have been used but some earlier manuscript materials in several repositories have been overlooked. The life and verse of a former slave is reconsidered in William H. Robinson's "Phillis Wheatley: Colonial Quandary" (*CLAJ*, IX, 25–38). The poet's divided loyalties and curious silence on the subject of human freedom particularly are examined. One explanation may be that she considered Negro slavery "providential," but there are apparently conflicting evidences which indicate that she merits further study.

Louis B. Wright looked once again at the minds of the first explorers and settlers in *The Dream of Prosperity in Colonial America* (New York, New York Univ. Press). The sixteenth- and seventeenth-century writings included in Hakluyt's *Navigations*, the records of the Virginia Company of London, John Smith, volumes on medicinal herbs to be found in strange places, the accounts of journeys into the interior by Bland, Clayton, and Spotswood, even the charter of the Ohio Company, are seen as indicative of the dreams of an economic utopia.

But again it was the Puritan mind that received greatest attention in the more general studies. Loren Baritz' *City on a Hill: A History of Ideas and Myths in America* (New York, John Wiley) attempts "to clarify the American qualities of thought in America." To do so, the author explores the writings of six major figures as indicative. Four of these, John Winthrop, Jonathan Edwards, John Adams, and John Taylor of Caroline, representing respectively political theology, theology, political theory, and agrarianism, fall within this period. The first two illustrate aspects of Puritanism: Winthrop the organic Christian community and the basic belief that some men are better than others and ought to be leaders; Edwards "the quintessential Protestant mind" and the original model for all later revivalism which has done permanent damage to the social history of the country. Adams was chosen over Franklin and Jefferson to represent the political mind because he was for Baritz the most systematic and interesting of the group. To balance Adams as political theorist is John Taylor of Caroline, who held in common with the three New Englanders the idea that Americans were God's guinea pigs and that this land was the hope of the world. The analyses of Adams and

Taylor frequently seem lacking in full perspective or background in the thinking of the period, and the conclusions regarding the men and their ideas are at least highly debatable.

More exclusively Puritan are the subjects of two essays. Howard H. Martin's "Puritan Preachers and Preaching: Notes on American Colonial Rhetoric" (*QJS*, L, 284–292) observes that the new clergy, while scorning Whitefield's arousing of the passions, placed their emphasis on warmth, naturalness, and appeal to human reasoning. Martin's assertion that few colonial preachers laid any importance on rhetoric is not convincingly supported by his evidence. Robert Middlekauf, "Piety and Intellect in Puritanism" (*WMQ*, XXII, 457–470), agreeing with those who believe Perry Miller gives too much attention to ideas and too little to religious emotion or piety, examines the writing of men such as Cotton Mather and Samuel Sewall to demonstrate that the "stretched passion" which was Puritanism had its origins in the mixture or fusion of piety and intellect in a complexity now impossible for us to understand fully. A third essay, J. J. McAleer's "Biblical Symbols in American Literature" (*ES*, XLVI, 310–322), devotes a small section to Puritanism as background for these symbols.

Irving Lowens' *Music and Musicians in Early America* (New York, W. W. Norton, 1964) devotes its initial chapters largely to the Puritan "Bay Psalm Book" and the Reverend John Tufts's *Introduction to the Singing of Psalm-Tunes (1721-1744)*, which he calls the first American music textbook. Not until Chapter V does he discuss a composer-librettist west of the Hudson. All the chapter-essays are informative, but the book is marred by the neglect of the music and composers of Williamsburg and Charleston and perhaps Philadelphia, who were as early and as active and able as most of those he does consider.

J. A. Leo Lemay, several of whose essays have been noted above, gives promise of producing a most valuable work on Southern writing in "A Literary History of Colonial Maryland" (*DA*, XXV, 7246), in which he outlines his treatment chronologically in ten chapters of a larger work on the major writers of the colony. The first three were producers of promotion literature (Andrew White, John Hammond, and George Alsop); then follow the poets and literati of eighteenth-century Maryland, including Ebenezer Cooke, Richard Lewis, Dr. Alexander Hamilton, James Sterling, Thomas Bacon, and Jonas

Green. This first literary history of colonial Maryland is being prepared for the press in book form. The résumé suggests that it will widen considerably our knowledge of the quantity and quality of Southern colonial literary expression.

Perry Miller's posthumous and fragmentary *The Life of the Mind in America from the Revolution to the Civil War* (New York, Harcourt, Brace and World) bears a misleading title, for only a few sparse references are devoted to the American intellect before 1800. The three sections, "The Evangelical Basis," "The Legal Mentality," and "Science—Theoretical and Applied," are repetitious, undocumented save in oblique references, and strongly in need of definitions. Miller's weakness in seeing New England's as *the* American mind is here accentuated, for he is concerned still largely with that region in a period when other sections were taking the lead in applied and philosophical thinking. The great intellectual historian's fractured reliques should never, in this reader's opinion, have been published without explanatory addenda.

University of Tennessee

10. Nineteenth-Century Fiction[1]

Louis J. Budd

Trends that were faintly discernible two years ago in the scholarship surrounding nineteenth-century fiction have now become clear and unmistakable. For example, we are witnessing a book explosion; evidently, more presses can afford to lose money on minor subjects. Likewise, openings abroad for commentary on American literature are multiplying, and the specialist aiming to read everything on his subject will soon need to know not only French and German but Italian and even Russian. Usually the interpretations done abroad depend on a critical pattern outmoded here, but one cannot be sure until he trudges through them.

In terms of the writers treated, some declines of reputation become more and more certain. Bret Harte challenges few modern minds; the heart of the Hamlin Garland matter has shrunk to whether he had integrity; William Gilmore Simms will not rise again before the scholarly edition of his works, if then. On the other hand, future attacks on Stephen Crane seem inevitable because he continues to get loving elaboration. Despite theories that only a masterpiece counts rather than its author, interest radiates from it to his lesser work. In a partly different case, James Fenimore Cooper is proving to be the most important rescue yet made by Natty Bumppo, whose admirers return to the entire range of Cooper's fiction with contagious gusto. As for William Dean Howells, 1965 brought another debunking essay but no slackening of persuasive appreciation.

i. Irving, Cooper, and Contemporaries

The year 1965 demonstrated Washington Irving's continuing ability to attract modest scholarly attention. As plans proceeded for the new authoritative edition of Irving's works, he was the benefi-

1. This essay excludes five major figures: Hawthorne, Poe, Melville, Mark Twain, and Henry James.

ciary of a major book: William L. Hedges' *Washington Irving: An American Study, 1802–1832* (Baltimore, Johns Hopkins Univ. Press). This work, which matches the eminence of Stanley Williams' biography, concentrates on the inward and the belletristic. Hedges deflates or drastically reshapes every generality about Irving, from the textbook notion that he founded the short story to the standard account of his final romanticism. Hedges demonstrates wide knowledge without faltering in his air of command, superbly merging aesthetic and—in its finest sense—socio-political analysis. He is especially cogent on the burlesque *History of New York*, the vital qualities of the "sketch" as Irving conceived and refined it, the strain of anti-progressive melancholy in our early literati, and the pose of "alienated observer" that dominated his later writing. By the time Hedges stops, one is convinced that his inventory of Irving is complete, that a basis for understanding the last books is triumphantly secure, even though the study ends with 1832. Hedges also draws so richly on Poe, Cooper, Hawthorne, and Melville that our early fiction seems, more than ever before, a shared grapple with New World experience.

Other work on Irving dealt with textual matters and influence. Eugene L. Huddleston, in "Washington Irving's 'On Passaic Falls' " (*AN&Q*, IV, 51–52), revived a little-known poem about a Paterson, New Jersey, landmark; John F. McDermott, in "An Unpublished Washington Irving Manuscript" (*PELL*, I, 369–373), uncovered a manuscript from his western trip; Peter Whyte, in "Deux Emprunts de Gautier à Irving" (*RLC*, XXXVIII, 1964, 572–577), demonstrated Irving's passing impact on Gautier.

Merit aside, the literary historian likes to trace the beginnings of American types. This he could do last year through an article by Joseph Arpad on Irving's contemporary Paulding: "John Wesley Jarvis, James Kirke Paulding, and Colonel Nimrod Wildfire" (*NYFQ*, XXI, 92–106). Arpad argues that Paulding's play *The Lion of the West* breaks ground in its use of an "original" or idiosyncratic character as its hero, a westerner given to Munchausen-like tales. Paulding also received further attention in a careful summary of his ideas on public values and manners: Ralph M. Aderman, "James Kirke Paulding as a Social Critic" (*PELL*, I, 217–229).

Cooper studies had an even richer year, keynoted by the willingness of Robert E. Spiller to come back to the dialogue with *James*

Fenimore Cooper (UMPAW, No. 48). With ripe wisdom and in spite
of his suggestion that Cooper developed toward the "realistic novel
of social purpose," this résumé follows the belief that "codified analysis" will miss Cooper's function as a "growing, vital and expressive
force" in a period when our culture stepped up its self-discovery. Another liberating insight comes from Sydney J. Krause, "Cooper's
Literary Offences: Mark Twain in Wonderland" (*NEQ*, XXXVIII,
291–311), which exposes the satanically unfair ridicule that too many
have enjoyed as germane to Cooper rather than revealing about
Twain. Also partly corrective, Richard E. Cunningham's "James Fenimore Cooper and the New England Mind" (*DA*, XXVI, 366–367)
concludes that Cooper "was basically more a Puritan than a Demo-
crat, and his long quarrel with New England was at its roots a case
of mistaken identity." To facilitate judging the real Cooper at this
very point, Warren S. Walker has edited *The Sea Lions* (Lincoln,
Univ. of Neb. Press), a preachy yarn for which others have claimed
too much lately.

Cooper's mind played vigorously through all his books, yet the
Bumppo legend keeps to the forefront. The inevitability of this
appears again in Kay Seymour House's "*The Pioneers*" in *The American Novel* (pp. 1–12). Though essays in that collection were hobbled
by the format for the Voice of America, Miss House elicits the
crammed richness in the first of the Leatherstocking novels. Mean-
while, taking up the one least discussed, Donald Darnell, "Uncas as
Hero: The *Ubi Sunt* Formula in *The Last of the Mohicans* (*AL*,
XXXVII, 259–266), contends that Natty is eclipsed by Uncas, "whose
movement to the position of dominance . . . Cooper skilfully develops" through investing the young chief with epic and mythic
qualities transcending the breathless plot. Two other essays on the
least admired of the five novels offer more provocative arguments.
Sargent Bush, Jr., "Charles Cap of *The Pathfinder*: A Foil to Cooper's
Views on the American Character in the 1840's" (*NCF*, XX, 267–
273), immerses it in Cooper's social battles, which inspired the tedi-
ously rigid Cap as a warning against "insusceptibility to new ideas
and a too ready willingness to base . . . judgments on insufficient
evidence." Returning to Natty as the center, G. Dekker, "*The
Pathfinder*: Leatherstocking in Love" (*BAASB*, No. 10, pp. 40–47),
feels that having Natty tempted to settle down as a husband reflects
Cooper's nostalgia over turning away from a naval "vocation" and

that committing him to a love affair forced changes in the patterns
of idea and structure that shaped the first three novels. In *Frontier:
American Literature and the American West* (Princeton, Princeton
Univ. Press), Edwin Fussell makes the Leatherstocking tales serve
for all of Cooper in arguing that he disengaged the frontier "metaphor" from its "literal origins" while eventually fusing questions of
"nature" with those of "highest civilization."

Natty also looms large in Kay Seymour House, *Cooper's Americans* (Columbus, Ohio State Univ. Press), which is particularly good
on *The Last of the Mohicans*, where—she demonstrates—he does
gain complexity despite his ceaseless tracking. Though organized
around Cooper's cultural types, her study does best by showing
that his memorable characters grew beyond their mold, that he
understood the age-old predicament of human nature much more
sensitively than we have thought, and that this understanding con-
tinually plumbed back to classical wisdom. She leaves us pondering
his grasp of inner tensions rather than drawing historical diagrams.

The latter kind of patterning, however, guides L. Moffitt Cecil in
the one significant piece of work on Simms last year: "Simms's Porgy
as National Hero" (*AL*, XXXVI, 475–484), which makes the plot of
Woodcraft teach that "through a natively inspired resourcefulness,
through a self-interest tempered by democratic idealism, through
determination, hard work, and faith, the colonists achieved unity and
strength." Whether anybody can expound Simms as a creator of in-
ternally viable characters remains to be seen.

Certainly no such approach works for Simms's inferiors, though
attempts persist, as in Edward Wagenknecht's *Harriet Beecher
Stowe: The Known and the Unknown* (New York, Oxford Univ.
Press). Ironic yet sympathetic toward Mrs. Stowe's inner life, he may
persuade some to give her fiction another chance. He particularly
upholds the quality of her topical masterpiece, as does Egbert S.
Oliver ("The Little Cabin of Uncle Tom," *CE*, XXVI, 355–361),
who declares that its "central and dominating metaphor," a "cabin
image," gives artful "form and meaning" to what so many find an
amateurish chronicle; still, as Albert Kaspin shows tangentially in
"*Uncle Tom's Cabin* and 'Uncle' Akim's Inn: More on Harriet
Beecher Stowe and Turgenev" (*SEEJ*, IX, 47–55), its appeal was
humanitarian. In *Theodore Winthrop* (TUSAS), Elbridge Colby

takes on an even steeper task of eulogy; well-prepared beyond question, he nevertheless gives ground on the fiction and finally rests Winthrop's fame on his swift-pacing style and his outdoor sketches. More a coincidence than sign of a boom, though again stressing the sparely vigorous style, Harold Dean Propst's "Theodore Winthrop: His Place in American Literary History and Intellectual History" (*DA*, XXV, 6600) deems him "one of the most attractive minor writers in his century" as well as a transitional figure between romance and realism.

ii. Local Color, Humor, and Post-Bellum Fiction

Nobody seems happy with local color nowadays. Choosing to pass over its sentimentalism, Claud B. Green, "The Rise and Fall of Local Color in Southern Literature" (*MissQ*, XVIII, 1–6), decides that the term itself, which has acquired a connotation of "second-rate," obscures the links between post-bellum and twentieth-century writers. Still, the once-acclaimed stories hold worthwhile point. Eugene F. Timpe, "Bret Harte's German Public" (*JA*, X, 215–220), reminds us that they continue to affect the image of America abroad; in a sound example of local color's value for social history, Robert Bush, "Richard Malcolm Johnston's Marriage Group" (*GaR*, XVIII, 1964, 429–436), codifies a "great deal about wedlock . . . as it was practised by the yeoman class of Middle Georgia." Virtually the only local colorist allowed much intrinsic merit, however, is Sarah Orne Jewett. In *Pioneers & Caretakers: A Study of 9 American Women Novelists* (Minneapolis, Univ. of Minn. Press), Louis Auchincloss praises her untangling of human motives; Jean Boggio-Sola's "The Poetic Realism of Sarah Orne Jewett" (*CLQ*, VII, 74–81) praises with more emphasis an "exceptionally refined emotive sensibility." A former rival, Mary Wilkins Freeman, endures primarily for a single story, in which David H. Hirsch ("Subdued Meaning in 'A New England Nun,'" *SSF*, II, 124–136) details rich subtleties before insisting on mythic and Freudian systems mostly foreign to her. Another rival receives a finely tooled monument in George McMichael's *Journey to Obscurity: The Life of Octave Thanet* (Lincoln, Univ. of Neb. Press), which strikes sparks between her Republican complacency and his implicit liberalism and catches her pathos in out-

living her relevance and wide prestige. The definitive study of the
local colorists, yet to be attempted, will find at least one sector
charted.

They usually had the saving grace of comedy, however, as Wade
Hall recognizes by including generous excerpts from them in *The
Smiling Phoenix: Southern Humor from 1865 to 1914* (Gainesville,
Univ. of Florida Press). Unfortunately he casts his net far too wide,
ending up with myriad sources, some clearly amateur; furthermore,
he merely hopes to display them as a "mirror of an age." *The Smiling
Phoenix* will serve mainly as a museum of scarce materials. Also
welcome for its generous excerpts, Robert L. Morris' *Opie Read:
American Humorist* (New York, Helios Books) genially takes a
third-rate wit on his own grounds; in many ways Read, we discover,
was a Mark Twain without the genius or self-torture, often good
copy yet bound to lose his appeal. Equally useful as a sampler, James
C. Austin's *Petroleum V. Nasby (David Ross Locke)* (TUSAS) fills
in the record of Locke's career and his endeavors to move into conventional fiction.

For George Ade (TUSAS) Lee Coyle reviews the mostly dull
facts in a breezy manner meant to fit his subject's style; instead of
trying to establish lasting merit for the prose fables, he squanders
two-thirds of his space, with many excerpts, on plays which dominated the commercial stage for a few seasons. A sharp contrast,
Milton Rickels' *George Washington Harris* (TUSAS) is packed, cogent, and original. It throws new light on Harris' life while adding
to the mystery: he was more talented yet more tormented than we
have realized. Likewise, it illuminates Sut Lovingood as the surrogate
for harsh, anarchic impulses otherwise repressed and uncovers an
"abyss of strange meanings" beneath his antics. Harris further gains
stature through M. Thomas Inge, who is digging out his stray pieces
for a scholarly edition, and reprints, in "G. W. Harris's 'The Doctor's
Bill': A Tale about Dr. J. G. M. Ramsey" (*THQ*, XIV, 185–194), a
hilarious, non-Sut sketch after the manner of Longstreet and Baldwin.

Local color could flourish in the post-bellum years partly because
competition was weak. Even so close a survey as Robert Falk's *The
Victorian Mode in American Fiction, 1865–1885* (East Lansing,
Mich. State Univ. Press) finds only Howells and James worthwhile
after a chapter on John William DeForest. Falk does accept DeForest
as the earliest sign that our novelists, while still conservative politi-

cally and hobbled by prim sexual mores, had started learning from the detached objectivity of European realists. James F. Light's *John William DeForest* (TUSAS) intends to judge his novels kindly, allotting equal space to any that are bearable; however, its ruling thesis is that DeForest, disheartened by reviewers and anxious to sell, wasted his talent by diluting realism with romance. In *"Miss Ravenel's Conversion"* in *The American Novel* (pp. 35–46), Claude M. Simpson, Jr., praises his masterpiece for its candidness so soon after the war and its mostly unflinching view of character.

Of DeForest's generation Tourgée is currently the most newsworthy because of his enthusiasm for civil rights long after the fervors of Reconstruction. Authoritative politically, Otto H. Olsen's *Carpetbagger's Crusade: The Life of Albion Winegar Tourgée* (Baltimore, Johns Hopkins Univ. Press) too seldom discusses his novels, in which his humane goals encouraged a weakness for melodrama. But his enemies in fiction who aimed to persuade as well as entertain now seem utterly empty. In *The Literary Career of Maurice Thompson* (Baton Rouge, Louisiana State Univ. Press), Otis B. Wheeler concedes that his subject is mired in "mediocrity"; still, instead of baiting Thompson fruitlessly, he gracefully restates that one-time Southerner's critical principles as typical of the genteel tradition adapted to Indiana. William K. Bottorff's *James Lane Allen* (TUSAS) spurns any falling back on social or even literary history. Proclaiming Allen a "minor master" with unique talents, Bottorff approves his theory of "romance" and his conveying of "myth" in modern dress; at least this may serve him better than appeals to his local-color qualities.

iii. Howells and His School

Criticism on William Dean Howells breathes determination to take a new look, marked by the title of Edwin H. Cady's "The Howells Nobody Knows" (*MRR*, I, 3–25). Though Cady had already alerted us to this Howells, he now highlights the sudden, unexpected turn into irrational psychology; he tends to fuse pre-Freudian delvings with taste for the occult yet earns the right to conclude that the "best of what Howells wrote in the twentieth century was neither untypical nor unworthy of it." The other extreme of the new look, William Wasserstrom, "Howells' Mansion and Thoreau's Cabin"

(*CE*, XXVI, 366–372), argues that he is finally admired as a self-made intellectual and that his aspirations came perilously close to those of Silas Lapham. More helpfully suggestive, Robert Falk's *The Victorian Mode* (see above) examines his first mature phase through then-current perspectives rather than later patterns or mere hindsight. Falk isolates an early kind of realism crucially different from the modern sense of the Howellsian vision.

Judging all of Howells, but using a late backdrop of ideas, Robert W. Schneider, *Five Novelists of the Progressive Era* (New York, Columbia Univ. Press), cuts down to his fondness for a saving remnant identifiable by "good" family and polished manners. With corollary insight Arthur M. Boardman, "Social Status and Morality in the Novels of William Dean Howells" (*DA*, XXVI, 1036), finds him favoring the upper social rank as the most moral and "deeply" committing his fiction to the status quo he criticized. Further implying his half-heartedness as a reformer, Phyllis-Joyce Holzschlag, "Howells' Portraits of Artists" (*DA*, XXV, 5906–5907), decides that his novels rang most true when ascribing "alienation, estrangement, and other artistic ills to individual failings." Clara M. Kirk's *W. D. Howells & Art in His Time* (New Brunswick, N. J., Rutgers Univ. Press) offers few such judgments and passes over the social complexities of taste; yet year by year, she piles up his reactions to the plastic arts, heightening our reading of countless passages in the fiction. Tracing a simple figure in the carpet, James Ellis, "William Dean Howells and the Family Home" (*CLAJ*, VIII, 240–245), cites instances of Howells' use of the domestic life as the touchstone for inward qualities.

Exploration of Howells is widening, although *The American Novel* (pp. 73–85) inevitably settles on "*The Rise of Silas Lapham*" by Robert Lee Hough, who concentrates on the tactical problems of that "antiromance." Nathalia Wright, *American Novelists in Italy* (Philadelphia, Univ. of Pa. Press), searches many books to map his lifelong, somewhat enigmatic taste for Italian ways. Digging deep on native grounds, Kermit Vanderbilt's "*The Undiscovered Country*: Howells' Version of American Pastoral" (*AQ*, XVII, 634–655) strikes unexpected nuances without claiming to unearth a major novel; it is eloquently persuasive about Howells' grasp of abnormal sexuality as well as pastoral motifs. It makes us decide that his ambition and craft had matured gratifyingly by 1880, but two other essays in

effect shake the usual notion that he was a slow bloomer. Daniel
Aaron, "Howells' Maggie" (*NEQ*, XXXVIII, 85–90), prints a fine
early sketch and points up its contrasting of maudlin fancy with
sordid fact. Compatibly, Myron Simon, "Howells on Romantic Fiction" (*SSF*, II, 241–246), bares layers of anti-sentimental irony in an
item from *Suburban Sketches* (1871).

Though setting a long example Howells had few working dis-
ciples. If Henry Blake Fuller had persisted, he could have headed
them, as proved by *With the Procession* (1895), which the University of Chicago Press reprints with an introduction by Mark Harris
keyed to the viably indecisive characters. Garland was eager, indeed
anxious, to assume Howells' or some other mantle, so anxious as to
incur the charge that his radicalism cooled too easily. But Kathryn
Whitford, "Crusader without a Cause: An Examination of Hamlin
Garland's Middle Border" (*MASJ*, VI, 61–72), pleads that he simply
realized that the farmers were not so beleaguered after all and that
the Single Tax had little relevance to the Midwest. More effectively,
Owen J. Reamer, "Garland and the Indians" (*NMQ*, XXXIV, 1964,
257–280), honors his support of the Plains tribes against encroach-
ment and his respect for their way of life. Still, these are extra-
literary grounds, while on the other hand Harold Frederic's admirers
now emphasize his art. In the process of drawing a strong link from
Frederic's characters to Sinclair Lewis', Charles V. Genthe, *"The
Damnation of Theron Ware* and *Elmer Gantry"* (*RS*, XXXII, 1964,
334–343), increases respect for the weight and penetration of Frederic's best novel. Tom H. Towers, "The Problem of Determinism
in Frederic's First Novel" (*CE*, XXVI, 361–366), offers a sound base
for *Seth's Brother's Wife* by finding it realistic in style yet incipiently
naturalistic in its "vision of humanity." Nothing much was heard of
Kirkland or Howe or Boyesen during 1965.

iv. Stephen Crane

The several biographies of Crane that must be in progress are getting
basic help. Marston LaFrance, "A Few Facts about Stephen Crane
and 'Holland'" (*AL*, XXXVII, 195–202), proves that he was gaining
repute during his darkest years; Joseph Katz, "Some Light on the
Stephen Crane–Amy Leslie Affair" (*MRR*, I, 43–62), fills in Crane's
hazy imbroglio with a neurotic; William Randel, "From Slate to

Emerald Green: New Light on Crane's Jacksonville Visit" (*NCF*, XIX, 357–368), nails down many details about his movements. As for his mental journeys, debate is focusing on whether his stripped-down ethic kept a religious core. Though alert to the vestiges of Christianity in *fin de siècle* rebels, Robert W. Schneider's *Five Novelists of the Progressive Era* fails to unlock any Crane riddles; heedless of Edwin H. Cady's warning that he blazed through many *isms*, Schneider discusses Crane as though his ideas never changed. Actually the exact reverse is true.

Crane early tried out a naturalism that clashed with his interest in radical protest. In "Stephen Crane and 'The Eternal Mystery of Social Condition'" (*NCF*, XIX, 387–394), Maurice Bassan makes "An Experiment in Luxury" nearly as intriguing as "An Experiment in Misery" for its method and cross-grained attitudes; Bassan's "An Early Draft of *George's Mother*" (*AL*, XXXVI, 518–522) uncovers a tentative sketch that clarifies the issues of Crane's last novelette about urban defeat. Donald Pizer, "Stephen Crane's 'Maggie' and American Naturalism" (*Criticism*, VII, 168–175), ably confronts his best known display of social conscience, declaring that it "is not so much about the slums as a physical reality as about what people believe in the slums and how their beliefs are both false to their experience and yet function as operative forces," that Maggie is destroyed not by her physical but her false moral environment. Here at least, Pizer detects Crane working more like a critical realist than a pupil of Zola.

Putting aside social morality or literary creeds—and again assuming a static problem—Neal J. Osborn, "The Riddle in 'The Clan': A Key to Crane's Major Fiction?" (*BNYPL*, LXIX, 247–258), decides that Crane followed a "cryptically but specifically religious, a Christian metaphysic and ethic" centered on brotherhood. Crane's other tales are virtually given a sabbatical, except for one seldom held vital despite Crane's satisfaction with it. Robert G. Cook, "Stephen Crane's 'The Bride Comes to Yellow Sky'" (*SSF*, II, 368–369), explicates its "funnel" image as the "perfect visual summation" for motifs that converge "inconclusively." But, feeling that it "has perhaps been misread more often than any other" of his stories, A. M. Tibbetts, "Stephen Crane's 'The Bride Comes to Yellow Sky'" (*EJ*, LIV, 314–316), warns against taking its comedy too portentously. Grappling directly with its intricate tones, Overton P. James, "The

'Game' in 'The Bride Comes to Yellow Sky'" (*XUS*, IV, 3–11),
suggests that Scratchy and the marshal realize that they have been
playing out an obsolete ritual.

Crane's most famous narrative is still getting almost overwhelmingly solemn scrutiny. In *The American Novel* (pp. 86–96) John
Berryman's "*The Red Badge of Courage*" emphasizes its uniqueness
of total effect. Eric Solomon adds a wry sidelight from a Union general who interpreted favorable reviews as disparagement of his army
("Stephen Crane, English Critics, and American Reviewers," *N&Q*,
XII, 62–64); and Solomon also finds anticipations of Crane in a magazine essay ("Yet Another Source for *The Red Badge of Courage*,"
ELN, II, 215–217). The record of influences takes a much bolder
step in Neal J. Osborn's "William Ellery Channing and *The Red
Badge of Courage*" (*BNYPL*, LXIX, 182–196), which matches passages to assert borrowings from the apostle of Unitarianism, especially from his discourse on "War" (1816); more broadly, Osborn
contends that the "extent of Crane's separation from pre-Darwinian
literary tradition is often exaggerated in contemporary criticism." Yet
Daniel Weiss, "*The Red Badge of Courage*" (*PsyR*, LII, 32–52, 130–
154), again looks forward—or much further back—in a Freudian
analysis that sets up a sophisticated Oedipal pattern for Crane and
then explains Henry Fleming from it, implying that Crane unraveled
the id with fine insight; as a grace note, Weiss extends his pattern to
"The Blue Hotel" with more success. However, a fresh cycle of Crane
readings may be the firmest prognosis, because William L. Howarth,
"*The Red Badge of Courage* Manuscript: New Evidence for a Critical
Edition" (*SB*, XVIII, 229–247), demonstrates that current texts are
not so meticulous as could be, and he underlines problems that involve key passages for the explicators.

Textual problems are surely uppermost for the poetry at present.
Charging "there is not even an adequate listing of the true editions
of the writings," Joseph Katz, "Toward a Descriptive Bibliography
of Stephen Crane: *The Black Riders*" (*PBSA*, LIX, 150–157), illustrates by correcting, refining, and extending the record for his first
important book of poems. Similarly, Katz's "Cora Crane and the
Poetry of Stephen Crane" (*PBSA*, LVIII, 1964, 469–476) tackles the
dismaying question whether her transcriptions are "faithful"; he concludes that they are "fairly dependable," though "prepared by one
with less sensitivity than a regard for established standards of 'cor-

rectness.' " Implicitly seconding the call for a definitive edition, Richard E. Peck, "A New Stephen Crane Poem" (*N&Q*, XII, 64–66), adds to the canon an item much closer to poetry than to any other standard genre although it has so far been treated as prose. In "Stephen Crane and Baudelaire: A Direct Link" (*AL*, XXXVII, 202–204), Peck also proves that another Crane poem condensed a recent translation of a prose-poem by Baudelaire. Presumably, Peck's two articles grew from "Method and Meaning in the Poetry of Stephen Crane" (*DA*, XXV, 5938).

v. Naturalism and Beyond

Partly because of the paradoxes in Crane, naturalism is being redefined. Insisting that it can be grasped best aside from realism or philosophic systems, Donald Pizer, "Nineteenth-Century Naturalism: An Essay in Definition" (*BuR*, XIII, 1–18), elicits two patterns common to *The Red Badge of Courage*, *Sister Carrie*, and *McTeague*: first, a tension between dully sordid doings and the excessive emotions they nevertheless betray; second, a tension between determinism and individual worth or an "affirmative ethical conception of life." Sister Mary Joanna Fink, "The Concept of the Artist and Creative Genius in American Naturalistic Fiction" (*DA*, XXVI, 2209), implicitly agrees with the second pattern when she concludes that Crane and Frank Norris, among others, diverged from "fatalistic" determinism by allowing one kind of character to function as a "self-made existential entity." Pointing up another divergence, Carvel Collins, "*McTeague: A Story of San Francisco*" in *The American Novel* (pp. 97–105), shows that Norris could drift into a sentimental, fuzzy primitivism. With the result of pushing him almost beyond serious regard, Robert W. Schneider's *Five Novelists of the Progressive Era* accuses Norris of echoing mostly conventional ideas about evil and retreating to a Spencerian notion of progress.

Warner Berthoff's *The Ferment of Realism: American Literature, 1884–1919* (New York, Free Press) virtually discards naturalism as a category. His title denies, in effect, that the heels of Howellsian realism were trod hard by one or more qualitative changes. Furthermore, though obviously undaunted by critical theory, he defines "realism" very flexibly as the drive to fathom objective and social reality—a definition that can apply to varied periods and genres. In fact he sees this drive, for the period staked out, as triumphing in the "literature of argument" by Sumner, Veblen, and William James. Acknowledging no major novelist except Henry James, he judges sternly not only Norris but also Howells and even Crane. But his discussion of them and many lesser authors is rewarding, even down to the local colorists. He further serves later nineteenth-century fiction by bracketing it with the rush onward, by ignoring 1900 as a supposed turning point. In short, he shakes us up, leaving no illusion of stability as scholarship and criticism roll on into 1966.

Duke University

11. Nineteenth-Century Poetry

J. Albert Robbins

Editions, rather than criticism, have constituted the most impressive work on nineteenth-century poets during the year. N. Scott Momaday's scholarly edition of Frederick Goddard Tuckerman seems to me to be of the greatest significance, for we have not until now had so complete and so thorough an edition of all of Tuckerman's work. Floyd Stovall has produced a useful new edition of Poe's poems, and Edd Winfield Parks and Aileen Wells Parks a variorum edition of Timrod's. Geoffrey Rans's short book on Poe and Albert J. Gelpi's longer one on Dickinson are sound and substantial. Of the shorter pieces, an article by Hyatt H. Waggoner on Dickinson (destined to become a chapter in a new study of American poetry) is perhaps the most ambitious and the best.

i. Edgar Allan Poe

a. **Texts and general studies.**   A scholarly edition is an event in any year, and this year brings the first one of Poe's poetry in almost half a century. Floyd Stovall has edited *The Poems of Edgar Allan Poe,* with an introduction, variant readings, and textual notes, and the University Press of Virginia, Charlottesville, has produced it in elegant format. The text is set in leaded ten-point italics, with titles in blue. Though there are line numbers, they are unobtrusive with such generous margins. Collations, textual notes, and variant texts are quite out of the way, but readily available through the index.

Stovall has included all of the poems in Poe's four volumes and the posthumous volume edited by Griswold, plus six poems now believed to be his and five of less sure pedigree. The record of textual changes is "reasonably complete," the editor says. Stovall's publication data are, of course, more complete than the record in Killis Campbell's fine pioneering edition (1917), for many printings have since been discovered; but Stovall has not attempted to duplicate, correct, or expand Campbell's background facts, critiques, or explications of words. Campbell, for example, has three hundred words on the term "Nicéan" in "To Helen"; Stovall has none. Stovall has, for the first time, printed *Politian* with act and scene divisions.

The introduction is a conservative one, summarizing the life (superfluous by now, it seems to me, in a volume of this sort), discussing the poetry as it changed during Poe's career, reviewing the reputation, and assessing the achievement. The tone of this essay is "academic" rather than critical, though these two terms need not necessarily be separate and discrete. In even a brief view of criticism it is odd to find two references to W. C. Brownell and none to Richard Wilbur. The volume is admirably conceived and executed and will quickly become the standard edition for scholars and, I would hope, general readers as well.

A good sampling of the *Literary Criticism of Edgar Allan Poe* can now be had in a paperback of some 150 pages. It is edited by Robert L. Hough (Lincoln, Univ. of Neb. Press), whose introduction places Poe as our first significant critic, "the first great American example of a romantic prototype—the writer as rebel, as defier, the artist inside society but not of it." He usefully sums up, both in the introduction and in the selections, Poe's theories of poetry and short fiction. All of the standard longer pieces are here and a sampling from reviews and "Marginalia." There is only one excerpt from Poe's criticism on drama, although Poe wrote extensively on the theater and has been called our first serious drama critic.

Two new Poe letters have appeared. One written to Eli Bowen October 18, 1848, is printed from a transcript which Thomas O. Mabbott received years ago from J. H. Whitty. He long thought it a forgery, but now considers it genuine ("Poe Letter about 'The Raven,'" *AN&Q*, III, 67). After a passing remark about his poem, Poe says, "I am willing to accept your offer about the Correspondence," but no paper with which Bowen was associated in 1848 shows any evidence of Poe's having contributed. The other is a one-sentence note to E. L. Francher, his attorney in the Thomas Dunn English lawsuit, authorizing payment of damages to Mrs. Clemm. It is dated Fordham, N. Y., March 28, 1846 (Floyd Stovall, "An Unpublished Poe Letter," *AL*, XXXVI, 514–515).

I find much to admire in Geoffrey Rans's *Writers and Critics* volume, *Edgar Allan Poe* (Edinburgh, Oliver and Boyd). On the

first page of the biographical first chapter Rans doubts that total
illumination can come from such a careful biography as A. H. Quinn's
for, he says, "One can imagine Poe, the solver of the mystery of
'Maelzel's Chess Player,' enjoying the puzzle of his own life." Later,
in a discussion of *Pym*, he wonders whether the "novel" is just abor-
tive or whether it is "a monstrous joke, always a possibility with Poe."

There is good reason, too, to open an evaluation of Poe's work
with a chapter on *Eureka* and Poe's criticism, for from the beginning
he was the compulsive, and the professional, critic. It is well to have
these convictions in mind before we look at the poetry and the fiction. It is well to have on record such dicta as these: "The poet aims
then, for a moment, to free man from the shackles of time, and rein-
state him in the eternity he has lost, to present man with a vision of
unity in his world of chaos" (p. 28); "The interpenetration of Poe's
sense of universal harmony and symmetry with his aesthetic can
hardly be overstressed, for it is, in this work [*Eureka*], and in his
work as a whole, obsessive" (p. 37). There is, as Mr. Rans observes,
a "sense of the corruption of the world" or, as Poe put it, "the cir-
cumscribed Eden of [our] dreams."

As to the poetry, Mr. Rans believes that, by design, "the reader
must guess, reach through the poem." "When the reader feels that he
has been led to an encounter with some strange other world that
defies explanation, Poe has succeeded" (p. 41). Poe's "point of departure is always a time-ridden, fallen, rationalistic world, to which the
imagination is an ambassador of eternity" (p. 45) and, with language,
he is "thrusting beyond denotative meaning, an attempt to force
words to do what is beyond their design" (p. 64).

On Poe's fiction, he says: "His disgust with the world in which
he lived is shared by many of his American contemporaries, although
he does not share their disappointment, for, from the beginning, he
did not share their hopes." Like Emerson and Cooper he pledged
allegiance to the intuitive, not the rational. "He shared with them
also a yearning for a lost world. Poe's is a Glimmerglass entirely of
the mind; both Cooper and Poe needed a myth to set against their
sense of man's inadequacy" (p. 94). As a last chapter, Mr. Rans surveys scholarship and criticism perceptively.

A comparative article by Nathan Lyons on "Kafka and Poe—and
Hope" (*MinnR*, V, 158–168) has interesting things to say about both

authors. There are obvious similarities: they suspect the "real" world they inhabit and see it often in terms of horror; they "create no characters in any traditional sense" and their protagonists are plagued by "an inexorable loneliness," friendship being impossible; "their tales exist out of time"; and their brand of humor is "odd."

b. Tales. Style is not always easy to describe and explain, but with such a writer as Poe, who is especially alert to the force that can be had by stylistic effects, it is of essential importance. Donald B. Stauffer ably explores "Style and Meaning in 'Ligeia' and 'William Wilson'" (*SSF*, II, 316–330), noting the incantatory quality, metrical effects, parallelism, repetition, inversions, and parenthetical expressions that characterize the former. Words, rhythms, sentence patterns in "Ligeia" all work to evoke, not to enlighten. Except for the emotionalism of the opening and closing paragraphs of "William Wilson," the style is analytical and intellectual. Poe's purposes demand an air of rationality and logic as the narrator strives to tell precisely what happened. Here we have the language of analysis, not the language of emotion, and so find Poe writing an ordered prose, thoughtfully periodic, with measured rhythm and mannered, often Latinate, diction. The two stories serve beautifully to illustrate Poe's virtuosity and firm control of differing styles.

In an eighteen-page pamphlet Susan Solomont and Ritchie Darling offer a reading of *Four Stories by Poe* (Norwich, Vt., Green Knight Press). They discuss "The Pit and the Pendulum" interestingly, but in "The Masque of the Red Death" the conclusion ("art will fail if it does not include all") seems to me forced. Comments on "The Cask of Amontillado" seem weakest of all (Mr. Randall's analysis [see *ALS, 1964*, p. 124] I find much more convincing). They consider "The Tell-Tale Heart" a profound and timeless study of insanity in which the lantern is "a symbol of consciousness (within) and projection (without)." The projection is first upon the screen of the blind, filmy eye; later, with removal of the eye, it needs no natural screen, transforms itself into auditory form, and moves swiftly to self-destruction.

The nature of the psychological themes principally concerns E. Arthur Robinson in his examination of "Poe's 'The Tell-Tale Heart'" (*NCF*, XIX, 369–378). "The thematic repetition and variation of incident" form the architectural principle of the tale, and the subjective, psychological handling of time gives it its force. Of the three elements—stimulus, internal response, and action—Poe dwells upon the second to an extreme degree and the greatest intensity comes when the relation between objective and subjective time sense falters or fails. Finally, the ultimate intensity comes with psychological identification of the man murdering with the man murdered: mistaking his own heartbeat for that of his victim, the "Evil Eye" becoming an "evil I."

And now we have the fall of the house of Usher as a parable of "the faltering Enlightenment orientation." Madeline is a "child of the Enlightenment" placed by her twin in a place of *no* light. As the house splits and sinks out of sight, "the Enlightenment orientation and the Enlightenment man are swallowed up together." So argues Michael J. Hoffman in "The House of Usher and Negative Romanticism" (*SIR*, IV, 158–168).

c. **Source studies.**   Parallels, echoes, conjectural sources, and influences are, in general, a grubby business and Poe has always seemed to attract more of this sort of scholarly attention than most of his contemporaries. Still, the accretion of findings and hunches may, for someone, some day, yield unforeseen results. Three articles seem significant or interesting to me. The others I shall refer to briefly.

"Poe's Reading of the British Periodicals" was extensive and his use of ideas, concepts, and even phrases found there was probably extensive. J. Lasley Dameron (*MissQ*, XVIII, 19–25) tells us that Poe made a total of ninety-one references to the titles of British magazines and newspapers in his letters and formal writings. Not only are there stylistic similarities but also the same critical terminology. A thorough examination (beyond the five samples given here) might show that Poe learned, here, more than we generally think.

The assumption that William Godwin's influence on Poe came through an intermediary such as, for example, Charles Brockden Brown, is wrong, according to Burton R. Pollin ("Poe and Godwin," *NCF*, XX, 237–253). In fourteen instances, here described, Poe showed a direct knowledge of and respect for Godwin's fiction, though he largely ignored, or was ignorant of, Godwin's social ideas.

David L. Carson's article "Ortolans and Geese: The Origin of

Poe's *Duc de L'Omelette*" (*CLAJ*, VIII, 277–283) is ingenious but ingenuous in proposing it as *the* origin. The thesis is that the tale is a disguised barracks satire based on the West Point days. An escapade in which Poe was involved forms the basis of the narrative: a roommate, Gibson, went surreptitiously to an adjacent inn and brought back a goose, which he bloodily decapitated outside the room. Poe arranged the hoax: Gibson came in and vowed he had killed a particularly hated officer, produced the knife that he had used, and flung the bloody goose at the sole candle in the room. A visitor from another barracks fled through the window and the third roommate, Jones, cringed in horror in a corner. In the tale, the Duc expires before the ortolan (goose); the austere cot of Jones becomes the "notorious ottoman of Cadêt" (remove the circumflex and you have cadet); the home of the ortolans, "far Peru," derives from Peru, New York, a city noted, according to a 1911 gazetteer, for the production of victuals; etc. It is all fascinating but unconvincing. Mr. Carson is aware that the tale has been seen as a satire on N. P. Willis (and it *is* difficult to bring Willis into the West Point context), but he is unaware of K. L. Daughrity's article (1933), "Poe's 'Quiz on Willis.'" That piece explains far more details in the tale than Carson's does.

As to the other articles, Burton R. Pollin finds "the major source" of "The Spectacles" in a London literary-fashion magazine of 1836 (*AL*, XXXVII, 185–190). Sinclair Snow sees "The Similarity of Poe's 'Eleonora' to Bernardin de Saint-Pierre's *Paul et Virginie*" (*RomN*, V, 40–44). Lodwick Hartley proposes a real-life model of the house of Usher in the eccentric John Hall-Stevenson's seat of residence in Yorkshire, familiarly known as "Crazy Castle" ("From Crazy House to The House of Usher: A Note Toward a Source," *SSF*, II, 256–261). Gerald E. Gerber notes the ingredients of aristocratic setting, masquerade festivities, and appearance of death in a book of etiquette which Poe reviewed ("Additional Sources for 'The Masque of the Red Death,'" *AL*, XXXVII, 52–54). L. Moffitt Cecil feels that the multi-colored Virginia springs, widely discussed in the *Southern Literary Messenger* and elsewhere, are converted into the unnatural water on the island of Tsalal in *Pym* ("Poe's Tsalal and the Virginia Springs," *NCF*, XIX, 398–402). Bulwer Lytton's "Monos and Diamonos" has been proposed as a source for three tales, and Burton

R. Pollin suggests a fourth in "Bulwer Lytton and 'The Tell-Tale Heart'" (*AN&Q*, IV, 7–9). Finally, Schiller's "Song of the Bell," proposed by Killis Campbell as a source of Poe's poem, could have come to Poe's attention, Kenneth Walter Cameron says, in Romberg's musical version of the poem, either in concert performance or in the 1837 printed score. J. O. Bailey's introduction to John C. Symmes's *Symzonia, A Voyage of Discovery (1820)* (Gainesville, Fla., SF&R) summarizes Poe's use of this curious work on polar holes and intra-terrestrial civilizations and proposes it as "the earliest American Utopian fiction."

d. **Miscellaneous.** Arnold Smithline contends (without convincing me) in "*Eureka*: Poe as Transcendentalist" (*ESQ*, No. 39, pp. 25–28) that he came very close to the position of the Transcendentalists. The more proper term for Poe's views may be pseudo-Transcendentalism, for Poe's fixation is not upon man but upon an all absorbing (hence destructive) Unity. Poe's "final vision," says Mr. Smithline, "is not a descent into the maelstrom of nothingness but a positive assertion of man's divinity."

An Italian article by Sergio de Marco, " 'Eureka' di Edgar Allan Poe (per una interpretazione)" (*RLMC*, XVII, 1964, 265–284), contributes little. It contends that the ideas and the interest in astronomy were a phenomenon of the times; that, in view of these interests, *Eureka* is not an eccentric work; and that, considered with Poe's tales, it is not unique in his own body of writing.

A fellow Virginian and a writer disposed to favor Poe wrote a review of the first two volumes of Griswold's edition of Poe's *Works*. Apparently it was never printed, but Richard Beale Davis has resurrected it from the manuscript copy in the Library of Congress ("Moncure D. Conway Looks at Edgar Poe—Through Dr. Griswold," *MissQ*, XVIII, 12–18). Conway criticized what was omitted, not aware that a third volume was coming, and said that the volumes will fall "very far short of public expectation." What is notable is that Conway does not detect Griswold's slanders.

A dissertation done at Fordham measures Poe against a concept expounded by the contemporary German theologian, Rudolf Otto (Seaborn L. Varnado, "The Numinous in the Work of Edgar Allan Poe," *DA*, XXVI, 3964–3965). The numinous is "a feeling of mystery, awe, and fascination that arises in man when he encounters the

Wholly Other." It can apply to both sacred and profane. The numinous can be found in Poe's poetry and prose; thus, the curious conclusion: this helps "to exonerate Poe from charges of immaturity"!

ii. Tuckerman, Holmes, Lowell, Longfellow, Whittier, Higginson, Read, Bryant, Cottle

The most significant publication by or about New England poets is N. Scott Momaday's edition of *The Complete Poems of Frederick Goddard Tuckerman* (New York, Oxford Univ. Press). Perhaps it will help to bring this fine poet into fuller recognition. It has long distressed me that the routine college anthologies consistently ignore Tuckerman (the remarkable exception being George F. Whicher's *Poetry of the New England Renaissance*).

We shall long be indebted to Witter Bynner for his 1931 edition of the sonnets but, as this volume makes clear, Bynner took some liberties with the text and had access to only a portion of Tuckerman's work. Mr. Momaday gives us a complete (but not a variorum) edition and, as he takes care to explain, he himself has taken certain liberties with the printed and manuscript texts, so that even now we read Tuckerman through the judgment of an intervening editor. Momaday's introduction is thoughtful and illuminating, but the foreword by Yvor Winters is unnecessary.

In 1857 Holmes sent a long poem to John Lothrop Motley for criticism. Motley's annotations reveal much about the taste of the time and about the rigid concepts of the Ideal and the Actual derived from German sources and from Blair's *Lectures on Rhetoric*, Eleanor M. Tilton says in "Holmes and His Critic Motley" (*AL*, XXXVI, 463–474). Motley's taste—impeccable then but ridiculous now—approved of trite stereotypes, encouraged the insipid, and rebelled against any hint of realistic details. Holmes dutifully followed the advice, and emasculated many good lines and details. "Ho! lazy boatman, scull your dory here!" Motley found too direct and too imperative, so Holmes changed it to "A boat shall waft us from the outstretched pier." Such preference for the trite "Ideal" over the more forceful "Actual" derives from a critical formula, not from prudery or the genteel tradition, Miss Tilton believes. This may be a more potent force than we generally realize. Regarding "Holmes' 'The Deacon's Masterpiece'" (*Expl*, XXIV, Item 17), Howard Webb says that it does more than attack such logical systems as Calvinism; it suggests, in stanza three, a system that may "*break down*, but doesn't *wear out*." This "emphasis on healing, sets forth the same theological empiricism as that of the physician in *Elsie Venner*." Lyle H. Kendall, Jr., in "Dr. Holmes, Allibone's *Dictionary*, and Dr. Mackenzie" (*PELL*, I, 181–183) prints an unpublished letter of 1858 in reply to Holmes's receiving proof of an article on his father and himself for Allibone's *Critical Dictionary of English Literature*. It principally shows Holmes's desire for some notice of his later work (pieces in the *Atlantic Monthly* and particularly "The Chambered Nautilus") to offset "my early and sometimes immature and trivial efforts."

In an article that is short but admirably selective in its details, C. M. Lombard discusses "Lowell and French Romanticism" (*RLC*, XXXVIII, 1964, 582–588). After a glance at his opinion of earlier French writers, Mr. Lombard admits Lowell's disapproving views of Hugo (a ludicrous would-be "re-organizer of the moral world"), Chateaubriand (an "arch-sentimentalist"), Lamartine (the "mere lackey of fine phrases"), and Rousseau (founder of a school with a "sickly taint"), but he calls attention to Lowell's more approbatory moments in which, for example, he could see Rousseau as father to such remarkable lineage as Cowper, Wordsworth, Byron, Chateaubriand, Victor Hugo, and George Sand. "Impatience . . . with the immature whims and moods of the Romantics did not keep Lowell from acknowledging they produced works replete with harmony and color." In general, "throughout Lowell's analysis of French Romanticism there is an intermingling of Yankee common sense and a highly developed literary cosmopolitanism." A dissertation by William J. De Saegher (*DA*, XXV, 1964, 3551) looks at Lowell's use of the Bible and observes that, although Lowell's mature view was to deny it as God's final word to man, he did recognize its ethical and literary worth.

The Longfellow scholarship for the year consists of an involved German argument for conjectural authorship, two articles on foreign interests, and an explication. In "Der Autor von 'David Whicher' und das Geheimnis der grünen Brille" (*JA*, X, 106–125), Alfred Weber reviews, reasons, argues, and speculates. Hans-Joachim Lang, who discovered the anonymous story in the *Token* for 1832, proposed John Neal's authorship. Irving T. Richards thinks it might be Hawthorne's.

Weber proposes Longfellow for several reasons: his being at Bowdoin at the time (the story is dated, "Bowdoin College, June 1, 1831"), his possibly having visited the locale of the story, his having planned a New England sketch book in which this tale might fit, Longfellow's known contributions to the *Token*, and so on. Nothing is finally demonstrable, beyond the zeal of the scholars. Harvey L. Johnson thinks that Longfellow's awareness of Portuguese literature is generally unnoted and corrects the matter in "Longfellow and Portuguese Language and Literature" (*CL*, XVII, 225–253) by noting his awareness of the Portuguese language as early as 1830 and substantial recognition of Portuguese literature in *The Poets and Poetry of Europe* and in *Poems of Places*. Johnson quotes a letter to James E. Hewitt, not generally known, on a translation of Camões and gives brief attention to Portuguese translations of Longfellow's work. How pervasive Longfellow's international influence could be Samuel A. Golden illustrates in "Longfellow, Potgieter, and Pijnappel" (*AL*, XXXVII, 312–315) by telling us the lengths to which the romantic and nationalistic Dutch poet, Everhardus J. Potgieter, went in repeatedly citing Longfellow's poetry as a model of fruitful poetic expression of the present. These efforts to redirect Dutch poetry succeeded generally, and specifically with one Jan Pijnappel, who heeded the message and produced a masterful Dutch translation of "The Village Blacksmith." The direction which Dutch poetry took after 1860 owes much to Longfellow—and Potgieter. G. Thomas Tanselle disagrees with George Arms that "Longfellow's 'Serenade' " (*The Spanish Student*, I, iii, 8–31)—the well-known "Stars of the summer night!"—could be better rearranged (*Expl*, XXII, Item 48). As it stands, the pattern of the lyric "is an intricate play on the meanings of the remote and the near, of the concrete and the abstract, a reflection of the corresponding intense subjectivity, heightened imagination, and shifting values characteristic of a lover's state of mind."

Scholars' Facsimiles & Reprints (Gainesville, Fla.) has added Whittier's *Legends of New England (1831)* to its list. In his introduction, John B. Pickard largely agrees with the general view that it is an imperfect first work. "Most of the tales . . . are marred by Whittier's crude technical execution, digressive structure, and moralizing tone," with the poems being "far superior" to the prose sketches. Pickard agrees with others that "The Black Fox" is the best of these. John M. Moran, Jr., has found "Eight Ungathered Whittier Poems"

in Garrison's *Liberator* and photographically reproduced them
(*ESQ*, No. 38, pp. 92–95).

For twenty-seven years Higginson reviewed contemporary poetry. It was a slack time for the muse, with people like Taylor,
Aldrich, Carman, Gilder, and Van Dyke in business. In examining
this enterprise, Edgar L. McCormick ("Thomas Wentworth Higginson, Poetry Critic for the *Nation*, 1877–1903," *Serif*, II, iii, 15–20)
tries to tell us that he was not as bad—as typical of the weak side of
the genteel tradition—as he is generally regarded. Granted, his materials were shoddy, in large part; but when such a new voice as
Stephen Crane appears, Higginson cannot abide its violent thrust,
though he does sense real promise in the early Robinson. The summary, however, is useful and there is an author checklist of Higginson criticism covering sixty-three names.

In two articles in the *CLQ*, five of Higginson's letters are printed,
with editorial comment. In Donald H. Williams' "T. W. Higginson
on Thoreau and Maine" (Ser. VII, pp. 29–32) a letter written in
1908 concerns Thoreau's *Maine Woods* and a recent article on it.
Higginson refers to H. G. O. Blake as "Thoreau's most intimate
friend & outdoor companion." In Richard Cary's "More Higginson
Letters" (Ser. VII, pp. 33–48) are four more letters, written from
1886 to 1889 on matters too routine to concern us here.

The William H. Venable who wrote *Beginnings of Literary Culture in the Ohio Valley* (1891) read a paper on Read to "The Literary Club" of Cincinnati in 1894. It is here first published, edited
with an introduction by Gene D. Lewis, as "Personal Recollections
and Anecdotes of Thomas Buchanan Read" (*CHSB*, XXIII, 273–
285). Being a discursive recollection by an acquaintance, it gives a
sense of the warmth and affability of Read, who longed to write one
immortal poem, but never did.

A dissertation by Rebecca Rio Jelliffe on Bryant's theory and
practice of poetry (*DA*, XXV, 4148–4149) considers the former as
being "an integrated system of principles founded on the basic conception of eighteenth-century associationism in England and Scotland: poetry is primarily the communication of emotion, the 'language of passion,'" and nature is the chief source of creative emotion.
In theory and practice, Bryant's was "the first systematic formulation
and application in America of associational aesthetics."

Finally, a curious, rough, and at times charming autobiographical

poem is published and its author described by William G. McLough-
lin in "The Life of Elder Jabez Cottle (1747–1820): A Spiritual Autobiography in Verse" (*NEQ*, XXXVIII, 375–386). Here in 294 lines
of verse, chiefly in heroic couplets, is a piece of true genre poetry
full of fact and piety. After a long life of whaling, soldiering, farm-
ing, preaching, and fathering ten children—and now that he is sev-
enty-three and infirm, so that he has "opportunity and time" for
writing his story in verse—he sets it down so that "When this you
read you will remember me."

iii. Emily Dickinson

The year's most ambitious work is *Emily Dickinson, The Mind of
the Poet* (Cambridge, Mass., Harvard Univ. Press). It is no work to
consult for concentrated readings of individual poems, for Albert J.
Gelpi is interested in Dickinson in motion: her repeated forays out
from consciousness and back again in restless search for self and the
place of self in the larger (but not greater) world without—the Me
and the Not-Me; her evolving personality and relationships with
others; and Dickinson's place historically from Taylor to Ginsberg.
It is in this latter movement that we find the book's central thesis.
Mr. Gelpi's chief views here are in Chapter IV, "Seeing New Eng-
landly: From Edwards to Emerson to Dickinson," and in Chapter
VII, "The Tightening Circle." As regards poetic craft, "she did not
belong to the prophetic or Dionysian strain of American poetry which
derived palely from Emerson and descended lustily through Whitman to Carl Sandburg and Jeffers"; rather she is associated with "the
diverse yet Apollonian tradition which proceeds from Edward Taylor
through her to Eliot, Stevens, Frost, and Marianne Moore, and thence
to Robert Lowell and Elizabeth Bishop" (p. 146). More than once
the author claims a pivotal role for Dickinson. In one instance he
puts it this way: her tiny poems "express—more than *Walden* or
Leaves of Grass—the crucial struggle within the American sensibility.
In the perspective of history Dickinson is the pivotal point in the
tension between Edwards' perception of types and Stevens' elaboration of tropes" (p. 161). Which is to say that she stands between a
colonial symbology of meaning or revelation and a modern symbology of world-cult and doubt. Looking, of course, more to the
latter than to the former; more to the modern than to the traditional.

"Her peculiar burden," he tells us, "was to be a Romantic poet with a Calvinist's sense of things; to know transitory ecstasy in a world tragically fallen and doomed" (p. 91).

Chapters V and VI consider the other large issue of consciousness. It is here that we see the essential Dickinson, the problem that is her chief concern. With her there is a unique fusion of self and art and again Mr. Gelpi claims the pivotal function for her: more than her two great predecessors, Emerson and Whitman, words—indeed, *the* word was vital. Her astringent economy of language becomes the key to unlock meaning, or display vision, just as it is at the same time the means of aesthetic power.

A more modest book is one in the Writers and Critics series (Edinburgh, Oliver and Boyd) in which Douglas Duncan examines *Emily Dickinson*. It serves adequately as a brief introduction of the poet to the general British reader, but there is not much here to inform scholars or the knowledgeable reader. The final chapter, reviewing scholarship and criticism, is too abridged to be very helpful.

Richard B. Sewall's *The Lyman Letters: New Light on Emily Dickinson and Her Family* are doubly available in *MR* (VI, 693–780) or as a hardcover book (Amherst, Univ. of Mass. Press). Family papers still in the hands of descendants tell us much about Joseph Bardwell Lyman (1829–1872), who was distantly related to the Dickinsons, was a schoolmate of Austin, a house guest in the Dickinson home in 1846, and one of Vinnie's beaus. It is in his letters to Laura Baker, his future wife, that we learn of his deep attachment to the Dickinson family and of his fond memory of pleasant days in Amherst. Laura must have tired of all the references to his early love. Vinnie he called "my Maud in her garden of roses by the old Manorial hall." He remembered "her kisses—those kisses!—It is 7 years ago now since I kissed her among the crocus flowers." And he recalled "gentle, tender, white armed Vinnie!" But Vinnie was not enterprising enough to break home ties and win such a handsome, ambitious, and worthy man as he, he thought immodestly. The letters give us glimpses of happy carefree days in the Dickinson home in the forties, and even austere Father Dickinson has his pleasant side.

The original letters from Emily and Vinnie are lost, but enough survives in Joseph's memory to give us a good sense of the Dickinson family and of his courtship of Vinnie. Emily figures incidentally, except for one piece in Lyman's hand that shows his more than

casual interest in the sister. It is headed "EMILY." Lyman recalls
her hands as "small, firm, deft but utterly emancipated from all clasp-
ings of perishable things" and her "mouth made for nothing & used
for nothing but uttering choice speech, rare thoughts, glittering,
starry misty figures, winged words." There are excerpts from her
letters, in which Father "seems to me often the oldest and the oddest
sort of a foreigner" and in which she asserts that "My Country is
Truth." She speaks of wide excursions in the Bible, which she finds
"infinitely wise" and "merry"; of words ("I dont know of anything
so mighty"); and of bumble bees. One excerpt clears up the speculation about her telling Higginson about "a terror" she had "since September." It is not a reference to Wadsworth's leaving for California
but to the trouble with eyesight which exiled her for a time from
books. "Some years ago," she told Lyman, "I had a woe, the only
one that ever made me tremble. It was a shutting out of all the
dearest ones of time, the strongest friends of the soul—BOOKS."

The most general article on Dickinson is a preview of a chapter
from a new history of American poetry by Hyatt H. Waggoner,
"Emily Dickinson: The Transcendent Self" (*Criticism*, VII, 297–
334). It is an excellent piece and it covers much ground: Dickinson's
response to liberal, Transcendental thought; the overwhelming significance of Emerson in her thought and art (and, pre-eminently, of
"Circles"); how we may explain a seeming lack of consistency in her
belief; the direction of her growth; and Dickinson's relationship to
predecessors and successors. Regarding the second item, Waggoner
discusses "Circles" as a call for self-transcendence and says that

> the key ideas revolve around the delusiveness of the safety sup-
> posedly provided by any dogma, the superiority of new truth to
> old, the law that the only alternative to continued personal and
> intellectual growth is death, the superiority of the possible over the
> actual in a reality whose limits are shrouded in mystery, the imagi-
> nation as the key to growth, poetry as the supreme embodiment of
> imagination and so the best aid to the soul's growth, and the
> superiority of action to comprehension . . . .

All these became doctrine to a woman who had denied more traditional doctrines. As to the third item, Waggoner contends, she
replaced allegiance to the rational and the believing self with faith
in a deeper, less tangible self "with no known or knowable circumference." The seeming lack of consistency comes, of course, from her

poetry's recording the process of her thought. As to the fourth item
—the direction of her growth—most of her poems relate to one of
three subjects: "she debated with her father on the subject of the
validity of his faith, she debated with Emerson on the validity of
his, and she debated with both of them, her *two* fathers as it were,
on the question of whether there could be any valid faith at all,
as they both thought." There was a form of resolution. Not one poem
after 1879 "returns to the question of whether *any* sort of religious
faith is possible for one both informed and honest with himself."
This redefining of faith was a "commitment in the manner of later
Existentialists" and was "agonizingly difficult." Finally, regarding her
place in American poetry, Waggoner believes that Dickinson, better
than any other, represents the uniquely American concerns of our
poetry. "There are very few important American poets either before
or after her whose work is not suggested somewhere in hers, whose
images she did not try out, whose insights she did not recapitulate,
criticize, or anticipate." Waggoner would agree with Gelpi that she
is pivotal, bridging the anterior gap between Taylor and Emerson
and the posterior one between Emerson and Eliot and Stevens,
though he might not subscribe to the Dionysian-Apollonian distinction.

A natural pair of poets for comparison are Edward Taylor and
Emily Dickinson. Jared R. Curtis ably notes the resemblances in
"Edward Taylor and Emily Dickinson: Voices and Visions" (*SUS*,
VII, 1964, 159–167). Both, of course, were private yet remarkably
original poets and both "found poetry both a cerebral and a cardial
playmate." Both are seclusive poets to whom, in differing ways, God
and the world produce an essential tension and a doubleness of tension. Both deal in the domestic and the abstract, the finite and the
infinite. Both "prefer a packed line to a melodious one." Both prefer
the vigor of juxtaposition and compression. There are differences,
of course. Her "range of experience is neither so wide nor so rich
as Taylor's; and unlike Taylor, she "has absorbed the New Eng-
lander's parsimony, and the key board of a single poem does not
sound half the notes Taylor exuberantly plays at full organ."

Dickinson's reliance on Isaac Watts is nothing new, but Martha
Winburn England in "Emily Dickinson and Isaac Watts: Puritan
Hymnodists" (*BNYPL*, LXIX, 83–116) looks into the relationship
with more knowledge of hymnology than usual. The Connecticut

Valley was a Watts enclave, though by Dickinson's time Watts was becoming old-fashioned. She grew up to the tone and tune of Watts's hymns and like his hymns her poems "are written, *par-odia*, to an existing tune." She utilizes the metrical range and thought span of the hymn—even its vocabulary, but in a spirit of parody. "From first to last in all her writings, she never consciously alluded to him [Watts] in any tone but criticism, any spirit but one of refutation." So, while the indebtedness is clear, the substance is rebelliously divergent: "irrefutable logic was his organizing principle; hers was her own sensibility; timeless verities were his theme; hers was the supreme importance of the fluctuating moment." His was a most public art, hers a most private one. There are metrical similarities and here Mrs. England has useful observations about individual poems. In generalizing on the topic she notes that the two "were well matched as metrists, with delicate ears for nuance, . . . and audacity to revolutionize a metrical situation. In all hymnody they are the two notorious offenders with false rhyme. They loved it."

In "Emily Dickinson: The Formative Years" (*MR*, VI, 559–569), David T. Porter considers her view of herself and of her art at the crucial moment of the appeal to Higginson. His "Letter to a Young Contributor" in the April, 1862, *Atlantic Monthly* (here photographically reproduced, pp. 570–580) doubtless moved her to seek his advice. The most suspect of his dicta was his affirming that public taste and opinion form a valid judgment of literary worth. Implicitly Dickinson must have suspected any such belief. The letters and the poems she enclosed show an unwillingness to test her worth by any such measure and the very "rhetoric of the letters constitutes a stylistic declaration of independence." This article, with adaptations, becomes Chapter I of the author's *The Art of Emily Dickinson's Early Poetry* (Cambridge, Mass., Harvard Univ. Press, 1966).

Living in an era of rapid economic growth and of speculative fever, "Emily Dickinson and the Acquisitive Society" were not strangers, Robert Merideth says (*NEQ*, XXXVII, 1964, 435–452). In almost 10 per cent of the poems, the worldly values of the market place are employed, critically and ironically in large part. As one would expect, her range in this theme is wide and varied—from the familiar world of shopping in Amherst stores, to the speculator's watching "The Stock's advance and Retrograde / And what the Markets say," to the cosmos measured by the materialist's values ("Is

Heaven an Exchequer?"). These concerns ally her with such critiques of contemporary values as Thoreau's "Economy" in *Walden*,
Emerson's "Ode" to Channing, and Lanier's "O Trade! O Trade!
would thou wert dead!"

Beyond these three books and five essays, the published scholarship is less impressive. Professor Biancamaria Tedeschini Lalli discusses some facts about Dickinson's vocabulary ("Sul vocabolario
poetico di Emily Dickinson," *SA*, X, 1964, 181–200), based in part
on the work of American scholars, in part on her work and that of
two Italian students who have done theses under her direction. She
compares Dickinson's word use with that of such poets as Keats and
Emerson, noting Dickinson's greater range, use of fewer compound
words, and heavily recurrent use of words of Anglo-Saxon origin
(little recurrence of words of Latin origin). She insists upon the
utility of studying the poet's word use by basic chronological periods,
by which view her evolving art takes on greater clarity and more
meaning.

Virginia Ogden Birdsall considers aspects of the mind in "Emily
Dickinson's Intruder in the Soul" (*AL*, XXXVII, 54–64). She selects
five poems which have in common two elements—actual or hoped-for
intrusion and house imagery. There is no doubt that the mind is
paramount in Dickinson's poetry, but these readings somehow leave
me unconvinced.

While most critics assume the "I" to be the poet, Cecil D. Eby in
" 'I Taste a Liquor Never Brewed': A Variant Reading" (*AL*, XXXIV,
516–517) proposes that the first person refers to a hummingbird,
whose "liquor never brewed" is nectar, whose "inns of Molten Blue"
are blue flowers, etc. Such a reading makes this a sprightly nature
poem, not one of self-revelation.

In rejoinder to Suzanne M. Wilson's "Structural Patterns in the
Poetry of Emily Dickinson" (see *ALS*, *1963*, p. 127), D. L. Emblen
offers a "Comment" on that article (*AL*, XXXVII, 64–65). While not
denying the value of her study, he does question her "discovery" of
a tripartite structure in her poetry of statement, elaboration, and
conclusion. Is this not the age-old patterning of discourse from Aris-
totle forward?

Thomas W. Ford tries to prove an essential relationship between
"Emily Dickinson and the Civil War" (*UR*, XXXI, 199–203), con-

tending wrongly that the war brought "a heightened awareness of death" and "made her realize the universality of death." (Mr. Ford should consult Rosenbaum's Concordance and read the hundreds of pre- and post-bellum poems that deal with "dead," "death," and "die.") Her high creativity in these five years is not, as claimed, the result of concern over the war and there is no real diminution of creative skill after the war. This article has little merit.

There are four dissertations, one by William R. Sherwood (*DA*, XXVI, 2193) on circumference and circumstance and shifting uses of these concepts during four periods of her work; one by Sister Peter Marie Anselmo (*DA*, XXVI, 2178) on her forms of renunciation; one by John Emerson Todd (*DA*, XXVI, 3309–3310) on a number of pure ("non-Emily") personae; and one by Ralph William Franklin (*DA*, XXVI, 3335) on "Editing Emily Dickinson." In this last study, Franklin has used all the relevant documents to test editions of Dickinson's work and he concludes, in part, that about one-third of the packets at the Houghton Library need revision and that the variorum edition is in need of revision.

iv. Timrod, Hayne, Lanier, Riley, Miller

Southern and Western poets have had little attention this year, with the notable exception of *The Collected Poems of Henry Timrod, A Variorum Edition*, prepared by Edd Winfield Parks and Aileen Wells Parks (Athens: Univ. of Ga. Press). With Edd Parks's edition of *The Essays* and Guy Cardwell's edition of *The Uncollected Poems*, this volume fills all need for texts of his writing. The introduction, which summarizes Timrod's life and calls attention to his better poems, forms a good short essay on the poet. The poems are arranged in chronological order, as they should be; and notes and variants are segregated unobtrusively at the back of the volume. Two uncollected poems have been found, but neither is of substantial merit.

John Williams has located "Hayne's 'The Prostrate South to the Radical North,'" originally published in an Augusta, Georgia, paper in 1869. He reprints it (*GaHQ*, XLIX, 98–101) without comment or analysis—nine stanzas of vituperative rant.

Elmer A. Haven's dissertation on Lanier's concept of nature (*DA*, XXV, 7268) examines his doctrine of "etherealization" (man's moral and spiritual progress is inherent in an evolving and spiritualizing nature), its influence on the moralistic function of art, and the bases of Lanier's agrarianism.

The mischievous side of Riley gets attention in William R. Cagle's "James Whitcomb Riley: Notes on the Early Years" (*MSS*, XVII, ii, 3–11), especially the hoax by which Riley's "Poe" poem, "Leonainie," purportedly found on the flyleaf of an old volume in Kokomo, Indiana, duped Edmund Clarence Stedman and many a metropolitan and provincial newspaper editor. This volume and the large Riley collection of correspondence, now in the Lilly Library, are noted.

How Miller reacted to the passing of the northwest frontier and the change in the tone of western life is discussed in Lewis E. Buchanan's "Joaquin Miller on the Passing of the Old West" (*RS*, XXXII, 1964, 326–333). He vastly idealized the original settlers—of whom he was one—and deplored the invasion of the railroads and the new generation of materialists; but he was of two minds: he could view it as a disaster, and on the other hand could see it as something inevitable that would, in turn, pass. Both prose and verse reflect these views.

v. General

Two dissertations treat broad issues in nineteenth-century poetry. Gerald E. Gerber (*DA*, XXV, 1964, 3553) seeks "to identify a pattern of thinking about the relationship of science and poetry." He finds that the impact of science upon such poets as Wordsworth, Emerson, and Poe is not as total as one might think, and believes that they objected more noticeably to "the modern economic system of commodity production and the socio-political changes coincident with the growth of the capitalistic system." Looking into "The Metaphysical Strain in Nineteenth-Century American Poetry" (*DA*, XXVI, 4631–4632) Karl Keller claims a clear metaphysical tradition from about 1836 to about 1870, which turned to seventeenth-century models for "greater freedom of thought, bolder language, a homelier and more precise idiom, a finer intellectuality of approach, and especially greater spiritual emphasis." These poets were Emerson, Thoreau, Melville, and Dickinson.

The greater part of a brochure called *Three Centuries of American Poetry: An Exhibition of Original Printings* (Bloomington, Ind., Lilly

Library) focuses attention in short essays upon the "Bay Psalm Book" and upon seventeen poets from Bradstreet to Stevens. In the choice of 522 titles J. A. Robbins attempted to demonstrate the range and variety of our poetry, suggesting thirty-two titles from the "Bay Psalm Book" to Williams' *Paterson* as classic volumes; presenting a chronological sampling of 310 titles from Nathaniel Ward to Louis Zukofsky; and including selections of debut volumes, quondam poets, anthologies, and popular verse. To the eighteen short essays David A. Randall, Lilly Librarian, has added bibliographical notes and has contributed prefatory "Notes on Rarity."

Indiana University

12. Fiction: 1900 to the 1930's

C. Hugh Holman

Now that two-thirds of the twentieth century has passed, a little order is beginning to emerge from the chaos of the fiction produced in America during the first third of the century. The ruthless winnowing of time and the capricious selections of changing literary fashions have conspired to give us an uncertain but reasonably distinct canon of fiction writers who either flowered or whose career got under way during the first three decades of this century. The major figures of the period now appear to be, in order of their appearance on the literary scene, Henry James, Edith Wharton, Ellen Glasgow, Theodore Dreiser, Willa Cather, John Dos Passos, Sinclair Lewis, F. Scott Fitzgerald, Ernest Hemingway, William Faulkner, Thomas Wolfe, and John Steinbeck. Of these dozen novelists, enough work is currently being done on James, Faulkner, Fitzgerald, and Hemingway for them to merit separate treatment in this annual review. Gradually the task of basic historical and critical study of the others is being accomplished; some, like Dreiser and Wolfe, have had much of that fundamental work done; for others, these basic tasks, too long neglected, are underway. The host of other writers of the age, significant primarily for what they contribute to the cultural and social history of their period, are being examined by a substantial group of young scholars.

During 1965 the fiction writers of the first three decades of the century—exclusive of James, Faulkner, Fitzgerald, and Hemingway —received a substantial amount of serious examination, and they bid fair to receive even more in the years immediately ahead. In 1965 DA reported twenty-six doctoral theses on these writers—three each on Willa Cather (XXV, 2980–2981; XXVI, 2205–2206), Theodore Dreiser (XXV, 3573; XXVI, 367 and 2223–2224), and Ellen Glasgow (XXV, 2991; XXVI, 2745 and 2751); two each on Sherwood Anderson (XXV, 7247; XXVI, 372–373), Katherine Anne Porter (XXV, 3571–3572; XXVI, 2201 [on *Ship of Fools!*]), and Thomas Wolfe (XXVI,

370 and 1043); and one each on James Boyd (XXVI, 1675), Holman Day (XXV, 3572-3573), John Dos Passos (XXV, 2510), James T. Farrell (XXV, 5285), John P. Marquand (XXV, 7271-7272), Upton Sinclair (XXV, 2959), John Steinbeck (XXVI, 2201-2202), James Thurber (XXV, 7261), Edith Wharton (XXV, 3571), Stewart Edward White (XXV, 3566-3567), and Edmund Wilson (XXV, 3569).

The most important work of the year on the fiction writers of this period was in book form, with twenty biographical and critical studies, two collections of letters, one bibliographical work, and six new editions and collections of works of fiction. Three of these twenty-nine books were clearly distinguished works: W. A. Swanberg's *Dreiser*, a monumentally detailed biography; Millicent Bell's *Edith Wharton & Henry James: The Story of Their Friendship*; and *Letters from Jack London*, edited by King Hendricks and Irving Shepard. Other books were generally series studies—seven in the Twayne series and two in the University of Minnesota Pamphlets series—or were monographs. The bulk of the articles were by young scholars and appeared in relatively minor journals.

The new editions included the winner of the National Book Award for fiction, *The Collected Stories of Katherine Anne Porter* (New York, Harcourt, Brace and World) containing all her earlier books of stories plus four stories not before collected. The series "Chicago in Fiction," under the general editorship of Saul Bellow, added *Windy McPherson's Son*, by Sherwood Anderson, with an appreciative introduction by Wright Morris, and *Gullible's Travels, Etc.*, by Ring Lardner, with an introduction by Josephine Herbst (Chicago, Univ. of Chicago Press). Louis Auchincloss edited *The Edith Wharton Reader* (New York, Scribner's), a large volume uniform with *The Thomas Wolfe*, *The F. Scott Fitzgerald*, and *The Ring Lardner Readers*; and he wrote an interpretive and appreciative introduction to Mrs. Wharton's most Jamesian novel *The Reef* (New York, Scribner's).

i. General Studies

Only three general studies dealing primarily with the fiction of this period appeared in 1965. Roy W. Meyer, in *The Middle Western Farm in the Twentieth Century* (Lincoln, Univ. of Neb. Press), did an admirably thorough job of examining a special genre in a regional setting. After reviewing novels written in the nineteenth century and laid on middle western farms, he examined the fictional pictures of farm life in novels laid in the Middle West between 1891 and 1962 and in an appendix treated briefly but carefully 140 representative examples of such novels. Despite the fact that only Willa Cather and O. E. Rölvaag are novelists who command serious attention among those with whom he dealt, Mr. Meyer's book is a useful and highly informative study.

Robert W. Schneider's *Five Novelists of the Progressive Era* (New York, Columbia Univ. Press) dealt with the ideational patterns in the work of Howells, Stephen Crane, Frank Norris, Dreiser, and Winston Churchill, only the last two of whom belong to this essay despite the fact that the Progressive Era falls in significant part in this period. Mr. Schneider is a historian and his study tends to be cultural rather than literary. His thesis is that "Progressivism" mediates between the traditional American view in which man is good and society corrupt and late nineteenth-century determinism which is thoroughly pessimistic, holding rather that man has some measure of freedom and that modern society allows him to realize his goodness. A measure of the literary weakness of Schneider's position is that Winston Churchill emerges as the novelist closest to the spirit of the Progressive movement. Although illuminating in parts, this study proves to be of very limited value to the literary student.

Louis Auchincloss' *Pioneers & Caretakers: A Study of 9 American Women Novelists* (Minneapolis, Univ. of Minn. Press) consists of brief studies of Sarah Orne Jewett, Edith Wharton, Ellen Glasgow, Willa Cather, Katherine Anne Porter, Elizabeth Madox Roberts, Carson McCullers, Jean Stafford, and Eudora Welty. He sees these novelists as "conservatives who are always trying to conserve" and believes they have struck more affirmative notes than male novelists of recent years. The essays on Edith Wharton and Ellen Glasgow are only slightly revised versions of excellent work earlier published in separate form in the UMPAW series. His treatment of Willa Cather is interesting and provocative. The examination of Miss Porter's work is sensitive, and that of Miss Roberts' richly and perhaps overly appreciative. Although markedly limited and often tentative, these essays—while they sometimes seem to overpraise their subjects—constitute a useful study of an often ignored trend in modern fiction, that of the serious though seldom experimental writer who is affirmative about life but who sees it in essentially social contexts.

A fourth book, which dealt with seven of these novelists, was a collection of essays, originally designed as talks on the Voice of America program, *The American Novel from James Fenimore Cooper to William Faulkner,* edited by Wallace Stegner (New York, Basic Books). These essays are always well-done but by their very nature are doomed to be good statements of relatively standard positions.

ii. Major Writers

a. **Ellen Glasgow and Edith Wharton.** Ellen Glasgow, for the first time in several years, received scant attention in 1965, aside from the work of the three doctoral candidates who wrote dissertations on her. She was the subject of two minor articles. William F. Heald examined "Ellen Glasgow and the Grotesque" (*MissQ*, XVIII, 7–11); John J. Murphy skirted the edge of missing Miss Glasgow's comic intention in "Marriage and Desire in Ellen Glasgow's *They Stooped to Folly*" (*Descant*, X, 35–40), which sees her as embracing the Victorian idea of mutual responsibility in marriages. She was the subject of a book-length study, *Ellen Glasgow's American Dream,* by Joan Foster Santas (Charlottesville, Univ. Press of Va.), an attempt to determine the philosophical content of Miss Glasgow's mind, to use her fiction as a source for such research, and to construct from these data a "Southern dream"—Calvinistic, Platonic, aristocratic—and contrast it with the "American dream" of which it is a part. The weakness of the work is that the author handled Miss Glasgow's fiction with too little respect for its aesthetic qualities and the qualifications which they place on philosophical interpretations. Although disappointing and finally unsatisfying, Miss Santas' study contains much of interest to the serious Glasgow student. But the reprinting of Mr. Auchincloss' essay in *Pioneers & Caretakers* was the major event in Glasgow study in 1965.

On the other hand, 1965 was a year in which Edith Wharton came very close to coming into her own as a major figure in the American novel. Louis Auchincloss' *Edith Wharton Reader* gives the student approaching her on slight acquaintance over seven hundred judiciously selected and impressively written pages of her work. Millicent

Bell's *Edith Wharton & Henry James: The Story of Their Friendship* (New York, Braziller) is a long (384 pp.), thorough, and very detailed recounting of the personal relationship between these two novelists and is also a closely reasoned and thoroughly convincing study of the literary relationship between the two. Mrs. Wharton was not a simple Jamesian, a fact which Professor Bell forcefully demonstrates, and although she certainly admired the Master and some of his work, she found herself unable to read the novels of what has come to be known as "The Major Phase"; yet the friendship of the two was closest in the decade ending in 1904. James might have been a Wharton hero and she a James heroine, yet the two had relatively little influence on each other. In demonstrating this thesis, Professor Bell used much unpublished material, traced the personal backgrounds of each writer with great care, and produced a remarkably fine piece of historical scholarship.

M s. Wharton was not so fortunate in another full-dress biography which appeared in 1965. Grace Kellogg's *The Two Lives of Edith Wharton: The Woman and Her Work* (New York, Appleton-Century-Crofts) was the outgrowth of a master's thesis, she tells us. It is highly speculative, often almost fictional in its approach, and treats as proven fact many assumptions that rest on facts which quite a few readers will consider to be subject to other and less overheated interpretations. There can be little question of Mrs. Kellogg's dedication to her subject, but she lacks the respect for primary data which a truly useful biography must always show.

Mrs. Wharton was also the subject of several briefer studies. Richard Poirier's "Edith Wharton, *The House of Mirth*," in *The American Novel* (pp. 117–132), gives a graceful critique which contributes nothing that is new. Louis Kronenberger, in "Edith Wharton's New York: Two Period Pieces" (*MQR*, IV, 3–13), studied *The Age of Innocence* and *The House of Mirth* as trenchant analyses of New York social life. Robert L. Coard examined the "Names in the Fiction of Edith Wharton" (*Names*, XIII, 1–10). Abigail Ann Hamblen studied "Edith Wharton in New England" (*NEQ*, XXXVIII, 239–244), found that she knew it only as a summer visitor, and concluded that she painted its life unsympathetically in *Summer* and *Ethan Frome*. Miss Hamblen also briefly explored "The Jamesian Note in Edith Wharton's *The Children*" (*UR*, XXXI, 209–211). John J. Murphy, in "Edith Wharton's Triptych: *The Valley of Decision*"

(*XUS*, IV, 85–94), found that the novel "suggests a painting," with the figures in the foreground representing three panels of the Italian social order. James W. Tuttleton's essay "The President and the Lady: Edith Wharton and Theodore Roosevelt" (*BNYPL*, LXIX, 49–57) argues that the principles of her social criticism of the New York aristocracy are like those reflected in the life and writings of her friend Roosevelt.

b. **Theodore Dreiser and Willa Cather.** Theodore Dreiser was the subject of the best biography done in 1965 of any figure in this chapter—indeed, W. A. Swanberg's *Dreiser* (New York, Scribner's) is an outstanding piece of work. The research that went into writing it was immense, and its abundance of factual detail is impressive. Memoirs, letters, interviews, and public records all contributed to the making of this massive study, and the data were well selected and ordered and the book adequately written. The result is about as thorough a study of Dreiser's unhappy, unpleasant, and fascinating life as we are likely to have. Mr. Swanberg declares himself to have no critical ambitions, and the huge task of showing how this suspicious, lecherous, greedy, contentious, and egotistical man came to be a major novelist remains for others to do. Mr. Swanberg in his relentless "truth-telling," however, seems to have settled the factual biographical record and the result is an impressive book. An example of the kind of data which Mr. Swanberg skilfully wove together from many such places is the reminiscences of Marguerite Tjader, *Theodore Dreiser, A New Dimension* (Norwalk, Conn., Silvermine). In addition to Robert W. Schneider's treatment of Dreiser as a pessimist in *Five Novelists of the Progressive Era*, H. Wayne Morgan, in *American Writers in Rebellion from Mark Twain to Dreiser* (New York, Hill and Wang), examined skilfully his role as an end-of-the-century rebel against Victorian mores and the pattern of American life, and Claude M. Simpson, Jr., in his Voice of America talk, "Theodore Dreiser, *Sister Carrie*," in *The American Novel* (pp. 106–116), said gracefully and well what he and others have already said. Vern Wagner, in "The Maligned Style of Theodore Dreiser" (*WHR*, XIX, 175–184), defended Dreiser's style as the successful effort to fit language to subject matter, arguing that his banal language is consciously used to create a sense of reality. His defense is more gallant than convincing.

The effort to make the primary data available is particularly notable in the case of Willa Cather. *Willa Cather's Collected Short Fiction, 1892–1912*, edited with an introduction by Mildred R. Bennett (Lincoln, Univ. of Neb. Press), assembles all the known stories by Miss Cather written during the years of experiment and discovery. These stories were rejected for republication by Miss Cather; their collection here, with a good introduction and scrupulously fine editing, certainly contributes nothing to her literary stature but does give us data to illustrate how—and *how much*—she grew. The present volume is a part of a Willa Cather project in which the University of Nebraska Press will publish three other volumes—a collection of her criticism written 1893–1896, a collection of her articles and reviews written 1893–1903, and a bibliography.

Wallace Stegner's Voice of America talk, "Willa Cather, *My Ántonia*," in *The American Novel* (pp. 144–153), is a perceptive treatment of the novel. Curtis Whittington, Jr., found form reinforced by imagery in one of her best novels, "'The Stream and the Broken Pottery': The Form of Willa Cather's *Death Comes for the Archbishop*" (*McNR*, XVI, 16–24). James Schroeter examined anti-Semitism in a Willa Cather novel and in Dreiser, Anderson, Fitzgerald, and Thomas Wolfe in "Willa Cather and *The Professor's House*" (*YR*, LIV, 494–512), and concluded that its presence was in part the result of there being few Jews in the Middle West. In a very good example of cross-disciplinary study, Clinton Keeler, in "Narrative Without Accent: Willa Cather and Puvis de Chavannes" (*AQ*, XVII, 119–126), found that Puvis' painting of Ste Geneviève not only provided the historical point of view which Miss Cather developed in the novel, but that his method in his frescoes of handling light and space, of using stasis rather than accent and distance rather than perspective was also analogously used in the novel. Several studies of Miss Cather's work originated at Notre Dame University. Sister Peter Damian Charles's "Love and Death in Willa Cather's *O Pioneers!*" (*CLAJ*, IX, 140–150) was drawn from her Notre Dame dissertation examining these themes in all Miss Cather's novels. Professor Joseph X. Brennan in two articles, "Willa Cather and Music" and "Music and Willa Cather" (*UR*, XXXI, 175–183 and 257–264), gave a general view of a topic explored in Richard Giannone's 1964 dissertation, which has been appearing as a series of articles: "Music in *My Ántonia*" (*PrS*, XXXVIII, 346–361), "Music in *The Professor's House*" (*CE*, XXVI, 464–469), "*One of Ours*: Willa Cather's Suppressed Bitter Melody" (*SAQ*, LXIV, 72–86), "*The Professor's House*: A Novel in Sonata-Form" (*CLQ*, Ser. VII, pp. 53–60), "Willa Cather's *My Mortal Enemy* and Bellini's *Norma*" (*NS*, XIV, 401–411), "*O Pioneers!*—Song of the Earth and Youth" (*SDR*, II, 52–69). These articles deal not only with Miss Cather's direct use of musical materials in her novels but also with how music reveals the intangible qualities of characters and situations. Although informative and valuable, when taken collectively, they have an air of the stating of a minor theme as major.

c. Dos Passos, Lewis, Wolfe.   Of the writers whom we have listed as major, none has received shorter shrift in recent years than John Dos Passos. In 1964 John Lydenberg gave him judicious treatment as a determinist in "Dos Passos's *U.S.A.*: The Words of the Hollow Men," in *Essays on Determinism in American Literature*, edited by Sydney J. Krause (Kent, Ohio, Kent State Univ. Press, 1964, pp. 97–107). In 1965 Walter Borenstein inquired into Spanish influences on and in his works in "The Failure of Nerve: The Impact of Pío Baroja's Spain on John Dos Passos" in *Nine Essays in Modern Literature*, edited by Donald E. Stanford (Baton Rouge, Louisiana State Univ. Press, pp. 63–87). Thomas Richard Gorman examined his playwriting efforts in "Dos Passos and the Drama" (*SM*, XXXII, 420–426). But the most useful piece of the year was J. M. Lalley's review-article, "John Dos Passos and the Reviewers" (*ModA*, IX, 296–301), which examined Dos Passos' shifting political stances and their effect on the views of him taken by the "Establishment." He concludes that Dos Passos has always been a true revolutionary and has always been opposed to whatever "Establishment" existed at a given time.

Sinclair Lewis also received little serious attention in 1965, although he has been treated handsomely in recent years. Daniel Aaron wrote excellently of *Main Street* as a social novel and as "an explosive cultural event" in his Voice of America talk in *The American Novel* (pp. 166–179). Benne B. Alder dealt with Lewis as a public speaker in "Sinclair Lewis: The Novelist Who 'Hated' Lecturing" (*QJS*, LI, 276–285). Charles Angoff added his recollections to the already substantial body of reminiscences of Dorothy Thompson and

Lewis in "A Kansan in Westchester" (*UR*, XXI, 283–288). And Thomas C. Kishler recorded a literary usage in " 'The Sacred Rites of Pride': An Echo of 'The Rape of the Lock' in *Babbitt*" (*SNL*, III, 28–29).

Thomas Wolfe was the subject of an appreciative book-length Italian study that was centered on his theme of and obsession with loneliness, *Thomas Wolfe o della solitudine*, by Guido Botta (Naples, Fiorentino). American students of Wolfe will find little that is new in it. C. Hugh Holman, in the introduction to *Of Time and the River: Young Faustus and Telemachus* (New York, Scribner's), argued that Books II and III of the novel have a separate identity and unity as continuations of the *bildungsroman* theme of *Look Homeward, Angel.*

The most important contribution to Wolfe studies was the Thomas Wolfe Special Number of *Modern Fiction Studies*, containing nine articles and an excellent checklist of "Criticism of Thomas Wolfe," prepared by Maurice Beebe and Leslie A. Field. Richard S. Kennedy, in "Thomas Wolfe and the American Experience" (pp. 219–233), gave useful data from Wolfe's notebooks and emphasized anew both their significance (Kennedy and Paschal Reeves are editing them for publication) and the centrality of America in Wolfe's thinking. Mark D. Hawthorne examined the use and distortion of quotations in Chapter XXIV of *Look Homeward, Angel* in "Thomas Wolfe's Use of the Poetic Fragment" (pp. 234–244). John S. Hill used the function of the ghost of Ben in Chapter XL of *Look Homeward, Angel* to argue that it is Eugene and not his brother to whom the refrain, "O Lost, and by the wind grieved, ghost, come back again," refers in "Eugene Gant and the Ghost of Ben" (pp. 245–249). Larry Rubin, in "Thomas Wolfe and the Lost Paradise" (pp. 250-258), sees "the lost paradise" expressing itself in a quest motif as "the central and controlling concept in Wolfe's thematic pattern." Thomas E. Boyle argues that there is need for a new reading of Wolfe, a reading based upon a study of images that are characteristic of Wolfe's basic beliefs. In his article "Thomas Wolfe: Theme through Imagery" (pp. 259–268), he argues that Wolfe is attempting to find a provisional solution to the untenability of subjective idealism for the individual in American society and that his imagery must be read in these terms. A provocative article in its method, Mr. Boyle's piece reaches conclusions that are surprisingly standard in Wolfe criticism and have been since Herbert Muller's small book in 1947. Richard Walser, in "An Early Wolfe Essay—And the Downfall of a Hero" (pp. 269–274), reprinted an essay by Wolfe from a 1919 issue of the *Tar Heel*, the University of North Carolina student newspaper, and compared it with the use of the same subject matter in *The Web and the Rock*. Paschal Reeves, in "Thomas Wolfe: Notes on Three Characters" (pp. 275–285), dealt with Mr. Rosen in Chapter XXVII of *The Web and the Rock*, James Burke in *You Can't Go Home Again*, and Esther Jack. Clyde C. Clements, in "Symbolic Patterns in *You Can't Go Home Again*" (pp. 286–296), argued for a greater formal structure for the novel than most critics have been willing to assign it. Wolfe accomplished this structure, Clements believes, by creating symbolic patterns. Clements' assertion of this "patternation of the artistic endeavor" (Clements' phrase) is not presented with sufficient supporting evidence to overcome the customary objections to the novel's structure. Morris Beja's "Why You Can't Go Home Again: Thomas Wolfe and 'The Escapes of Time and Memory' " (pp. 297–314) studies the roles of time and memory in Wolfe's fiction and the problems they produced for an autobiographical novelist. This essay must be considered seriously as a contender for honors in the category of efforts to explain Wolfe's failure to realize his obviously great talent.

Thomas C. Moser's treatment of *Look Homeward, Angel* in *The American Novel* (pp. 206–218) was routine. Thomas Gardner, in "The Form of 'Look Homeward, Angel' " (*Archiv*, CCII, 189–193), attempted to disprove the charge of formlessness for the novel, declaring that the charge results from too much emphasis being put on the last chapter and on the title, a point also made by John S. Hill in "Eugene Gant and the Ghost of Ben" cited above. Anthony Channell Hilfer used Chapter XIV of *Look Homeward, Angel* to show how Wolfe used a dense texture and a firm structure to present "the ground of Being in a North Carolina town," in "Wolfe's Altamont: The Mimesis of Being" (*GaR*, XVIII, 451–456). Paschal Reeves, in "Thomas Wolfe on Publishers: Reaction to Rejection" (*SAQ*, LXIV, 385–389), pointed out that in Wolfe's novel *You Can't Go Home Again*, James Rodney & Co. is a portrayal of Scribner's and the satiric picture of Rawng & Wright is aimed at Boni & Liveright. The Polish scholar Helena Norwid, in "Thomas Wolfe et les courants littéraires en Amérique d'entre-deux-guerres" (*KN*, XII, 255–270), places Wolfe in the literary history of his era and displays a substantial amount of learning and several fresh viewpoints.

d. John Steinbeck. Although there was a book-length study by Helmut Liedloff, *Steinbeck in German Translation* (Carbondale, Southern Illinois Univ. Press), which was an exhaustive analysis of the German translations of *The Grapes of Wrath, Cannery Row, The Red Pony,* and "The Chrysanthemums" and a listing of German translations of all Steinbeck's books between 1940 and 1961, the most important single Steinbeck publication was the John Steinbeck Special Number of *Modern Fiction Studies.* This issue consisted of a valuable bibliography by Maurice Beebe and Jackson R. Bryer, "Criticism of John Steinbeck: A Selected Checklist" (pp. 90–103), and ten articles. Peter Lisca, in "Steinbeck's Image of Man and His Decline as a Writer" (pp. 3–10), saw his decline in part as a function of the shift from his image of man as biologically naturalistic to an image based on more conventional notions of Christian morality and integrity. When Steinbeck was "deprived of pervasive naturalistic metaphor, the formal qualities" of his fiction worsened. Arthur F. Kinney, examining "The Arthurian Cycle in *Tortilla Flat*" (pp. 11–20), took Steinbeck's letter comparing the novel to the Arthurian cycle as a key to the book and concluded that *"Tortilla Flat* is quite possibly the best Arthurian story for which a modern society can serve as basis"—which seems an extravagant claim. Howard Levant, in "The Unity of *In Dubious Battle*: Violence and Dehumanization" (pp. 21–33), saw the novel as the story of Nolan's "specific education in violence" fused with a "general narrative of a strike of apple pickers in the Torgas Valley in the early 1930's," and concluded that Steinbeck so harmonizes these elements that he succeeds artistically, although he fails to attain "a thoroughly philosophical level of absolute insight." Jules Chametzky, in one of the finest short critical studies of the year, "The Ambivalent Endings of *The Grapes of Wrath*" (pp. 33–44), sees three possible endings to the novel: one with the picture of life at the government camp (the "New Deal" ending), one in the deserted boxcar when the migrants work together to stop the flood (the "proletarian" ending), and the ambiguous one actually used, which makes a difficult choice of human dignity over the other and simpler conclusions. John Antico, in "A Reading of Steinbeck's 'Flight'" (pp. 45–53), insisted that the "Christ story" element is subordinate to the theme of man's emergence from his prehuman origins. Mordecai Marcus examined "The Lost Dream of Sex and Childbirth in 'The Chrysanthemums'" (pp. 54–58) and decided that the story is a great and subtle exploration of Eliza Allen's lost dream. Donna Gerstenberger, in "Steinbeck's American Waste Land" (pp. 59–65), considered *The Winter of Our Discontent* as based on conscious parallelisms to T. S. Eliot's poem. Warren G. French, in "Steinbeck's Winter Tale" (pp. 66–74), said that *The Winter of Our Discontent* grows from a 1956 *Atlantic Monthly* story, has some apparent debts to Salinger's fiction, and fails, although the example of Scott Fitzgerald's methods could have helped Steinbeck to achieve his goal. Curtis L. Johnson, in "Steinbeck: A Suggestion for Research" (pp. 75–78), used a letter Steinbeck wrote him as a student inquiring about *East of Eden* to propose the examination of a recurrent "Maja" figure in his books. Why this note was published eludes my understanding. James W. Tuttleton studied "Steinbeck in Russia: The Rhetoric of Praise and Blame" (pp. 79–89), demonstrated that the Russian reception of Steinbeck's novels has shifted from high praise of *The Grapes of Wrath* to condemnation of his more recent work, and concluded convincingly that this is a political as well as an aesthetic shift.

Wilfrid Paul Dvorak, in "Notes Toward the Education of the Heart" (*IEY*, No. 10, pp. 46–49), concluded that Dr. Burton, in *In Dubious Battle*, unsuccessfully propounds a philosophy which Jim Casy teaches successfully in *The Grapes of Wrath*—that man's personal and social problems can be solved only by trust in brotherly love. Warren G. French asserted that "The First Theatrical Production of Steinbeck's *Of Mice and Men*" (*AL*, XXXVI, 525–527) was a dramatization that followed the novel closely; it was performed in 1937 in San Francisco. Arnold L. Goldsmith's study, "Thematic Rhythm in *The Red Pony*" (*CE*, XXVI, 391–394), argued the unity of the four parts of the work in terms that must have been used by thousands of those who teach the story, although he states his case very gracefully. Ernest E. Karsten, Jr., in "Thematic Structure in *The Pearl*" (*EJ*, LIV, 1–7), said that the central theme of the story is that "man emerges as good or evil because of the ways men use other men" and that this theme is represented through symbols. Joan Steele's "John Steinbeck: A Checklist of Biographical, Critical, and Bibliographical Material" (*BB*, XXIV, 149–152, 162–163) covers the

period 1930–1960 and includes doctoral dissertations and some critical essays by Steinbeck. Its treatment of other materials is less useful than that in the checklist in the Steinbeck Number of *MFS*.
Clearly Steinbeck, a recent Nobel Prize winner, is receiving serious
attention from some of our academic critics, yet much of what they
write is defensive or apologetic, as the fine Steinbeck issue of *MFS*
plainly shows.

iii. Lesser Writers

a. **Anderson, Katherine Anne Porter, London.** Of those writers who
appear at present to be lesser figures than those just treated, three
received unusual amounts of treatment during 1965: Sherwood
Anderson, for whom rumors of a small revival are being heard, Katherine Anne Porter, still enjoying the prestige of *Ship of Fools*, and
Jack London, to whom scholarship is at last doing justice.

Anderson had his novel *Windy McPherson's Son* reprinted in the
"Chicago in Fiction" series, was the subject of a good discussion—
although understandably one that contained little that was new—by
Irving Howe in *The American Novel* (pp. 154–165), had his correspondence with August Derleth published by G. Thomas Tanselle
in "The Letters of Sherwood Anderson and August Derleth" (*N&Q*,
XII, 266–273), and had readings of four of his short stories published: "A Reading of Sherwood Anderson's 'The Man Who Became
a Woman'" by Howard S. Babb (*PMLA*, LXXX, 432–435); "The
American Triumph of the Egg: Anderson's 'The Egg' and Fitzgerald's *The Great Gatsby*," by Joseph Gerhard (*Criticism*, VII, 131–
140); "Mature Identity in Sherwood Anderson's 'The Sad Horn-
Blowers,'" by Ben Lucow (*SSF*, II, 291–293); and "The Silent Father
in Anderson's 'I Want to Know Why,'" by John E. Parish (*RUS*, LI,
i, 49–57). All of these readings find Anderson's stories to be concerned—understandably—with the maturing process. Mr. Gerhard is
also interested in Anderson's use of the "American dream" and what
it tells of his strengths and his weaknesses.

Katherine Anne Porter was the subject of a book-length study by
George Hendrick, *Katherine Anne Porter* (TUSAS), which gives a
brief biographical sketch and careful readings of her short stories and
a very qualified approval of *Ship of Fools*, a work which Louis

Auchincloss had called a nearly "perfect novel" in *Pioneers & Care-takers*. Hendrick's readings of the short stories tend to find a high assay of autobiographical material in them, and some of it may seem trivial to the skeptical reader. His book is, however, the best treatment of her total work to date. Robert Penn Warren and Eudora Welty assessed her short stories as a group. Warren, in "Uncorrupted Consciousness: The Stories of Katherine Anne Porter" (*YR*, LV, 280–290), saw them as both modern and "fixed" against changing fashions and found her value in the success of her efforts to reveal truth through the process of living rather than through stasis. Miss Welty, in "The Eye of the Story" (*YR*, LV, 265–275), saw the interior of lives, a deep moral sense, and a quality of outrage as her most often expressed emotions in her stories. Time, she declared, is the "eye" of her tales and it functions as the time of the spirit which is eternity. Cleanth Brooks—"On 'The Grave'" (*YR*, LV, 275–280)—Dale Kramer—"Notes on Lyricism and Symbols in 'The Grave'" (*SSF*, II, 331–336)—and Vereen M. Bell—"'The Grave' Revisited" (*SSF*, III, 39–45)—explicated in varying ways one of Miss Porter's most often discussed stories. Brooks was particularly convincing in his assertion of the philosophical and social content of the story. Robert L. Perry gave "Hacienda" a close reading in "Porter's 'Hacienda' and the Theme of Change" (*MQ*, VI, 403–415) and concluded that it was blurred by topicality. J. Oates Smith praised one of Miss Porter's *novelle* very highly in "Porter's *Noon Wine*: A Stifled Tragedy" (*Renascence*, XVII, 157–162). Paul W. Miller, in "Katherine Porter's *Ship of Fools*, A Masterpiece Manqué" (*UR*, XXXII, 151–157), found that the reasons for her failure in the novel result from her inadequate assimilation of the art of the novel. Robert N. Hertz, in "Sebastian Brant and Porter's *Ship of Fools*" (*MQ*, VI, 389–401), used *Das Narrenschiff* as a way to view *Ship of Fools*; he declared the novel to be "a kind of twentieth century 'philosophy'" that argues that every human philosophy is incomplete.

Jack London was the subject of a useful essay by Franklin Walker, "Jack London, *Martin Eden*," in *The American Novel* (pp. 133–143). The publication of Volume III, *Martin Eden*, of *The Bodley Head Jack London*, with introductions by Arthur Calder-Marshall (London, Bodley Head) occurred in early 1965, and the fourth volume of this excellent edition, *The Klondike Dream*, is promised for 1966.

But the major event involving London was the publication of *Letters from Jack London, Containing an Unpublished Correspondence between London and Sinclair Lewis*, edited by King Hendricks and Irving Shepard (New York, Odyssey). These four hundred letters, edited well from manuscript, form the best collection of London material available and almost constitute an autobiography. The usefulness of the work is further enhanced by an excellent index. It is a pity that the publishers gave the book a poor physical format and made the title page reference to correspondence with Lewis, which is really a minor part of a very fine work.

b. **Other writers: books.**   There were sixteen books about the other fiction writers of this period published during 1965. Six of them were in the Twayne series, with its pattern of brief biographical sketches followed by chapters examining the works of the writer and by bibliographies. One of the most uneven series ever produced, the Twayne volumes have the virtue of giving book-length treatments to many relatively obscure writers and giving publication to a number of young scholars. T. M. Pearce, in *Mary Hunter Austin* (TUSAS), dealt with an almost forgotten but significant writer, giving considerable attention to biographical and background data. Perry D. Westbrook, in *Mary Ellen Chase* (TUSAS), made a competent but too generous treatment of a minor contemporary New England regionalist. Joseph M. Flora, in *Vardis Fisher* (TUSAS), did a good job of bringing order out of the large output of an ambitious and prolific novelist of limited success. Eugene Current-Garcia's *O. Henry (William Sydney Porter)* (TUSAS) is a compact, accurate, relatively complete, and critically sound introduction. Edward Lueders' *Carl Van Vechten* (TUSAS) gives adequate treatment to a once important but quite minor figure. William H. Rueckert's *Glenway Wescott* (TUSAS) is a conscientious and competent study which frankly acknowledges Wescott's shortcomings.

Two of the 1965 University of Minnesota Pamphlets on American Writers deal with fiction writers of this period. The Minnesota Pamphlets form a very well-edited series, designed to give rapid but accurate summaries for non-specialists here and abroad. Otto Friedrich's *Ring Lardner* (UMPAW, No. 49) is a graceful biographical sketch and an astute critical evaluation of its subject. C. Hugh Holman's *John P. Marquand* (UMPAW, No. 46) for the first time examines all Marquand's novels in an effort to assess the serious elements of a popular magazine writer's work and asserts that he is a fine craftsman and ironic novelist of manners.

Wilson M. Hudson's *Andy Adams, His Life and Writings* (Dallas, Southern Methodist Univ. Press, 1964) is an excellent and thorough treatment of a minor but significant Southwestern regionalist. *Ingénue Among the Lions: The Letters of Emily Clark to Joseph Hergesheimer,* edited by Gerald Langford (Austin, Univ. of Texas Press), reprints letters from the editor of the Richmond 'little magazine" *The Reviewer* to the novelist between 1921 and 1924. These letters and the introduction give much good information about the literary scene in the early twenties. Ronald E. Martin, in *The Fiction of Joseph Hergesheimer* (Philadelphia, Univ. of Pa. Press), studied the career of a popular novelist but spoiled his study, which has interesting data along the way, by indecisive conclusions and leaving in it too much of the mark of a dissertation. Josephine Herbst's introduction to Ring Lardner's *Gullible's Travels, Etc.,* in the "Chicago in Fiction" series, argues persuasively for Lardner's importance. Malcolm Goldstein's *The Art of Thornton Wilder* (Lincoln, Univ. of Neb. Press) is intended as a guide to Wilder's novels and plays. Its biographical matter is minimal and sketchy, and the book is basically a series of brief—but very good—essays on individual works. Sherman Paul, in *Edmund Wilson, A Study of Literary Vocation in our Time* (Urbana, Univ. of Illinois Press), depended entirely on published material in an attempt to define Wilson's role in American literary life. Unexpectedly large—and welcome—emphasis is placed on *I Thought of Daisy* and *Memoirs of Hecate County.* And that old master of the pulp writing factory, the creator of Tarzan, came in for two books: Henry H. Heins's *A Golden Anniversary Bibliography of Edgar Rice Burroughs* (West Kingston, R. I., Donald M. Grant, 1964) and an appreciative study by Richard A. Lupoff, *Edgar Rice Burroughs, Master of Adventure* (New York, Canaveral Press).

c. Other writers: Articles. Of the twenty-four periodical articles on the lesser fiction writers of this period, most appeared in relatively minor journals and contributed little to the serious study or criticism of their subject. In general, the quality of the articles bore a fairly direct relationship to the quality of the writers being examined; thus Thurber, Cozzens, Farrell, Marquand, and similar writers fared better than Upton Sinclair or Harry Harrison Kroll.

In the best of these articles, "The Rich in Fiction," by Robie Macauley (KR, XXVII, 645–671), representation of the rich in the fiction of Fitzgerald, James, Louis Auchincloss, Edith Wharton, and John P. Marquand was examined, and the conclusion was drawn that the world of the very rich was fairly consistently portrayed as a "fairy tale" realm and not realistically. In a very good essay, "James Thurber and the Art of Fantasy" (YR, LV, 17–33), Charles S. Holmes argued that Thurber's central theme is man's precarious life in a world of women and organizations, where he is aggressively menaced on every hand; it is the need for irrational compensation, Mr. Holmes feels, that forms the basis of his fantasy. A brief study of allusion in Thurber was also made by James Ellis in "The Allusions in 'The Secret Life of Walter Mitty'" (EJ, LIV, 310–313). Abigail Ann Hamblen, in "The Paradox of James Gould Cozzens" (WHR, XIX, 355–361), saw Cozzens' novels as a "careful blend of traditionalism and modernity" and declared his themes to be the impossibility of human equality and the concept of original sin. His view of life is finally an old-fashioned one. E. Hudson Long, working from deeply informed knowledge of W. S. Porter's work and of the Southwest, wrote convincingly of "Social Customs in O. Henry's Texas Stories," in A Good Tale and a Bonny Tune, edited by Mody C. Boatwright, Wilson M. Hudson, and Allen Maxwell (Dallas, Southern Methodist Univ. Press, 1964). Hermine I. Popper wrote persuasively of "The Universe of Thornton Wilder" (Harpers, CCXXX, No. 1381, 72–78, 81), and Franz H. Link studied Wilder's plays in "Das Theater Thornton Wilders" (NS, XIV, 305–318).

James T. Farrell, whose contribution to the American novel has been great, has fallen of late on bad critical days. Wallace Douglas, in Tri-Quarterly (No. 2), attempted to evaluate his status and the reasons for his low standing, and argued cogently for a serious reexamination of his work, in "The Case of James T. Farrell" (pp. 105–123). The same journal also published a Farrell fragment, "A Preface to the Death Fantasy Sequence of 'Judgment Day'" (pp. 127–138) with an introduction by Newton Berry (pp. 124–126), and Farrell himself supplied "A Note on Future Plans" (pp. 139–140). Gerhard T. Alexis studied the period of Farrell's alleged decline in "Farrell

Since *Our Days of Anger"* (*CE*, XVII, 221–226), and Edgar M. Branch brought an informed and wise judgment to bear on the problem of "Freedom and Determinism in James T. Farrell's Fiction," in *Essays on Determinism in American Literature* (pp. 79–96).

Cabell's early works and his conservatism were studied in Frank Durham's "Love as a Literary Exercise: Young James Branch Cabell Tries His Wings" (*MissQ*, XVIII, 26–37) and in Robert H. Canary's "James Branch Cabell and the Comedy of Skeptical Conservatisms" (*MASJ*, VI, i, 52–60). Durham also examined seven hitherto unnoticed stories in "DuBose Heyward's 'Lost' Short Stories" (*SSF*, II, 157–163). Upton Sinclair received attention in Russia in a reprinting of some of his letters to *Priboj*, in I. Šomrakova's "Pis'ma Èptona Sinklera v izdatel'stvo *Priboj*" (*Rlit*, VIII, ii, 184–187), and in a study of his novel *The Jungle* in Anatas Venclova's "*Džiungles*—gyva knyga" (*Pergalé*, No. 6, pp. 158–168). Alessandro Pellegrini studied Edmund Wilson's criticism in "L'opera critica di Edmund Wilson" (*OPL*, XI, iv, 69–96). The Flemish writer Eugene De Bock, in "Nog eens Frank Harris en Conscience" (*NVT*, XVII, 1964, 1220), found recent praise of Harris' literary judgment a further strengthening of Harris' high opinion of the Flemish novelist Hendrik Conscience. Mildred Y. Payne studied "Folk Characters in Two [Harry Harrison] Kroll Novels" (*TFSB*, XXXI, 16–22), and Sidney Shyet studied the early years of an unjustly neglected figure in "Ludwig Lewisohn in Charleston (1892–1903)" (*AJHQ*, LIV, 296–322).

This is my third annual summary of writings about American authors of fiction during the first third of this century, and I cannot conclude it without a brief retrospective glance. Much too much casual critical statement is still being written about these men, who, if not major figures in the foreground of American letters, form indispensable elements of the immediate background against which the major figures must be viewed. This period, in which the shape and temper of much of modern fiction was made—in subject matter, in manner, and in freedom from Victorian convention—is beginning to be examined seriously by a number of young scholars. And the task of sound biography, of thorough bibliography, of editions, and of collections of letters is underway. As it progresses we shall all be the richer.

University of North Carolina at Chapel Hill

13. Fiction: 1930 to the Present

William T. Stafford

In surveying the scholarship in the field of modern American fiction
for the year 1964, I measured the *quantity* of material then examined
in feet and inches. In 1965 that quantity had diminished somewhat—
except in one remarkable area, that of dissertations completed in the
field. Completed dissertations are certainly one reliable indication of
things to come—to wit, the probable need of a yardstick. Twenty dissertations in this area were abstracted during late 1964 and 1965.
Seven of them were devoted in whole or in part in a broad way to
modern American fiction in general. Three were devoted to the fiction
of Nathanael West, two to that of John O'Hara, one to a comparative
study of the fiction of Mailer and Styron. Dissertations on single
authors included (in alphabetical order): Agee, Algren, McCullers,
Miller, Richter, Peter Taylor, and Warren. Consider, if you will, what
they would collectively measure (in many senses of the word) if
the dissertations themselves, not their concise abstracts, were stacked
in neat order in front of one.[1]

i. General Studies

The single contribution during 1965 to the growing shelf of book-
length surveys of the American novel since World War II (those, for
example, of Hassan, Eisinger, and Klein) is Jonathan Baumbach's
*The Landscape of Nightmare: Studies in the Contemporary American
Novel* (New York: New York Univ. Press). Mr. Baumbach's method
(after the manner of Dorothy Van Ghent and the late Richard Chase)
is generally to examine in detail only a single novel of each of the

1. Perhaps another indication of things to come is the some thirty studies in
this field during 1965 in modern foreign languages—Italian, German, Dutch,
French, Spanish, and Russian—most of which I am equipped neither to see nor
properly to evaluate.

nine writers he covers in order to savor the whole. His chapters are
on Warren, Bellow, Salinger, Ellison, O'Connor, Malamud, Styron,
Wallant, and Morris. Stating that since World War II we have perhaps "more good novelists" if "fewer great ones," he sees in the fiction
of these writers a concern for a loss of innocence more thorough than
had been the case before. He thus sees continuing themes from our
past, "adamic falls and quixotic redemptions." He acknowledges his
use of Chase's classic definition of romance in American fiction and
adapts it for his own: "Its concerns tend to be cosmic rather than
societal, its view of the world hallucinatory rather than objective, its
moral alternatives metaphysical rather than practical." Hence (for
him), "the best of the post-second-World-War novelists have taken
as their terrain the landscape of the psyche—that lonely and terrifying
sanctuary where the possibilities of heroism and love and nobility
comfort our fantasies." His analyses of these writers are far less pre-
scriptive in fact than his introduction might lead one to expect. And
although guilt and redemption are in effect the themes for him most
pervasive in recent fiction, he is nowhere dogmatic; he admits to the
arbitrariness of his method and his selections; he reads with tolerant
sensitivity; he writes with verve. Thus qualified, this is a good book,
even if one regrets the selected bibliography at the end that lists
only the novels of the authors discussed in the book.

Also important is Louise Y. Gossett's *Violence in Recent Southern
Fiction* (Durham, N. C., Duke Univ. Press). It may well be mis-
named, however, for the fine studies of the eight recent Southern
writers whose works are the subject of the bulk of this book could almost as well have been called, say, "Order in Recent Southern Fiction," or "Love . . . ," or "Family . . . ," or "Rhetoric . . . ," or "Place
. . . ," to name only *some* of the possibilities. In short, the eight recent
Southern writers here examined—Warren, O'Connor, Welty, Styron,
Goyen, Capote, McCullers, and Grau—are seen far more comprehen-
sively than her title would indicate. Each chapter, to be sure, is
brought to a kind of focus on violence; but "violence" interpreted as
broadly as it is here strikes one as no more the central interest of
these writers than any number of other broad concerns commonly
held by them as tools or themes. Its introductory chapter is on Wolfe,
Caldwell, and Faulkner—predicating in their practice a milieu and
standard against which their younger contemporaries are not so much

measured as simply defined. Violence, as she views it, is a very broad concept indeed, for "it elucidates theme, intensifies mood, and delineates character." It is a means whereby aesthetic value is derived from the "incongruous, the ugly, the repulsive, and the chaotic. . . . It expresses the suffering of inarticulate and dispossessed persons. It questions an optimistic faith in progress and human self sufficiency." It "affirm[s] . . . order through the very disorder which violates it." In seeing, in her brief conclusion, less overt violence in younger writers like Shirley Ann Grau than in an older contemporary like Warren, Miss Gossett wisely refuses the easy generalization with the exception of the apparent conviction that Southern writers of the last two decades are either ending one tradition or starting another. She does, however, perceive changes—in devices "which condense the narration but expand its allusiveness" and in a heavier reliance upon metaphor and symbol than on luxuriant vocabulary and involved syntax. These younger Southerners, moreover, hold in common a kind of affirmation, but only in their mutual respect for a kind of "order," one whose absence is commonly "painful'; yet, in the "anguish of trying to achieve it" is seen "purpose" and "points of meaning."

The remaining book relevant to our concern is Louis Auchincloss' gracefully written *Pioneers & Caretakers: A Study of 9 American Women Novelists* (Minneapolis, Univ. of Minn. Press, 1964), which devotes three of its chapters to Jean Stafford, Carson McCullers, and Mary McCarthy, Mr. Auchincloss provides only the briefest kind of introductory statement, suggesting that our women novelists "have struck a more affirmative note than the men" and that the more recent of them, although critical enough of our past, nonetheless embody "strong elements of nostalgia." His slight introductory essay does a real disservice to his Jamesian-like dissection of each writer, for the perceptive analyses of the three writers in this period are introduced with no more than an observation about their common "comic" view of vulgarity, which "did not magnify it by taking it too seriously."

The remaining scholarship about modern American fiction is all in the form of articles and can be conveniently grouped into broad thesis-statements about the area or else tied to ethnic groups, specifically the Negro and the Jew.

Into that first category would surely fall the following three articles: Ihab Hassan's "The Novel of Outrage: A Minority Voice in Postwar American Fiction" (*ASch*, XXXIV, 239–253), Stanley Trachtenberg's "The Hero in Stasis" (*Crit*, VII, ii, 5–17), and David D. Galloway's "Clown and Saint: The Hero in Current American Fiction" (*Crit*, VIII, iii, 46–65). Hassan's view is in some ways the most sweeping of the three, even if what he finds he considers to be "a minority voice." He briefly examines a work or works of nine contemporary authors, grouping them into three triads composed of Styron, Baldwin, and Ellison; Bowles, Purdy, and O'Connor; Mailer, Hawkes, and Burroughs. What he finds in this structure is an intensifying order of nihilism, from the "outrage" that contains some humanity, in the first triad, to what he calls an "apocalyptic destruction of creation," in the last. He finds this a disturbing development, even if a minority development in contemporary fiction; for nothing less than "the threat of nothingness" is the issue, assailing as it does even time, finding even in terror "no usable content." Stanley Trachtenberg contends that there has developed a new kind of modern novel, one mediating between "the compulsive affirmation" of one group and "the surrealistic agony" of another—"a novel of compromise . . . in which heroic mode is static, lacking either motion or confirmation of inactivity, surrendering the options of experience by default." He detects a touch of this in Salinger's *The Catcher in the Rye* and then goes on to examine first novels by P. Roth, Peter Cohen, Alfred Grossman, and Herbert Lobsenz. For David Galloway, heroes of modern American fiction veer toward the condition of clown (as in Southern's Candy, Heller's Yossarian, or Bellow's Henderson) or that of saint (as in Wallant's Moonbloom, Updike's Rabbit and Caldwell, or Kerouac's Gerard), all reactions, with others, to "the variety of insidious threats to personal integrity . . . offered by modern society."

Actually, those studies I have characterized above as special studies of ethnic groups in modern American fiction are far less numerous than the *PMLA* bibliographical listing would suggest. For example, of the four studies there of *apparent* concern with the subject of the Jew and contemporary fiction, only one is truly appropriate to our concerns, one other only tangentially concerned. Bernard A. Sherman's "The Jewish-American Initiation Novel" (*CJF*, XXIV, 10–14) surveys a half-century of novels written by American Jews that are concerned with the initiation theme, but the "vitality and viability" that Sherman finds therein are not too convincing. Allen Guttmann's "The Conversion of the Jews" (*WSCL*, VI, 161–176), although not restricted in its concerns to Jewish fiction, or even creative literature, finds in the increasing assimilation of Jewish writers to the American community less and less likelihood "of a significant and identifiably *Jewish* literature" in America.

Probably more impressive than any of these articles, and in a different direction, is Hoyt W. Fuller's "Contemporary Negro Fiction" (*SWR*, L, 321–335), which is an extensive and rather impressive survey of fiction written by American Negroes over the past twenty years. He considers the ambivalent results when Negroes refrain from writing about Negroes, the necessity and the destructiveness (in Baldwin, Wright, and LeRoi Jones, for example) of assimilation; but he is also intent upon pointing to less widely known talent in the fiction of Julian Mayfield, John A. Williams, and Ernest J. Gaines. Fuller obviously knows Negro literature very well indeed.

A special study of an entirely different kind is Stanton Hoffman's "The Cities of Night: John Rechy's *City of Night* and the American Literature of Homosexuality" (*ChiR*, XVII, ii-iii, 1964, 195–206). Hoffman studies three recent novels of homosexuality—Vidal's *The City and the Pillar*, Baldwin's *Giovanni's Room*, and Rechy's *City of Night*—to show how their respective "gay" worlds are now increasingly seen to be microcosms of America itself and its failure to love. All this is then contrasted with earlier treatments of homosexuality in American fiction where society's cruelty to nonconformity was the usual intent and with treatments of the subject in current French literature where, for Hoffman, perversion is more effectively "used."

American short fiction is the subject of a single study during 1965 —and that in the most peripheral way. Sister M. Joselyn, O.S.B., in "Edward Joseph O'Brien and the American Short Story" (*SSF*, III, 1–15), gives us an appreciative sketch of the famous compiler of the annual American and British anthologies, *Best Short Stories*. She goes into considerable detail about O'Brien's biography, the compilations themselves, what famous stories of what famous authors were included or recommended when, and so on. It is a rather impressive job.

Variety and productivity, however, (as has already been suggested) are to be found more in dissertations than anywhere else, and more of them in this general area than in any other. Since to abstract an abstract approaches absurdity, perhaps a list of titles is support enough for my contention: Stephen Alan Shapiro's "The Ambivalent Animal: Man in the Contemporary British and American

Novel," Sister Mary Joanna Fink's "The Concept of the Artist and Creative Genius in American Naturalistic Fiction," Ralph Armando Ciancio's "The Grotesque in Modern American Fiction: An Existential Theory," Jonas Spatz's "Hollywood in Fiction: Some Versions of the American Myth," Howard Morrall Harper's "Concepts of Human Destiny in Five American Novelists: Bellow, Salinger, Mailer, Baldwin, Updike," Stuart LeRoy Burns's "The Novel of Adolescence in America: 1940–1963," and Lewis Allen Lawson's "The Grotesque in Recent Southern Fiction."

A final footnote on American literary scholarship on contemporary American fiction for 1965 is Marilyn Meeske's "Memoirs of a Female Pornographer" (*Esquire*, LXIII, No. 4, 112–115)—a priceless account of how Miss Meeske, under the pen name of Henry Crannach, wrote pornography on prescription for the Olympia Press in Paris, with amusing sideline anecdotes of Miller, Curso, Burroughs, Nabokov, Southern, and others.

ii. Henry Miller

George Wickes's edition of the Durrell-Miller correspondence, which appeared late in 1963 but has not yet been discussed in these pages, strikes me as one of the great collections of modern literary letters: *Lawrence Durrell—Henry Miller, A Private Correspondence* (New York, Dutton). Begun in August of 1935 from Corfu, with the initial letter from Durrell in praise of *Tropic of Cancer*, it recounts a twenty-five-year course of this sensitive, engaging, and (for me, at least) really astounding friendship. Only one letter in the collection reveals candid disagreement between the two men;[2] most of the delightful talk is enthusiastic praise of one another's work, talk about their own work, their lives, the times, their strange mutuality of interest. The Miller who reveals himself here has few surprises: he is still the great "innocent" of modern American fiction—exuberant, indiscriminate, insatiably curious, enthusiastic, lovable. Coupled as he here is with the more restrained, art-conscious, and yet admiring Durrell, Miller makes an unforgettable picture of how the Emersonian and Whit-

---

2. P. 264, Durrell to Miller regarding the just completed *Sexus*: "But my dear Henry, the moral vulgarity of so much of it is *artistically* painful. These silly, meaningless scenes which have no raison d'être, no humor, just childish explosions of obscenity. . . . What on earth possessed you to leave so much twaddle in?"

manesque modern residue somehow still has its appeal to an older, more sophisticated "Europe," however "young" the specific example.

Falling hard upon the Durrell–Miller correspondence, Gunther Stuhlmann's edition of *Henry Miller's Letters to Anaïs Nin* (New York, Putnam's) is somewhat disappointing—not because the picture of Miller himself is any less engaging than elsewhere—but simply because of the zestful counterbalance provided in the "dualness" of the above. This volume is better edited, with a much fuller introduction and notes; and although the Miller we see here has all the same appeals that so attracted Durrell, unrelieved enthusiasm *can* approach the tedious. His appeal to Miss Nin, however, has its obvious affinities to his appeal to Durrell, and his day-to-day accounts of events that later appear in his books (his school teaching in Dijon, for example, or his trip across America—to reappear respectively in *Tropic of Cancer* and *The Air-Conditioned Nightmare*) have a special relevance all their own.

Two studies on Miller appearing in 1965 are Edward Bell Mitchell's dissertation, "Henry Miller: The Artist as Seer" (*DA*, XXVI, 1047), and Thomas Robischon's "A Day in Court with the Literary Critic" (*MR*, VI, 1964–1965, 101–110). The latter is an old-fashioned attack on the issue of obscenity, an account of Robischon's reaction to a day in court when Mark Schorer, Harry Levin, and Harry T. Moore were defending *Tropic of Cancer* in Massachusetts. Robischon's conclusion is that literary critics have no business in such matters, for they tend to "foster a morally irrelevant approach to literature"!

iii. James Baldwin

The critical attention to James Baldwin in 1965 is greatly diminished from what it was in 1964, especially if one excludes a spate of studies in foreign languages. Moreover, all of the general articles appear to have severe reservations about Baldwin's future. Robert A. Bone, for example, in "The Novels of James Baldwin" (*Tri-Quarterly*, No. 2, pp. 3–20)—probably the best-informed article of the year on Baldwin—is mercilessly critical of *Another Country* and *Giovanni's Room*. Lack of distance from his material is his ultimate failure, contends Bone, and Baldwin's essays are thus far still his best work. Theodore

Gross's "The World of James Baldwin" (*Crit*, VII, ii, 139–149) is an equally feaiful report, contending that for him Baldwin's talent seems likely to be submerged in "the very myth (of power and wealth and prestige, of American heroism) which he has criticized so earnestly." For Gross, Baldwin appears on the edge of taking on the role of "prophet and . . . literary priest" before "he has discovered the fictional referents for his ideological passions." And for John S. Lash, in "Baldwin Beside Himself: A Study in Modern Phallicism" (*CLAJ*, VIII, 1964, 132–140), Baldwin's apparent substitution of homosexual love for a religion has not brought with it the recognition that "sex *in any form* is not the ultimate answer to self-fulfillment."

Somewhat more tentative is John Rees Moore's estimation, in an essay-review, "An Embarrassment of Riches: Baldwin's *Going to Meet the Man*" (*HC*, II, v, 1–12). The new collection of short stories, Moore sees as a "testing out of experience that is writ large in the novels," and in the novels generally, he concedes, Baldwin is clearly revealed as a man with "brains, talent, and a conviction of what art should do: make us change our lives."

Two additional items have their clear uses: Russell G. Fischer's "James Baldwin: A Bibliography, 1947–1962" (*BB*, XXIV, 127–130), and Kathleen A. Kindt's "James Baldwin: A Checklist, 1947–1962" (*BB*, XXIV, 123–126).

iv. Saul Bellow

In another of those remarkable essay-reviews in the *Hollins Critic*, George Garrett, who wrote the beautiful essay there on John Cheever in 1964, is author of clearly the most important article on Bellow to have appeared in 1965. As is the custom of that journal, a new book is the occasion, but an over-all estimate of the author is the practice. "To Do Right in a Bad World: Saul Bellow's *Herzog*" (II, ii, 1–12) is no exception. The issue which Garrett addresses, with some intrigue and some incredulity, is Bellow's ability to be good and to be popular, to be admired by the critics *and* the public, to go his own way and yet be "given credit for being a good boy and going theirs." Garrett sees Bellow as having done this through his sense of the comic, his authentic if changing demands on both the minds and emotions of his readers, and his variety of competencies in technique without any obvious need for flashy innovation. And *Herzog*, he concludes, is probably his finest achievement, making as it does the greatest demands on his talent and on our perception. Jonathan Baumbach's chapter is equally favorable, in "The Double Vision: *The Victim*" (*The Landscape of Nightmare*, pp. 35–54), and, again like Garrett, although his detail is on one novel, he looks at the whole canon. But everywhere, says Baumbach, Bellow deals with the "sufferer, the seismographic recorder of world guilt who, confronted by a guilt-distorted correlative of himself, seeks within the bounds of his own hell the means to his heaven." In so doing, Bellow has caught, especially in *The Victim*, "one of the profound moral myths of these anguished, bomb-haunted times." For Baumbach, Bellow, after Faulkner, is no less than "our major novelist." A final article on Bellow's range is that by Irving Malin, in "Saul Bellow" (*LM*, IV, x, 43–54), who examines what he calls the "tensions" in Bellow's fiction, those between "theme and use of style," those between "Prophecy and Preaching."

The four articles constituting the special Saul Bellow Issue of *Crit* (VII, iii) are widely uneven: James Dean Young's "Bellow's View of the Heart" (pp. 5–17); Robert D. Crozier's "Theme in *Augie March*" (pp. 18–32); Allen Guttmann's "Bellow's *Henderson*" (pp. 33–42); and James C. Mathis' "The Theme of *Seize the Day*" (pp. 43–45). Young's approach is what he calls a "prismatic" analysis of *Herzog*, the method by which the novel's title, point of view, use of letters, and so on coalesce into Bellow's "finest novel." More convincing is Crozier's perception of a "pentagonal pattern" in the theme-complex of *Augie March*, a pattern "characterized by an objectification of action, character, and comment in centers of reflection upon character-fate, power, money, love, and urbanization." Guttmann is also rather good on *Henderson*, seeing the movement of the novel, in the great tradition of the romance in America, from a conception of *want* to one of *imagine*, of *love*—and doing so through "the ironic hyperboles of the comic mode, the qualifications dramatized in the dark tradition of Hawthorne and Melville" (and many others). Mathis' is a brief note contending that the line from Shakespeare's Sonnet No. 73—"love that well which thou must leave ere long"—is both the source of the title and a guide to the form of the narrative in *Seize the Day*.

Two other articles on Bellow include Malcolm Bradbury's "Saul

Bellow's *Herzog*" (*CritQ*, VII, 269–278), which contrasts Bellow's
novel with Burroughs' *Naked Lunch* as preface to his belief that the
one novel by Bellow that is "widest in scope"—*Herzog*—is the one
that "balances more exactly than the other novels," even if it is not
"his most lucid or most inventive." In John Enck's "Saul Bellow: An
Interview" (*WSCL*, VI, 156–160) we do not learn much that we do
not already know.

v. Bernard Malamud

Two general articles on Malamud in 1965 are at opposite ends of the
critical spectrum. Mark Gold, in "Bernard Malamud's Comic Vision
and the Theme of Identity" (*Crit*, VII, i, 92–109), is concerned
with the affirmative in Malamud's fiction, an "affirmative" com-
pounded with the "comic" and realizable through an ultimate understanding of self made possible only through an ability to love. Samuel
Irving Bellman, on the other hand, in "Women, Children, and Idiots
First: The Transformation Psychology of Bernard Malamud" (*Crit*,
VII, ii, 123–138), seems more interested in the despair, defeat, and
pain he reads in Malamud's fiction. Bellman does more, of course,
finding in Malamud, for example, an ability to see America's dilemma
as that of the Jew in particular. But there is also in Malamud the
"human" possibility for starting again, even if the "New Life" may
indeed repeat pain and death. Bellman wonders, however, after seeing ties with Joyce and James, if Malamud's language is equal to his
themes. Ruth B. Mandel, in "Bernard Malamud's *The Assistant* and
A New Life: Ironic Affirmation" (*Crit*, VII, ii, 110–121), might well
be fitted in between these two positions, seeing in the earlier novel
Malamud's non-secular affirmation as a process of redemption, and
in the latter a theme "undercut so much" that the irony may leave
too little for credibility of character or of meaning.

   The article on this writer I found most rewarding was Earl R.
Wasserman's "*The Natural*: Malamud's World Ceres" (*CRAS*, IX,
438–460), which examines in beautiful detail how "baseball has given
Malamud a ritualistic system that cuts across all our regional and
social difference," how "the assimilation of the Arthurian myth defines the historical perspective," and how "the Jungian psychology
. . . locates the central human problem where it must always be, in
one's human use of one's human spirit." Wasserman shows better than

most, moreover, how Ray's flaw, his failure, results from his infantilism and how "it is the infantilism of the American hero that Malamud is concerned with." Jonathan Baumbach's fine chapter on Malamud in his *The Landscape of Nightmare* ("All Men Are Jews: *The Assistant*," pp. 101–122) is essentially the same as that appearing in *KR* in 1963.

vi. Carson McCullers

Two books devoted chapters to the fiction of Carson McCullers in 1965. In Louis Auchincloss' *Pioneers & Caretakers* ("Carson McCullers," pp. 161–169) we find, in addition to a brief survey of her life and works, a perceptive focus on the "strange sweet taste, like that of a sticky soft drink shot with whiskey, or of a kiss ending in a bite, that evokes the nightmare combination of brutality and sentimentality" everywhere present in the world she depicts. Louise Y. Gossett's focus, instead, is on the meaning of violence and love in Mrs. McCullers' world, in her *Violence in Recent Southern Fiction* ("Dispossessed Love: Carson McCullers," pp. 159–177). Although for her, says Miss Gossett, violence is primarily a tool for "external description" of the condition of her characters, and although "in each of the novels an act of violence forms the climax," that act often represents "tensions not so much resolved as openly expressed and rearranged." New arrangements of love will thus provoke new arrangements of violence. Mrs. McCullers is also the exclusive subject of a completed dissertation, Simeon Mozart Smith, Jr.'s "Carson McCullers: A Critical Introduction" (*DA*, XXV, 1964, 3583–3584).

In addition, *The Heart Is a Lonely Hunter* is the subject of two separate analyses. In "Carson McCullers: The Heart is a Timeless Hunter" (*TCL*, XI, 71–81), Jack B. Moore is concerned with Mrs. McCullers' "ability to fuse the demands of verisimilitude and romance" in the novel which for him is at once a retelling of the initiation rite and a convincing picture of a young girl's loss of her virginity and her girlhood. In "The Case of the Silent Singer: A Revaluation of *The Heart Is a Lonely Hunter*" (*GaR*, XIX, 188–203), Oliver Evans contends that the realistic aspects of the novel have been overemphasized at the expense of its allegorical ones, especially as the latter are revealed in how Antonapoulos relates to Singer as a key structural device.

vii. Wright Morris

Jonathan Baumbach's chapter in his *The Landscape of Nightmare* ("Wake Before Bomb: *Ceremony in Lone Tree*," pp. 152–169) is, surprisingly, the single critical study of Wright Morris in 1965. Baumbach turns to two great contemporary masters in an effort to define Morris' achievement, seeing his total attempt as not unlike Faulkner's in Morris' "founding of a self-contained mythic world in which the universe can be dissected and examined in miniature," and as not unlike Hemingway's in the "limited" reality of the world he depicts. His special talent, says Baumbach, is in his "courage to say no in a civilization whose euphemistic yea-saying in the face of potential annihilation has been indicative in itself of the profound reaches of its self-denial."

More important perhaps are two comments made by Morris himself, in "Letter to a Young Critic" (*MR*, VI, 93–100) and in "The Lunatic, the Lover and the Poet' " (*KR*, XXVII, 727–737). The first is a set of answers sent to a set of questions asked by David Madden about his novelistic theories and practices, his influences, and his high, high hopes for *Love Among the Cannibals* in the over-all scheme of his fiction. His second is a playful objection to current critical objections to the creation of so-called "grotesques" in contemporary fiction.

viii. Flannery O'Connor

Studies proliferated in 1965 on Flannery O'Connor, possibly, of course, because of her recent death, possibly too, however, because of an increasing awareness of the relevance of her "ultimates" to the dilemmas of modern man. (It is a rare critic who does not discuss her fiction in terms of its religious designs.) Whatever the reasons, attention to her work was extensive.

Jonathan Baumbach's chapter on her in *The Landscape of Nightmare* ("The Acid of God's Grace: *Wise Blood*," pp. 87–100) is one of his best. Her central characters, he maintains, do not fall from innocence. "They are fallen from the outset and move, doomed, through an infested world proliferating its evils, until at the heart of darkness they discover light, or God, and through renunciation and

extreme penance achieve redemption for themselves, and, in extension, for all of us." For Baumbach, her world is both seriously absurd
and absurdly serious, but in it always, "at the last extremity of suffering, at the risk of everything, we discover the awesome judgment
(and love) of God." Interestingly enough, the chapter in Louise Y.
Gossett's *Violence in Recent Southern Fiction* ("The Test by Fire:
Flannery O'Connor," pp. 75–97) is also, in my opinion, one of her
best. Miss Gossett sees with beautiful clarity and conviction that
"deep in Miss O'Connor's fiction lies the wonder that man matters
sufficiently for God to care." She sees, moreover, how for Miss O'Connor "violence" is "a religious evaluation of modern life," how "brutality and savagery" are her means "to recall the readers' attention
to the uncompromising primacy of God's demands," how, in short,
"man can never dictate the conditions in which truth will be revealed." A final general assessment is that by Walter Sullivan who,
in "Flannery O'Connor, Sin, and Grace: *Everything That Rises Must
Converge*" (*HC*, II, iv, 1–8, 10), views her last work as an opportunity to survey the whole. What he finds pervasive is that her characters cannot be distinguished as good or bad, guilty or innocent,
only "those who know of God's mercy and those who do not . . .
those who think they can save themselves . . . and those who are
driven . . . to do God's purpose." Yet, observes Sullivan, "even the
apparent worst . . . is funny because . . . under the omniscience of
God, the position of all men is ironic . . ."

   Two additional studies of her work are in effect studies of her
devices. In "The Functional Gothic of Flannery O'Connor" (*SWR*,
L, 286–299), Ollye Tine Snow demonstrates the wide variety of
"gothic" devices in Miss O'Connor's fiction, and although the critic's
intention is to show their uses, they become here almost an interest
in themselves. In "The Moment of Grace in the Fiction of Flannery
O'Connor" (*CE*, XXVII, 235–239), Bob Dowell details several instances in the fiction when revelation comes to her characters in the
"grotesque parables" that underlie her themes.

   Richard Stern's "Flannery O'Connor: A Remembrance and Some
Letters" (*Shenandoah*, XVI, ii, 5–10) is a delightful if not very meaningful series of letters from Miss O'Connor and his account of a visit
she made to the University of Chicago.

   Four articles are exclusive studies of single works. Lewis A. Lawson, in "Flannery O'Connor and the Grotesque: *Wise Blood*" (*Renascence*, XVII, 137–147, 156), aptly describes Haze Motes of that novel as an "oxymoron," details his many attempts to fight off a belief in Christ, demonstrates some provocative parallels between Motes and St. Anthony, and concludes that the desperation of Miss O'Connor's convictions could have led her to no other theme. A less impressive analysis of Haze Motes's quest is Robert M. Rechnitz' "Passionate Pilgrim: Flannery O'Connor's *Wise Blood*" (*GaR*, XIX, 310–316) wherein the God Haze finally accepted is described as "a ruthless demanding God who will not let Haze lose his soul." Two comments on two stories include "Depth Psychology and Literary Study" (*MASJ*, V, 1964, ii, 50–56), Bartlett C. Jones's examination of how the psychoanalytic theories of Karl Abraham, M.D., provide one way of understanding the "perversions" in "Good Country People." The other is "O'Connor's 'A Good Man Is Hard To Find'" (*Expl*, XXIV, Item 19), Sister M. Martin's conviction that it is "a good woman" (the grandmother) who counterpoints the "good man" of the title and that her "goodness" is what produced her own ugly family life no less than the misfit who kills her.

ix. J. D. Salinger

James E. Miller, Jr.'s *J. D. Salinger* (UMPAW, No. 51) is quite possibly the best word yet written on the fiction of Salinger. This pamphlet of forty-five pages strikes me as the well-nigh perfect length for a subject matter of Salinger's quantity and texture. Miller knows his subject well, is articulate and lucid, and is sympathetic to Salinger's achievement without being blind to his limitations. He gives us what biographical information is available and apparently relevant, he sees well just what *The Catcher in the Rye* and its appeal are all about, he sees the order of *Nine Stories* and the apparent reason for it, and he is willing to face the Glass family stories with an open mind. Concerning those stories, except possibly for the very recent "Hapworth 16, 1924," he is self-assured, convincing, even if properly tentative in his conviction of Salinger's kinship there to the "mystical tradition of American letters."

At the same time, there is no dearth of other Salinger criticism: Lyle Glazier's "The Glass Family Saga: Argument and Epiphany"

(*CE*, XXVII, 248–251) finds parallel techniques at work in *Franny and Zooey* and *Raise High the Roof Beam, Carpenters and Seymour: An Introduction*. Glazier believes that the first half of each book ends with "poetic epiphanies," and the second half of each is devoted to a more "prosaic argument for humanism." William Wiegand's "Salinger and Kierkegaard" (*MinnR*, V, 137–156) is an extensive and convincing "case" to the effect that Kierkegaard is a bright illumination to both the ideas and the technique—the form *and* the content— of the entire Glass saga. This is a carefully researched, enlightening piece of scholarship—even to its Kierkegaardian defense of the technique of post-publication revaluation of Seymour's suicide in the "Bananafish" story. Daniel Seitzman's "Salinger's 'Franny': Homoerotic Imagery" (*AI*, XXII, 57–76) is an unconvincing effort to show that "Franny's hostility, her intense rivalry, and her scarcely-concealed wish to emasculate all men are the root of her problem."

Four comparative items on *The Catcher in the Rye* perhaps deserve mention. George C. Herndle, in "Golding and Salinger: A Clear Choice" (*WR*, CCXXXVIII, No. 502, 308–332), opts for what he calls an older "Christian humanism" in Golding, rather than the "Romantic primitivism" of Salinger. Eugene McNamara's "Holden as Novelist" (*EJ*, LIV, 166–170) focuses on Holden's role as narrator by way of an extended contrast with the first person technique of *David Copperfield*. Ronald Weber, in "Narrative Method in *A Separate Peace*" (*SSF*, III, 63–71), finds Knowles's novel more knowledgeable than Salinger's because Knowles sees that self-knowledge must precede accommodation to society. And Deane M. Warner produces still another "Huck and Holden" (*CEA*, XXVIII, vi, 4a–4b).

Robert P. Moore, in "The World of Holden" (*EJ*, LIV, 159–165), gives us a not very original analysis of the novel itself as a retort to those who would repress its distribution to high school students. Warren G. French, in "Holden's Fall" (*MFS*, X, 389), argues with a previous critic about the precise point in the novel where Holden's "fall" begins.

Warren G. French is also the author of "An Unnoticed Salinger Story" (*CE*, XXVI, 394–395), citing the discovery of "Go See Eddie" in *UKCR* (Dec., 1940, pp. 121–124), an early Salinger story previously uncited that has ties in technique and theme with other early and uncollected examples. In "Six, Sex, Sick: Seymour, Some Comments" (*TCL*, X, 170–171), Charles V. Genthe spoofs, I take it, critical method by way of extracting the number *six* from the reference to "Little Black Sambo" early in "A Perfect Day for Bananafish" as a key to the various "mysteries" in that story.

The Salinger industry rolls right along.

x. William Styron

Like Salinger, Styron is probably too young, the author of too little, to deserve the amount of critical attention being paid him. In 1965 he was nevertheless the subject of chapters in two books, a long essay (to be, no doubt, still another chapter in still another book), the central figure in an article in one of our popular monthlies, and at least half the subject of a doctoral dissertation. David D. Galloway, in "The Absurd Man as a Tragic Hero: The Novels of William Styron" (*TSLL*, VI, 512–534), makes a favorable, extensive, convincing survey of Styron's three novels as following with shocking regularity the themes of the absurd as Camus, in particular, prescribes them. In *The Landscape of Nightmare* Jonathan Baumbach reprints his "Paradise Lost: The Novels of William Styron" (pp. 123–137) from *SAQ* the year before (see *ALS, 1964*, p. 173). In one of the weakest chapters of *Violence in Recent Southern Fiction* ("The Cost of Freedom: William Styron," pp. 117–131), Louise Y. Gossett is conventional enough in seeing violence in Styron's fiction as marking "the clash of the individual with an organization impervious to his needs" or man's "struggle to live in the vacuum left by the dispersion of social or moral patterns." It is Styron's *Lie Down in Darkness* that Louis D. Rubin, Jr., points most extensively to (with Barth's *The Sot-Weed Factor*) in showing how Southern novelists differ from older contemporaries such as Faulkner, Warren, Porter, *et al.* in "Notes on the Literary Scene: Their Own Language" (*Harpers*, CCXXX, No. 1379, 173–175). And it is the first three novels of Styron that James Burton Scott contrasts with the first three of Mailer in his dissertation, "The Individual and Society: Norman Mailer Versus William Styron" (*DA*, XXV, 5942).

xi. Robert Penn Warren

In sharp contrast with work on Styron *and* Salinger is the comparative paucity of attention given to Warren during 1965. The edition by John L. Longley, Jr., *Robert Penn Warren: A Collection of Critical Essays* (New York, New York Univ. Press), is a very useful volume —in its sensible introduction, its bibliography, its gathering together of widely dispersed critical material. Its two original essays, moreover, are very good ones. George P. Garrett's "The Recent Poetry of Robert Penn Warren" (pp. 223–236) is a sensible and convincing defense of that late work, showing "a steady growth and blooming." And Longley's essay on *The Flood* ("When All Is Said and Done . . . ," pp. 169–177) presents an equally convincing brief on how this late "romance of our own time," its "pastoral mode" notwithstanding, contains all the old "metaphysical dimension."

Jonathan Baumbach, in his *The Landscape of Nightmare* ("The Metaphysics of Demagoguery: *All the King's Men*," pp. 16–34), has no trouble reading Jack Burden's salvation into the "redemptive" theme of his book. And Miss Gossett's use of Warren in her *Violence in Recent Southern Fiction* ("Violence and the Integrity of the Self: Robert Penn Warren," pp. 52–75) is simply a demonstration of the role violence plays in the often seen inadequacies-of-Eden themes in his work.

The most original essay of the year on Warren's fiction is James H. Justus' "The Use of Gesture in Warren's *The Cave*" (*MLQ*, XXVI, 448–460), an extended analysis of how Warren has diffused in that novel a single strong protagonist into the quests (for self) of seven major characters. In this "shared commonalty of weakness and imperfection," contends Justus, is perhaps constituted a shared commonalty of regeneration. One dissertation was completed on Warren: "Robert Penn Warren and History: 'The Big Myth We Live'" (*DA*, XXV, 5283–5284), by Littleton Hugh Moore, Jr.

xii. Eudora Welty

"Endlessly new, mysterious, and alluring" are the words of Miss Welty with which Alfred Appel, Jr., ends his *A Season of Dreams: The Fiction of Eudora Welty* (Baton Rouge, Louisiana State Univ. Press), an attempt "to examine Eudora Welty's fiction as completely as possible." The book is intricately organized into eight chapters that follow both a chronological and a thematic pattern, from the stories of human isolation in *Curtains of Green* (1941) through the "outside narratives" of *The Bride of the Innisfallen* (1955). Along the way we get chapters on the comic, on the grotesque and the gothic, on form and technique, on her Negroes, on the stories of the Natchez Trace, and on those in *The Golden Apples*. He is convincing enough on the unity of the stories in the last-named volume and on those of the "Trace," where, he says, we find a "fictive world that is elegiac, unearthly, timeless—a setting appropriate for characters who are striving to discover the most tenuous, fundamental mysteries about themselves." But other critics have been equally convincing before him, especially Ruth M. Vande Kieft, whose *Eudora Welty* (TUSAS, 1962) is not unlike Mr. Appel's study in its organizational scheme, its coverage, and at least some of its critical conclusions.

Miss Gossett's chapter on this writer in her *Violence in Recent Southern Fiction* ("Violence as Revelation: Eudora Welty," pp. 98–117) is also competent, even if a little more restricted to her theme than some of her others. Violence is for Miss Welty a device in characterization for an "affirmation of their distinctiveness," contends Miss Gossett, and we are thus often taken by it and grotesqueness "into a new dimension where they are controlled by the needs of the states of mind which she wishes to portray."

Remaining studies are much more limited. Kurt Opitz, like Appel, in his "Eudora Welty: The Order of a Captive Soul" (*Crit*, VII, ii, 79-91), is concerned about what he feels is a deterioration in her fiction after *The Golden Apples* because of a "programmatic imaginative determinism" that forced upon her an inability to continue to see life whole. In "A Progression of Answers" (*SSF*, II, 343–350), Ruth Ann Lief analyzes "The Mystery" in terms of its encompassing in growth both happiness and sorrow, anguish and ecstasy. And Appel's "Powerhouse's Blues" (*SSF*, II, 221–234) follows the same lines as his treatment of this story in his book in seeing it as "a comment upon the Negro race itself" and as a "paradigm of *all* human isolation, and all attempts to transcend it."

xiii. Others

Scholarship on the authors listed in this section came pretty much in bits and pieces in 1965—very little bits, in fact, and scattered pieces.

James Agee, for example, is the subject of a dissertation and a bibliography—but nothing more: Peter Hakan Ohlin, "James Agee: A Critical Study" (*DA*, XXV, 5284), and Genevieve Fabre, "A Bibliography of the Works of James Agee" (*BB*, XXIV, 145–148, 163–166). William Burroughs provokes a fascinating biographical sketch by Ronald Weston, in "William Burroughs, High Priest of Hipsterism" (*Fact*, II, vi, 11–17), but it tells us nothing about his fiction. Richard Kostelanetz, on the other hand, in "From Nightmare to Seredipity [*sic*]: A Retrospective Look at William Burroughs" (*TCL*, XI, 123–130), tells us more about one of his fictions, *Naked Lunch*, than we will probably accept—that it is "perhaps among the greatest literary works of our time."

Truman Capote, Shirley Ann Grau, and William Goyen are all given chapters in Louise Y. Gossett's *Violence in Recent Southern Fiction*, with varying degrees of success. The best of the three is the chapter on Goyen (pp. 131–144), for it relates violence to something truly central in his work, his reflected "refractions," which "enhance the distance from the norm which grotesque characters already represent." In her chapters on Capote and Grau there is less to enlighten us, although she sees well enough Capote's weakness (pp. 145–158) for dealing with the "lovable" and "diabolical" in "separate compartments" and "the new innocents of modern literature" in the fiction of Miss Grau (pp. 177–195).

Jonathan Baumbach's fine chapter on Ralph Ellison in his *The Landscape of Nightmare* ("Nightmare of a Native Son: *Invisible Man*," pp. 68-86) is not blind to the weakness of Ellison as a realist —"talky, didactic, even at times . . . tedious"—but neither is he blind to the ambivalent implications at the end of *Invisible Man* where a "final loss of illusion forces the protagonist underground into the coffin (and womb) of the earth," for it is entirely possible for him "to be either finally buried or finally reborn."

Novels by three more recent writers—John Hawkes, Joseph Heller, and Ken Kesey—are also treated well. W. M. Frohock's "John Hawkes's Vision of Violence" (*SWR*, L, 69–79) is a model study of this novelist, for Frohock sees exactly how Hawkes is doing what he is even as he retains his distance and perspective about Hawkes's worth. For example, Hawkes's specialty, says Frohock, "is weaving little bits of authentic reality into a deep-textured nightmare." His method: suppressing information and obfuscating point of view (but in a new way). Also useful is John Enck's "John Hawkes: An

Interview" (*WSCL*, VI, 141–155), for the candor with which Hawkes talks about his writing habits, intents, hopes, and practices is refreshing indeed. Two views of *Catch-22* qualify somewhat the initial uncritical reaction to that novel. Sanford Pinsker, in "Heller's *Catch-22*: The Protest of a *Puer Eternis*" (*Crit*, VII, ii, 150–162), sees the novel as beginning where novels of World War I left off, that is, with futility; and they are concerned, not with initiation, but with survival. The book has ties with both Tom Sawyer and Holden Caulfield—and, of course, with the absurd. For Joseph J. Waldmeir, in "Two Novelists of the Absurd: Heller and Kesey" (*WSCL*, V, 1964, 192–204), the novel suffers when compared to Kesey's *One Flew Over the Cuckoo's Nest* by virtue of its naïveté, its absence of point of view, its episodic repetitiveness, its pseudo-absurdity. Kesey's novel, says Waldmeir, has all the marvelous comic qualities of Heller's but also a much tighter structure and "point"—absurd though the point is. These are all good essays.

Norman Mailer's new novel elicited opposing responses in two thoughtful reviews. Brom Weber, in "A Fear of Dying: Norman Mailer's *An American Dream*" (*HC*, II, iii, 1–6, 8–11), views it as Mailer's finest achievement—in conception and execution. For Weber, the upside-down movement of the novel, the protagonist's "effort to revivify his cauterized sensibilities," is a true "existential metamorphosis"—and in a style far advanced over the pseudo-Hemingway which dominated Mailer's prose for so long. Mordecai Richler, however, in "Norman Mailer" (*Encounter*, XXV, i, 61–64), tries very much to like it, but the novel "is a big bad book, a novel so obviously appalling" that even after rereading, he can find nothing good in it except narrative skill. (For a dissertation partly on Mailer, see Styron above.)

Mary McCarthy and Jean Stafford are the subjects of two fine chapters in Louis Auchincloss' *Pioneers & Caretakers* (pp. 170–186, 152–160). Auchincloss is graceful but astringent on the achievement of both women. Miss McCarthy, for example, is desperately in need of the authority of her own voice, for while there is more of herself in her fiction than she perhaps realizes, her "fire and drive" are at their best in her non-fiction, her autobiographical *Memories of a Catholic Girlhood*, or her travel books on Italy. He sees Miss Stafford as, like himself, a great disciple of James. She is one whose special gift is "to place vulgar detail in the center of the picture without making the picture vulgar, making it, on the contrary, something at once more vivid, faintly humorous, accurate, and at the same time fantastic."

Vladimir Nabokov is not so fortunate. Appearing in 1965 was one brief study of his short fiction, "Duplexity in V. Nabokov's Short Stories" (SSF, II, 307–315), wherein L. L. Lee demonstrates the writer's use of doubles (from examples in three or four stories from *Nabokov's Dozen*). In these stories Lee observes a dialectic spiral at work as in his novels—to reveal the ambiguity of his fictional world no less than that in ourselves and our own worlds. Two studies of *Lolita* turn to English writers of the eighteenth century: Harold J. Harris, in "*Lolita* and the Sly Foreword" (MRR, I, ii, 29–38), points to Nabokov's debts to Defoe for his "sly" foreword which, however, is misleading, for it invites the reader to a comic mode that is not ultimately sustained; and Paul M. Zall's subject, in SNL (III, 33–37), is "Lolita and Gulliver."

John O'Hara and Nathanael West, however little else they have in common, appear to have cornered the dissertation market in 1965. Charles Walker Bassett and Robert Pierce Sedlack both completed studies of the former, in, respectively, "The Fictional World of John O'Hara" (DA, XXVI, 363–364) and "Manners, Morals, and the Fiction of John O'Hara" (DA, XXVI, 2224). West surpassed O'Hara, however, for we have Gerald Ivan Locklin's "A Critical Study of the Novels of Nathanael West" (DA, XXV, 1964, 3576–3577); Thomas M. Lorch's "The Peculiar Half-World of Nathanael West" (DA, XXVI, 2218); and Marcus Ayres Joseph Smith, Jr.'s "The Art and Influence of Nathanael West" (DA, XXV, 4155–4156). We find, moreover, insofar as their abstracts can be relied upon, no great differences in their results—if we make an exception of the writers listed by Smith as influenced by West: Bellow, Bourjaily, Ellison, Hawkes, Heller, Mailer, Malamud, O'Connor, Purdy, Salinger, and Wolfe! Two other studies of West include A. M. Tibbetts' "Nathanael West's *The Dream Life of Balso Snell*" (SSF, II, 105–112), which sees parts of a single entity in the "fractured fictional personalities" of three of the episodes in that novel. More significant is Daniel Aaron's "Late Thoughts on Nathanael West" (MR, VI, 307–317). Aaron is concerned with the indifference of the liberal critics of the thirties to West's fiction, in spite of West's own liberal leanings, and with his

explicitly anti-capitalist spoof, *A Cool Million*, which was much too
zany for the "left" to understand then. An unexpected fillip to Aaron's
article is a delightful little-known tongue-in-cheek prose portrait of
West by S. J. Perelman (from *Contempo*, III, July 25, 1933, 1, 4).

In the studies of J. F. Powers and Philip Roth special pleading
appears to be involved. In "Brother Juniper, Father Urban, and the
Unworldly Tradition" (*Renascence*, XVII, 207–210, 215), Leo J.
Hertzel shows how pervasive is the irony with which Powers shows
the worldly ways of his various priests, but he also sees Powers as
"a serious religious writer," one whose fiction is "a kind of affirmation of the traditional Christian contempt of the world." Something
of the same point is made in Rabbi Dan Isaac's "In Defense of Philip
Roth" (*ChiR*, XVII, ii–iii, 1964, 84–96), which is a reply to Jewish
critics of Roth who have not seen his pictures of a corrupting American-Jewish life as a means of purifying it. Sister Mary Sandra, S S.A.,
in "The Priest Hero in Modern Fiction" (*Person*, XLVI, 527–542),
makes a comparative study of novels by Powers, Edwin O'Connor,
George Bernanos, and Graham Greene, especially as they relate to
conflicts between their respective cultures and their religions.

The world of James Purdy, says Thomas M. Lorch in "Purdy's
Malcolm: A Unique Vision of Radical Emptiness" (*WSCL*, VI, 204–
213), is one "inhabited by stylized, artificial masks and behavior,
exaggerated, even ridiculous conventions and clichés, which im-
perfectly conceal a terrifying emptiness within which all familiar
logic and meaning have been perverted or destroyed." And *that*
perhaps is world enough.

In nice contrast is the world of Edward Wallant, where, according to Jonathan Baumbach in his *The Landscape of Nightmare* ("The
Illusion of Indifference: *The Pawnbroker*," pp. 138–151), a ritual
structure repeats itself again and again, as "a man cut off from the
source of himself, in a delicate truce with the nightmare of survival,
slowly, terrifyingly, at the risk of everything, rediscovers the possibility of feeling."

And finally, only a single study appeared in 1965 on the fiction of
John Updike: Norris W. Yates's "The Doubt and Faith of John Updike" (*CE*, XXVI, 469–474), a demonstration of how central some
sort of search for religious faith seems to be throughout this novelist's
fiction.

xiv. And Still Others

Despite this lengthy discussion of scholarship on recent American fiction, some two or three dozen items remain untouched. For most of these items I can only refer the indefatigable students of fiction to the appropriate pages of the *PMLA* bibliography for 1935. Though thick in bulk, this final grouping seems less important, and space remains only for a highly selective gleaning: two TUSAS volumes, a book on Margaret Mitchell, and three articles.

The two Twayne books are *not* among the better examples in that series. Peter Doyle's *Pearl Buck* (TUSAS) makes no more than a questionable defense of Miss Buck's worth as a serious novelist, for he himself declares that only *The Good Earth* and her two biographies of her parents—the real reason she was awarded the Nobel Prize—constitute the "literature" of consequence she has produced. Edwin W. Gaston, Jr.'s *Conrad Richter* (TUSAS) is somewhat better, although I do not think we are really convinced by his invocation of Cooper, Willa Cather, and Elizabeth Madox Roberts as worthy comparisons to the achievement of Richter's historical fiction. He views, as most readers probably would, Richter's Ohio trilogy, his *The Sea of Grass, The Waters of Kronos, A Simple Honorable Man*, and one collection of short stories, *Early Americana*, as the important work, ties them in with their autobiographical sources with much more detail than we either want or need, and sees in parts of them —in the epic frontier heroine, in the created landscape of the South west and of Ohio, and in the revived folklore of those two regions— the "detail" of that achievement.

Finis Farr's *Margaret Mitchell of Atlanta: The Author of* Gone with the Wind (New York, Morrow) is also a pedestrian book. The account here of *Gone with the Wind* is much more interesting than the account of the author, who nonetheless somehow "comes through" Mr. Farr's not very distinguished prose. He makes no attempt to judge the quality of the book, or even to explore some of the implications its widespread popularity had for the times in which it appeared. He provides no notes, no references, no sources, and, indeed, not even a very appealing portrait of Miss Mitchell, although his intention is clearly not to debunk. In short, the complex cultural phenomenon that was Margaret Mitchell and her one book is never seen in much depth. The sometimes uneasy relationship with Macmillan, her publisher, is approached from time to time, but never really explored in any meaningful sense. The ties between the exploitation of the book and the ultimate destruction of Miss Mitchell and her family are backed away from as often as they are approached. The possibil.ties of his subject, in short, are only occasionally realized.

Finally, three articles complete this report: Gordon E. Bigelow's "Marjorie Kinnan Rawlings' Wilderness" (*SR*, LXXIII, 299–310) is an extraordinarily sensitive account of Miss Rawlings' "sylvan, bucolic, pastoral" Florida wilderness and the uses she makes of it in her fiction. And Bernard Benstock's "On William Gaddis: In Recognition of James Joyce" (*WSCL*, VI, 177–189) sees with clarity both the meaningful debts of *The Recognitions* to Joyce and its explorations of new terrain. James M. Keech's "Trilling's 'Of This Time, of That Place'" (*Expl*, XXIII, Item 66) is worth mentioning for the ties it cites between that story and Book III of Wordsworth's *The Prelude*.

Purdue University

14. Poetry: 1900 to the 1930's

Ann Stanford

i. Ezra Pound

By far the bulk of criticism for 1965 is on Pound. This year, his eightieth, has produced two collections in his honor. Noel Stock, *Ezra Pound Perspectives: Essays in Honor of His Eightieth Birthday* (Chicago, Henry Regnery), has gathered a miscellany of old and new essays on Pound, letters to the poet, and photographs. Several essays recall personal encounters. Conrad Aiken, Herbert Read, Tom Scott, and Wyndham Lewis comment on the significance of Pound in shaping modern poetry. Even Allen Tate, critical of Pound's ideas and the lack of order in his poetry, finds that Pound has "done more than any other man to regenerate the language." Christine Brooke-Rose draws parallels between the structure of the *Cantos* and *Piers Plowman*. In both, she finds a spiral construction which views again and again the center, which is, in Langland, the Field of Folk, in Pound, the modern wasteland. Two essays discuss Pound as a translator. That by A. Alvarez finds Pound "at his best when . . . putting the strengths of another language into English." Hugh Kenner too finds as "the central Poundian act" the art of "mimetic homage." Donald Gallup gives a lively account of a successful search for a missing Pound manuscript. A transcript of a page from a Fenollosa notebook is also included, with the poem Pound composed from it.

Agenda, a British literary magazine, hails the poet with an issue (IV, Oct.-Nov.) containing brief essays, notes, messages of congratulations, and reviews of books by Pound. Among the essays, Michael Alexander's points out that the *Cantos* are romantic and elegiac. Robert Creeley speaks of Pound's contributions to the measure of contemporary poetry, as does Robert Duncan. Duncan finds Pound using the phrase as his base in contrast to the syllabic base of Marianne Moore and the earlier Williams. Hugh Kenner's essay on Pound's economic theories is reprinted here from an earlier volume. Another significant essay by Kenner, "Ezra Pound and Chinese," shows that Pound in his translations from the Chinese worked from available translations, improving them, rather than from ideograms, except for his 1936 notes to Fenollosa's "Chinese Written Characters." When the ideograms influenced his poetry they were "visualizations of a structure of imagery congenial to him on other grounds."

The most important biographical material this year is found in *Ezra Pound's Kensington: An Exploration, 1885–1913*, by Patricia Hutchins (London, Faber and Faber; Chicago, Henry Regnery). This is a detailed account of the places Pound lived and his contacts with people, books, and ideas, as well as his own comment on those years. In "An Interview with Ezra Pound" (*EWR*, I, 1964, 212-217), Kōjirō Yoshikawa describes an afternoon visit to Pound at St. Elizabeth's. In "Pound at the Wake or the Uses of a Contemporary" (*JJQ*, II, 204–216), David Hayman finds Pound to be the model for certain aspects of the characters of Shaun and HCE in Joyce's novel and shows how certain of his ideas and linguistic idiosyncracies appear in the *Wake*.

The part played by Pound in Vorticism is the subject of an excellent article by William C. Wees ("Ezra Pound as a Vorticist," *WSCL*, VI, 56–72). Wees finds that by early 1914 Pound was deserting the cool image for a more violent mode. Vorticism allowed artist and poet to express themselves through one *ism*. Pound actually extended his imagism to include a spatial concept of poetry. Ultimately his use of visual form influenced his *Cantos* by providing a structure of overlying planes.

Two essays on *Hugh Selwyn Mauberley* take opposite views of its value. William V. Spanos ("The Modulating Voice of *Hugh Selwyn Mauberley*," *WSCL*, VI, 73-96) defends the unity of the poem by demonstrating that the whole sequence is spoken by Mauberley, though at times his voice is identical with Pound's. The identity occurs when both poets attack the age; the separation of voices is widest when Mauberley is most personal and becomes greater as the poem progresses. On the other hand, A. L. French ("'Olympian Apathein': Pound's *Hugh Selwyn Mauberley* and Modern Poetry," *EIC*, XV, 428–445), after pointing out various oversimplifications and ambiguities, declares that it is no defense of the poem's weaknesses to say that Pound put it into the mouth of "an unimportant writer."

In "Ezra Pound and the Haiku" (*CE*, XXVI, 522–527), Richard Eugene Smith points out that traditionally the haiku uses a lesser image to compare and contrast with a greater image. Hence Pound's "In a Station of the Metro" is not a true haiku, though his "Fan Piece" is.

There is much critical comment this year on Pound as translator. John C. Wang, in "Ezra Pound as a Translator of Classical Chinese Poetry" (SR, LXXIII, 345–357), finds Pound's translations closer to the spirit of the original than other translators', particularly in gaining a quality of motion. Pound's ability in translation is discussed in several essays on *Homage to Sextus Propertius*. J. P. Sullivan has produced three perceptive works on this subject. *Ezra Pound and Sextus Propertius: A Study in Creative Translation* (London, Faber and Faber; Austin, Univ. of Texas Press, 1964), "Pound and Propertius: Some Techniques of Translation," *Hereditas: Seven Essays on the Modern Experience of the Classical* (Austin, Univ. of Texas Press, 1964), and "Pound's *Homage to Sextus Propertius*" (*Agenda*, IV, ii, 57–61). For Sullivan, Pound in the *Homage* was not merely translating, but creating a new work which used Propertian themes, particularly themes that marked a parallel concern between Pound in his society and Propertius in that of Rome. Pound has emphasized Propertius' preoccupation with his art and the expectations of the artist in Roman society. His love poetry, though present, is subordinate to the larger aim. By his inclusions and exclusions, Pound is also serving as a critic of Propertius; he does not include elements, such as the mythological tales, for which he himself has no concern. Pound's techniques in translation move toward a modern diction which renders the hardness of Latin poetry. Sullivan finds Pound using units of sense rather than a rhythmic approximation of the elegiac couplet, and thus he contradicts part of the discussion of this poem by A. Alvarez (above). Sullivan points out the influence of the image and of "associative structure" on the poem, defending the latter as comprehensible even though it omits certain formal connective devices. Sullivan's defense of the "mistranslations" is extensive and convincing. His work on the *Homage* takes somewhat the same position as Hugh Kenner's less detailed commentary on the body of Pound's work in his article "Leucothea's Bikini: Mimetic Homage" in the Stock anthology. Thomas Drew-Bear in his note, "Ezra Pound's 'Homage to Sextus Propertius'" (*AL*, XXXVII, 204–210), analyzes the translation of the first two stanzas of the second poem of the *Homage* and also explains the translation on the basis of vitality and irony.

Of the several essays on the *Cantos*, the most extensive is Thomas Clark's "The Formal Structure of Pound's *Cantos*" (*EWR*, I, 1964, 97–144). Clark finds a didactic purpose in the *Cantos*; he says Pound believes that there are universals running through cultures of different places and times and wishes to translate past events into the present through "effective signs or symbols." The concrete images he presents are the particulars by which he arrives at universals. Pound does not separate these, but juxtaposes a particular from one thematic series to one from another series. Like Christine Brooke-Rose, Clark finds a spiral structure in the *Cantos*, with the arcs of thematic material becoming smaller. Clark illustrates his thesis by a close analysis of recurring themes in Canto LIII, showing, among other things, that the characters are allegorical, each representing a quality.

Leland D. Peterson's "Ezra Pound: The Use and Abuse of History" (*AQ*, XVII, 33–47) argues that in the early cantos—through Canto XLII—Pound's attitude toward history was disinterested. But Pound's attitude toward history changed. With the economic troubles of the thirties, Pound began to look at history as the record of a sick civilization. In the cantos after XLII he oversimplified history in his obsession with usury. In "The Adventures of Messire Wrong-Head" (*ELH*, XXXII, 238–255), Thomas H. Jackson comments on the character of Sigismundo in the Malatesta cantos as an illustration of the ideogrammatic method Pound uses throughout the entire work.

The influence of Yeats on Pound is discussed by Herbert N. Schneidau in "Pound and Yeats: The Question of Symbolism" (*ELH*, XXXII, 220–237). During 1911–1912 Yeats was the most important influence on Pound, though Pound has tried to obscure the traces of this period. Yeats passed along his interest in Symbolism and occultism through his own talks with Pound and through introducing Pound to such esoteric companions as Allen Upward and G. R. S. Mead. The metaphysical mysticism that Pound picked up in his associations with Yeats continues to be found in his work. Both poets were for a time interested in nō drama, and Lindley William Hubbell ("Yeats, Pound and Nō Drama," *EWR*, I, 1964, 70–78) points out briefly that Pound was limited in his translation of the plays by the brevity of Fenollosa's notes from which he worked. Roy E. Teele, "A Balance Sheet on Pound's Translations of Noh Plays" (*BA*, XXXIX, 168–170), also notes this limitation. Moreover, Pound does not distinguish between prose and verse in his translation, though this is an important distinction to the Japanese. Pound's nō plays may be read for their fine use of imagery, but not for a sound knowledge of the genre.

Some general comments on the qualities to be found in Pound's work are made by Elizabeth Jennings' 'Idea and Expression in Emily Dickinson, Marianne Moore, and Ezra Pound," in *American Poetry* (pp. 97–113). A dissertation by Alan Holder, "Three Voyagers in Search of Europe: A Study of Henry James, Ezra Pound, and T. S. Eliot" (*DA*, XXVI, 1646–1647), compares the three expatriates with regard to their discontent with America and their expectations of Europe.

ii. Edwin Arlington Robinson

Published work on Robinson has increased markedly this year. The *Selected Poems of Edwin Arlington Robinson*, edited by Morton Dauwen Zabel (New York, Macmillan), contains over a hundred of the short poems (none longer than "The Book of Annandale"), the first selection of Robinson's work since 1953. James Dickey's introduction discusses Robinson's techniques and accomplishment, his use of "devices usually thought to be unfruitful for the creative act." He concludes that Robinson's great virtue is that he arrives "at only provisional answers" and obtains "roundness and fullness" through his circumlocutions.

The most significant work on Robinson to be published this year is Chard Powers Smith's *Where the Light Falls: A Portrait of Edwin Arlington Robinson* (New York, Macmillan). Between two sections of reminiscences of the aging poet, whom Smith met in 1924, Smith has inserted a biography of Robinson which draws upon hitherto untapped sources. He has found material on the decline of the Robinson family fortune and, most important, he presents Robinson's sister-in-law Emma Shepherd Robinson as the object of the poet's lifelong devotion. Smith also gives a theory of the development of the inner and outer self of Robinson the artist as reflected in his art. The result of Smith's combination of aims is a book which is disunified. The sections of reminiscences, though they give some of the essential characteristics of the poet, are adulatory in tone. The most useful part of the book is the biography, to which Smith has added so many details important in understanding Robinson. Unfortunately, some of the names of witnesses, especially with regard to the reminiscences of Emma Robinson, cannot be revealed at present, though Smith has deposited them in the Yale library.

James G. Hepburn, in "E. A. Robinson's System of Opposites" (*PMLA*, LXXX, 266–274), explores the implications of Robinson's early claim that in some poems he is "creating a fictitious life in direct opposition to a real life which I know." Hepburn finds that the poems Robinson associated with his system of opposites did in fact speak for the poet. And he finds that some of his best poems (such as "Luke Havergal") embody a despair that is the opposite of the philosophy that Robinson claimed.

Two excellent articles treat Robinson's ethical and religious attitudes. In "The New England Conscience" (*The American Way of Poetry*, New York, Russell and Russell, 1964), Henry W. Wells explores Robinson's concern with the state of the soul, a concern which is an outgrowth of his inheritance of Puritan values. He elaborates on the theme of spiritual dryness "which may be thought of as one of spirit, of morals, or of nerves." Denis Donoghue, in 'Edwin Arlington Robinson, J. V. Cunningham, Robert Lowell," *Connoisseurs of Chaos: Ideas of Order in Modern American Poetry* (New York, Macmillan), admits the faults of Robinson: his limiting his poetic "property" to certain areas of experience, especially the distance between vision and action. His phrases are often "gray generalizations" made up of ironies. However, he has written a number of successful short poems, and there are remarkable passages in the long narratives. What Robinson did for other poets, says Donoghue, was to dramatize a lasting problem of ethics, sometimes seen "as the conflict between reason and passion," sometimes "as that between authority and the self."

In "E. A. Robinson's Poetics" (*TCL*, XI, 131–145), Lewis E. Weeks, Jr., draws on Robinson's works for specific answers to the questions: why does a poet write, how does he, what is poetry, what is poetry for? Weeks's conclusions, though not surprising, present a succinct summary of Robinson's position.

A further exploration of Robinson's "conservative critical ideas" of poetry has been made by Paul Nathan Zietlow in a dissertation, "The Shorter Poems of Thomas Hardy and Edwin Arlington Robinson: A Study in Contrasts" (*DA*, XXVI, 2765). Zietlow compares the shorter poems in their manner of mirroring reality, their sincerity of expression, their use of colloquial language, and their pessimism and regionalism.

Charles R. Morris suggests that an influence from Hardy is responsible for the large number of anglicisms in the portrait of Richard Cory ("Robinson's 'Richard Cory,'" *Expl*, XXIII, Item 52). Ralph E. Jenkins ("Robinson's 'Lost Anchors,'" *Expl*, XXIII, Item 64) shows that the sailor in the poem is simply giving an analogy between his own failure in life and that of the divers who find only rusted anchors.

Two bibliographies round out the work on Robinson. One is the excellent selected bibliography included by Morton Dauwen Zabel in the volume of Robinson's *Selected Poems*. The other is the more complete bibliography for the years 1941–1963 by William White: "A Bibliography of Edwin Arlington Robinson, 1941–1963" (*CLQ*, Ser. VII, pp. 1–26). This bibliography continues two earlier bibliographies by Charles Beecher Hogan published in 1936 and 1941.

iii. Hart Crane

The collection of Hart Crane's letters, edited by Brom Weber and first published in 1952, has been reprinted this year by the University of California Press (*The Letters of Hart Crane 1916–1932*, Berkeley and Los Angeles). The republication makes available one of the most significant literary documents of our period. The remaining work on Crane consists of critical evaluations and explications. The long essay by Monroe K. Spears (UMPAW, No. 47) discusses Crane's work as a whole. Spears notes the contrary pulls on Crane of mysticism and the American literary heritage, of the "Decadents"—Swinburne, Yeats, Wilde—and the new poets, especially Pound and Eliot. Almost as strong as the influence of the French Symbolists is that of the graphic arts. Spears points out that despite Crane's way of life, his attitude toward his poetry was disciplined. In his later work Crane presents an "absolutist' idea of poetry, which goes from the real world into "some absolute and timeless concept of the imagination." After a detailed discussion of Crane's total work, Spears concludes with the earlier consensus of Winters and Tate, that Crane was the "archetype of the modern American poet whose fundamental mistake lay in thinking that an irrational surrender of the intellect to the will would be the basis of a new morality" (Tate). But despite this Spears finds that he has a substantial number of great lyrics, unforgettable passages whose "haunting intensity and candor . . . are unlike anything else in English poetry."

Two essays deal with "Voyages." Maurice Kramer, in "Six Voyages of a Derelict Seer" (SR, LXXIII, 410–423), finds that in the "Voyages" sequence Hart Crane is "at peace with himself." He achieves a tone of serenity through the successive working out of the relationship with the lover and the sea. The poet "enthrones" his "passion in a vision of eternity; the vision in turn redeems . . . the passion." Robert A. Day, in "Image and Idea in 'Voyages II'" (*Criticism*, VII, 224–234), finds that the poem stands by itself as a dramatic monologue which fits into the other themes of the series, and that no elaborate mythic interpretation need "be forced upon it." He begins with the proposition that Crane meant the poem to be "grammatically and syntactically 'correct,' generally unified and coherent." Other points on which he bases his interpretation are that it is a love poem addressed to the man who inspired the six voyages and that the poetic statements which seem to require explication are really ordinary ones. Crane has enriched them by reversing the "normal relationships of things in space and time . . . and by leaving out, for the sake of condensation, several links in the chain of thinking." The result is a convincing and consistent interpretation of the images of the poem.

There are two essays on *The Bridge*. Thomas A. Vogler, in "A New View of Hart Crane's Bridge" (*SR*, LXXIII, 382–408), suggests that the poem is a failure only on Crane's terms—as an epic or myth of the movement of American history. But there actually is in the poem, according to Vogler, a theme which gives the poem "a high degree of organic unity." The poem is unified by the search for a mythic vision, which will bridge the gap between the "glorious past" and the future. The metaphor of the return from a quest bearing something of value is repeated in the poem. Alan Trachtenberg, in the chapters on Crane in his book *Brooklyn Bridge: Fact and Symbol*

(New York, Oxford Univ. Press), also notices the "myth of 'eternal return'" in *The Bridge*. For Crane, history is not a series of separate acts, but the repetition of certain archetypal acts, and all history culminates in self-discovery. But Trachtenberg feels that Crane was not able to fulfil the double insight suggested by his epigraph. In the conclusion of the poem, he is unable to show a bridge which has its ends anchored in reality; it is not a link to anything. Hence it cannot be a symbol that the American people can live by.

Joseph Evans Slate, "William Carlos Williams, Hart Crane, and 'The Virtue of History'" (*TSLL*, VI, 486–511), also finds that Crane, as well as Williams, rejects history as chronological detail. He draws parallels between the careers of the two men and their books, *The Bridge* and *In the American Grain*. Though the men were not friends during Crane's lifetime, Williams apparently admitted a historical relationship between his work and Crane's in *Paterson*.

Robert J. Andreach's *Studies in Structure: The Stages of the Spiritual Life of Four Modern Authors* (New York, Fordham Univ. Press, 1964) attempts to show that *The Bridge* can be read as representing stages in the spiritual life, classically defined as purgative, illuminative, and unitive. Though the progression of *The Bridge* leads through these stages, Crane himse'f is not a mystic. In the poem Crane is affirming man's responsibility for his own spiritual growth.

In "America and the Poet: Whitman, Hart Crane and Frost" (*American Poetry*, pp. 45-67), J. Albert Robbins briefly touches on the differences between the Americas in which Whitman and Crane found themselves. The sources for trade names and other specific references in "The River" are the subject of a lively article by John Baker, "Commercial Sources for Hart Crane's *The River*" (*WSCL*, VI, 45–55). Baker interviewed members of the advertising agencies where Crane worked and examined contemporary magazine advertising and the vaudeville of Bert Williams.

Two dissertations round out the work on Crane. Arnold Eugene Newman ("The Romantic Image in the Poetry of Hart Crane," *DA*, XXV, 5935–5936) places Crane in the romantic tradition in his mode of thinking and techniques and examines his symbols of the tower, the eagle-serpent, and the sea as controlling the types of imagery used in his poems. Margaret Dickie Uroff ("Hart Crane's *White Buildings*," *DA*, XXVI, 3354) finds that this book shows Crane's search for a description of the transcendent state. "Voyages" defines his vision of the ideal world "as the Christian vision of God" (a position which seems opposed to the interpretation of the two articles on this poem discussed above), and it is this vision which underlies *The Bridge*.

iv. Robert Frost

Reminiscences by those who knew Frost continue to make up a large part of the writing on the late poet. Most important of these is *Robert Frost: Life and Talks-Walking* (Norman, Univ. of Okla. Press) by Louis Mertins. Mertins, a long-time friend of Frost's, has gathered the recollections of Frost and others into a book which considers the life of the poet decade by decade. Frost's own words—or, at any rate, Mertins' reproduction of them—take on the wholeness and liveliness lacking in some other accounts. Daniel Smythe has also written of his meetings with Frost in *Robert Frost Speaks* (New York, Twayne, 1964). He has confined himself to the conversations and lectures he himself observed and has reported in minute detail the subjects of lectures and conversation, the mannerisms of Frost, and the decor of the rooms in which the events he describes occurred. Though he has recorded the conversations carefully, even down to Frost's jokes, and useful as the scenes he depicts may be to future biographers, the conversations do not have the brightness for the reader that they apparently did for the listener. Gordon S. Haight, in "Robert Frost at Yale" (*YULG*, XL, 12–17), also reports on the "glorious talk" that students and friends had with Frost after readings of his poetry at Pierson College, Yale. A single conversation with Harvey Breit is recorded in "Robert Frost Speaks Prose" (*Esquire*, LXIV, vi, 230, 308). The result is largely a series of aphorisms, some pungent, on freedom and poetry.

General essays, based in part on books and essays already published and which summarize Frost's achievement, include those of Albert E. Stone, Jr. ("Robert Frost," *EUQ*, XXI, 59–69) and André Le Vot ("La voix de Frost," *Langues Modernes*, LIX, 349–356).

Several critical articles define Frost's attitudes and style. In "A Parallel of Parablists: Thoreau and Frost" (*The Thoreau Centennial*, edited by Walter Harding, Albany, State Univ. of New York, 1964), Reginald L. Cook finds many likenesses in the two writers, but ultimately a differing "vision of reality." Both, according to Cook, are related "to a native story-telling tradition," in their colloquial diction and their attention to concrete details. But Thoreau reads moral purposiveness "into natural phenomena and human effort" whereas Frost has "no preformed conviction."

Isadore Traschen, "Robert Frost: Some Divisions in a Whole Man" (*YR*, LV, 57–70), defines the critical defect in Frost's work as a refusal to take risks; he shows this as a cause of disunity in Frost's work in several ways. The nature poetry tends to be divided between description and comment, rather than being fused by feeling into a whole. Frost does not adapt his tone to his various subjects, but speaks always in the same even voice. Moreover Traschen criticizes Frost for resisting nature; he refuses the encounter that would have defined his humanness. In this and in his refusal to consider the "complexities and contentions of our time," he preserves himself from a "passionate commitment."

An opposing view with regard to Frost's relation to nature is held by Nina Baym ("An Approach to Robert Frost's Nature Poetry," *AQ*, XVII, 713–723). This author says we must look at Frost as a carrier of a poetic tradition rather than "through ideological preconceptions." He deals with the respected poetic theme of "mutability." Frost finds a world not friendly to man, in which man must take the small human action of resistance. Hence his resistance to nature is really a virtue.

Two other writers, if not so critical of Frost as Traschen, at least have some reservations in their view of his work. Denis Donoghue's "Robert Frost," in *Connoisseurs of Chaos: Ideas of Order in Modern American Poetry* (New York, Macmillan), has some of the most pungent commentary on Frost. He finds Frost's persona putting himself in many of the poems with a kind of charm that means "communicative success." He is a poet of "the way things are," rather than a poet of the mind. His best poems, contends Donoghue, are those that depend upon a presentation of the facts, upon keeping close to the earth. Donoghue finds many of the tenets of the Social Darwinists in Frost's attitude: especially the ideas that in the natural world the best will survive and that there is no relevant value beyond survival itself.

Henry W. Wells ("Nearer and Farther Ranges," *The American Way of Poetry*, New York, Russell and Russell, 1964) finds that for

Frost "localism" is essential. But though he has captured the surface mannerisms of New England culture, he has not caught as much of the spirit of New England as have Emerson, Dickinson, and Robinson.

Brief comments on individual poems include a query as to whether Frost's line "Nature's first green is gold" may have some connection with Goethe's "*Grau, teurer Freund, ist alle Theorie, | Und grün des Lebens goldner Baum*" (Robert F. Fleissner, "Frost and 'Faust,'" *N&Q*, XII, 432). James Hoetker challenges Frederick L. Gwynn's statement (*CE*, XXVI, 1964, 223–225) that "the speaker reluctantly accepts a power greater than man's" with the interpretation that Frost thought the speaker was a fool ("Frost's 'The Draft Horse,'" *CE*, XXVI, 485). R. G. Malbone ("Frost's 'The Road Not Taken,'" *Expl*, XXIV, Item 27) finds humor in the contrast between the past and future attitudes of the speaker about the difference in the two roads at the time of the choice.

v. E. E. Cummings

Cummings' *A Miscellany*, has been republished as *E. E. Cummings: A Miscellany Revised*, edited by George J. Firmage (New York, October House). The original miscellany was a gathering of all the Cummings pieces not in book form; the new edition adds seven new pieces and some of Cummings' line drawings.

Charles Norman's 1957 biography *E. E. Cummings: The Magic-Maker* (New York, Duell, Sloan and Pearce, 1964) has also been revised. The new edition is shorter, with some of the documentation removed and a four-page chapter on the poet's death added. This readable biography concerns itself with the facts of the poet's life and the details of how his books came to be published.

A short book by Robert E. Wegner, *The Poetry and Prose of E. E. Cummings* (New York, Harcourt, Brace and World), presents his comments as an "appreciation" of Cummings. The book does not try to cover exhaustively any particular aspect of Cummings' work or style, but comments discursively on Cummings' view of the artist, his themes, and his forms. Wegner describes the progress of Cummings' work as a process of self-discovery in the course of which it became increasingly mature and powerful. Cummings was always concerned with the mystery of his subject and with the danger of thinking at the expense of feeling. Cummings' work moved from an early sensory exuberance to a later concern with the integrity of the individual. Against those who tried to stultify the individual he used the weapon of satire.

Two essays deal with filth and obscenity in the work of Cummings. In *"The Enormous Room* and *The Pilgrim's Progress"* (*TCL,* XI, 67–75), David E. Smith points out that *The Pilgrim's Progress* serves as the "organizing principle" for Cummings' book. Christian and the prisoner go on similar journeys, and Cummings a number of times refers to the parallels. Cummings, the initiate, enters the Interpreter's House, i.e., the Enormous Room. Entering the society there resembles conversion. The infernal Trinity of the room are "the erotic, urinary, and excremental," and these "symbolize the . . . mysteries of Christian brotherhood." In this society cleanliness is on the side of the fiend. In defense of this thesis, Smith argues the scumminess of the Slough of Despond in which man must wallow for a time. Like Gulliver, who could not bear the smell of his fellow men after being in Houyhnhnmland, the twentieth-century pilgrim needs to flee his deodorized, dehumanized surroundings by escaping into "a community of odorous human beings."

In "Obscenity and its Function in the Poetry of E. E. Cummings" (*SR,* LXXIII, 469–478), Fred E. H. Schroeder distinguishes between the obscene and the vulgar and pornographic. He finds that when Cummings uses obscenity it is always for the sake of satire or irony. His satire attacks "pompous hypocrisy," "literary idealized love," and "man's inhumanity to man." He does not use obscenity to be *avant garde* (he satirizes those who do), but as a moralist.

James Peter Thorne ("Stylistics and Generative Grammars," *JL,* I, 49–59) uses Cummings' "Anyone lived in a pretty how town" to illustrate his point that it is not economical to stretch the grammar of English to include certain sentences in this poem. Rather the linguist should consider the text a dialect—or better a language—and postulate rules for it.

Explications include William R. Osborne's comment on the precision of the use of the word "skilful" in "Cummings' 'The Bigness of Cannon' (La Guerre, I)" (*Expl,* XXIV, Item 28). The word includes both the pun on "killful" and an ironical use of skill. C. Steven Turner remarks of "Cummings' 'In Just—'" (*Expl,* XXIV,

Item 18) that the poem points toward the loss of childhood. George Wesolek's "e. e. cummings: A Reconsideration" (*Renascence,* XVIII, 3–8) is a very general commentary on the work of the poet.

vi. Aiken, MacLeish, Fletcher, Davidson, Masters, Dresbach

What Aiken and other poets learned at Harvard from the philosopher Santayana is the subject of a dissertation by Robert Henry Hunter Wilbur ("George Santayana and Three Modern Philosophical Poets: T. S. Eliot, Conrad Aiken, and Wallace Stevens," *DA,* XXVI, 2228). Aiken acquired the belief that poetry can replace religion in interpreting human life and that poetry should accord with a contemporary naturalistic view of the world. In such a scheme the greatest poetry must be poetry of ideas. Aiken held these ideas while working out his own theory of man's evolving consciousness. Mary Martin Rountree finds a similar belief in her study of "The Fiction of Conrad Aiken" (*DA,* XXVI, 3350). The artist assists mankind by explaining his "rich consciousness" for the benefit of the reader. One of Aiken's major themes is the exploration of the self through relationships with others. Another is the awareness of the irrational forces that menace man. Further relationships that Aiken finds significant are explored by Vance Mizelle in "Conrad Aiken's 'Music Strangely Subtle'" (*GaR,* XIX, 81–92). Taking *Ushant* as an example of Aiken's use of a musical structure based on counterpoint, the author explains that the transference from musical to literary form comes through the "interweaving of themes and subjects around one basic theme," which in *Ushant* is that of self-knowledge. This valuable article discusses the principal themes of ancestry, art, sex, and home that revolve about self-knowledge.

Archibald MacLeish, by Signi Lenea Falk (TUSAS), is a largely factual presentation of the career of this poet. Miss Falk discusses MacLeish's place in modern poetry and summarizes each of his major works of poetry, prose, and drama. Mary Stiles Maher's "Man and the Natural Condition: Some Aspects of Primitivism in the Poetry of Archibald MacLeish" (*DA,* XXVI, 1649) finds three phases in MacLeish's poetry. In all three he is concerned with man's relation to nature and the interpretation of that relationship for physical and moral good.

In "The Love Songs of John Gould Fletcher" (*MQ,* VII, 83–91),

Mary Graham Lund considers both his expression of love of nature and love of women. Fletcher was unfortunate in his first important love affair and to a certain extent in his literary contacts. Miss Lund finds Fletcher's work important to English poetry for his furtherance of clearness of imagery and the rhythmic possibilities of the language. Fletcher's voluminous correspondence has been made more available to scholars by the completion of the first half of an index to the John Gould Fletcher Collection of the University of Arkansas. The index was compiled by Oliver Leon Peters ("A Name, Works, and Selected Subjects Index of the Correspondence of John Gould Fletcher for Correspondents 'A' Through 'K,'" *DA*, XXVI, 1048–1049).

The "significant memories, motives, and attitudes" of Edgar Lee Masters as shown in his prose are studied by Mary Margaret Weeg ("The Prose of Edgar Lee Masters: Its Revelation of His Views and Its Significance in His Canon," *DA*, XXVI, 1052).

The stages of composition that Donald Davidson went through in writing his poem "Lee in the Mountains" are analyzed by Thomas D. Young and M. Thomas Inge in *Donald Davidson, An Essay and a Bibliography* (Nashville, Vanderbilt Univ. Press). The essay indicates the kind of help that members of the Fugitive group gave one another. The Davidson bibliography is thorough. In "Four Southerners" (*American Poetry*, pp. 11–43), Louis D. Rubin, Jr., finds Davidson using the Southern historical and agrarian traditions to such an extent that his work has not found as many readers as the other Fugitive poets.

The poet Glenn Ward Dresbach is the subject of an article by Edsel Ford, "Glenn Ward Dresbach: The New Mexico Years, 1915–1920" (*NMQ*, XXXIV, 78–96). Ford discusses the poet's life and the sources of his inspiration in the natural scenery of southwestern New Mexico.

Rounding out the period are some works on some of the magazines, movements, and personalities. J. J. Healy has written on the *Dial* in "*The Dial* and the Revolution in Poetry: 1912–1917: A Study in Controversy" (*BAASB*, No. 10, pp. 48–69). A. R. Jones, in "Imagism: A Unity of Gesture" (*American Poetry*, pp. 114–133), traces the history of imagism and points out that perhaps its greatest importance is in its Anglo-American character. After imagism, English and American poets are writing in a common tradition. Jean Starr Untermeyer's *Private Collection* (New York, Knopf) contains brief reminiscences of many literary figures of this period, colored by a highly personal point of view. In "American Poetry of the First World War (1914–1920): A Survey and Checklist" (*DA*, XXVI, 2212–2213), James Alfred Hart examines the work not only of soldier poets but of well-known civilian poets such as Sandburg, Lindsay, Masters, Frost, Robinson, Pound, Fletcher, and Stevens.

San Fernando Valley State College

15. Poetry: 1930 to the Present

Oliver Evans

i. General

The struggle which was described in some detail in *ALS, 1964* (between the "Establishment" and the newest form of romanticism) appears somewhat to have abated. One reason for this is that the more authentic of the younger talents have themselves begun to constitute an Establishment of sorts, as a glance at the more recent issues of Chicago's *Poetry* will confirm. Olson, Levertov, Duncan, and Creeley now appear in the most respectable anthologies; Miss Levertov is poetry editor of the *Nation*; Creeley gives lectures to academic audiences. Another reason is that a number of poets formerly identified with the Establishment have, quite recently, significantly changed their styles; among these we might mention James Merrill, Louis Simpson, James Wright, John Berryman (*mirabile dictu*), and of course Karl Shapiro.

The most important book-length study of the most recent American poetry is Stephen Stepanchev's *American Poetry Since 1945* (New York, Harper and Row). Between 1945 and 1953, he states, the poetry of public issues became virtually extinguished; poems with a social, political, and economic emphasis were succeeded by those of a psychological, archetypal, or mythological character. Wilbur, Merwin, and Jarrell wrote verse that was strongly influenced by the theories of the New Criticism, which Mr. Stepanchev rightly states was the "subtlest explicatory criticism in American literary history." After 1953, he maintains, three new tendencies emerged: a negation of mythological and psychological archetypes in favor of autobiographical subjects (Lowell, Snodgrass); a preference for free verse with a colloquial quality over traditional metrical forms (Olson, Levertov, Creeley, Duncan); and—most recently of all—an emphasis on the "subjective" or "depth" image, which arises from the poet's unconscious and generates in the reader powerful emotions beyond the reach of logic or analysis (Wright, Bly).

Though he is generally sanguine about the direction taken by American poetry in the last twenty years, and though he tends to prefer the new poetry to that produced by the Establishment-as-such, Mr. Stepanchev is not blind to its defects and excesses; his analysis of the weaknesses of Ginsberg's work and of Shapiro's most recent poetic output is both objective and perceptive. He has three complaints to make about the present scene: many of the modern poets have overlooked the importance of incident, action, and plot; the Objectivists, under the influence of Williams and Zukofsky, have neglected the creation of character ("One would like to find a larger population in contemporary poetry"); and the reaction against the intellectualism of metaphysical verse has resulted in an overemphasis on the merely physical and emotional aspects of human behavior.

Though its proper subject is American poetry as a whole, Henry W. Wells's *The American Way of Poetry* (New York, Russell and Russell, 1964) is partially concerned with the modern period. His thesis is that since 1920 American poetry, which had been dominated for nearly a century by sectionalism, has tended to become increasingly national in its sensibility, and that in this respect it resembles, and continues, the original poetic tradition established by Freneau, Poe, and Whitman; there are also signs, he claims, of an increased internationalism. Ransom, whom we tend to think of as a militant regionalist, is in fact a transitional figure; he cannot, as Wells correctly states, be said to have expressed the New South, and is "perceptibly Southern only as he remains traditionally so"; his influences, moreover, were international. According to Wells, the late Merrill Moore (to whom he devotes the better part of an entire chapter) deserted provincialism in favor of "a liberalism essentially cosmopolitan, a pragmatism characteristically American," and Tate has become attached to "critical ideas which leave the mind of the Old South far behind." It is good to see that extraordinary Renaissance character, Merrill Moore (so much admired by his professional colleague, Dr. Williams), done something resembling justice at last, and the chapter on Jeffers, another neglected poet of considerable power, is pertinent and perceptive. On the other hand, Wells exaggerates the value of such a minor poet as Stephen Vincent Benét. (Comparing Hardy's *Dynasts* with *John Brown's Body*, he says: "Hardy's poem is much more philosophical than Benét's. . . . In so far as epic poetry deals primarily with war, Hardy surpasses Benét,"

which must be among the critical understatements of the decade.)
Nor is the book up to date; it is unforgivable, writing in 1964, to
refer to the Fugitives as having "flourished some twenty years ago
in Nashville."

A most valuable collection of essays dealing with the modern
scene is *American Poetry*. The two essays which deal with the subject in general, and which are therefore our concern in this section,
are "Criticism and Poetry," by Walter Sutton, and "Against the
Grain: Poets Writing Today," by George Garrett.

Refuting with historical arguments the anti-intellectual thesis
(which has been upheld by, among others, Cummings and Frost)
that criticism is hostile to creativity, Sutton traces the relations between poetry and criticism in America from Emerson to the most
recent generation. He finds that the romantic tradition of English
criticism (as represented by Wordsworth and Coleridge) has been
most influential, particularly in its emphasis, via the *Biographia
Literaria* and Emerson's essay, "The Poet," upon an organic theory of
form. Whitman, he claims, was the first American poet to realize in
his practice the ideal of "open form"—allowing the content to find its
own unique and inevitable form with marvelous effect. Eliot and the
poets associated with the New Criticism, he argues, were influenced
by this tradition and this theory of form no less than were Williams,
Olson, Ginsberg, Levertov, Duncan, and Creeley. Of the latter he
says: "Most of this group of poets have concerned themselves with
theories of technique. . . . Most of the younger American poets are
committed to the romantic tradition of organic form as it has come
down from Emerson and Whitman through Pound and Williams."

In an interesting essay marred by an unfortunate style which, in
striving not to be stuffy, is instead facetious and frequently vulgar,
Garrett notes how the current social scene affects our poets. He
distinguishes four categories: the "General Motors Aesthetic," which
requires that poets, if they are to "grow," change their styles as often
as automobiles; the "Madison Avenue Madness," which reveals itself
in the blurbs which poets write for other poets' bookjackets; the
"Success Syndrome," which causes poets to list (again on the jackets
of their books) the various prestigious magazines wherein their
work has appeared, as well as fellowships, grants, and awards; and
"Status Seeking," whereby the better publishers, instead of taking
chances on new poets, prefer to republish books by authors who have

already appeared on their lists, with the result that "the overall situation is good for established poets, poor for new ones." The second part of Garrett's article, "Sitzkrieg, or the Phoney War," claims that the battle between the academicians and the rebels has reached a stalemate because the former now include many radicals in their ranks, while the latter have become increasingly obsessed with problems of form.

Of items in periodicals, perhaps the most interesting are "Poetry Since *The Waste Land*," by Cleanth Brooks (*SoR*, I, 487–500); "The New American Poets," by Kenneth Rexroth (*Harper's*, CCXXX, No. 1381, 65–71); "The Two Rooms: Humor in Modern American Verse," by Reed Whittemore (*WSCL*, V, 1964, 185–191); and "*Introduction à la* 'Beat Generation,'" by Alain Jouffroy (*TM*, XX, 1964, 961–980). Brooks's essay is easily the most substantial. With something of the same excitement with which, in the late thirties and early forties, he proclaimed the importance of irony and paradox, he now finds "un-analyzed juxtapositions" to be the structural basis of most modern poetry, and traces this technique back to Wordsworth: it began, he claims, as "an almost instinctive attempt on the part of Wordsworth and his fellow poets to circumvent what had seemed to them the numbing effects of misapplied reason." In support of this argument he cites Auden: "The real novelty in Romantic poetry is not its diction but its structure. If the Romantic poets, after rejecting Pope and Dryden, did not rediscover Donne and the metaphysical poets, this was because the latter, no less than the former, organized their poems *logically.*" In a brilliant explication (of the kind which he practices perhaps better than any living critic in English) of Frost's "Stopping by Woods on a Snowy Evening," Brooks shows how this poet uses such juxtaposition by contrasting, within the world of the poem, the man's relationship to nature with the horse's; and gives other examples of this device in Yeats, Eliot, Pound, MacLeish, Williams, Stevens, Lowell, Auden, and Warren. (The last two he acclaims "the most powerful poets of this generation.")

Brooks devotes the latter part of his article to the current reaction against Eliot and the modern school of wit; it is, he claims, a rebellion against "overt analogy" and "overt logic," and aspires toward poetry of the kind that Blake and Wordsworth had hoped to write, the former by the ecstatic projection of a personal vision, and the latter "with such naked austerity as to make the poem rise spontaneously, like an exhalation, from the minutely observed particulars." Brooks is clearly dubious of the attempt. Disagreeing with Donald Hall's statement, in the introduction to his anthology, *Contemporary American Poetry* (discussed in *ALS, 1963*) that a "new imagination" is at work in the most recent poetry, he maintains that the juxtapositions one finds therein are at least as old as Wordsworth: "The poet juxtaposes two images and hopes that the steel of the first will strike a spark from the flint of the second." Frequently, ignition fails to occur, and as a case in point he cites Williams' famous "Red Wheelbarrow": "I see the white chickens and the raindrops glazing the new paint, but I have to take on faith the author's statement that 'so much depends' on this scene."

Hall had written: "The new imagination reveals through images a subjective life which is *general*, and which corresponds to an old objective life of shared experience and knowing." But Brooks remains unconvinced:

> Genuine poetry has always united men by bringing them into a shared experience, but if Mr. Hall means more than this, if he finds in recent poetry something truly new, if he means for us to take his statements literally, then we are about to witness a shift in our whole cultural situation. For it was the split between the subjective and the objective—the chasm between the life of the emotions and attitudes within the poet and the universe outside him—that so much troubled the Romantic poets. The poetry of Wordsworth and the criticism of Coleridge are dominated by the attempt to bridge this chasm. It would be tidings indeed to learn that the American poets of the 1950's had finally spanned it.

This may well be, in its inclusiveness, the most important critical article of the year, but to one familiar with Brooks's earlier work the latter part of his essay strikes an oddly defensive note.

Rexroth's piece, intended for popular consumption, oversimplifies and exaggerates. Both in his poetry (derived from Pound and lacking the vitality of Williams', which was similarly derived) and in his criticism—which is really middlebrow journalism, judgment rather than illumination—Rexroth has for some years played the role of Tiresias to the younger generation of poets; like Tiresias, he is frequently blind. Examples: "The Imagist movement produced only a couple of poets of importance"; Cid Corman is "the most dedicated man in American literature"; Claude Vigée is "the most significant French poet ever to live in this country." His discussion of the current scene calls attention to the obvious (which, to be sure, may not always be obvious to readers of *Harper's*) but does little beyond that; one would scarcely call it enlightening in any general sense, though it is revealing of his personal tastes and those of his friends. (Of the dozen poets "of unquestioned ability" whom he asked to name their favorite poet, most chose Gary Snyder.) He does make one important point, that little of value has come out of the poetry of race relations: "The relation between the races in America is in fact a tragedy or a mortal sin, but artistically it is a bore. It is a shocking state of affairs, but it doesn't make for art."

Whittemore argues that the sharp division of modern American poetry into light and heavy verse is harmful to both: poets feel they must *choose*. Contrasting two "heavy" poems by Philip Booth and Lawrence Ferlinghetti with one of Kingsley Amis', he claims that English poetry lacks the stiffness of American; the English find it easier to be natural at the same time that they are serious. Jouffroy's essay is an intelligent and sympathetic discussion of Ginsberg, Corso, and Ferlinghetti. The American reader will not learn much about these figures *per se*, but there are valuable comparisons with French poets, particularly Michaux and Artaud.

ii. Individual Poets

Book-length studies were scarce. There were three books on Stevens, though one of them, *The Act of the Mind: Essays on the Poetry of Wallace Stevens* (Baltimore, Johns Hopkins Univ. Press), contains only four new essays as against eight which have previously been published. There was a book on Lowell, one on Roethke, and a pamphlet on Marianne Moore.

The Cosmological Eye, by Joseph N. Riddel (Baton Rouge, Louisiana State Univ. Press) is probably the most satisfactory full-length study of Stevens that has yet appeared. It is thorough, scholarly, objective. At the same time that he is aware of his subject's uniqueness, he is conscious of his limitations, and the major poems receive imaginative explication. Riddel notes that Stevens' reputation in the academies was slow in developing: "Among undergraduates, for whom *The Waste Land* is as common a title as *Macbeth*, Stevens is virtually unknown; and graduate students continue to 'discover' him year after year." Eugene Paul Nassar's *Wallace Stevens: An Anatomy of Figuration* (Philadelphia, Univ. of Pa. Press) is less ambitious, but it has the virtue of extreme compactness. Nassar is skeptical of Stevens' value as a philosopher, viewing him essentially as an "anti-rationalist who played with ideas, with the experience of thinking." Again, the explications are worthy of the best tradition of the New Criticism, and it is interesting to note that in his preface Nassar acknowledges his indebtedness to John Crowe Ransom. The four new essays in *The Act of the Mind* are "The Qualified Assertions of Wallace Stevens," by Helen Vendler; "On the Grammar of Wallace Stevens," by Mac Hammond; "The Climates of Wallace Stevens," by Richard A. Macksey; and "Nuances of a Theme by Wallace Stevens," by Denis Donoghue. The first two have a rather special approach; Macksey's essay is more inclusive, and Donoghue does a good job of presenting the predicament of the man on the park bench (who is the generic type of poet) in "Notes Toward a Supreme Fiction."

Jerome Mazzaro's *The Poetic Themes of Robert Lowell* (Ann Arbor, Univ. of Mich. Press) updates Hugh Staples' *Robert Lowell: The First Twenty Years* (1962) and is the first full-scale appreciation of this poet whom many critics now believe to be the most important talent living in America. The book does not make enough of Lowell's influences, perhaps; Milton is mentioned but not Donne, and Donne, by way of Allen Tate, was certainly one of Lowell's mentors. But it is systematic, observing a chronological approach, and full of fine insights; and the bibliography and index are excellent.

Theodore Roethke, whose reputation has risen steadily since his death, is the subject of a collection of essays edited by Arnold Stein (*Theodore Roethke*, Seattle, Univ. of Wash. Press). There are con-tributions by Spender, Snodgrass, Louis L. Martz, William Meredith, John Wain, Frederick J. Hoffman, Ralph J. Mills, Jr., Denis Don-oghue, and Roy Harvey Pearce. (Meredith's essay was discussed in *ALS, 1964.*) Donoghue and Pearce maintain that Roethke continued to grow until the end of his career; Snodgrass denies this. Pearce draws an interesting analogy with Blake, and suggests that had Roethke lived longer "he might have written a poem of power and identification, a *Jerusalem* for our age." According to Pearce, he could not take "the compulsive twentieth-century quest for identity via the route of alienation. . . . His was the way of sympathy, and he kept to it as long as he lived."

Jean Garrigue's pamphlet on Marianne Moore (UMPAW, No. 50) is a miracle of much-in-little; in the course of a brief forty-five pages she traces this poet's career from its beginnings right down to the present. In-depth discussion and explication of particular works are thus automatically excluded, and perhaps this is as well, for on the whole Miss Garrigue is a safer guide on matters of technique than of content and sensibility (as witness her judgment of "In Distrust of Merits").

Denis Donoghue's essay on Roethke, which appeared in Stein's collection, is reprinted (or vice versa) in his book *Connoisseurs of Chaos* (New York, Macmillan), which also contains an essay on Stevens wherein he compares this poet with Eliot (both men, he says, equate "the good with the conscious") and contrasts him to Williams. "It is unwise," he says, "to chart directions in Stevens' poetry or to say that he did this in the early poems and that different thing in the later poems. At any moment he was likely to write a poem that would confound the cartographer." This is a warning which has been heeded too seldom in Stevens criticism, as anyone who studies the mountainous mass of it—particularly the doctoral dissertations, which are very nearly legion—cannot but be aware.

Four essays concerned with individual poets also appeared in the anthology *American Poetry*. They are "The Age of Lowell," by Irvin Ehrenpreis; "The Diction of American Poetry," by David Ferry; "An Ironic Romantic: Three Readings in Wallace Stevens," by Malcolm Bradbury; and "Four Southerners," by Louis D. Rubin, Jr. Ehrenpreis states that in Lowell's early work he applied the great moral crises of history to his personal experience, while in his later work he reversed the process. Lowell's peculiar power, he suggests, derives from the fact that he is so completely of his time: "After outrage has exhausted itself in contempt, after the mind has got the habit of Dallas and South Africa, the shudder of curiosity remains." More than any other living poet writing in English, Ehrenpreis says, Lowell knows how to express this "shudder" in words. Ferry's essay is chiefly devoted to Williams, who he says rivals Frost in his use of language which is characteristically realistic and American. His analysis of the differences between Whitman and Williams (it is often assumed they had identical theories of diction) is particularly interesting. Bradbury offers original and intelligent explications of Stevens' "Bantam in Pine Woods," "The Sense of the

Sleight-of-hand Man," and "The Poem that Took the Place of a Mountain," and concludes that in most of Stevens' poems he uses *personae*, "colorful characters in whose profession or physical shape is implied an attitude towards the world, or more vaguely imagined agents . . . involved in significant moments of perception, in mobilities of the imagination, and often seeming to stand for himself." Rubin, one of the most active and astute critics of the Southern literary scene—particularly of the Fugitive and Agrarian group, whose official chronicler he might almost be said to be—appraises Ransom, Davidson, Tate, and Warren. While Tate and Davidson characteristically took their themes and images from Southern history, so that we associate them with ideas of order and stability, Ransom, he claims, is preoccupied with what is violent and irrational, and Warren's obsession with the themes of mortality and loneliness has cut him off from a *particular* history: "His poems are filled with images of the solitary individual contemplating his plight in time."

So numerous and so generally informative were the articles (in periodicals) devoted to specific poets in 1965, and to specific aspects of specific poets, that it is extremely difficult to choose among them: it is impossible to do justice here to all of them, even to all of them which are first-rate. Choosing almost at random, therefore, from the second group, I find that I must mention at least six. Three of them are devoted to Stevens, two to Williams, and one (in my opinion the best of the lot) to Yvor Winters. C. D. Cecil, in "An Audience for Wallace Stevens" (*EIC*, XV, 193–207), does not precisely set out to "get" Stevens (who since his death has been the object of almost as much hero worship as Dylan Thomas), but his analysis of this poet's limitations is the most penetrating that I have yet seen in print. "No recent major figure," he writes, "comes so close to being *le poète manqué.* The heritage of Symbolism is in his case an agony about the validity of words, and one gets a little tired of hearing about his self-sufficiency and indifference to all but an audience of one." Deploring Stevens' didactic tendencies, he states that the poems seem "almost to beg for a wide and not very perceptive audience that they can enlighten, especially concerning the arrogant presumptions that we call beliefs, attitudes, and opinions." According to Cecil, Stevens was frequently conscious that he had not completely realized his intentions in his poems: "Except possibly with 'Sunday Morning,' one never feels that the poet could join the reader in wholehearted admiration for his work." That fact, if it is one, is advanced as if it did not do the poet much credit, but it is possible to view the matter somewhat differently: how many good poets admire even their best work "wholeheartedly"? David P. Young's "A Skeptical Music: Stevens and Santayana" (*Criticism*, VII, 263–283) makes the general point that "if Stevens was not afraid to mix poetry with philosophy it was because he had accepted George Santayana's description of an ideal affinity between the two." Stevens, he claims, also shared Santayana's "radical skepticism" (hardly anyone would care to deny this). Some of Young's distinctions seem dangerously fine. In his first paragraph he states that Stevens' quest for an ideal poetry led him to write verse that "grew more and more insistently philosophical," and in the next paragraph we read: "For all his interest in philosophy, he never made poetry its vehicle." Patricia Merivale, in "Wallace Stevens' 'Jar': The Absurd Detritus of a Romantic Myth" (*CE*, XXVI, 527–532), makes a vigorous defense of Yvor Winters' controversial interpretation of "Anecdote of the Jar," according to which that object, so far from standing, as is usually thought, as a beneficent symbol of order in a universe of chaos (or, as an *artifact*, as an equally beneficent symbol of the perfection of art, like Keats's Grecian urn or one of Yeats's marvelous pieces of Byzantine jewelry), stands negatively instead as a symbol of *apparent* order—man-made, illusory, and incomplete. The argument is a difficult one to sustain, particularly in view of the explications of this poem by Howard Baker and J. B. Kirby. "Would we not," she asks, "be better off trying to grasp, to 'discover' the slovenly wilderness itself, rather than making experiments to mold it into our oversimplified image of perfection?" But is the question, even if we choose to answer it in the positive, really relevant?

A. Kingsley Weatherhead, in "William Carlos Williams and the World Beyond" (*ELH*, XXXII, 126–137), maintains that Williams in his later work not only creates a world (and himself in the process), but that he is able to look beyond it at another world, "no less real, which remains virginal to his approaches," a world suggested but not explored, composed of "raw materials that the poetry cannot, or cannot yet, or will not, encompass." Weatherhead makes his point by detailed references to specific poems, particularly "The Desert Music," and praises Williams' refusal to eliminate such raw materials from the poems for the sake of giving them a superficial order; he consistently avoids, he says, the "carefully finished frozen poem,"

and cites Williams' own definition of order: "not a little piss pot
for us all to urinate into," but "what is discovered after the fact."
This essay reminds us of the controversy over Stevens' jar, and suggests that—if Merivale's interpretation of that poem is correct—
Williams and Stevens are closer philosophically than we are accus-
tomed to think. Richard Gustafson's "William Carlos Williams: A
Map and Opinion" (CE, XXVI, 532–534, 539) is, rather surprisingly,
the first detailed systematic study of Paterson, whose five books,
Gustafson says, "show the various ways by which man tries to unlock his mind to find beauty." The moral of the first three books
of this important poem (and according to Gustafson Paterson is a
frankly didactic work) is that "personal striving for only oneself
ends in despair and failure," while the last two books teach that
"the best personal vitality leads away from the person to the per-
petuation of life and to art." Gustafson shows the great debt which
Williams owes to Whitman and to Pound, and concedes that the
poem suffers from inadequate revision, owing to the pressures of its
author's busy medical practice.

Paul Ramsey's essay, "Yvor Winters: Some Abstractions Against
Abstraction" (SR, LXXIII, 451–464), is brilliant. Noting Winters'
preference for literature in which a moral theme predominates, he
objects that this view of art "subsumes delight under instruction,
and omits many and legitimate kinds of delight." He also argues
that the sharp separation which Winters characteristically makes
between reason and impulse is meaningless: "He often speaks as
though one must choose between . . . rationalism (the priority of
reason) and voluntarism (the priority of will and consequently
emotion over reason)." I very much hope that one need not so
choose, as both theories seem to me rationally and practically impossible, and I have at least a good hunch, supported by some reasons, that the analysis of human experience which leads to the
disjunction is seriously at fault. But Ramsey's essay is by no means
wholly negative: he acknowledges Winters' distinction both as poet
and as critic, and his tone, even when he disagrees most radically
with his subject, never fails of being respectful.

San Fernando Valley State College

16. Drama

Malcolm Goldstein

i. Texts, Bibliographies, Reference

In 1965 the Indiana University Press completed its reissue of the "America's Lost Plays" series originally published by Princeton in the early forties. The wealth of material present in these ten double volumes is massive; however quaint most of the plays would look in the theater today, many of them still give pleasure in the library —to say nothing of their value as documents in our cultural history. Among the choicest items are several that receive comment in books and articles surveyed below: minor but enjoyable plays by James A. Herne, Bronson Howard's melodramas of the Gilded Age, and James O'Neill's popular *Monte Cristo*. Work remains to be done on these and other men represented in the series. Now that their "lost" plays have once more been regained, may it proceed!

An edition of William Bulloch Maxwell's *The Mysterious Father* prepared by Gerald Kahan (Athens, Univ. of Ga. Press) makes available another lost, but virtually unreadable, piece of the theatrical past. Maxwell's Italianate melodrama was first produced in Savannah in 1807; the editor observes that it resembles William Dunlap's *Ribbemont* of 1796.

Long overdue is the reissue of Hallie Flanagan's *Arena* (New York, Benjamin Blom), the history of the short-lived Federal Theatre project of the Works Progress Administration. The author, who served as Director of Federal Theatre, wrote her substantial account of its activities within months of the project's closing in 1939. Since it is primarily a piece of theatrical history rather than a study of dramatic literature, *Arena* comes only barely within the range of this annual report. To neglect it, however, would be to neglect an important aid to the understanding of the social drama of the thirties. In this regard the pages on the living newspapers and Negro drama are especially useful. To be sure, this book, for all its accuracy of detail and its seventy pages of production records and bibliography, is not an objective report. In view of the author's struggles with Congress to keep Federal Theatre alive, it could scarcely be other than a partisan account. What matter? Most books, after all, are bad; this one is not only good, but it is also a primary source of the greatest importance for students of the depression scene. And still there, for all to see, on page 342 is Miss Flanagan's famous exchange with Rep. Joseph Starnes on the political affiliations of Christopher Marlowe.

Two bibliographies appeared in 1965, each in a somewhat out-of-the-way place. Frances Manley's "William Inge: A Bibliography" (*ABC*, XVI, ii, 13–21) lists items on and by the playwright. The record of Inge's reviews for the St. Louis *Star-Times* will no doubt be of interest to his biographers to come. Of very limited usefulness is John C. McCloskey's "American Satires, 1637–1957: A Selective Checklist. Part I: Drama" (*SNL*, II, 101–109). The compiler lists various plays under their authors' names, but gives no indication of the subjects satirized in any of them. Presumably the omission of many titles that come to mind—for example, Kaufman and Ferber's *Dinner at Eight*—may be explained by the prefatory note that the bibliography includes "only works which are predominantly satiric in intent or effect and not those in which satire is merely incidental."

Walter J. Meserve's *An Outline History of American Drama* (Totowa, N. J., Littlefield, Adams) is a well-planned reference work covering the entire range of American writing for the stage without overemphasizing the period since World War I. Plot summaries are, of course, important in any book of this sort, but the author also provides thoughtful criticism, a mass of historical detail, and bibliographies as he describes the development of dramaturgy in this country.

ii. Eighteenth and Nineteenth Centuries

Of the year's two essays on eighteenth-century drama, both are concerned primarily with language. Ralph Borden Culp, in "Drama-and-Theater in the American Revolution" (*SM*, XXXII, 79–86), discusses the rhetoric and dramatic situations devised by Whig and Tory playwrights during the Revolution. The Whigs, he has discovered, were the more skillful propagandists. Studies in the period are so few that any sensible essay is welcome; nevertheless, a reviewer may complain about the uninspired style of this author, the hyphenation of "drama" and "theater," and the summary conclusion which merely rephrases the content of the essay. Superior to this is Roger B. Stein's "Royall Tyler and the Question of Our Speech" (*NEQ*, XXXVIII, 454–474). The author believes that Tyler was attempting in the play to develop a standard of speech for the independent American nation. He does not think that Tyler succeeded in the attempt, but he demonstrates that the playwright used language effectively for the individualization of his characters.

As always, good studies of nineteenth-century plays and their authors are scarce. Of the four items reviewed, three appeared in 1964, but too late, unfortunately, for mention until this year. One of the four is a biographical sketch quite remote from the field. Two, on Howard and Herne, are more encouraging; they continue the reassessment of end-of-the-century playwrights that has been in progress, if only limpingly, through the present decade.

The extra-theatrical activity of William Dunlap, a contemporary of Royall Tyler's whose career spanned the end of the eighteenth and the beginning of the nineteenth centuries, is the subject of an essay by Oral S. Coad: "William Dunlap: New Jersey Artist" (*PNJHS*, LXXXIII, 238–263). Coad, it will be remembered, is the author of the standard biography of the playwright; here he writes of Dunlap's range as a painter.

Michael R. Booth in "The Drunkard's Progress: Nineteenth-Century Temperance Drama" (*DR*, XLIV, 1964, 205–212) writes entertainingly on a staple of our forebears' theater. Booth describes the anatomy of the temperance play as it existed in America and Britain from about 1830 on through the century: the drunkard's knowledge of himself as a moral criminal, the important pledge-signing scene, and so on to the drunkard's melodramatic recovery or agonizing death.

Bronson Howard emerges as a talented commentator on his age in Maxwell Bloomfield's "Mirror for Businessmen: Bronson Howard's Melodramas, 1870–1890" (*MASJ*, V, 1964, ii, 38–49). The playwright, as Bloomfield points out, wrote his plays about American life at a time when producers preferred plots set in other lands. His best works are peopled with American businessmen and their families and reflect the concerns of a fortune-building age. The financiers are simple and industrious in Howard's depictions, even sentimental —for to the extent that Howard was a social critic, he was more inclined to criticize the private vices of businessmen than their business

affairs. The playwright receives fair treatment in this essay; Howard
was not a great writer, but without question his plays remain
readable.

Herbert J. Edwards and Julie A. Herne's *James A. Herne: The
Rise of Realism in the American Drama* (Orono, Univ. of Maine
Press) is a good critical biography of an engaging figure. The basis
of the book is a memoir by Julie A. Herne, the playwright's eldest
daughter, who died in 1955. Herne at the outset of his career lived
an almost typical actor's life of shuttling back and forth from one
stock company to another: in the sixties and seventies he played in
upstate New York, Baltimore, Washington, Philadelphia, and San
Francisco. He learned the repertory, married, got a divorce, and
married again. At the end of the seventies he began to write in col-
laboration with David Belasco, and thereupon began the development of a talent which was to contribute generously to American
drama. Friendships with Hamlin Garland, who introduced him to
Ibsen's plays, and with William Dean Howells were important in the
sharpening of his taste for realism, and he began in the eighties to
write social drama in a style then unfamiliar to the American public.
As is usual with writers who are in advance of their time, Herne
found it difficult at first to win approval for such plays as *Margaret
Fleming* and *Griffith Davenport*, produced, respectively, at the beginning and end of the nineties. But Herne's talent ultimately received the recognition it deserved, and the reputation continues to
grow. Readers of this book will find a just balance of biographical
detail with analysis of Herne's work and literary relationships.

iii. Twentieth Century

The books and essays on twentieth-century drama published in 1965
make a weighty bulk in the arms of the reviewer who must carry
them home to read. Fully half take up matters of no importance
or treat important matters inadequately. The favorite authors again
this year are Eugene O'Neill, Arthur Miller, Tennessee Williams, and
Edward Albee—and it is a safe bet that they will be the favorites of
1966 as well. Were all the studies of these four writers of good quality, no one could object to them on grounds of quantity. All too few,
however, repay the attention they ask of a reader.

Two new volumes of reprinted critical essays cover, between
them, most of the interesting playwrights from the nineties to the

present. *American Playwrights on Drama*, edited by Horst Frenz (New York, Hill and Wang), is a selection of twenty-two pieces by fourteen writers from O'Neill to Albee. While most will be familiar to specialists, the book is nevertheless a convenient gathering of important materials. *American Drama and Its Critics*, edited by Alan S. Downer (Chicago, Univ. of Chicago Press), is a selection of less familiar pieces which begins with Herne's "Art for Truth's Sake," an essay mainly on his own plays. Among other noteworthy pieces are George Jean Nathan's shrewd, prodding comments on O'Neill's plays for the old *American Mercury* from 1924 through 1929 and Robert Benchley's reviews of musicals for the old *Life* and the *New Yorker* from 1921 through 1936. Included among the seventeen items is one new essay: Malcolm Goldstein's "Clifford Odets and the Found Generation." The author expresses the opinion in this piece that Odets' decline was the result of his inability to alter his view of American society with the changing times.

a. **Rice, Barry, Sherwood.** The oldest living playwright of distinction in America is Elmer Rice, whose first play, *On Trial*, was produced over fifty years ago. Robert Hogan, in *The Independence of Elmer Rice* (Carbondale, Southern Illinois Univ. Press), attempts to rescue this writer from neglect. Hogan is to be praised for writing only a scant hundred and fifty pages on the prolific but uneven Rice. Nevertheless, to take away with the left hand what one gives with the right, the book is some forty pages longer than it need be. The unnecessary parts of the book are the first and last chapters, which are largely routine complaints about the commercial stage and journalistic criticism, and the next to last chapter, which is the author's memory of his unhappy experience as the director of a college production of Rice's *Love among the Ruins*, previously unproduced. But the central chapters offer helpful criticism of plays which ought not to be forgotten. Hogan views Rice as primarily a realist and notes that those of his plays which are not literal transcriptions of life do not so much depart from realism as extend its boundaries.

Philip Barry, with whom Rice once collaborated on a play, is also honored with a book this year. Joseph P. Roppolo's *Philip Barry* (TUSAS) will help to preserve the memory of a much better than average Broadway writer, such as the public too easily forgets, whose best work is a bright reflection of its period. Roppolo presents the biographical material conscientiously and well, offering a portrait of

Barry which resembles those he himself drew of wellborn persons
in his comedies. In the section on the playwright's student days,
Roppolo is especially interesting on Barry's relationship with George
Pierce Baker, from whose instruction he quite obviously profited. A
flaw in the book is that the analyses of individual works include far
more details of plot than are necessary. Such close retelling seems
to be required of contributors to the Twayne series.

John Mason Brown's *The World of Robert E. Sherwood, Mirror
to His Times, 1896–1939* (New York, Harper and Row) is the first
part of what is to be a two-volume biography. It is an "official" biography; Brown has had access to the Sherwood papers and the co-
operation of the playwright's widow. Like Arthur and Barbara Gelb
in their monumental life of O'Neill, Brown chooses to omit notes to
his sources; he is, however, at least as trustworthy as the Gelbs and,
again like them, gives a list of the many persons close to his playwright who have supplied information. Brown does not explore the
plays in depth, but otherwise does his job well. The truth is, however,
that Sherwood's life up to 1939 does not make strikingly interesting
reading matter to anyone who is already familiar with the theatrical
and literary scenes of the twenties and thirties. In all likelihood the
second volume, which will cover Sherwood's wartime activities, will
prove more stimulating.

b. **The twenties.** Four short essays cover, in a variety of styles, a
broad range of topics of the twenties. Thomas Richard Gorman, writing on "Dos Passos and the Drama" (*SM*, XXXII, 420–426), comments stodgily on Dos Passos as a critic of American theater, a
member of the New Playwrights' Theater, and as a social dramatist.
The piece adds nothing to the information already available in other
recent publications on the New Playwrights. In "Expressionism: 40
Years After" (*CEA*, XXVII, ix, 1, 7–8), Sister Ann Gertrude Coleman
discusses the expressionistic devices employed by O'Neill, Rice, John
Howard Lawson, and (later) Thornton Wilder. She believes that the
development of dramatic expressionism in America derived from the
influence of Strindberg on O'Neill and was not, as is sometimes
thought, influenced by German dramaturgy. John J. Sommers' "The
Critic as Playwright: A Study of Stark Young's *The Saint*" (*MD*, VII,
446–453) is a paper on a very slight subject. Sommers reviews
Young's play (produced unsuccessfully by the Provincetown Players
in 1924) with the purpose of discovering whether it is constructed in

accordance with Young's principles as a critic. His finding is that Young did indeed practice what he preached, but that his play is dull. Gerald Weales, in "What *Garrick Gaieties*? A Note on Reference and Source Material" (*MD*, VIII, 198–203), provides an amusing piece on the difficulty of reconstructing a musical revue from the published records of its production. Weales has looked at programs and reviews of the first (1925) edition of the Theatre Guild's famous revue, and, discovering that many changes of material and performers took place during the run, concludes that one cannot say precisely what such a production really was like. In passing, he takes a quite justifiable swipe at the popular historians of the musical theater.

c. O'Neill. Examinations of the work of O'Neill continue to pour from the presses. Authors of the new studies express, either tacitly or directly, a very high regard for the plays. It is the general assumption that O'Neill has reached the status of a classic writer, and therefore the more explications, the better. Regrettably, a few of the critics have begun to repeat themselves and one another, and some have allowed themselves to publish essays on decidedly minor points.

The best of the new studies—and indeed a very good book—is John H. Raleigh's *The Plays of Eugene O'Neill* (Carbondale, Southern Illinois Univ. Press). It is an investigation of the influences at work upon O'Neill's thought and the form of his plays, as well as an attempt to locate the playwright's position, so to speak, in the stream of modern literature and to present him as a great American writer. Raleigh's scrutiny and analysis of the work is extremely close; we are told, for instance, that the late plays "always take place on, or begin on, excessively hot days." The result is a most illuminating study, even when it covers such relatively familiar ground as the playwright's contrasts between night and day, sea and land, and city and country, and his use of biographical details. Among many points of interest is a section on O'Neill's attitude toward and skill in delineating various religious and national groups; Raleigh ranks him with Twain and Faulkner as a writer on the Negro. The author's essay of 1964 on O'Neill's debt to the theater of his father reappears, conveniently, and again stands out as an impressive contribution. The final chapter, on the playwright's affinities to other American writers, includes a comparison of his intellectual concerns with those of Melville.

John Gassner, in *Eugene O'Neill* (UMPAW, No. 45), covers

O'Neill's extensive output in a mere thirty-nine pages of text. Gassner observes that the plays may be divided into two general categories, the naturalistic works with which O'Neill began his career and wrote at intervals until the end and, beginning with *The Emperor Jones* in 1920, those which are "romantic, symbolist, and expressionistic"—in short, antinaturalistic. Paragraphs on the early expressionistic pieces should, though reserved in tone, stimulate the curiosity of students. Despite his disapproval of the great length of the late works, Gassner praises them for their humanity and theatricality. He is able, in his conclusion, to make the most of O'Neill's verbosity by describing the playwright as "the *master* of massive dramatic assault." Thoughtful readers may object to the reference to O'Neill as "the first American 'naturalist.'"

Two essays of interest are examinations of early plays. Charles Fish, in "Beginnings: O'Neill's *The Web*" (*PULC*, XXVII, 3–20), discusses material in this "lost" play which prefigures the works to come: the determination to portray reality as evident in the suffering of the heroine, the focus on low-life characters, and the conscientious effort to bring the dialect of New York into the language of the play. In "The Unity of O'Neill's S. S. *Glencairn*" (*AL*, XXXVII, 280–290), R. Dilworth Rust describes those elements of the four *Glencairn* plays which unite them. They are various dramatic themes, the treatment of the seamen as group hero, the reach for ideas above the purely personal (as evident in the titles), and the employment of pairs of iterative images.

Less rewarding are three essays on aspects of the playwright's thought. Arthur H. Nethercot, in "The Psychoanalyzing of Eugene O'Neill: Postscript" (*MD*, VIII, 150–155), merely brings together comments by O'Neill on psychoanalysts as reported by the Gelbs; the "postscript" of the title refers to an earlier article of his own. Robert C. Wright's "O'Neill's Universalizing Technique in *The Iceman Cometh*" (*MD*, VIII, 1–11) is an unnecessarily long and somewhat disjointed essay on the devices which make the play universally meaningful. These are the use of ritual and myth, the symbols of various sorts, poetic density (the multiplicity of themes), and humor; all have long been evident to students of the play. Sophus K. Winther, in "Eugene O'Neill: The Dreamer Confronts His Dream" (*ArQ*, XXI, 221–233), also comments on the dramatist's universal appeal. O'Neill, as Winther views his work, is appealing as a writer of the illusions

without which man cannot live. This, too, is familiar, but its application to *More Stately Mansions* is of interest.

Two essays which relate O'Neill's plays to the work of other writers are less than convincing. Egil Tørnqvist, in "Ibsen and O'Neill:
A Study of Influence" (*SS*, XXXVII, 211–235), pushes too hard. It
is, of course, evident that O'Neill knew Ibsen's plays, but no purpose
is served by the observation that a similarity between Ephraim Cabot
and Brand is "kinship, which may or may not be due to direct influ-
ence." Nor, to the present reviewer, do the resemblances of *Ghosts* to
Long Day's Journey into Night and *The Lady from the Sea* to *Anna
Christie* seem to be anything but, indeed, resemblances. Deena P.
Metzger writes, in "Variations on a Theme: A Study of *Exiles* by
James Joyce and *The Great God Brown* by Eugene O'Neill" (*MD*,
VIII, 174–184), that in their themes and the design of their characters
the two plays have much in common. The author does not claim that
Joyce the Ibsenite influenced O'Neill the Strindbergian, but merely
gives the two plays a comparison-and-contrast treatment at length.

Finally, among the O'Neill items, are two slim volumes which in
their quite different ways should prove very useful. Horst Frenz's
Eugene O'Neill (Berlin, Colloquium Verlag) is a concise introduction
to O'Neill's life and work in German. Jordan Y. Miller, in *Playwright's
Progress: O'Neill and the Critics* (Chicago, Scott, Foresman), offers
a casebook consisting of reviews published in newspapers and weekly
and monthly magazines during O'Neill's lifetime and on to the major
revivals of 1964. Miller divides the career into six periods and provides a separate introduction to each. The selection is excellent. Certainly no O'Neill enthusiast should miss Lionel Trilling's commentary
on the plays through *Days without End*.

d. **The thirties.**   Studies of the dramatic currents of the thirties, or
on writers whose theatrical reputations date from that decade, are few
this year. Most, moreover, are brief.

Although Thornton Wilder began to publish plays in the second
decade of the century, it was not until 1938, when *Our Town* was
produced, that he emerged as a major playwright. In *The Art of
Thornton Wilder* (Lincoln, Univ. of Neb. Press), Malcolm Goldstein
discusses all of Wilder's work to date, novels as well as plays. He
finds that a single theme, expressed in a variety of ways, runs through
it. Simply put, it is a plea to the human being to make the most of his

brief time on earth. This, Wilder insists, he can do only if he refuses to live in the past or spin fantasies about the future; otherwise he will miss the marvels of the present moment. Astute readers may suspect that Goldstein is more comfortable in the criticism of drama than in the criticism of fiction.[1]

Franz N. Link, in "Das Theater Thornton Wilders" (*NS*, XIV, 305–318), offers, in German, a brief examination of the plays. The paper is useful for the analysis provided of *The Alcestiad*; the play is Wilder's least familiar and has been published only in a German translation.

Four essays treat, in various ways, the social dramas with which many, if not most, dramatists of the depression decade were preoccupied. In "The Conclusion of *Night over Taos*" (*AL*, XXXVII, 318–321), Laurence G. Avery, who has examined the manuscript of Maxwell Anderson's tragedy, observes that the play as its author wrote it differs from the two printed versions (of 1932 and 1940). In the first, the final speech of the protagonist is cut; in the second, it is divided between him and a minor character. More is needed than this correction, however, to turn Anderson's hapless play into good theater. Warren G. French, in "The First Theatrical Production of Steinbeck's *Of Mice and Men*" (*AL*, XXXVI, 525–527), notes that a version of the play was given in May, 1937, by the San Francisco Theatre Union, one of the scores of workers' theaters then in operation, before the final version appeared on Broadway in November. In "The Living Newspaper as a Dramatic Form" (*MD*, VIII, 82–94), Douglas McDermott gives an analysis and short history of the form of documentary drama made popular by Federal Theatre. He also offers a reminder that many other examples exist than the few that were published commercially in the thirties. Malcolm Goldstein has a dual thesis in "Body and Soul on Broadway" (*MD*, VII, 411–421), an essay that spans the years from the thirties to the sixties. He attempts to demonstrate, first, that the drama of psychological motivation popular at present has grown directly out of the sociological drama of the depression period and, second, that it is no more honest in its presentation of ideas than was that earlier group of plays.

Like Wilder, Archibald MacLeish wrote plays before the thirties,

---

1. Joseph Firebaugh writes in *AL*, XXXVII, 507: "Mr. Goldstein writes well; his critical acumen illuminates the plays and novels"—Ed.

but first came into prominence as a dramatist in that decade. Although Signi L. Falk in *Archibald MacLeish* (TUSAS) does not overlook the writer's work for the theater, she is not, it would seem, greatly interested in it. She ignores *Union Pacific*, a ballet scenario, except for mention of the title, and *The Secret of Freedom*, a television play, receives nothing more than a listing in the bibliography. In her discussion of *Panic*, a depression play of substantial historical value, she makes no mention of the contribution of Martha Graham and does not recognize that the form of the play is a variety of "agitprop." *J. B.*, however, receives full treatment, including comment on some differences between the original and Broadway versions. The book leaves the present reviewer with the thought that a good essay on MacLeish as a political playwright remains to be written.

e. **Contemporary drama, Tennessee Williams.** With few exceptions, discussions of the drama of more recent years center on the work of the major figures. Two books have appeared which range over the field, but they are intended for the mass audience rather than for specialists. Allan Lewis' *American Plays and Playwrights of the Contemporary Theatre* (New York, Crown) is essentially a series of reviews covering plays produced both on Broadway and off since 1957, with chapters on all the principal writers. R. H. Gardner, drama critic of the Baltimore *Sun*, presents in *The Splintered Stage: The Decline of the American Theater* (New York, Macmillan) an unhappy view of the sociological and psychological drama of today and suggests that playwrights consider as subjects such stirring figures as President Kennedy, Martin Luther King, and John Glenn. Along with these, if anywhere, should be mentioned Howard Taubman's *The Making of the American Theatre* (New York, Coward-McCann), a whirlwind tour from the eighteenth century to the present, but with two-thirds of its contents given over to the twentieth century. A review of reviewers is offered by Nathan Cohen, the entertainment editor of the Toronto *Star* in "American Drama Criticism Today" (*TamR*, No. 34, pp. 42–56). Among those currently practicing, he admires only Harold Clurman in the *Nation* and Robert Brustein in the *New Republic*.

Tennessee Williams' long list of successful plays elicits annually a mass of reviews and investigations, along with, though less substantially, reports on his private life by persons who have known him.

Some are easily dismissed, such as Gilbert Maxwell's *Tennessee Williams and Friends* (Cleveland, World), a book of gossip whose style is embarrassingly arch. But to all his critics, whatever they wish to say about him, Williams is an important writer, even at his worst.

Esther Merle Jackson's respect for the playwright is evident on every page of her *The Broken World of Tennessee Williams* (Madison, Univ. of Wis. Press). Determined though she is to present Williams as a man of profound intellectual capacity, the author nevertheless writes with restraint. Her intention is to discuss the development of Williams' art. After providing a history of the evolution of dramatic form, which in fact the book does not need, she discusses Williams' technique as a fusion of expressionistic devices with traditional—that is, realistic—theatrical means. Among other topics of the book are Williams' ability to write from a particular character's point of view, his skill in the use of materials from the dance and other arts, and his image of man. On this last, large topic, the author observes that Williams has gradually developed a myth of modern man; his typical, suffering protagonist is an anti-hero embarked on a spiritual journey. In recent work, she believes, the search for God is the journey's goal. This is a clearheaded study.

In *Tennessee Williams* (UMPAW, No. 53), Gerald Weales writes briefly and well of the playwright as the creator of the "different" individual who can see the world clearly for the very reason that he stands outside it. Such an individual, Weales observes, may be an artist, a disturbed person, a cripple, a "sexual specialist," or a foreigner, and he may be menaced by others, by the universe, or indeed by himself. Yet, Weales notes, in these plays of troubled heroes and heroines, it is at times hard to tell who is the victim and who is the victimizer. Weales has also written two short pieces on Williams. In "Tennessee Williams Borrows a Little Shaw" (*ShawR*, VIII, 63–64), he points to some similarities between *You Touched Me!* and *Heartbreak House*. In "Tennessee Williams's 'Lost' Play" (*AL*, XXXVII, 321–323), he describes the one-act "At Liberty." The play first appeared in 1941 in *American Scenes*, an anthology edited by William Kozlenko, but has long been out of print and has been omitted from bibliographies of Williams' work.

In "*The Glass Menagerie*: From Story to Play" (*MD*, VIII, 142–149), Lester A. Beaurline traces the development of the work through four versions: short story, long one-act play, and the longer play as published first in 1945 and again in 1948, with later revisions in the mid-fifties. Beaurline describes three of the play's moments as Williams altered and improved them in the various treatments over the years.

Five additional essays of the year offer a variety of views. Durant Da Ponte, in "Tennessee Williams' Gallery of Feminine Characters" (*TSL*, X, 7–26), identifies three types: the Southern belle, the Latin, and the fading actress. Alan Casty, in "Tennessee Williams and the Small Hands of the Rain" (*MRR*, I, iii, 27–43), writes of "an archetypal dream of fusion" (of aspects of personality) that he finds in all the plays, though changing over the years. Marvin Spevack, in "Tennessee Williams: The Idea of a Theater" (*JA*, X, 221–231), comments on the personal quality in Williams' work: the "I-you" sense of the prefaces, the interest in relations among individuals. It is this which he believes to be important in Williams' plays, not the economic, social, or political ideas present in them. In "American Abelard: A Footnote to *Sweet Bird of Youth*" (*CE*, XXVI, 630–634), Bernard F. Dukore's principal point is that the affair of Chance Wayne and Heavenly Finley resembles that of Abelard and Héloïse; both relationships were forbidden, and Chance, more passive than later Williams characters, is to suffer emasculation. Robert B. Heilman, in "Tennessee Williams: Approaches to Tragedy" (*SoR*, I, 770–790), admires the plays, but describes them as "dramas of disaster" and melodramas, rather than as tragedies. Whether the plays end calamitously or not, the characters suffer from those "troubles that simply come upon human beings," not from the divided mind possessed by traditional tragic characters. He notes that in recent plays Williams has introduced a "nurse" or "savior" figure, whose presence obviously affects the outcome.

f. **Miller, Inge.** Sheila Huftel, in *Arthur Miller: The Burning Glass* (New York, Citadel), remarks that Miller is a man who, confronted with a problem, would take steps to cure it, whereas Williams would only loose pity on it. Although other critics of Miller's work have stressed many of the ideas which this author mentions—the theme of guilt, the commitment of the protagonists, the importance of the family, the individual as social being—her book gives much that is less familiar. Especially to be commended is the introductory chapter, with its carefully presented biographical material, including commentary on Miller's confrontation with the House Committee on Un-American Activities. Elsewhere, probing for clues to Miller's method, she compares his version of Ibsen's *The Enemy of the People* to the original, Sartre's film version of *The Crucible* to the play as Miller wrote it, and the two versions of *A View from the Bridge*—these also are among the book's best sections. Had the manuscript undergone a rigorous thinning out of details offered in the plot summaries, the book would be better for it. It is, nevertheless, an ably written study.

Authors of the year's essays on Miller treat problems of individual plays. So well liked is Willy Loman by most of his critics that he is now a real person for them, no longer a mere dramatic personage, as were the major characters of Shakespeare to certain Victorian critics. "It is impossible to speculate on what sort of influence Willy's mother had on him, but it is safe to say that Willy was deprived of the masculine influence which allowed Ben to so blithely head for Alaska and wind up in Africa," writes Barry Edward Gross in "Peddler and Pioneer in *Death of a Salesman*" (*MD*, VII, 405–410). The author comments on Miller's employment of certain qualities of the frontier life and the frontier mentality in characterizing Willy and his sons. A disapproving view of Willy is offered by Margaret Loftus Ranald in "*Death of a Salesman*: Fifteen Years After" (*Comment*, VI, iv, 28–35). The author refuses to accept the play as tragedy, finds it full of clichés, and believes that its language is at times bathetic. Arthur D. Epstein, in "A Look at *A View from the Bridge*" (*TSLL*, VII, 109–122), is mainly interested in the personality of Eddie Carbone and suggests that Miller feels something for Eddie despite the enormity of his crime. He believes, curiously, that Eddie's fellow workers on the dock are as much inclined as he to wonder about Rodolpho's masculinity.

R. Baird Shuman's *William Inge* (TUSAS) is a book for which there is no very great need at present. It is true that Inge has produced, all in all, as much work as Miller, but since the mid-fifties his career has been in decline. Shuman is aware that Inge's recent work is unsatisfactory, but he has nevertheless written an extended examination of all the plays, with ponderously detailed summaries.

g. Albee, Negro drama. Edward Albee now seems to have taken Inge's place alongside Williams and Miller. Although Albee has not created a successful play since *Who's Afraid of Virginia Woolf?*, he is still quite clearly someone to write about. From whatever points his critics start out, most of them mention in passing his vision of a decaying American society and his unsympathetic mother-figures. By no means are all of the essays favorable.

Among the authors on Albee this year are three who examine the plays with the purpose of discovering the traditions behind them. The title of the essay by Elizabeth C. Phillips, "Albee and the Theatre of the Absurd" (*TSL*, X, 73–80), indicates its content. The author names those conventions of the absurd which she has detected in the plays through *Virginia Woolf*. Charles Thomas Samuels, in "The Theatre of Edward Albee" (*MR*, VI, 187–201), gives the opinion, however, that Albee has taken only mannerisms from the absurdists. In "*Who's Afraid of Virginia Woolf?* and the Tradition" (*BuR*, XIII, i, 27–36), Emil Roy observes that naturalism and the absurd are combined in the play, and also that it is allegorical and allusive. He is concerned as well to defend Albee's morality; it is his belief that Albee offers shocking material only to uphold goodness and to decry the puritanical moral code.

Additional speculations on the plays treat, among other matters, Albee's characterization of the family and his obscurantism. Lee Baxandall, in "The Theatre of Edward Albee" (*TDR*, IX, iv, 19–40), an essay longer than need be, writes of Albee's use of the family to express his view of the debilitation of society. The archetypal family as it appears in the plays is made up of three generations: "then"— the powerful older generation of pioneer stock; "now"—the generation of the daddy who has abandoned leadership and the mommy who must take over; "nowhere"—the generation of such figures as the insensitive Nick of *Virginia Woolf*, who may control the future. Melvin L. Plotinsky, in "The Transformations of Understanding: Edward Albee in the Theatre of the Irresolute" (*DramS*, IV, 220–232), observes that Albee writes of a world in which intellectual understanding is impossible and that for this reason the plays are without resolution, adding, however, that the most recent plays have begun to approach it. (Yet it is possible to argue against the author's notion that *Virginia Woolf* ends irresolutely—that is, without the establishment of truth in the place of the illusions which George and Martha have held.) With the help of a more than generous supply of quotations, Marion A. Taylor provides an essay whose title sums up its contents: "Edward Albee and August Strindberg: Some Parallels Between *The Dance of Death* and *Who's Afraid of Virginia Woolf?*" (*PELL*, I, 59–71).

Two authors write enthusiastically of Albee's most controversial play. Thomas B. Markus, in "*Tiny Alice* and Tragic Catharsis" (*ETJ*, XVII, 225–233), admires the play as a tragedy; as he interprets it, the action concludes with catharsis for Julian, who dies serenely, and simultaneously with catharsis for the audience as it responds to his death. In "The Social Theatre of Edward Albee" (*PrS*, XXXIX, 248–262), Peter Wolfe focuses on Albee's investigation of social malaise in such matters as the shallow life of Peter, the family man in *The Zoo Story*, and the destructive role of the American woman as she appears in other plays. He believes that Albee may be altering the woman's role, since Miss Alice appears to be working toward the redemption of Julian, not his destruction. How many persons, one wonders, who have sat through *Tiny Alice* would agree with him that in it Albee demonstrates "magnificent showmanship"?

No theatrical phenomenon of the sixties, not even the rise of Albee, is so remarkable as the rapid development of a strong body of plays by Negroes on the position of the Negro in American life. These have ranged in mood and method from *Purlie Victorious*, a satiric folk comedy by Ossie Davis, to *The Slave*, LeRoi Jones's fantasy of revenge. Waters E. Turpin comments on these and other writers— among them, James Baldwin and the late Lorraine Hansberry—in "The Contemporary American Negro Playwright" (*CLAJ*, IX, 12–24). In his essay Turpin provides, in brief, a history of twentieth-century drama on the Negro from the plays of the white Ridgely Torrence to those of Baldwin and Jones. Few plays written before very recent times come in for praise. Those that the author admires provide strong, unsentimental portraits of the Negro: William DuBois' *Haiti*, Paul Green and Richard Wright's *Native Son*, Robert Ardrey's *Jeb*, and Arnaud d'Usseau and James Gow's *Deep Are the Roots*. In discussing the relatively young, embattled Negro writers of the present, he realizes that their work is harsh, but is willing to excuse them for making it so. A topic as important as this, though well treated here, cannot be exhausted in one essay. It is to be hoped that other critics and scholars are at work on it now.

Queens College

17. Folklore

John T. Flanagan

The year 1964 saw the appearance of the final volume of the *Frank C. Brown Collection of North Carolina Folklore* (Durham, N. C., Duke Univ. Press), the whole admirably edited by a variety of specialists and including an extraordinary compilation of the ballads, tales, proverbs, traditions, and superstitions of a single state. Wayland D. Hand's edition, Volume VII, of the *Popular Beliefs and Superstitions from North Carolina*, brought to a successful end a project which began in 1952 and which makes available the most complete collection of regional American folklore. Nothing comparable was published in 1965, but the year's work illustrates convincingly the amazing scope and complexity of scholarship in American folklore.

A survey of the American folklore material published during 1965 reveals an astonishing diversity and range. In substance the material varies from studies of ballad theory and examinations of individual songs to compilations of beliefs and superstitions, interpretations of folktales, analyses of myths or legends, and explorations of the use of folklore in American literature. In the process, connections between folklore and such fields as history, biography, musicology, and anthropology are convincingly demonstrated.

i. Bibliography

Four bibliographical compilations are of special merit. For the September issue of the *Tennessee Folklore Society Bulletin*, a mimeographed periodical published at Nashville, William J. Griffin compiled an index of the first thirty volumes, a useful work which confirms the wide variety of material appearing in the *Bulletin*. Many of the articles indexed refer to the folklore of Tennessee and Kentucky, but peripheral regions are included and some of the interpretive and analytical discussions have a wider frame of reference.

The quarterly *Abstracts of Folklore Studies* digests current periodical material, each item including full bibliographical information and providing a paragraph of summary or comment. The general arrangement is alphabetical according to the journals cited. The September issue, devoted to the Annual Bibliography for 1964, was compiled by W. Edson Richmond and is arranged by topics from general folklore to peripheral material. Within each category the material is presented alphabetically by the names of authors.

Each March issue of the *Southern Folklore Quarterly* is devoted to the folklore bibliography of the preceding year. Thus the March, 1965, number contains the folklore material for 1964 and with the index of contributors runs to 125 pages. The compilation is divided into ten sections and extends beyond verbal folklore to include ritual, dance, and material culture. Moreover, a substantial number of the references are not related to the United States, since items from all over the world and from periodicals in many languages are included. Since the arrangement is based on folklore types, the seeker of American material (whether it be an article dealing with Hart Crane's symbolism, Thomas Wolfe's folk heritage, or fiddle tunes in the Southern Appalachians) must disregard a considerable number of foreign items during his quest for native scholarship in order to profit by it. Yet this bibliography, since it includes both periodical articles and books, is the most substantial and comprehensive annual listing available.

The December issue of the *New York Folklore Quarterly* contains an unusually valuable "Bibliographical Introduction to American Folklore" by the Swiss scholar Robert Wildhaber. The author is the director of the Swiss Museum for Folklore in Basel and has long been interested in American folklore. His compilation originally appeared in German in a Swiss periodical (*Schweizerisches Archiv für Volkskunde*) and was both revised and enlarged for the English version. Because of the extraordinary comprehensiveness of the bibliography, an enumeration of the subheadings seems desirable:

> Intentions and Tendencies of American Folklore
> University Courses, Archives, and Libraries
> Festschriften
> Periodicals and Serial Publications
> Bibliographies
> Folklife Museums
> Introductions to Folklore
> Cultural History, History of Ideas, and Sociology
> Sects and Folk Religion
> Immigration and Settlement
> Regional Ethnic Groups

Negro Folklore
Regional Folklore
Folk Tales
Heroes, Outlaws, and Cowboys
Humorous Anecdotes, Funny Stories, Tall Tales
Popular Reading Matter
Folksongs, Ballads, and Folk Music
Folk Dance
Proverbs, Sayings, and Riddles
Folk Drama and Folk Theater
Children's Games and Toys
Almanacs, Weather Lore, Animal Lore, and Plant Lore
Folk Medicine
Folk Beliefs, Superstitions, and Witchcraft
Calendar Customs and Customs of the Life Cycle
Folk Art
Imagery and Popular Painting
Santos, Bultos, and Retablos
Folk Architecture
Furniture
Handicrafts
Everyday Life, Daily Work, Tools and Utensils
Costume and Textiles.

Wildhaber's list has two very obvious limitations, one its very comprehensiveness and the other a deliberate exclusion. European folklore scholars pay more attention to the material arts than do American scholars, with the result that such sections as those dealing with furniture, painting, costume, and textiles would normally be omitted from any American bibliography of a similar nature while such a section as that dealing with immigration would more properly be relegated to a bibliography of history. Again, Wildhaber's list is limited to books, so that for the vast accumulation of periodical references the scholar must utilize other guides. Nevertheless, this bibliography, which embraces forty-three pages and includes terse and concise evaluations of most of the items included, is immensely useful.

ii. Ballad and Folksong

David C. Fowler's article "Toward a Literary History of the Popular Ballad" (*NYFQ*, XXI, 123–141) covers familiar ground but carefully re-examines some of the Child ballads with the intention of dating their composition more accurately. The author takes issue with Child's theory that the oldest ballads are those with refrains and emphasizes that the eighteenth century was the golden age of balladry in England and Scotland. By the time the minstrel tradition had merged with the folksong tradition, Fowler argues, the narrative style had changed and ballads themselves had become shorter and more concise, while a reservoir of stylistic commonplaces or clichés had made composition easier.

Ben Gray Lumpkin provides a careful study of a familiar historical song in " 'The Happy Land of Canaan': An Unpublished Civil War Song" (*CWH*, XI, 44–57). He surveys the development of this once popular minstrel song, one version of which was attributed to the Southern singer Harry Macarthy, and points out topical variants. The text which he prints in full is a sixteen-stanza ballad including choruses which was preserved in a manuscript book kept originally by a schoolgirl in Holly Springs, Mississippi, in the early 1860's. No music accompanied the text, but the words seem to fit the tunes of several standard versions.

In *WF* (XXIV, 77–85), John Q. Anderson prints the original ballad of Graham Barnett, composed as late as 1935 by cowboys who had known the hero, a western gunfighter and badman who served for some years in the Texas Rangers. The ballad has no music and is rather conventional in diction and action, but the account of its genesis suggests that communal composition is neither impossible nor a lost art. Robert E. Gyemant in the same journal (XXIV, 105–108) draws an interesting parallel between one of the best-known lumberjack ballads of Michigan, "The Flat River Girl," and a Jim Haggarty who was an itinerant lumberjack employed in California mills and who, involved in a dispute with his foreman, murdered the boss with a saw and then disappeared. The California legend persists as a horror tale told to young campers.

The year saw the appearance of the fourth volume of Helen Hartness Flanders' compilation, *Ancient Ballads Traditionally Sung in New England* (Philadelphia, Univ. of Pa. Press). American variants of sixteen Child ballads are presented, with critical analyses by Tristram P. Coffin and musical annotations by Bruno Nettl. Biographical material about the original singers is carefully included. Among the ballads receiving lengthy attention are "The Farmer's Curst Wife," "Sir Andrew Barton," and "The Sweet Trinity or the Golden Vanity." Of the last, some thirty-six variants are printed and an extensive bibliography is provided.

Robert L. Wright's collection *Swedish Emigrant Ballads* (Lincoln, Univ. of Neb. Press) is a valuable contribution to the study of emigration. Unfortunately none of the ballads that Wright prints here comes from oral tradition since all have literary sources—broadsides, leaflets, or even songbooks. Most are obscure, although, as the editor points out, both "We Sold Our Farm" and "Petter Jönnson" have had considerable currency. The Swedish texts are given first followed by the translations, which are the work of many hands. The ballads are grouped topically into songs of justification, songs of warning, songs of disillusionment, songs of nostalgia, and songs of disaster, the last group generally involving shipwrecks. An appendix provides a few melodies. The ballads are literal and rough, but they reveal the real problems facing the emigrants from Sweden and they often suggest interesting aspects of the folk mind.

George Boswell's article "Folksongs in Northern Kentucky" (*KFR*, XI, 65–75) cites eight Child ballads reported in Kentucky counties as well as many other songs ranging from occupational and disaster ballads to lullabies, drinking and temperance songs, and sentimental ditties. James C. Downey contributed a substantial article to *Ethnomusicology* (IX, 115–125) entitled "Revivalism, the Gospel Songs and Social Reform," which examines the familiar gospel songs used by such evangelists as Dwight L. Moody, Charles Finney, and Billy Sunday in services from 1875 to 1930. Ira Sankey's songs effectively illustrated many of Moody's sermons and reinforced the words of the preacher. The gospel songs were designed to rally the audience and to establish a suitable mood, to convey the basic message, and often to prod sinners to come to the mourners' bench. Their role in the ultimate conversion of the evildoer was significant. Another article in *Ethnomusicology* (IX, 100–114), Robert B. Cantrick's "The Blind Men and the Elephant: Scholars on Popular Music," deals with various misconceptions in the field of popular music and discusses the terminology generally employed. The author points out that today jazz, rock and roll, blues, and country music are loosely combined as popular music but that the term eludes definition and the history of the form has never been written. Writers dealing with the subject are compared to the wise men in the fable who strove to describe the elephant on the basis of single details known to each.

The July-September *JAF* (LXXVIII, 195–286) is a Hillbilly Issue with D. A. Wilgus serving as guest editor. Archie Green, Norman

Cohen, L. Mayne Smith, and Ed Kahn discuss various aspects of the subject and Wilgus also contributes a review of hillbilly recordings. In his editorial introduction Wilgus traces the history of hillbilly music and explodes two myths about it: that it is solely Southern and that it has been foisted on the public by metropolitan music vendors. To Wilgus the hillbilly musician and the music he plays represent "one of the most significant fields for the student of twentieth-century American folk music."

Green's article "Hillbilly Music: Source and Symbol" (pp. 204–228) is a thoughtful and well documented account of the term "hillbilly" itself and of the players who originally performed hillbilly music. His discussion concentrates on the twenties. Absolute priority in such a disputed field is hard to establish, but it is undoubtedly true that Ralph S. Peer of Okeh records was the pioneer promoter of this kind of music. Not only did Peer arrange for the recording of hillbilly tunes under the Okeh label but he went outside New York City to get the services of country musicians. In Atlanta the Okeh company in 1923 recorded Fiddlin' John Carson for the first time. A quartet known as the Hill Billies became Okeh performers and eventually "Pop" Stoneman joined them. Soon afterward both the Vocalion and Victor companies recorded hillbilly music with such fiddlers and singers as "Uncle" Dave Macon and Vernon Dalhart. By 1930 hillbilly records were listed in the catalogues of both Sears, Roebuck and Montgomery Ward.

Norman Cohen's article "The Skillet Lickers" (pp. 229–244) is equally well documented but deals with a more limited subject. Cohen traces the career of Gid Tanner, whose Skillet Lickers band recorded under the Columbia label from 1926 to 1931. Other important hillbilly musicians with a wide radio vogue were Riley Puckett and Clayton McMichen. It is interesting that all three were native Georgians, Tanner a farmer and fiddler, Puckett a blind banjoist, and McMichen a fiddle player who won many contests and subsequently became familiar as a television performer and disk jockey.

L. Mayne Smith's "An Introduction to Bluegrass" (pp. 245–256) defines the special kind of hillbilly music known as "bluegrass," which is usually played by bands consisting of bass, guitar, banjo, fiddle, and mandolin. The term has been in general use since 1950. Smith emphasizes that bluegrass music is hillbilly music played in the South by professional white musicians and is not used for dance music. It also gives the banjo a special role. Smith analyzes the style and the instrumentation and gives a brief historical account of the major musicians involved. The dominant figure in the bluegrass movement is Bill Monroe, although the banjoist Earl Scruggs and the guitarist Lester Flatt have since achieved considerable fame. Smith points out finally that like Southern culture in general, "hillbilly music has moved away from its traditional origins and increasingly incorporated elements of national popular music." A useful complement to Smith's article is Ed Kahn's "Hillbilly Music: Source and Resource" (pp. 257–266), which discusses recordings, published texts, biographical compendiums, and some of the little magazines like *Caravan* and *Sing Out!* devoted to folk music. Kahn also provides an extensive bibliography, arranged alphabetically by authors, of books and magazine articles relevant to the subject.

iii. Folk Narrative

During the year two volumes of the Folktales of the World series, published by the University of Chicago Press, appeared: Wolfram Eberhard's *Folktales of China* and Linda Dégh's *Folktales of Hungary*. To each collection Richard M. Dorson contributed a valuable foreword which traces the history of folktale scholarship and collecting in the two countries concerned. Moreover, the tales are carefully annotated and tabulated, thus paralleling earlier collections devoted to Israel, Japan, and Norway. At least one collection of American tales was published, Ruth Ann Musick's *The Telltale Lilac Bush, and Other West Virginia Ghost Tales* (Lexington, Univ. of Kentucky Press), a volume containing some hundred stories which reflect an older or pioneer period and provide many details regarding the settlement of the region as well as coal mining and early railroading.

Interest in the important role of the Negro and the Indian in American folklore is reflected in several articles. Bruce Jackson's "Stagolee Stories: A Badman Goes Gentle" (*SFQ*, XXIX, 188–194) points out that the famous Negro folk hero is usually either a badman or a trickster, both of which roles Stagolee clearly exemplifies. But certain stories which Jackson secured from John Hurt present Stagolee in quite a different light; indeed the protagonist changes from a vicious or sadistic bully to a hero. In "African Tales Among the North American Indians" (*SFQ*, XXIX, 207–219), Alan Dundes contends that most of the animal tales found among the North American aborigines can be traced back to African Negro origins despite the fact that early investigators of the subject tended to accept the contrary theory. Dundes surveys such earlier discussions as those of Joel Chandler Harris, T. F. Crane, and James Mooney and refutes any theory of Indian provenience. As clinching evidence he cites six stories, in at least two of which a trickster dupes another animal, which resemble Indian tales but are clearly of African origin. Ernest J. Moyne's "Manabozho, Tarenyawagen, and Hiawatha" (*SFQ*, XXIX, 195–203) reviews the old Schoolcraft-Longfellow controversy and reexamines the confusing identification of Hiawatha with Manabozho. The evidence, Moyne contends, exculpates Longfellow. The poet was not a specialist in aboriginal mythology but "depended upon Schoolcraft, whose works were the best source for Indian material available at the time." Longfellow's own inferences were sound; Schoolcraft was in error when he combined an Iroquois statesman and an Ojibwa mythical character into one person. In an article of somewhat broader scope, "The Moon and the American Indian" (*WF*, XXIV, 87–100), Eddie W. Wilson surveys beliefs about the moon held by various Indian tribes and recorded by missionaries, army officers, or anthropologists who visited them. To some tribes the moon was a deity or the symbol of a deity. The pantheon of the Plains Indians included the moon with the sun, the wind, and the morning star. Because of the worship which various tribes accorded the moon, elaborate rituals were frequently developed, an excellent example being the famous Navajo "Beautyway." The moon also figured in creation stories and was frequently personified. American Indians were aware of lunar eclipses for which they advanced mythological explanations; to some tribes also the moon was gentle, being both friendly and beneficent.

iv. Verbal Folklore

Various articles which are basically compilations appeared during 1965. Tabulations of beliefs, cures, omens, superstitions, or proverbs and proverbial comparisons collected in certain localities, they are frequently repetitious and trivial and probably appeal more to the editors of folklore journals than to the average reader. But if the material is often familiar and trite, the slant of the collectors differs and many of the lists have considerable sociological or psychological interest.

Gordon Wilson's "Mammoth Cave Words" runs through four issues of the *KFR* (XI, 5–8, 28–31, 52–55, 78–81) and presents examples of household and neighborhood words or phrases collected by the author from the Mammoth Cave region of Kentucky. The same author contributed a list of folk remedies and plant and animal beliefs to the *TFSB* (XXXI, 33–41, 57–67). Kenneth Porter's "Humor, Blasphemy, and Criticism in the Grace Before Meat" (*NYFQ*, XXI, 3–18) is an amusing tabulation of comic or satiric prayers before eating which the author remembered from his Kansas youth or collected during residences in various parts of the country. William E. Koch collected lore about the pursuit of birds and animals on the plains in "Hunting Beliefs and Customs from Kansas" (*WF*, XXIV, 165–174). Two collections of superstitions from the Far West appear in issues of *WF*. Donald M. Hines, in "Superstitions from Oregon" (XXIV, 7–20), presents material gathered in the metropolitan region of Portland, mostly from migrants to the area. The superstitions relate to personal health, birth, death, marriage, preparation of food, and the weather. Pat Bieter, in "Folklore of the Boise Basques" (XXIV, 263–270), gives interesting details about herding practices, games, and holiday customs of the people imported from Spain to herd sheep in Idaho.

Several other articles reveal the wide disparity of interest among those specialists in the field of verbal folklore. Alta Jablow and Carl Withers, in their study "Social Sense and Verbal Nonsense in Urban Children's Folklore" (*NYFQ*, XXI, 243–257), report the results of their investigation of the folklore collected from urban middle-class children generally in Manhattan and Brooklyn. By means of interviews and questionnaires they secured many examples of tongue twisters, riddles, rhymes, play chants, insult or banter formulas, as well as songs and stories. The investigators noted the frequency of alliteration, cumulative items, and chain or circular items, not to mention the expected parodies. Some of the riddles cited are far out (What weighs one thousand pounds, has four wings, and flies? Answer: two five-hundred-pound canaries), and some of the humor is either warped or hostile. Even more bitter than such adolescent folklore is the language utilized by convicts and revealed by Bruce Jackson in "Prison Folklore" (*JAF*, LXXVIII, 317–329). Jackson visited prisons and interviewed their inmates in Massachusetts, Indiana, and Texas. He discovered first of all a kind of social hierarchy among the convicts since the prison population included the non-criminals (that is, those who were criminals by accident), thieves, and the hard-core recidivists. It is the last group, of course, who have generated their own idiom. The habitual convict uses a language all his own, rich in argot and a limited slang, often obscene, and generally with a high sex interest. Also those convicts who have access to metal-working equipment become ingenious in their forging of knives. The inmates of one Missouri penitentiary identified their crude products by size and shape as *shank, shiv, shotgun,* and *mutton.*

The vocabulary of the worker figures prominently in Archie Green's "American Labor Lore: Its Meanings and Uses" (*Industrial Relations,* IV, 51–68), although the scope of the article is considerably wider. Green develops the thesis that labor lore has been strangely neglected and that it is not only interesting in its own right but that it sheds considerable light on the development of unionism. He discusses four categories of material: tales, dialect, ritual, and custom or belief, and utilizes data garnered from his years as a building trades worker on the San Francisco waterfront. Several paragraphs are devoted to the term *scissorbill,* of which the derivation remains doubtful, and to other words of derision or contempt such as *fink, rat,* and *scab.* Green concludes that an industrial society will continue to produce folklore and that an intelligent study of labor lore "adds a dimension of understanding to unionism."

By studying the language of Henry Thoreau's daily jottings, Leo A. Pederson has taken an interesting verbal approach to the work of a major American author. In "Americanisms in Thoreau's Journal" (*AL,* XXXVII, 167–184), Pederson presents the conclusions of a careful examination of the fourteen volumes of Thoreau's journal and divides his material into four lists. The first and longest tabulation consists of words or terms which antedate the earliest citations in the chief historical dictionaries. The second list includes variants of familiar forms not recognized by the lexicons. The third list includes outright coinages, often hyphenated adjectives or nouns. The fourth compilation consists of localisms which Thoreau picked up or imitated in New England and Canada. Many of these items, to be sure, are trivial variants or suggest differences only in spelling or tense from standard forms. But the extensiveness of the compilation underscores again Thoreau's ever-acute verbal ear.

A more ambitious project in the assembling of verbal folklore resulted in the publication by Frances M. Barbour of *Proverbs and*

Proverbial Phrases of Illinois (Carbondale, Southern Illinois Univ. Press). This florilegium of proverbial material is the product of many years of collecting from college students at Carbondale and Urbana. The material is arranged alphabetically by important words or key words in the quotations. The editor lists the basic bibliographical sources and cites analogues from the standard collections when they seem relevant. Occasionally explanations are provided, sometimes rather naïvely (surely few readers would need to be told the meaning of "to be snowed under" or "to act as if one is hit by lightning"). The majority of the items seem to be of rural origin and are obviously not peculiar to Illinois nor even to the Middle West. Certainly many of the stock comparisons or clichés are current throughout the country.

v. Folklore in the Fine Arts and Literature

Folklore appeals to a widely diversified audience, of course, and one of its most fascinating aspects is its occurrence in the fine arts, in painting and in music, but especially in literature. A beautifully illustrated article by Mitchell A. Wilder entitled "Santos" in the *American West* (II, 37–46) gives some account of the religious folk art of New Mexico and describes the figures of the Virgin or of various saints which once adorned the obscure parish churches but have now been removed to museums. Made generally of cottonwood and covered with native plaster or some coarse fabric, the garishly painted figures retain their primitive charm and at the same time reveal some unusual aspects of hieratic art. A number of articles deal with the literary use of folklore or rather with the introduction of folklore material into storytelling and fiction. Readers of James Fenimore Cooper's *Satanstoe* (1845) have long been curious about the novelist's description of Pinkster, the Negro holiday which he claims was celebrated in New York City in 1757. James H. Pickering's note, "Fenimore Cooper and Pinkster" (*NYFQ*, XXII, 15–19), convincingly suggests that although Pinkster was probably not a Negro celebration in New York City as late as the action of the novel, it did survive in Albany and Cooper undoubtedly saw the festival there in his youth. Joseph M. DeFalco's "Frost's 'Paul's Wife': The Death of an Ideal" (*SFQ*, XXIX, 259–265) deals with Robert Frost's use of the Paul Bunyan theme in his poem and contends somewhat unconvincingly that "Frost's hero embodies more complex aspects of man's

nature. He has a spiritual and chthonian nature, and represents the
perennial conflict in man that issues from such a duality."

A carefully reasoned and more significant article is Jan Harold
Brunvand's "Sailors' and Cowboys' Folklore in Two Popular Classics"
(*SFQ*, XXIX, 266–283), in which a comparison is made between
Dana's *Two Years Before the Mast* and Adams' *The Log of a Cow-
boy*. Singularly enough, despite the differences in the occupations of
the characters and in the geographical settings of the stories, the
author finds striking similarities. Sailors and cowboys have apparently
similar views of nature, share attitudes toward daily routine (different as that routine may be), employ stock nicknames, strive to
banish boredom through storytelling, are prone to gamble, and speak
directly and bluntly. The two books deal with long journeys and
with tasks requiring strength and endurance; neither narrative has
much place for women. As Brunvand concludes, both Dana and
Adams used folklore skilfully and unobtrusively, "weaving together
strands of invented, reported, and traditional material into scenes of
pleasing variety and balance."

Three studies of individual authors are of special interest. Thomas
W. Ford's "Ned Brace of *Georgia Scenes*" (*SFQ*, XXIX, 220–227)
identifies the model of a character named Ned Brace in Longstreet's
famous *Georgia Scenes* and points out that the author merely exaggerated the foibles of a personal friend to achieve one of his best
characterizations. Tristram P. Coffin's "Harden E. Taliaferro and the
Use of Folklore by American Literary Figures" (*SAQ*, LXIV, 241–
246) generalizes on the appearance of folk themes in American fiction and cites as a particularly good example the volume of back
country tales published in 1859 by "Skitt," the pseudonym of Taliaferro, and entitled *Fisher's River Scenes and Characters*. Taliaferro,
a North Carolina Baptist clergyman, dealt with Surry County materials because he had grown up with them: "the tales, the proverbs,
and the superstitions are used just as persons in a folk community
would use them." According to the author, *Fisher's River Scenes and
Characters* might serve as a casebook for the study of the proper use
of folk themes and language in fiction. Richard Walser's "Ham Jones:
Southern Folk Humorist" (*JAF*, LXXVIII, 295–316) is a lengthy discussion of the work of Hamilton Chamberlain Jones, a North Carolina
lawyer and journalist who in 1831 contributed to a Philadelphia
paper the famous comic sketch "Cousin Sally Dilliard." The tale won

wide currency, became one of Lincoln's favorite stories, and was reprinted in many collections of Southwestern humor. Jones was the author of other sketches in a similar vein, notably "The Lost Breeches" and "A Buncombe Story," both of which are reprinted in Walser's article, but none achieved the fame of "Cousin Sally Dilliard."

Two brief studies emphasize the folklore material in twentieth-century regional fiction. Mary W. Clarke's "Proverbs, Proverbial Phrases, and Proverbial Comparisons in the Writings of Jesse Stuart" (*SFQ*, XXIX, 142–163) is a tabulation of verbal material culled from the work of the Kentucky novelist and poet. In a brief introduction Mrs. Clarke stresses the Scotch-Irish or English and the Evangelical Protestant background of Stuart's characters and calls attention likewise to the predominantly rural sources of the language. Mildred Y. Payne, in the article "Folk Characters in Two Kroll Novels" (*TFSB*, XXXI, 16–22), points out that significant figures in two novels by H. H. Kroll, *Fury in the Earth* and *Rogues' Company*, were actually modeled on backwoods worthies of the Mike Fink type.

Donald M. Winkelman, in a study entitled "Three American Authors as Semi-Folk Artists" (*JAF*, LXXVIII, 130–135), examines superficially the folk material utilized by Mark Twain, Manly Wade Wellman, and Charles W. Chesnutt (whose name is misspelled throughout the article). Grace Pleasant Wellborn, in "The Golden Thread in *The Scarlet Letter*" (*SFQ*, XXIX, 169–178), returns to the color imagery in Hawthorne's novel and points out not only the frequent use of black and white (which previous commentators have emphasized) but the rather extraordinary use of yellow and red or scarlet. The reader may recognize the stress on the symbolic value of gold and sunshine as a bit of special pleading but will be less disposed to quarrel with the significance attached to images of red. In a general evaluation of John G. Neihardt's work (*ArQ*, XXI, 7–20), John T. Flanagan calls attention to Neihardt's prose books and suggests that both *Black Elk Speaks* and *When the Tree Flowered* are interesting and authentic narratives of Sioux life in which a good deal of the mythology of the plains Indians is introduced.

Two TUSAS volumes appeared during the year which include folklore material. T. M. Pearce's *Mary Hunter Austin* gives a succinct account of the author's life and summarizes her fiction; it also praises Mrs. Austin's regional interpretation in such books as *The Land of*

Little Rain. But although Pearce states that Mrs. Austin "tried, in fact, to make the Indian folklore of America as vital and as interesting to readers as the folk tales of the Grimm brothers or those of Hans Christian Andersen," he does not develop his thesis substantially. Milton Rickels' *George Washington Harris*, on the other hand, devotes considerable space to Harris' use of tradition and of earlier folk patterns. His famous backwoods figure Sut Lovingood, the "natral born durn'd fool," derives in part from the rural clowns of the Southwestern frontier and in part from both Tyl Eulenspiegel and Shakespeare's Touchstone and Launcelot Gobbo. As Rickels points out, "He is no simple poor white, and he goes considerably beyond Davy Crockett and the Big Bear of Arkansas in his grasp of his world." Moreover, Sut's pranks, his practical jokes, his defiance of respectability and decorum place him within an ancient and vivid tradition. Harris' originality lay not so much in the conception of Sut as a malicious, interfering rustic but as a fool who was also his own spokesman. Before Twain introduced Huck Finn with his marvelous control of various dialects, Harris portrayed a character who symbolized "the essential poverty and mortality of human life" and became the irrational comic figure who could survive being made a scapegoat. In addition, Harris, as Walter Blair has observed, "had greater genius than his contemporaries for transferring the unique artistry of the oral narrative to the printed page."

vi. Miscellaneous

During the year several provocative articles of considerably wider range appeared. Herbert Weisinger contributed "Before Myth" to the *JFI* (II, 120–131), an article which attempts to reconstruct the human imaginative processes even before the establishment of ritual and myth. Weisinger reviews the theories of such folklore scholars as Propp, Eliade, and Von Sydow but does not always carry the reader with him during tenuous and overly elaborate arguments. Arthur L. Campa, in "Folklore and History" (*WF*, XXIV, 1–5), compares the folklorist to the historian: each has the function "of saving the past from oblivion by retelling events from it." But he points out that the two necessarily differ in their treatment of facts and that while the teller of a good tale can be admittedly subjective the reliable historian must strive for objectivity. Thus, while the two fields touch at many points, they cannot be identical. William Bascom, in "The Forms of Folklore: Prose Narrative" (*JAF*, LXXVIII, 3–19), returns to a subject which has occupied folklore specialists for many years. What, he asks, is the precise meaning of "folktale" and what is its relation to such widely recognized genres as myth and legend? All are prose in form, all are narrated orally, and all possess some kind of credibility. Bascom reviews earlier discussions of the terminology and pleads for the rejection of such foreign words as *conte* and *märchen* and for the precise definition of the basic forms of prose narrative. He provides examples of both the terminology and the narratives from primitive cultures and in conclusion quotes Jacob Grimm's distinctions. Readers will certainly agree with Bascom that some kind of fixed and clear definition of these basic terms is essential.

American folk heroes, as might be expected, continue to attract attention. While no major discussion of Mike Fink or Davy Crockett appeared, John Henry did not escape notice. In an excellent article entitled "The Career of 'John Henry'" (*WF*, XXIV, 155–163), Richard M. Dorson reviews the story of the famous Negro track worker and ballad hero and discusses in this connection the contributions of Guy B. Johnson, Louis W. Chappell, and Roark Bradford. Dorson stresses two important aspects of the John Henry story: the historicity of the steam-drilling contest at the Big Bend Tunnel on the Chesapeake and Ohio Railroad in West Virginia which began it all, and the necessary separation of John Henry from the Negro badman John Hardy. He then illustrates the remarkable way in which the John Henry legend has persisted and proliferated. Not only has the ballad in one form or another found its way into innumerable anthologies; it has been recorded countless times, it is still sung by folksingers and by groups, and with various embellishments it has reached the musical stage.

A different approach to the American frontier hero is illustrated by Kent Ladd Steckmesser's book, *The Western Hero in History and Legend* (Norman, Univ. of Okla. Press). Steckmesser chooses four representative figures: Billy the Kid as outlaw, Wild Bill Hickok as gunfighter, Kit Carson as mountain man, and George A. Custer as soldier. He states succinctly the facts of their careers as far as a careful historian can ascertain them and then admits that history alone cannot account for their fame. Tradition and legend have swollen the

reputations of all four men until today it is difficult to separate folklore from fact. The posthumous celebrity of Billy the Kid is a particularly good example since certain publicists have tried to turn this
moronic little killer into a western Robin Hood.

Revisions of two important books appeared during 1965. Ray M.
Lawless' *Folksingers and Folksongs in America*, originally published
in 1960, was reissued with a supplement of eighty pages (New York,
Duell, Sloane and Pearce). This remains the most useful handbook
for students of the folksong and provides an excellent bibliography
and discography besides biographical data. Daniel Hoffman's *Form
and Fable in American Fiction*, published first in 1961, was reissued
after careful revision which eliminated most of the proofreading
errors that disfigured the earlier edition (New York, Oxford Univ.
Press). Hoffman touches on a good many literary works in his perceptive study but concentrates on the fiction of Hawthorne, Melville,
and Mark Twain. Many of his judgments are acute and will aid the
reader in assessing such works as "My Kinsman, Major Molineux"
and *The Confidence Man*.

vii. Two Anthologies and a Festschrift

Two folklore anthologies also appeared during the year. One, *A
Folklore Reader* edited by Kenneth and Mary Clarke (New York,
A. S. Barnes) is disappointing despite the fact that it contains useful and diverse items. The authors tried to cover too much in one
volume, both the theory of folklore and significant examples of folklore in literature, so that many of the selections are thin and scrappy.
Of the five major sections of the anthology, one deals with what
might be called the rationale of folklore (collecting, myth, archives),
one presents folklore samples of all ages and regions, one illustrates
the work of modern collectors such as Vance Randolph and Franz
Boas, one is devoted to folksong but includes only two ballad texts,
and the final one is deliberately peripheral and even reprints a popular article on Eskimo soapstone carving from the *Reader's Digest*.
Some of the essays chosen for inclusion are truncated and the proof-
reading is often unreliable.

The other anthology, *The Study of Folklore*, edited by Alan
Dundes (Englewood Cliffs, Prentice-Hall), is in some ways the most
useful single work dealing with folklore published during the year.

Designed as a textbook, it nevertheless presents within a reasonable scope (481 pp.) the essential aspects of the study of a subject which is rapidly exceeding its bounds. Definitions begin the volume and William J. Thoms's coinage of the term "folklore" is the proper initial selection. The second section illustrates various origin theories while the third part is given over to a discussion of basic structural patterns—in folk narrative, in myth, in riddles, in folktales, and in music. Other parts of the anthology deal with the transmission of folklore (by tradition or by publication) and with its functions. The final portion represents the extraordinary range of interest in one of the newest of disciplines. Over thirty specialists contributed to the anthology, and selections from the work of such distinguished folklorists as Stith Thompson, Albert B. Lord, C. W. Von Sydow, and Archer Taylor are included. The essays themselves vary in theme and complexity. The reader will find interpretations of "The Three Bears" and "Jack and the Beanstalk" as well as a discussion of the significance of Pennsylvania Dutch barn symbols and a sixty-page monograph by Stith Thompson on "The Star Husband Tale" which will try the reading patience even of specialists. The introductory notes to the various selections by Alan Dundes are invariably helpful and informative; frequently they provide additional bibliographical information. A kind of postscript entitled "Suggestions for Further Reading in Folklore" is not only an annotated bibliography but also a listing of the important folklore journals currently being published. Guides to folksong discography are cited and the institutions in the United States which offer graduate curricula in folklore are enumerated.

It is perhaps appropriate to conclude this survey of American folklore scholarship in 1965 with the citation of a festschrift, *Folklore Studies in Honor of Arthur Palmer Hudson* (Chapel Hill, North Carolina Folklore Society). Professor Hudson came to the University of North Carolina in 1930 and was subsequently an important member of the Department of English and a mainstay of the North Carolina Folklore Society. His own work in folksong and ballad scholarship was distinguished. The festschrift edited in his honor by Daniel W. Patterson contains eleven contributions by associates or students of Professor Hudson. The range of the papers included confirms a statement made in the first paragraph of this essay, namely, that folklore scholarship is both ramifying and complex. Stith Thompson is the author of an evaluation of folktale and folk motif indexes in which he points out the lacunae that still exist for the specialist: neither China nor Southeast Asia has been adequately studied. John E. Keller pays tribute to an early medieval folklorist, King Alphonso X of Spain, known as "El Sabio." Alton C. Morris examines the proverbial lore in an obscure Elizabethan play, Henry Porter's *The Two Angrie Women of Abington* (1599), and Archer Taylor presents a small additional list of nineteenth-century American proverbs as a postscript to the definitive dictionary of such material which he and Bartlett J. Whiting compiled in 1958. Holger O. Nygard discusses English, Danish, and French balladry with special attention to the relationship between Child and Grundtvig. Philip H. Kennedy surveys ballad collecting in North Carolina on a geographical basis and points out that even today certain areas of the state are under-collected. Wayland D. Hand, drawing on the unparalleled *Frank C. Brown Collection of North Carolina Folklore* which he did so much to make available in print, discusses cures and the magical transference of disease. Daniel W. Patterson directs his attention to the hitherto neglected Shaker balladry and Richard Walser describes the importance of *The Rasp*, a comic newspaper published in Raleigh during 1841 and 1842. John T. Flanagan calls attention to the importance of the mounted man in myth and legend and suggests that the cavalier who appears in so many of the tales of William Faulkner provides "connotative values far beyond the literal." The festschrift ends with an essay by Guy Owen, a North Carolina novelist, who illustrates the fictional use of folklore by citing his own practices and contends that the incorporation of folk themes, folk speech, and folk characters in fictional narrative adds to the honesty and accuracy of the work.

University of Illinois

18. Miscellaneous: 1964, 1965

Harry Finestone

Once again this reviewer has attempted to separate the embarrassingly large number of essays listed in the bibliography under the rubric *Miscellaneous* into a series of fairly homogeneous groupings. A semblance of order, it is hoped, is thereby achieved, if one does not hold too strictly to precise principles of unity. American scholars and critics generally continue to follow interests similar to those noted in this section two years ago.

i. The Nineteenth Century and Earlier

Probably the most stimulating recent book in American studies, and the one most likely to exert an influence on the direction of scholarship, is Leo Marx's *The Machine in the Garden* (New York, Oxford Univ. Press, 1964). The subtitle "Technology and the Pastoral Ideal in America" presents the basic paradox of the book's motif. As Marx puts it, "The contrast between the machine and the pastoral ideal dramatizes the great issue of our culture." An examination of the major writers of the nineteenth century explores the tensions and repercussions which developed as an essentially simple, agrarian country was transformed into a complex, industrialized civilization.

Two works which follow definitely in its path are Alan Trachtenberg's *Brooklyn Bridge, Fact and Symbol* (New York, Oxford Univ. Press) and Edwin Fussell's *Frontier: American Literature and the American West* (Princeton, Princeton Univ. Press). Trachtenberg acknowledges his debt to Leo Marx's *The Machine in the Garden* and to Henry Nash Smith's *Virgin Land: The West as Myth and Symbol.* He traces the history of the idea of a bridge across the East River to New York, from its inception in 1800 in a note by Jeremiah Johnson, who became the mayor of New York and first citizen of Brooklyn after the War of 1812, to its active formulation in plans by John Augustus Roebling. The history of the company formed to construct the bridge in 1865 is one of scandals becoming successively larger in scope. In part three, "Fact and Symbol," Trachtenberg tells of the bridge's completion and its conversion to myth; he includes a section on Hart Crane's *The Bridge*. Sixteen pages of excellent photographs are collected in the center of the book.

Edwin Fussell's volume is a study of the writing of Cooper, Hawthorne, Poe, Thoreau, Melville, and Whitman as writers "through whom the frontier passed into American culture and became a formal principle in our literature." By the frontier Fussell means no precise area since he sees it often as merely a state of mind, but the word "West" is cited as the key to an understanding of American literature from 1820 to 1860, with literature an effect of the frontier as well as itself a real cause in the shaping of American character.

Robert Falk's *The Victorian Mode in American Fiction, 1865–1885* (East Lansing, Mich. State Univ. Press) develops the thesis of his essay "The Search for Reality: Writers and Their Literature" which had appeared in *The Gilded Age, A Reappraisal*. The first chapter, "Gilt and Innocence," continues the reassessment of the Gilded Age, which Falk sees not so much as a time of moral scandalousness and aesthetic vulgarity, but as a period of great growth and development in American history. In general he rejects the findings of Parrington, Van Wyck Brooks, the Beards, and others as oversimplification, caused by their political leanings and reformist attitudes. E. L. Godkin's term "chromo-civilization," which he used in an editorial in the *Nation* in 1874 to describe the mental and moral chaos which pervaded the notorious Theodore Tilden-Henry Ward Beecher trial, is likewise dismissed as fanciful and as an unfortunate exaggeration. The major portion of the book aims to isolate and define the phenomenon which has been called "Victorian Realism." Falk explores the "vision of reality" of the time and the steps by which it was given expression, primarily in the fiction and critical theory of its major literary figures—Henry James, Howells, DeForest, and Mark Twain.

In a very long chapter on the seventies which bears the subtitle "A Decade of Hesitation and Literary Experiment," we find a brief, but highly perceptive passage on DeForest, a statement on Howells' significant role in the early growth of realistic fiction, an intelligent glimpse of the early James and his almost precocious efforts in the direction of a new realism, and a survey of a number of Victorian critics and their responses toward the "New Novel." Falk sees the eighties as a period of social adjustment and literary fulfilment, particularly as evidenced in Howells and James. He sees Mark Twain as outside the pattern, with his nostalgic angle of vision; but his humor, which did much to puncture literary charlatanism, and his attention to accurate local color also contributed positively to the development of realism.

Falk concludes that after 1885 the intensification of social problems led to a shift from moderation to what can be called "The Year of Protest." He finds Howells' later novels, with the exception of *A Hazard of New Fortunes*, inferior to his novels of moderate realism. Twain became embittered, James turned away from the American scene and lost touch. He points out quite accurately that "another and greatly altered concept of realism" began to develop.

H. Wayne Morgan's *American Writers in Rebellion from Mark Twain to Dreiser* (New York, Hill and Wang) focuses on certain writers whose work displays both the unity and variety of American literature in the late nineteenth and early twentieth centuries. In addition to the authors whose names circumscribe the title, Morgan devotes chapters to Howells, Garland, and Norris. All the essays in this volume suffer somewhat from over-simplification. A writer as complex and self-contradictory as Twain is described as "the Optimist as Pessimist." Howells is "the Realist as Reformer," and his drift toward "mild Socialism" is stressed; what is not stressed is the accompanying deterioration of his talent. Norris and Dreiser are treated in terms of their Naturalism, the former as a "romantic naturalist," the latter as "naturalistic humanist." With both these writers Morgan sees quite properly that a quarrel over their defects of style seems petty when contrasted with the questions they asked and the worlds they created.

A similar work is Warner Berthoff's *The Ferment of Realism: American Literature 1884-1919* (New York, Free Press), the first of a new seven-volume history. Berthoff examines the theme of revolt which he finds common to the poetry, fiction, philosophy, sociology, history, and criticism of the period. The goals of realism he finds not easily determinable; he finds it easier to state what the new realists were in revolt against. He examines Howells, Twain, James, Bierce, and their successors, and in "The Literature of Argument" he studies William James, Thorstein Veblen, William Graham Sumner, and Henry and Brooks Adams. Contrary to most critics Berthoff feels that the realistic mode will continue to function as an influence on future writing in America.

R. W. Chambers' "The Influence of Magazine Journalism on the Rise of Realism in America, 1870–1890" (*DA*, XXV, 6619-6620) asserts a healthy relationship between the rise of realism and the flowering of the general monthly magazine. A decline in partisanship among the journals corresponded to the championship of the realist movement, and journalists of the leading monthlies exerted a major influence on its development. Chambers argues that after 1890 realism lost its dominant position and the literary journals lost their leadership to cheaper, more popular magazines.

Robert W. Duncan's "The London *Literary Gazette* and American Writers" (*PELL*, I, 153–166) sets out to disprove the contention that the *Literary Gazette*, a powerful critical journal in the first half of the nineteenth century, was intensely anti-American. Irving, Franklin, and Cooper were all treated with approval, and, although Poe and Melville were not admired, Bryant was welcomed and Emerson favorably compared to Carlyle. Duncan finds this general fairness toward American writers particularly notable in the face of hostility from America, and he concludes that the editors of the *Literary Gazette* were busy looking for new talent from any source and tended to judge American writing on its literary merits.

A group of studies of nineteenth-century periodicals are both historical and critical in nature. See Dale Kay Doepke, "St. Louis Magazines before the War, 1832–1860" (*DA*, XXV, 1964, 1191–1192); Randolph Hudson, "*Atlantic Monthly* Authorship, 1857–1861" (*AN&Q*, III, 1964, 6–7, 22–23, 36–37, 56–57), a study to be continued serially, in six-month periods; and Norman la Cour Olsen, Jr., "The *Forum* as a Magazine of Literary Comment: 1886–1907" (*DA*, XXIV, 1964, 4702–4703).

Paul R. Baker, in *The Fortunate Pilgrims: Americans in Italy, 1800–1860* (Cambridge, Mass., Harvard Univ. Press, 1964), using letters, diaries, travel accounts, and journals, traces the American interest in Italy during the first half of the nineteenth century. Baker points out that by 1858 nearly two thousand Americans paid annual visits to Florence and that a permanent colony of about two hundred was established in Rome between 1840 and 1900. By the middle of the century difficulties of travel had so lessened that the trip to Italy no longer was limited to those of aristocratic privilege. The book is primarily interesting as a careful study of the impact of Italian life and culture on American writers, painters, and the American middle class.

Perry Miller's *The Life of the Mind in America from the Revolution to the Civil War* (New York, Harcourt, Brace and World), though left unfinished at the time of his death, is a brilliant examination of religion, law, and science in America. Book I, "The Evangelical Basis," and Book II, "The Legal Mentality," are complete, while Book III, "Science—Theoretical and Applied," contains only the first chapter with an outline for remaining chapters which were to have examined technological America. An appendix outlining the nine-book plan is also included.

The Examined Self by Robert F. Sayre (Princeton, Princeton Univ. Press, 1964) is a study of the autobiographies of Benjamin Franklin, Henry Adams, and Henry James. It is not a history of American autobiography, but a careful study of the three writers, the latter two of whom were strongly attracted toward Franklin's *Autobiography*. In several chapters Sayre substantiates his claim that all three autobiographies are profound comments on the American scene.

Two New England worthies and an immigrant who became a great power in American publishing are dealt with in the following volumes. Henry Wyman Parker, in *Henry Stevens of Vermont: American Rare Book Dealer in London, 1845–1886* (Amsterdam, N. Israel, 1963), provides a glimpse of book collecting in the United States and England in the nineteenth century. Stevens' great service to scholarship lay in his bringing large numbers of important books to America from Europe. Among his American clients were James Lenox, John Carter Brown, and the Smithsonian Museum. W. S. Tryon's *Parnassus Corner, A Life of James T. Fields* (Boston, Houghton Mifflin, 1963) traces the rise of Fields from a hard-working village boy to his position as the most important publisher in Victorian Boston. Ticknor and Fields published Longfellow, Lowell, Bayard Taylor, Hawthorne, Julia Ward Howe, Whittier, Thoreau, and Emerson. The list of English writers included Tennyson, Browning, De Quincey, Leigh Hunt, Charles Kingsley, Charles Reade, Thackeray, Dickens, and Arnold. Of particular interest is the account of the Charles Street salon presided over by Annie Fields, which Willa Cather has also so movingly recalled in her essay "148 Charles Street." Peter Lyon, in *Success Story: The Life and Times of S. S. McClure* (New York, Scribner's), traces the life of McClure, an Irish immigrant boy who rose in Horatio Alger fashion to become an important magazine editor and publisher. His unceasing efforts in organizing a newspaper syndicate for fiction brought success, and by means of it he met and aided the careers of prominent writers of the day. The longest section of the book is devoted to a description of *McClure's Magazine*, which was highly profitable from 1895–1910, containing fiction and the muckraker articles by Lincoln Steffens and others. Debts and machinations by his associates ultimately lost him his magazine, and he spent a long later life relatively unappreciated and in poverty.

McClure's great qualities were his enthusiasm, his knowledge of what people wanted to read, and his facility for promoting things at the right time. His main motivation was not money but to be busy, important, and admired. Included in the book are narrations of his personal encounters with many writers, including his friendship with Willa Cather.

Budd Leslie Gambee's *Frank Leslie and His Illustrated Newspaper, 1855–1860* (Ann Arbor, Univ. of Mich., Dept. of Lib. Sci., 1964) is a fascinating study in biography and business as they were related to each other in the life of Frank Leslie, another important nineteenth-century editor. It also provides a study of the technique of illustrating newspapers by the use of wood blocks in assembly line production.

ii. Literary History and Criticism

Frederick J. Hoffman's "The Scholar Critic: Trends in Contemporary British and American Literary Study" (*MLQ*, XXVI, 1–5) suggests that scholars and critics are currently in the process of making major changes in their approaches and emphases. He approves of the post-New Critical world, discusses the problems of choosing the appropriate text of a work for critical study, and inveighs against the increasing tendency to gather for republication in collections essays by various writers on the grounds that such activity creates a false sense of creative energy.

In the same volume, Willard Thorp's "Exodus: Four Decades of American Literary Scholarship" (*MLQ*, XXVI, 40–61) presents a thoroughgoing survey of American scholarship, which includes the persistent efforts to correct literary falsifications, the writing of accurate and objective biographies, the clear accounts of literary movements, the breakthrough in the study of language, the publication of responsible histories, the emergence of the American Studies movement, and the attempts to publish accurate texts. Thorp sees all these efforts as the major achievements of American literary scholarship in our time.

A number of works employ the resolvable paradox as a means of developing diverse topics. Tony Tanner's *The Reign of Wonder: Naivety and Reality in American Literature* (London, Cambridge Univ. Press) does not actually discuss naïveté and reality in American literature, as the title suggests, but rather is an investigation of certain authors' styles and their use of naïve language in an attempt to produce reality. He states three basic interests: the naïve eye with its unselective wonder, the vernacular with its immediacy and concrete directness, and the effort to slough off the past and concentrate exclusively on the present moment. Mr. Tanner concentrates heavily on his first two concerns but neglects his third interest.

R. W. B. Lewis, in "The Aspiring Clown" (*Learners and Discerners: A Newer Criticism*, ed. Robert Scholes, Charlottesville, Univ. Press of Va., 1964, pp. 63–108), uses Hart Crane's "Chaplinesque" as a focus for his study of the clownish element in the work of Whitman, Crane, Wallace Stevens, and Nathanael West. Crane felt that Chaplin's comic gestures embodied a transcendence into "a new kind of tragedy, eccentric, homely and yet brilliant." Lewis generalizes the element of self-mockery and mockery at the world in Chaplin as the controlling mode of transcendence for a whole group of writers.

Frederick J. Hoffman's *The Mortal No: Death and the Modern Imagination* (Princeton, Princeton Univ. Press, 1964) is an ambitious study of the metaphors associated with death. Part I, "Grace," is concerned with nineteenth-century backgrounds of modern negativism; the second part, "Violence," with twentieth-century manifestations, and the final part, "Self," concludes with a discussion of the strategies of rehabilitation, "of reconstituting the self," in a time of crisis. Hoffman "offers a set of major speculations upon the condition of 'no' and the desperate interest in the 'yes' that underlies it." Part II is particularly filled with startling insights into many modern classics, but the clear meaning and design of the whole keep just below the horizon of the understanding.

In his introduction to *Essays on Determinism in American Literature* (Kent, Ohio, Kent State Univ. Press, 1964), presented for the most part at the December, 1963, MLA meeting in Chicago, Sydney J. Krause defines deterministic naturalism, gives reasons for its decline, and says that determinism is the one element that contemporary naturalists disavow. The paradox of deterministic naturalism, centering on the refusal of the human to be overcome, is affirmed by the statement that "these essays presuppose that the freedom sought by characters in deterministic literature is what makes determinism worth writing about."

Geoffrey Moore, in *American Literature and the American Imagination* (Hull, England, Univ. of Hull Press, 1964), discusses the problem of typical English reactions to the *idea* of American literature. Literature, Moore says, should be judged on its merits, not on how it reveals national traits. He points out, however, that the physical environment and the national-social-historical situation have created in America a literature with its own characteristics. He talks of "Hunt the Symbol" as an American university game symptomatic of a basic American quality. To the question whether American literature is primarily a literature of myth, allegory, symbolism, Moore answers in the negative, but he asserts that American writing has always had the tendency to search for the principle rather than the particular. He quotes Henry James, Whitman, Wallace Stevens, and Faulkner's Nobel Prize speech to support the point that the American imagination always is fired with the spirit of anguish over the discrepancy of the way things are and the way things should be. American writers are the "custodians of its conscience."

An additional evaluator of American fiction is Pierre Brodin. Brodin's *Présences contemporaines: Écrivains américains d'aujourdhui* (Paris, Nouvelles ed. Debresse, 1964) deals with the heirs of Hemingway and Faulkner. The writers on whom he comments seem to him to have "enlarged" his horizons through their wide experience; each is deeply concerned with problems of style and form, with a content generally tragic, violent, filled with evil and alienation. The common subject is the victim treated with irony rather than rancor. Brief plot summaries and a chronology follow comments on each book. Brodin concludes each section with remarks on the writer's work as a whole, his achievements, style, and his place in American literature. An appendix of letters received by Brodin from writers replying to his questions about French influences on them is followed by a bibliography of general articles on American literature and on the specific people he has treated, including a record of translations into French.

Donald Heiney, in *America in Modern Italian Literature* (New Jersey, Rutgers Univ. Press, 1964), examines the Italian myth of America as a country of easy wealth and facile, irresponsible love. Pavese saw America as "pensive and barbaric, blissful yet quarrelsome, dissolute, fecund; burdened with all the past of the world, yet youthful, innocent." To the average Italian, however, the movies represented the America they wanted to believe in, even if they dimly felt it was a dream. Although under fascism many writers discovered America through its literature and were influenced by it (it was, as Pavese said, "the first breathing hole to liberty"), by 1950 an anti-American strain developed among writers, and the literature of resistance and liberation was ambivalent toward America and what it represents.

An appendix contains three documents on America which the author considers especially revealing. These are Pintor's "Americana" (1943), Pavese's "Yesterday and Today" (1947), and Soavi's preface to "America All at One Breath" (1959). A bibliography is included.

Paths of American Thought, edited by Arthur M. Schlesinger, Jr., and Morton White (Boston, Houghton Mifflin, 1963), presents a group of scholars and writers who deal with salient aspects of the evolution of the American mind. With no pretension to total coverage, the essays concern themselves with political thought, education, economics, literature, religion, and broad aspects of science.

The book is set up in a historical framework, the four division headings ranging from the colonial phase to the present. The final part includes sociological essays by Edward Shils and Daniel Bell and three essays on the American image abroad. In "European Images of America," Marcus Cunliffe asserts that although America has never been "real" for Europeans, European images of America have usually been either highly favorable or markedly pejorative. Pejorative images, however, have prevailed lately over favorable ones. He concludes that America has never been quite "real" for Americans either. In an epilogue, "The One Against the Many," Schlesinger decries the ideologist with his tidy models and extols the American democratic tradition which sees the world as many, not as one. There are notes and a guide to further reading.

The American Reading Public: What it Reads, Why it Reads, The Daedalus Symposium, edited by Roger H. Smith (New York, R. R.

Bowker, 1964), deals for the most part with the publishing business. The first three articles, however, are of interest to the teacher of literature. Among interesting papers, "Of Textbooks and Trapped Idealists" by Frank Jennings is a tirade against current, standard textbooks. He offers, as a startling solution, the use of paperbacks. "Book Reading and Reading of Books" by Reuben A. Brower tries to explain why students do not read. He deplores the difference between the materials used by teachers of reading and the materials chosen by college professors.

While "A Criticism of Commercial Publishing" by Jason Epstein is critical of commercial book publishers because they are not imaginative, "The Publisher as an Individualist" by Frederick A. Praeger complains that a publisher can no longer be an individualist because paperbacks have made the industry big business. "The Professors and Their Publishers" by Roger W. Shugg suggests that a program be instituted wherein professors could publish shorter works in pamphlet form; this co-operation of professor and publisher would be a "dedication to intellectual ends and pleasure in serving a learned world." "What is Wrong with American Book Reviewing?" by Henri Peyre reminds us that while no one is content with the current art of book reviewing, reviews are essential because they mean publicity. He concludes that we need critics who will enlighten the reading public. "Some Animadversions on Current Reviewing" by John Hollander claims that nothing is worse for an author than to be praised by someone whom he thinks a fool. If the foundations, which spend huge sums of money for academic and creative work, were to invest their money in a weekly review, it would "improve cultural and intellectual morale."

Counterparts (Chicago, Rand McNally, 1964) by Roy Newquist also explores the problems of reviewing and the state of criticism in America. A series of interviews reveals startling juxtapositions. Harper Lee believes that "we have no literary critics in the sense that they exist (for instance) in England. . . . We have," she adds, "few journals that begin to compare with English periodicals like *The Spectator* and *The Economist*." Doris Lessing complains about the abysmal standard of criticism in England and asserts that "very few writers have any respect for the criticism they get." Dwight Macdonald, after dismissing the hack reviews of the *Saturday Review* and the New York *Times*, reminds us of the extremely good critics in this country who write for the little magazines, and, of course, of Edmund Wilson. Irwin Shaw says that "criticism in America could be more or less wrapped up in one name: Edmund Wilson," and then adds, "Oddly enough, the British literary reviews are, in general, worse than ours, and they don't have the massive example of Wilson to lead them on. . . . Maybe this just isn't the age for criticism." Morris L. West, the author of *The Shoes of the Fisherman*, has "no complaints at all about American critics" and finds them "enlightened and, in the main, just. And even when they haven't been just I find them very agreeable fellows to have a drink with."

Various writers interviewed in *Counterparts* take a stand on the *New Yorker*, a popular target for years. Maxwell Geismar finds James Jones's *The Thin Red Line* among the best books written during the past ten years, but complains that it is "scarcely noted in high and serious quarters because Jones is concerned with the common man." He finds John Howard Griffin a "splendid" writer, but dislikes intensely the *New Yorker* school. He reserves most of his dislike, as usual, for Henry James and his "cult."

A very moving discussion of the *New Yorker* by the late A. J. Liebling is one of several defenses also made by Lillian Ross, Dwight Macdonald, and Peter De Vries, who answered Newquist's often repeated question of how he would like to be evaluated a hundred years from now: "We know now what they couldn't see then. He was six months ahead of his time."

iii. The West and the Southwest

The West and Southwest continue to prove popular subjects for revaluation. In *The Western Hero in History and Legend* (Norman, Univ. of Okla. Press), Kent Ladd Steckmesser presents four American folk heroes as classic examples of how history and legend mingle in our picture of the Far Western frontier. Kit Carson represents the mountain man; Billy the Kid typifies the outlaw; Wild Bill Hickok is the civilizer; and General Custer is the soldier. They are all symbols, men who through publicity caught the public's imagination. The growth of fiction about them has made history hard to come by. Besides the development of the legends of the four main heroes, insights are given into the development of the legends of John Smith, Daniel Boone, Mike Fink, Davy Crockett, and various mountain men.

A typical section discusses the hero, how he acquired fame, how he was changed in literature by the building of the legend, and the way in which he is viewed today. Kit Carson was in fact "short, plain featured, and walked with his toes turned in." But in legend he became another Hercules. A careful student of the history of the American West must view biographies of the hero with much skepticism since the writers treated truth casually, and in each legend the beautiful eclipses the true.

The American Frontier: A Social and Literary Record (New York: Holt, Rinehart and Winston), edited by C. Merton Babcock, sheds light on various facets of the frontier. Cooper, Irving, Thoreau, Twain, and Garland are discussed, among others. In his introduction Babcock provides a brief history of the movement of westward expansion and points out that while the American West seemed a land of promise to the hopeful first frontiersmen, others called it a desert, similar to the steppes of Tatary or Siberia. Advocates of territorial expansion, however, clung to the cornucopia myth as a means of furthering their own ends, and the doctrine of Manifest Destiny was a rationalization and justification of America's highhanded method in acquiring western territories.

Religion was an important force on the frontier, but the scarcity of churches made for a decrease in religious bigotry. The frontier was not the lawless place it was reputed to be; however, frontier politics, like frontier religion, were "impassioned, emotional and rampageous." It followed naturally that the language of the frontier was full of tall talk and bombastic outspokenness. Emerson, Whitman, and Melville thought that a true American literature must reflect the ideas and moods of the West.

Clarence Gohdes, in "The Earliest Description of 'Western' Fiction?" (*AL*, XXXVII, 70–71), reports that an address delivered in 1858 by William T. Coggeshall, librarian of Ohio State, attempted to define "Western" fiction. The address was published the following year with the title "The Protective Policy in Literature: A Discourse on the Social and Moral Advantages of the Cultivation of Local Literature." The discourse presents a history of authors and periodicals in the Ohio Valley and an appeal to sectional pride in the encouragement of local writing, arguing that a republic of letters may be a "Confederacy of individualities," and asserting that the rest of the nation had failed to notice favorably the fiction and poetry of the West.

An interesting bibliographical entry dealing with the West is

Archibald J. Hanna, Jr., "The Yale Collection of Western Americana and The Benjamin Franklin Collection" (*YULG*, XXXVIII, 1964, 160–166). See also Don D. Walker, "Freedom and Destiny in the Myth of the American West" (*NMQ*, XXXIII, 1964, 381–387), and Louis B. Wright, "Culture and Anarchy on the Frontier," in *Literary Views: Critical and Historical Essays*, edited by Carroll Camden (Chicago, Univ. of Chicago Press, for William Marsh Rice Univ., 1963).

The studies of the Southwest merge into a discussion of its relation with the tradition and development of humor. *Humor of the Old Southwest*, edited by Hennig Cohen and William B. Dillingham (Boston, Houghton Mifflin, 1964), is an anthology including J. K. Paulding, Davy Crockett, Longstreet, Hooper, Twain, and lesser-known figures. In a very fine introduction the editors assert that "So similar were these writers that a composite portrait is possible. The typical Southwestern humorist smiled easily but was no clown. He was a man of education and breeding who felt deeply and spoke with conviction." The language of the humor is seen to be especially rich in comic similes. An explanation of the origins of Southwest humor is made in terms of the psychology of laughter as well as the history of the westward movement. This book is an excellent and useful volume, offering a survey of the entire field.

For two additional studies with a comparative slant see John Q. Anderson, "Scholarship in Southwestern Humor: Past and Present" (*MissQ*, XVII, 1964, 67–86) and John K. Bettersworth, "The Humor of the Old Southwest: Yesterday and Today" (*MissQ*, XVII, 1964, 87–94).

iv. Humor

The general topic of humor is continued in a particularly fine study by Willard Thorp, *American Humorists* (UMPAW, 1964, No. 42), which points out that even earlier than the 1830's native humor was developing. The writings of William Byrd, the poems of Freneau, and Benjamin Franklin's *Poor Richard's Almanac* show that humor and satire were part of the colonial heritage as well as part of the Revolutionary arsenal. The tall tale perhaps begins with Franklin's letter in 1765 defending the right of the colonists to manufacture their own goods. The volume traces the development of humor in its various forms down to present times. Thorp concludes that Americans are listening to and looking at humor more than they are reading it.

Television, records, and night club acts have pre-empted older forms.

Two more studies of American humor seem worth noting. Mark Sidney Steadman, Jr., in "American Humor: 1920–1955" (*DA*, XXV, 1964, 486), studies modern American humorists and their character-istic themes and attitudes and discusses theories of humor, similari-ties of comic figures, reactions against the rural character, and the decline of the conventional stereotypes. In the final chapter he argues that the seemingly negative tone of modern humorists comes from their opposition to the mechanized society which threatens the in-dividual.

Don Mark Hausdorff's "Depression Laughter: Magazine Humor and American Society: 1929–1933" (*DA*, XXV, 1964, 1913) examines *Judge, Life, New Yorker, New Masses, Ballyhoo, Esquire*, and other magazines, and discovers that the bulk of the humor of these maga-zines revealed basically conservative attitudes. The study argues that the subtle approach to moral questions which developed during the period was accompanied by a lessening of commitment and an in-creasing vagueness in the system of values.

v. The South

Richmond Croom Beatty in his scholarship and teaching inspired a very large number of Southern writers and critics who flocked around him from 1927 until his death. The volume of essays titled *Reality and Myth: Essays in American Literature in Memory of Richmond Croom Beatty* (Nashville, Vanderbilt Univ. Press, 1964), edited by William E. Walker and Robert Welker, is intended as a tribute to the memory of the man.

Part I is devoted to Richmond Croom Beatty. Donald Davidson has written a memoir and Theodore C. Hoepfner a critical estimate of his work, which is followed by a selection of his poems and a bibliography.

The second section consists of thirteen essays on reality and myth in American literature, but the truly unifying element in the volume is its concern with the literature produced in the South. There are essays on Evelyn Scott, Caroline Gordon, Jesse Stuart, Donald David-son, Sidney Lanier, William Faulkner, the New Orleans *Double Dealer*, Scottish ballads transformed and anglicized in the hills of Kentucky and other parts of the South, John Peale Bishop, Ellen

Glasgow, and two New Englanders—Herman Melville and Nathaniel Hawthorne. The critical approaches vary from the historical and social to the aesthetic and analytical and there are "critiques" as well as "impressionistic celebrations."

Clement Eaton, in *The Mind of the Old South* (Baton Rouge, Louisiana State Univ. Press, 1964), seeks to give a glimpse of the process of historical change in the Old South and to increase understanding of some of the decisions made there by focusing on the lives of individual men. Those who were chosen for case histories are not well-known today and are not completely typical or consistent in their attitudes, but they represent major points of view in the ante bellum South. Of the fifteen men, only four clearly favored secession, only four practiced the code duello, only one was unorthodox in religion, only three were against slavery, and all but one were affected in varying ways by the Romantic movement. All but two owned plantations.

In the last chapter on the dynamics of the Southern mind, the author states that, although most of the old Southern values have largely disappeared or are disappearing, certain traits remain. These are religious orthodoxy, conservatism, the feeling of Negro inferiority, the necessity for segregation, and the martial spirit. Eaton hopes for a new type of Southerner combining the virtues of the bygone South with those of the present.

Susan B. Riley's "Southern Literary Magazines of the Mid-Nineteenth Century" (*THQ*, XXIII, 1964, 221–236) describes in detail a number of literary magazines, with emphasis on Tennessee periodicals. She reminds us that magazines, "naturally sensitive to factors affecting patronage, furnish some interesting barometric readings of the intellectual climate of the times." Southern magazines, hindered by a Southern preference for Northern publications, never had real vitality. She concludes that what marks the entire period is the consistent apathy of the public.

This position is largely supported by Arlin Turner, "Review of North Carolina Fiction, 1962–63" (*NCHR*, XLI, 1964, 226–230), who begins with the view that the South has never been generous in its support of its writers, "generally valuing a book by the remoteness of its origins." He suggests that Southern literature was hampered in its development by convention and that great literature generally flourishes when authors feel free to follow their inclinations. On the other hand, Richard Beale Davis' *Intellectual Life in Jefferson's Virginia, 1790–1830* (Chapel Hill, Univ. of N. C. Press, 1964) describes a period of intellectual stimulation in the South, before the defense of slavery against the attack of abolitionists began to close Southern minds.

A provocative essay by Louis D. Rubin, Jr., is "The Literature of a Changing South" in *The Deep South in Transformation*, edited by Robert B. Highsaw (University, Univ. of Alabama Press, 1964, pp. 147–175). Quoting C. Alphonso Smith's observation that the tension resulting from industrialization creates great literature, Rubin suggests that this is only a partial truth and that the flowering of literature in the South during the twenties and thirties, and possibly after, resulted from tensions between values and circumstances at a time when men were both changing and attempting to resist change. Appended to the essay are comments by Carl Benson, Hudson Strode, and Walter Sullivan.

L. Hugh Moore, Jr., "*The Sunny South* and Its Literature" (*GaR*, XIX, 176–185), notes that the *Sunny South*, a literary magazine in Atlanta from 1875 to 1907, was the most distinguished Southern magazine to achieve a circulation of over a hundred thousand before 1885. An illustrated weekly miscellany, it published poetry, sermons, moralistic stories, serialized novels, and an occasional essay. The taste in poetry of the editors seems typically Southern Victorian. They considered Longfellow the greatest American poet, with Poe denigrated for lacking moral seriousness. They admired Wordsworth and Byron, but not Shelley or Coleridge. Hardy's *A Laodicean* was published under the more appealing title, *Her Two Lovers: Or The Lady in Her Castle*.

Ray M. Atchison provides another study of a nineteenth-century Southern periodical in "*Scott's Monthly Magazine*: A Georgia Post-Bellum Periodical of Literature and History" (*GaHQ*, XLIX, 249–305). William J. Scott launched the miscellany in December, 1865, and Paul Hamilton Hayne and Henry Timrod were among its earliest contributors. Scott attempted to publish as much Southern writing as possible and only passing notice was given to Northern writers. Atchison suggests that this was one of the most important magazines devoted to the Lost Cause and notes that both Jay Hubbell and Merton Coulter have frequently used it as a source for their studies of the period.

See also Dewey W. Grantham, Jr., "Interpreters of the Modern South" (*SAQ*, LXII, 1964, 521–529); William J. Handy, *Kant and the*

Southern New Critics (Austin, Univ. of Texas Press, 1963); Virginia Jean Rock, "The Making and Meaning of *I'll Take My Stand*: A Study in Utopian-Conservatism, 1925–1939" (*DA*, XXIV, 1964, 4197–4198); and George B. Tindall, "The Benighted South: Origins of a Modern Image" (*VQR*, XL, 1964, 281–294).

vi. The Twenties

Alms for Oblivion (Minneapolis, Univ. of Minn. Press, 1964) by Edward Dahlberg collects a group of literary essays and personal reminiscences mostly of the twenties into a volume which depends for its excitement on vivid portraits of his friends in New York and Paris: Steiglitz, Anderson, Dreiser, Ford, Robert McAlmon. Of particular interest is "The Expatriates: A Memoir." An essay on *Moby-Dick* is of considerably less value.

Malcolm and Robert Cowley, in "Memoranda of a Decade" (*AH*, XVI, Aug., 33–40), present a pastiche of the twenties, with excerpts from Cowley's own *Exile's Return*, Warren Harding's Inaugural Address, *Babbitt*, Grantland Rice describing the Four Horsemen, Harold Ross's prospectus for the *New Yorker*, a New York *Daily News* story on the Hall-Mills case of 1922, *The Great Gatsby*, Cummings, Hemingway, etc. The article presages a larger anthology and catches the spirit of the times.

The retrospective view of American literary periodicals of the twenties begun in recent years continues with *A History of* The Freeman by Susan J. Turner (New York and London, Columbia Univ. Press, 1963), a model of historical accuracy and critical acumen. The chapters analyzing the contents of the magazine, which was a true intellectual complement to the *Dial*, are extremely fine. An interesting footnote to this volume is provided by G. Thomas Tanselle, "Unsigned and Initialed Contributions to *The Freeman*" (*SB*, XVII, 1964, 153–175).

The resumption in January, 1920, of the *Dial* after thirty years as a fortnightly was a significant harbinger of the Jazz Age. It remains a discriminating record of what the twenties looked like to a group of intelligent men and women who lived through those years. Nicholas Joost, *Schofield Thayer and The Dial: An Illustrated History* (Carbondale, Southern Illinois Univ. Press, 1964), is a highly documented addition to its history with the bias expected of a commissioned study.

William Wasserstrom continues his work in "Marianne Moore, *The Dial*, and Kenneth Burke" (*WHR*, XVII, 1963, 249–262).

Leonard Aaron Greenbaum's "*The Hound and Horn*: Episodes in American Literary History, 1927–34" (*DA*, XXIV, 1964, 2031) describes the history of the magazine and is directed toward an understanding of the role of the "little magazine" in promoting individual writers and trends. The magazine's major interests during its seven years were humanism, agrarianism, Marxism. It attempted to be a humanist journal, but failed as Babbitt and More refused to publish in it. It was an outlet through Allen Tate for the Agrarians, but in 1934 a policy change ruled out all political articles. The study is of bibliographical interest, since it gathers together previously unpublished materials. It demonstrates that although the commitment to specific causes was a matter of personalities, *Hound and Horn* was a literary quarterly that sought to justify literature on moral grounds, in terms of some ultimately useful purpose.

An interesting comment on the history of *Hound and Horn* is "Literary Quarterlies in the 1960's" (*CE*, XXVII, 153–156) by John H. Hicks, who examines the major literary magazines of the period, comparing them with their predecessors. He attacks the coterie impulse among journals and notes that both the *Partisan Review* and *Kenyon Review* have outlived their original purpose. The essay is primarily valuable as a description of the founding and development of the *Massachusetts Review*, which had as its models Emerson and Parker's *Massachusetts Quarterly Review* and *Hound and Horn*.

vii. The Radical Movement and the Thirties

David Mar Chalmers, in *The Social and Political Ideas of the Muckrakers* (New York, Citadel), fights the stereotyped view of the muckrakers. George K. Turner, Ida M. Tarbell, Ray Stannard Baker, Upton Sinclair, and Lincoln Steffens are discussed, and Chalmers points out that they formed their general attitudes by a painstaking series of investigations. They concerned themselves with a variety of vice from the white slave trade to corruption in oil, Wall Street, municipal and state governments, and were interested in labor and pure food and drug legislation. They were apparently not frightened by the prospect of "big government" and, in general, were totally lacking in a broad knowledge of economics.

Christopher Lasch's strategy for *The New Radicalism, 1889–1962: The Intellectual as a Social Type* (New York, Knopf) is that of social biography. Though not necessarily typical, key radicals such as Jane Addams, Randolph Bourne, Mabel Dodge Luhan, and Lincoln Steffens are placed in their sociological and intellectual contexts. Each figure was rebellious, disillusioned, in conflict with and engaged in an indictment of society, but Lasch shows the subtle changes which occurred in the shifts both of attitudes and in the society criticized. The early radicals of the period had in common a strong sense of rebellion against their upper middle-class advantages. Lincoln Steffens is seen as typifying the transition to the new type of anti-intellectual intellectual. The book closes with an examination of the intellectual as part of the Establishment, with Norman Mailer chosen for the final portrait. The fantasies of omnipotence with corresponding fears of hostility and persecution and the "secret self-contempt" that underlie Mailer's career are seen by Lasch to be typical of much of twentieth-century intellectual life.

Alfred Kazin's *Starting Out in the Thirties* (Boston, Little, Brown) is a volume of reminiscences organized chronologically. There are six parts representing a survey from 1934 to the end of the decade and an epilogue, dated 1945. Kazin describes his entry into the leftist literary world of New York. There are also memoirs of the *New Republic* and brief and often brilliantly clear delineations of a number of significant figures, such as Otis Ferguson, Malcolm Cowley, V. F. Calverton, Max Eastman, and William Saroyan. There are critical notes on works which had, because of social meaning, great and immediate relevance, such as *Man's Fate, Fontamara, Studs Lonigan,* and *Awake and Sing.* The book is remarkably successful for its evocation of the radical literary world, with its feuds, its plots and counterplots, and its moving portraits of his family life.

The major problem with Sidney Finklestein's *Existentialism and Alienation in American Literature* (New York, International Publishers) is that in the application of his definitions almost everybody is included as either existentialist, or alienated, or both. For the author existentialism is deeply bound to alienation because it attempts to confront the absurdity of man's existence which results from his consciousness that his " 'essence'—his consciousness of his 'being'—is surrounded by 'nothingness' and will dissolve into death." He sees Marxist ideology as the most successful existentialist solution to the hopelessness of alienation. Of particular interest is a well-mounted, if not entirely convincing, attack on T. S. Eliot and a Marxist reading of *A Long Day's Journey into Night.*

A thoroughly hostile account of the thirties may be seen in Richard Kostelanetz' "Men of the '30s" (*Commonweal,* LXXXIII, Dec. 3, 266–267). "No other cultural generation," he writes, "has lived to see so much completely dismissed as duped and irrelevant." The decade not only espoused fallacious ideas but succeeded in killing off budding talent. Aaron Copland and the "Action Painters" he feels were the only artists to survive the era. Memoirs by Alfred Kazin, Lionel Trilling, Philip Rahv, F. W. Dupee, and Granville Hicks are coolly offered as evidence of the inferiority of the men who came to maturity at the time.

A more balanced account than Kostelanetz' is Malcolm Cowley's "The Sense of Guilt" (*KR,* XXVII, 259–278), in which he analyzes the guilt of the intellectual left wing after its disillusionment with Communism. He sees the first half of the thirties as one of intellectual ferment, with the last half typified by stagnation, brought on primarily by the debilitating struggle between the Stalinists and Trotskyites.

The *Carleton Miscellany* (VI, i) presents a symposium on the thirties. Malcolm Cowley provides a reminiscence of a period in the history of the *New Republic* in its old brownstone in the Chelsea district of New York. Jack Conroy derides the rueful confessions of flirtation with the Left by Murray Kempton and James Wechsler. R. A. Botkin, August Derleth, Ben Hagglund, David Ignatow, and John Rood recall their experiences with little magazines.

Malcolm Cowley's "A Remembrance of the Red Romance" (*Esquire,* LXI, 1964, iii, 124–130; iv, 78–81) is a similar reminiscence, and the same author's "While They Waited For Lefty" (*SatR,* LXII, June 6, 1964, 16–19, 61) discusses proletarian literature. See also Marshall Van Deusen, "Criticism in the Thirties: The Marxists and the New Critics" (*WHR,* XVII, 1963, 75–85).

viii. Mostly Ethnic

A collection of critical essays, *Waiting for the End* (New York, Stein and Day, 1964), by Leslie Fiedler begins with "The Death of the Old Men," a reflection on the meaning to American letters of the deaths of

Faulkner and Hemingway, both of whom he concludes are essentially comic writers. *The Torrents of Spring* remains for Fiedler one of Hemingway's central achievements. His influence on American writing is diffuse, "found everywhere and nowhere, more often in nuance and reflection than in overt imitation." Faulkner has become the universal favorite, whose works have greatest general significance for the United States, his treatment of the relation of the races, the chief symbol of evil for our time. A significant number of these essays deal with what is, if one is to judge by sheer numbers, the most chic subject in nonacademic criticism: the Jew as American Writer.

Irving Malin, in *Jews and Americans* (Carbondale, Southern Illinois Univ. Press), develops this theme into a book-length study, but he is generally less provocative than Fiedler and less imaginative than Jonathan Baumbach whose book *The Landscape of Nightmare* (New York, New York Univ. Press) includes several chapters on the problems of the Jewish writer.

Jules Chametzky, in "Notes on the Assimilation of the American-Jewish Writer: Abraham Cahan to Saul Bellow" (*JA*, IX, 1964, 173–180), dates the importance of the question from the early fifties. He seeks an explanation in the change of status of the Jewish community in America, which had at last freed itself of "awkward self-consciousness . . . crippling defensiveness, sentimentality and hatred." The direction of the article is toward an understanding of how assimilation affects the American Jewish writer. With Saul Bellow the writer could begin to utilize elements of the Jewish experience without obsession, creating a strong link with a secure Americanism. Also there was at the same time the search toward the securing of an identity independent of either all-embracing experience, Jewishness or Americanism. The Jewish writer is seen to be in a unique position; his search for self-identity begins from the security of a defined position. Assimilation as an experience for the American Jewish writer means not the abandonment of diversity for conformity, but the discovery by the Jew of the richness of differences beyond his parochial, secure position.

Mary Jean DeMarr's "In a Strange Land: Contributions to American Literature by Russian and Russian-Jewish Immigrants" (*DA*, XXV, 1964, 1907–1908) presents a historical view, and Marie Syrkins' "Jewish Awareness in American Literature," a chapter in *The American Jew: A Reappraisal*, edited by Oscar J. Janowsky (Philadelphia,

Jewish Publication Society of America, 1964), continues that author's generally first-rate comments on similar themes. It is interesting to recall that many of the ideas being advanced on this topic seem often at best to echo Isaac Rosenfield's remarks collected in *An Age of Enormity* (Cleveland and New York, World, 1962).

Breakthrough, A Treasury of Contemporary American-Jewish Literature, edited by Irving Malin and Irvin Stark (New York, McGraw-Hill, 1964), offers a remarkably fresh collection of stories, poems, and essays. The schematization offered in the editors' introduction is somewhat forced and artificial.

Norman Podhoretz' collection of essays, *Doings and Undoings: The Fifties and After in American Writings* (New York, Farrar, Straus, 1964), is valuable for a fine essay entitled "Jewish Culture and the Intellectuals," as well as for sympathetic responses to James Baldwin as novelist and essayist and for the painfully honest "My Negro Problem—and Ours."

Saunders Redding's "The Problems of the Negro Writer" (*MR*, VI, 1964, 57–70) continues a discussion begun in a symposium by Langston Hughes, John Williams, and LeRoi Jones (*SatR*, XLVI, April 20, 1963, 19–21, 40) on limitations placed on the Negro dramatist and novelist.

Loften Mitchell, in "Three Writers and a Dream" (*Crisis*, LXXII, 219–223), also asserts that the Negro writer is not permitted freedom or artistic expression through the mass media. He uses as examples of this denial William Branch and Alice Childress, both of whom have failed to get the hearing they deserve. He suggests what has in fact been done both in Harlem and Watts, that Negro businessmen support theater in the ghettos which would draw on Negroes in the area both for audience and production crews.

And finally, Miles M. Jackson, "Significant Belles Lettres by and about Negroes Published in 1964" (*Phylon*, XXVI, 216–227), contrasts the new group of Negro writers with the Harlem group of an earlier day. He comments favorably on new novels by Ernest J. Gaines, Robert Boles, and Kristin Hunter, short stories by William Melvin Kelley, and poetry by Audre Lorde, Julian Bond, and Allen Polite. Ralph Ellison's essays, *The Shadow and the Act*, are particularly praised.

San Fernando Valley State College

Index

The 1965 index, like the preceding *ALS* indexes, gives references to literary and historical figures who are referred to throughout the book, as well as to authors of the literary scholarship therein surveyed. Works are cited only for those authors given chapter coverage (Part I). Literary movements and genres are not indexed as such, since the organization of the book makes pertinent pages clear for most such studies.

Joseph M. Flora